DEVELOPING SKILLS & KNOWLEDGE

FOR

Social Work Practice

Sara Miller McCune founded SAGE Publishing in 1965 to support the dissemination of usable knowledge and educate a global community. SAGE publishes more than 1000 journals and over 800 new books each year, spanning a wide range of subject areas. Our growing selection of library products includes archives, data, case studies and video. SAGE remains majority owned by our founder and after her lifetime will become owned by a charitable trust that secures the company's continued independence.

Los Angeles | London | New Delhi | Singapore | Washington DC | Melbourne

DEVELOPING SKILLS & KNOWLEDGE

FOR

Social Work Practice

MICHAELA ROGERS, DAWN WHITAKER, DAVID EDMONDSON & DONNA PEACH

Los Angeles | London | New Delhi
Singapore | Washington DC | Melbourne

2ND EDITION

Los Angeles | London | New Delhi
Singapore | Washington DC | Melbourne

SAGE Publications Ltd
1 Oliver's Yard
55 City Road
London EC1Y 1SP

SAGE Publications Inc.
2455 Teller Road
Thousand Oaks, California 91320

SAGE Publications India Pvt Ltd
B 1/I 1 Mohan Cooperative Industrial Area
Mathura Road
New Delhi 110 044

SAGE Publications Asia-Pacific Pte Ltd
3 Church Street
#10-04 Samsung Hub
Singapore 049483

Editor: Kate Keers/Catriona McMullen
Assistant editor: Ruth Lilly
Production editor: Martin Fox
Copyeditor: Jane Fricker
Proofreader: Bryan Campbell
Marketing manager: Camille Richmond
Cover design: Wendy Scott
Typeset by: C&M Digitals (P) Ltd, Chennai, India
Printed in the UK

First edition published 2016. Reprinted 2017
(three times), 2018
This second edition published 2020

Library of Congress Control Number: 2019949837

British Library Cataloguing in Publication data

A catalogue record for this book is available
from the British Library

ISBN 978-1-5264-6324-1
ISBN 978-1-5264-6325-8 (pbk)

At SAGE we take sustainability seriously. Most of our products are printed in the UK using responsibly sourced papers and
boards. When we print overseas we ensure sustainable papers are used as measured by the PREPS grading system. We
undertake an annual audit to monitor our sustainability.

Contents

List of Figures and Tables   viii
About the Authors and Contributors   x
Acknowledgements   xiv
Online Resources   xv

Introduction   1

Part I   Core Skills   9

  1 Person-Centred Communication   11
     Dawn Whitaker

  2 Active Listening Skills   22
     Michaela Rogers

  3 Communicating with Children   32
     Donna Peach

  4 Emotionally Intelligent Social Work   42
     Donna Peach

  5 Developing Empathic Skills   52
     Donna Peach

  6 Reflection and Reflexivity   63
     Michaela Rogers

  7 Understanding Values, Ethics and Human Rights   73
     Dawn Whitaker

  8 Valuing Difference and Diversity   84
     Michaela Rogers

  9 Resilience and Self-Care   95
     Ciarán Murphy

 10 Time Management   107
     Ciarán Murphy

Part II   Skills and Knowledge for Assessment and Interventions   **119**

11 Assessment Skills   121
    Michaela Rogers

12 Interviewing Skills   133
    Michaela Rogers

13 A Positive Approach to Safeguarding: Risk in Humane Social Work   143
    Donna Peach

14 Working with Service Users and Carers   152
    David Edmondson

15 Building Resilience in Others   167
    Michaela Rogers

16 Conflict Management and Resolution   175
    David Edmondson and Charlotte Ashworth

17 Research-Informed Practice   186
    Donna Peach

18 Writing Skills for Practice   194
    Michaela Rogers

19 Inter-Professional Practice and Working Together   203
    David Edmondson and Charlotte Ashworth

20 Maximising Supervision   212
    Michaela Rogers

21 Review and Evaluation   221
    David Edmondson

22 Court Skills   230
    Dawn Whitaker

Part III   Key Social Work Theories and Methods   **241**

23 Strengths-Based and Solution-Focused Approaches   243
    Michaela Rogers

24 Systems Theory and an Ecological Approach   251
    Michaela Rogers and Jennifer Cooper

25 Narrative Social Work   259
    Jennifer Cooper

26 Task-Centred Social Work Practice   269
    David Edmondson

27 Person-Centred Social Work   279
    Dawn Whitaker

28 Group Work   291
    Michaela Rogers

29 Attachment Theory: Examining Maternal Sensitivity Scales   300
    Donna Peach

30 Grief and Loss   309
    Julie Lawrence

31 Crisis Intervention   318
    Donna Peach

32 The Social Models of Disability and Distress   327
    Dawn Whitaker

33 Social Work Activism   338
    Donna Peach

Conclusion   347

References   348
Index   362

List of Figures and Tables

FIGURES

1.1	Collins's communication cycle	13
3.1	What young people say about starting a conversation	38
4.1	Ingram's intelligent social work model	45
5.1	Marshall and Marshall's (2011) revised model of empathy	55
5.2	Neuronal basis of imitation	56
5.3	The input and representational systems involved in understanding one's own emotion	58
6.1	Gibbs's reflective cycle	66
7.1	Thompson's PCS model	77
II.1	Social work practice cycle	120
11.1	The Assessment Framework	123
13.1	The triangular relationship of state–child–parents	147
17.1	Features of systemic planned practice and single system designs	188
18.1	GAS model	199
20.1	Reflective learning model	216
24.1	The ecological model	253
24.2	The Assessment Framework	254
25.1	One-page profile for Bob	267
30.1	Social work interventions during times of grief and loss	316
31.1	Roberts's seven-stage crisis intervention model (1991)	320

33.1   Campaigners walked 100 miles to highlight the negative impact
        of austerity on families   342
33.2   Typology of activism in the digital age   343

TABLES

1.1   Different forms of communication   13

2.1   Active listening skills   24
2.2   Case study: Marian I dialogue   25
2.3   Case study: Marian II dialogue   27

5.1   Marshall et al.'s (1995) four-stage model of empathy   54
5.2   Social work model of empathy   59

7.1   The Human Rights Act   80

10.1   Example time diary   110

11.1   Five purposes of social work assessment   122
11.2   Professional judgements and danger zones   131

12.1   Case study: Joshua dialogue   136
12.2   Cognitive distortions   141

15.1   Characteristics associated with good levels of resilience   171

18.1   Examples of poor communication   196

21.1   Features to consider when preparing to review your work   223
21.2   Intervention impacts   224

22.1   Key principles for the format of written work   235
22.2   Key principles for the content of written work   236
22.3   Formal court etiquette   237

23.1   Benefits and limitations of strengths-based and solution-focused work   249

24.1   Benefits and limitations of systemic thinking in social work   257

28.1   Benefits and limitations of group work   298

31.1   Key principles of trauma-informed approaches   324

About the Authors and Contributors

Michaela Rogers is a registered social worker and Senior Lecturer in Social Work at the University of Sheffield. Michaela has a professional background in the fields of social work and social care and her research spans the areas of equality and diversity, safeguarding, interpersonal abuse and gender-based violence. These projects typically aim to explore social problems in terms of everyday experiences or assess the impact of service delivery or specific policy initiatives. For example, her work on gender-based violence and domestic abuse has a focus towards the experiences of marginalised groups (LGBTQ communities and older people for example) exploring the barriers and enablers to accessing support. Michaela's current projects examine social norming approaches with young people in prevention programmes which promote healthy relationships.

Dawn Whitaker is an independent lecturer and social work consultant. Dawn worked as a mental health social worker for many years, before joining a local authority training department in the north west of England to deliver teaching on the Mental Capacity Act 2005. Dawn subsequently joined the NHS as a locality Mental Capacity Act implementation lead, with particular responsibility for implementing the Deprivation of Liberty Safeguards. More recently, Dawn has led on implementing systemic approaches with children and families across the north west. Dawn also works as an independent social worker (ISW) and has been regularly instructed by the Official Solicitor in the Court of Protection. Dawn continues to undertake ISW work and has been involved in a number of high-profile cases.

David Edmondson previously worked as a qualified mental health social worker and service manager in central Manchester, before finishing his career teaching social work at Manchester Metropolitan University. His book, *Social Work Practice Learning*, was published by SAGE in 2014.

Donna Peach is a registered social worker with more than 30 years' experience of working with children and families. Since 2013, Donna has worked part-time as a lecturer in social work and integrated practice at the University of Salford. In addition, Donna acts as an independent social work consultant undertaking reviews and investigation of practice for local authorities and the police. Her PhD examined the experiences of prospective adoptive parents but most of her research is focused on better understanding child sexual abuse and exploitation both nationally and internationally. Donna is an elected member of Council for the British Association of Social Work and a member of the editorial board for the *British Journal of Social Work*.

We would like to thank all contributors for their wonderful and valuable contributions by way of case studies, commentaries and reflections.

Charlotte Ashworth is a Team Manager of a frontline child protection team in Manchester.

Jennifer Cooper qualified as a social worker in March 2015 having completed the Step Up to Social Work programme through the University of Salford with Distinction. Jennifer is employed as a Advanced Practitioner in a Child Protection and Court Team based in the North of England in a local authority. Jennifer also has experience of delivering training and education for social work students. Prior to commencing her social work training, Jennifer obtained an LLB (2:1) (Hons) from the University of Birmingham and an LLM in International Law and International Relations (with Merit) from Lancaster University. Jennifer has previously worked in the NHS as well as for the Equality and Human Rights Commission (EHRC) and the General Medical Council (GMC).

Fazeela Hafejee qualified as a social worker within the children and families area and has worked as Assistant Director with adults who experience mental health problems (including those in forensic settings), learning disabilities, physical disabilities and with older people. Fazeela holds considerable experience of engaging with socially excluded and vulnerable people and communities and undertaking organisational diagnostics and development. Fazeela holds significant professional practice and strategic development in Leadership and Management, with specialism in Equality and Diversity. She is a hands-on consultant, working at all levels of the organisation to identify and address the barriers to improvement and change – including areas of strategy, culture, structure, relationships or performance.

Clare Jackman's academic and professional background centres on social work within child protection practice. She entered full-time education at the age of 34, a single parent to two children. Following the successful completion of her degree in social work (2014) she obtained full-time employment with her local council within a child protection team. Clare's practice enabled her to work with vulnerable children and adults. Her areas of practice include: mental health issues, CSE (child sexual exploitation), child abuse and neglect, drug and alcohol misuse, domestic abuse and assessments for court. Her practice requires effective policy and procedure implementation, completion of thorough and comprehensive assessments and positive and effective child-centred practice. Underpinning Clare's practice is a child-centred approach based on evidenced-based practice and theory.

Her interest in current research, social work themes and critical debates has kept her practice current, effective and informed. Currently, Clare works as a schools organiser for the NSPCC, which has enabled her to transfer important advice and information to children directly on how to keep safe and know their individual rights.

Ian Joddrell is a registered social worker in the Midlands.

Shani Kilasi is a registered Social Worker in the North West of England, working as a Senior Practitioner in an NHS mental health service.

Julie Lawrence has been a lecturer in social work at the University of Salford since 2010. In addition, Julie is a registered social worker and has a professional and academic background in criminal justice, probation and social work with people who have complex health needs and learning disabilities. Her previous work within the statutory sector as a social worker and team manager has involved working with young people in transition to adulthood. She has developed and coordinated services for vulnerable adults who had a variety of learning disabilities. She has also worked alongside bereaved parents and carers, who mourned the loss of their adult children, in terms of long-term illness and/or unexpected deaths, relating to complex health needs. Julie's PhD research focused upon social work and learning disabilities, and the contribution of social work within a statutory learning disabilities multidisciplinary team. Julie is a member of the Sustainable Housing & Urban Studies Unit at the University of Salford and is currently the Principal Investigator for the Help through Crisis Project, which is a Big Lottery Community Funded project until 2021.

Vicky Lowe has considerable experience of working within advocacy, initially providing non-statutory advocacy to older people in residential and nursing care. Since then she has worked with adults who have learning disabilities, carers, older people, and people with physical and sensory disabilities. In addition to this she has worked as an Independent Mental Health Advocate and Independent Mental Capacity Advocate and now manages a team which provides both statutory and non-statutory advocacy services. Vicky has a strong belief that working in partnership with practitioners from other agencies results in more positive and person-centred outcomes for clients whilst also promoting the development of self-advocacy and its benefits. With this in mind she ensures a proactive approach in building local relationships whilst remaining independent to offer a strategic voice which aims to influence decision-making in social policy, both locally and nationally.

Dr Ciarán Murphy is Senior Lecturer in Social Work at Edge Hill University, Ormskirk. He is a qualified and registered social worker, having specialised in child care/protection. Ciarán practised for 10 years in the areas of child protection, substance misuse and education welfare. He formerly sat on the Greater Manchester Family Justice Board subgroup for improving outcomes for children in the Family Court. In his previous role as a consultant social worker, Ciarán was instrumental in developing and implementing new assessment models for children and families social work across Greater Manchester.

His previous research publications have pertained to the evaluation of substance misuse treatment services. His current area of focus is the discretionary space of the child protection social worker. Ciarán is also an avid Houston Texans fan – #WeAreTexans!

Jo Shaw is a mental health practitioner at 42nd Street in Manchester.

Victoria Shevlin qualified as a social worker in 2015, after completing the MA Social Work course at Manchester Metropolitan University. She has a background in support work with both children and adults, and has previously worked with community theatre companies for individuals affected by homelessness. Victoria is employed as a Child Protection Social Worker in the South of England in a local authority that has implemented Signs of Safety as a social work model.

Maya von Käss is a member of 42nd Street in Manchester.

Sarah Wright qualified as a social worker in 2015 having completed the Step Up to Social Work. Sarah is currently employed as a children and families social worker in the Midlands. Sarah is coming to the end of her Assessed and Supported Year in Employment and since qualifying has also obtained a Master's in Social Work (Distinction). During this time, she has completed primary research exploring leadership development in social work. Prior to commencing social work training, Sarah obtained a BSc in Criminology and Social Policy (2:1) and a Professional Certificate in Effect Practice: Youth Justice (Distinction). Sarah's pre-qualifying practice experience has been in youth justice, where she focused on improving service delivery for young people with additional needs within the criminal justice system.

Acknowledgements

Michaela – Thank you to everyone who supported me to work on this book including, as always, the Ryans (Mick and my gorgeous children, Noah and Daisy), who provided sustenance, love and nurturing. Thank you to Kate Keers, Catriona McMullen and Talulah Hall at SAGE who offered support and useful nudges; as always, it's been a pleasure. Thank you to my excellent friends who have supported me in getting this second edition complete when things have taken unusual turns and life has been busy; you know who you are!

Dawn – Thank you to my husband, family, friends and colleagues for their unwavering encouragement, support and proofreading.

David – Thank you to all the excellent and dedicated social work practitioners, educators and students in Lancashire, Manchester and beyond, who have inspired and guided me over the years. Thanks, once again, to the team at SAGE for their unceasing positive encouragement. Finally, I would like to thank Christine and Daniel for their enduring patience, love and support.

Donna – To all the children, parents, families, students and colleagues that I have been honoured to know throughout my social work career; I thank you for sharing what will become a lifetime of learning and appreciation that I can share with others.

Online Resources

Visit the SAGE companion website at **https://study.sagepub.com/rogers2e** to find a range of free tools and resources that will enhance your learning experience.

- **Read more widely!** A selection of FREE SAGE journal articles supports each chapter to help expand your knowledge and reinforce your learning of key topics.
- Downloadable **'How to …' guides* and templates** to be used on the go and to support your revision.
- **Watch relevant video** clips from the SAGE Social Work Video Collection and **answer the discussion questions** to develop critical thinking and reflection.
- **Weblinks** which direct you to relevant resources to broaden your understanding of chapter topics and expand your knowledge.
- The **Glossary** will further your understanding of key terminology used in the book.

*'How to …' guides were written by Michaela Rogers and Jennifer Cooper.

Introduction

Social work has been a profession in flux for a long time. There are continual changes in terms of its infrastructure and practice contexts. For example, currently the regulation and registration of social work sits with the Health and Care Professions Council (HCPC) but at the time of writing this second edition, we are waiting for the new regulator, Social Work England (SWE), to come into being. SWE will introduce a whole new set of standards and regulatory requirements. The Professional Capabilities Framework for Social Workers (hereafter referred to as 'the PCF', the profession's framework for social work education and practice) may remain with the British Association of Social Workers (BASW), or it may be replaced with a new framework. There are many uncertainties in this period of change. Additional shifts are occurring in social work education as during 2019 a new social work programme, the integrated degree apprenticeship for social work, has been introduced and will gain momentum in the coming years. The apprenticeship scheme brings another new and different set of standards in addition to those currently implemented via the HCPC. Despite these shifts, one thing remains constant and that is the need for a skilled workforce. Indeed, the PCF was introduced as a keystone of developing a skilled workforce and we have integrated the PCF domains into this book.

The PCF, along with the 'Knowledge and Skills Statements' (KSSs), discussed below, set out what are considered to be the core areas of skills and knowledge for social workers to have attained and maintained on their career pathway. The purpose of this book is to introduce the reader to what we consider to be the core skills and knowledge that are required for social work practice, and each of these map onto the PCF and KSSs. Please note, however, that the areas of skill and knowledge that are covered in this book are by no means exhaustive, but indicative of some of the fundamental ones needed from the point of entry into social work education through to the early stages of a social work career.

In terms of mapping this more formally, the PCF is the overarching professional standards framework, originally developed by the Social Work Reform Board (SWRB, 2010). The PCF is currently managed and delivered by BASW and serves to:

- set out consistent expectations of social workers at every stage in their career;
- provide a backdrop to both initial social work education and continuing professional development (CPD) after qualification;

- inform the design and implementation of the national career structure;
- give social workers a framework around which to plan their careers and professional development. (BASW, 2016)

There are nine domains of capability contained within the PCF and these are as follows:

Professionalism: Social workers are members of an internationally recognised profession. Our title is protected in UK law. We demonstrate professional commitment by taking responsibility for our conduct, practice, self-care and development. We seek and use supervision and other professional support. We promote excellent practice, and challenge circumstances that compromise this. As representatives of the profession, we safeguard its reputation. We are accountable to people using services, the public, employers and the regulator. We take ethical decisions in the context of multiple accountabilities.

Values and ethics: Social workers have an obligation to conduct themselves and make decisions in accordance with our Code of Ethics. This includes working in partnership with people who use our services. We promote human rights and social justice. We develop and maintain our understanding of the value base of our profession throughout our career, its ethical standards and relevant law.

Diversity and equality: Social workers understand that diversity characterises and shapes human experience and is critical to the formation of identity. Diversity is multidimensional and includes race, disability, class, economic status, age, sexuality, gender (including transgender), faith and belief, and the intersection of these and other characteristics. We understand that because of difference, and perception of difference, a person's life experience may include oppression, marginalisation and alienation as well as privilege, power and acclaim. We identify this and promote equality.

Rights, justice and economic wellbeing: Social workers recognise and promote the fundamental principles of human rights, social justice and economic wellbeing enshrined in national and international laws, conventions and policies. These principles underpin our practice and we use statutory and case law effectively in our work. We understand and address the effects of oppression, discrimination and poverty. Wherever possible, we work in partnership with people using services, their carers and families, to challenge inequality and injustice, and promote strengths, agency, hope and self-determination.

Knowledge: We develop our professional knowledge throughout our careers and sustain our curiosity. As a unified profession, we develop core knowledge that relates to our purpose, values and ethics. We also develop specific knowledge needed for fields of practice and roles. Our knowledge comes from social work practice, theory, law, research, expertise by experience, and from other relevant fields and disciplines. All social workers contribute to creating as well as using professional knowledge. We understand our distinctive knowledge complements that of other disciplines to provide effective services.

Critical reflection and analysis: Social workers critically reflect on their practice, use analysis, apply professional judgement and reasoned discernment. We identify, evaluate and integrate multiple sources of knowledge and evidence. We continuously evaluate our impact and benefit to service users. We use supervision and other support to reflect on our work and sustain our practice and wellbeing. We apply our critical reflective skills to the context and conditions under which we practise. Our reflection enables us to challenge ourselves and others, and maintain our professional curiosity, creativity and self-awareness.

Skills and interventions: Social workers engage with individuals, families and communities, working alongside people to determine their needs and wishes, and what action may be helpful. We build productive working relationships and communicate effectively. Using our professional judgement, we employ appropriate interventions, promoting self-determination, support, protection and positive change. We develop and maintain skills relevant to our roles. We understand and take account of power differentials and use our authority appropriately. We evaluate our own practice and its impact, and how we improve outcomes for those we work with.

Contexts and organisations: Social workers are informed about and proactively respond to the challenges and opportunities that come from changing social, policy and work contexts. We fulfil this responsibility in accordance with our professional values and ethics, as individual and collective professionals and as members of the organisations in which we work. We collaborate, inform and are informed by our work with other social workers, other professions, individuals and communities.

Professional leadership: We develop and show our leadership, individually and collectively, through promoting social work's purpose, practices and impact. We achieve this through diverse activities which may include: advancing practice; supervising; educating others; research; evaluation; using innovation and creativity; writing; using social media positively; being active in professional networks and bodies; contributing to policy; taking formal leadership/management roles. We promote organisational contexts conducive to good practice and learning. We work in partnership with people who use services and stakeholders in developing our leadership and aims for the profession. (BASW, 2018a)

We recognise that skills, qualities and knowledge are not applied in isolation and that these intersect, interact and complement each other. Therefore, at the start of each chapter we list the PCF domains that we think are pertinent to the area of skill under scrutiny so that it is clear to the reader which skill relates to which domain. We also explore some of the practical issues that face social workers in terms of tensions and limitations. Hopefully, you will find useful the practical tips that are contained within the book and the 'How to …' guides that accompany the book (found on the companion website). Thus, we see this book as a resource and a guide to be used for trainee social workers and those new to professional practice.

As referred to briefly above, the social work profession has experienced a recent addition to the infrastructure that supports and guides the profession by the way of 'Knowledge and Skills Statements' (KSSs). There are two KSSs: one for social workers in adults-oriented services (www.gov.uk/government/uploads/system/uploads/attachment_data/file/411957/KSS.pdf), which was developed by the Chief Social Worker for Adults, and one for children's social workers, which was developed by the Chief Social Worker for Child and Family Social Work (www.gov.uk/government/uploads/system/uploads/attachment_data/file/338718/140730_Knowledge_and_skills_statement_final_version_AS_RH_Checked.pdf). Both statements have been developed in partnership with key stakeholders, including the now defunct College of Social Work, BASW, Skills for Care, Social Care Institute for Excellence (SCIE) and others. Along with other frameworks (the PCF for example) the KSSs are intended as a national framework for the education of trainee social workers and the assessment of social workers at the end of their first year in practice. The statements should be used by social workers and their employers to build a wider framework for induction, supervision and the continuing professional development of social workers and the social work profession. In addition to indicating which PCF domains are relevant to each chapter, we also indicate which areas of the KSSs are relevant too.

ORGANISATION OF THE BOOK

The book is structured over three parts: Part I 'Core Skills'; Part II 'Skills and Knowledge for Assessment and Interventions'; and Part III 'Key Social Work Theories and Methods'.

Focus across the book

Each of the three parts of the book has a specific focus:

- *Part I* includes chapters on core skills for relationship-based and person-centred social work. These are the key skills and qualities that student social workers should have at the start of their practice experience, but that can be practised and developed throughout training and into the early years of their career. In order to recognise these skills and qualities, there is a strong focus upon the value of reflection, use of self and self-care as integral to skills development.
- *Part II* urges the reader to consider the core areas of skill and knowledge that are necessary to the processes of social work. This section uses the ASPIRE model (Sutton, 1999) to organise the chapters into particular areas of social work from initial assessments to reviewing plans and intervention. There are chapters that span the different aspects of the ASPIRE model (for example, Chapter 17 'Research-Informed Practice' may be relevant at the 'assessment' or the 'intervention' stage).

Parts I and II provide a backdrop to the core skills and knowledge, along with practical tips, essential for social work practice.

- *Part III* builds on this knowledge by providing a discussion of some of the key social work theories and methods that underpin the majority of social work and that are congruent to our framework of relationship-based practice (RBP) and a person-centred (PC) approach.

Chapters in each part of the book

Part I

As noted above, the content of the chapters in Part I are underscored by two theoretical approaches to social work: relationship-based practice and person-centred thinking. Part I is divided into 10 chapters.

Chapter 1 introduces the notion of person-centred communication in relation to achieving a personalised approach to support. Chapter 2 then explores a more generic communication skill – active listening – which is integral to relationship-building and the chapter advocates the value of developing skills in attunement and listening. In Chapter 3, there is a focus on communication with a specific group of people – children – to provide a foundation for understanding in relation to the importance of communicating with children and young people and of providing the right environment to facilitate and enhance this, not only as an aspect of good practice but as a legal and moral duty. Chapters 4 and 5 are similar in that they both offer an exploration of key personal qualities and skill-building in relation to emotional intelligence and developing empathy. Chapter 6 builds on the insights offered by the chapters so far to promote the ever-important activity of reflection and reflexivity in social work practice and for the process of developing skills. Chapters 7 and 8 build on the notion of reflexivity further by highlighting the importance of values, ethics and human rights in the context of difference and diversity. These chapters highlight the centrality of anti-oppressive practice in relation to direct work with service users and carers. Chapters 9 and 10 focus on practical skills in two essential areas: building professional resilience and self-care; and time management.

Part II

This part of the book is divided into 12 chapters (11 to 22) focusing on social work skills and knowledge that contribute to the practice of social work process. The different elements of Sutton's (1999) ASPIRE model (assessment, planning, intervention, review and evaluation) give structure to this section and each chapter relates to one or more stages in the model.

Chapter 11 explores some of the basic skills needed for undertaking assessments. This chapter acknowledges that various frameworks and tools exist but there are generic skills and techniques that apply to any form of assessment. Chapter 12 discusses a specific aspect of the assessment process: interviewing. Chapter 13 considers the intersection of risk and safeguarding as central to the task of social work assessment. This chapter advocates for a humane approach that emphasises the themes of RBP and PC work. In Chapters 14 and 15, a lens is used to consider the service-user and carer experiences of assessment. Chapter 14 looks at skills of engagement and takes a perspective that values the input of service users as experts in their own lives. Chapter 15 takes a different path by exploring the skills needed to help service users and carers to build resilience. In Chapter 16, the focus remains on the relational aspects of the assessment process but considers conflict. This chapter includes lots of practical tips for managing conflict, whether this be a minor argument or a major dispute.

Still contemplating the assessment process, but also moving to the planning and intervention stages of the ASPIRE model, Chapter 17 explores the value and limitations of research-informed practice. Chapter 18 also moves across the different stages in a discussion about the writing skills needed during the ASPIRE processes, focusing on case records and report writing. Chapter 19 moves away from the individual work of producing written work, to consider the skills needed to engage in multi-agency contexts. As inter-professional practice is an intrinsic aspect of social work, this is an important chapter that draws on many of the core skills explored throughout each section of this book. Chapter 20 considers the skills needed for maximising supervision. In the context of Part II and the ASPIRE model, supervision is seen as a crucial environment in which practitioners have the opportunity to reflect on and review their assessments, planning and intervention. Chapter 21 draws the ASPIRE model to a close with a discussion of the value of completing a review and evaluation following a piece of work. However, this does not bring the section to a close.

There is one final chapter, which considers court skills as intrinsic to the social work process. Whilst a chapter on court skills does not necessarily have a place in the ASPIRE model (although it might as the assessment itself may be court ordered), the skills needed for court work are integral to any student or newly qualified social worker. In addition, if the assessment and subsequent intervention does not evoke positive change, the individual or family that you are working with might find themselves in the court arena, with you acting as an agent of the state; then court skills will be necessary.

Part III

Part III is divided into 11 chapters and illuminates the importance of using theory in everyday practice. Chapter 23 explores the value of the ever popular strengths-based and solution-focused approaches. The chapter emphasises the value of partnership in helping service users to move forward in their lives. The next chapter (Chapter 24) also considers a contemporary influence – systems theory – drawing on a practitioner's reflections and a case study to illustrate the value of this theoretical model. Chapter 25 advocates for the value of a narrative approach to social work. In Chapter 26 a discussion of task-centred practice demonstrates a model that can be useful with individuals or groups. The discussion of task-centred practice illustrates a very practical model of social work that promotes change and, again, is premised on the principle of partnership. Chapter 27 revisits person-centred thinking to explore the value of RBP and learning from the important work of Carl Rogers. Chapter 28 offers a departure in terms of the intimate, one-to-one approach to social work to advocate for the benefits of group work. Next, Chapter 29 explores attachment theory, described as 'a cornerstone' of social work. This chapter takes a critical stance and urges the reader to recall that all theories have limitations. Chapter 30 introduces the concepts of grief and loss, which are central to social work practice. Then Chapter 31 offers a view of a practical model but more specifically for people who are considered to be in crisis. This chapter highlights some of the complexities of practice by noting that 'crisis' can have both/either internal or external sources. The social models of disability and distress are discussed in Chapter 32.

Part III ends with Chapter 33, which discusses social work activism as a means of challenging social injustice and discrimination.

FEATURES OF THE BOOK

Each chapter will begin by directing the reader to the relevant domains of the PCF and elements of the KSSs that particularly relate to the topic of that chapter. This is followed by 'key messages' which help to sum up the chapter's contents and show the relevance for social work practice. There are a number of additional features to be found throughout too and these include:

- *Commentaries*: Peppered throughout the chapters there are commentaries from social workers and newly qualified social workers.
- *Case studies*: Chapters may contain a case study which illustrates the chapter topic in action.
- *Reflective activities*: Most chapters will contain reflective activities that are included as prompts to help the reader apply the chapter topic to practice situations, or to consider the chapter topic in relation to themselves and their experiences to date.
- *Recommended reading*: Every chapter will highlight key reading that complements the chapter topic. In addition, links to relevant SAGE journal articles are to be found on the companion website.
- *Glossary terms*: To support and develop your understanding, throughout the book you will see key terms highlighted in bold. The full Glossary can be found on the website.

Not all chapters will contain the same additional features. The content is chosen to reflect the chapter's topic.

ONLINE RESOURCES

Each chapter has a webpage on the website. These will provide additional material relevant to the chapter topic. Throughout the book you will see these icons in the margin:

These icons indicate that there is additional material and there will be links or text to explain what this is. This may be a weblink to a site relevant to social work (for example, our regulator body [currently the HCPC], or a link to more practical aids), or a signpost to a video with accompanying discussion questions. There are a number of 'How to …' documents that have been written to provide you with succinct guides to tools and techniques that can be used with service users and that enhance the processes and interventions in social work. These short guides can be accessed through portable devices and are therefore useful when 'in the field'. Finally, you will also be able to locate the full Glossary on the website (https://study.sagepub.com/rogers2e).

CONCLUSION

In writing this book we have aimed to produce a practical handbook for students and newly qualified social workers that can help in the development of core skills and knowledge. Where we have included examples from a specific area of practice (child and family, adults or mental health social work), we urge the reader to remember to 'Think Family' and in doing so be mindful that the areas of skills and knowledge contained within this book are transferable across practice areas (SCIE, 2012).

We have set out the theoretical underpinning that we have taken as our point of departure in terms of a relationship-based practice (RBP) and person-centred (PC) approach, exploring the value of these throughout in terms of core skills and in relation to skills for assessment and intervention. Finally, we have identified key theories and models for practice that we feel complement RBP and a PC approach. Moreover, we hope that students and newly qualified practitioners will be able to see how the work that they do is underpinned by a theoretical basis (whilst noting the benefits and limitations of such). We hope that you enjoy this book and find its content to be relevant and accessible.

PART I

CORE SKILLS

The first section of this book will introduce ten key themes. These encompass the core skills required for social work which is underpinned by a commitment to humane, relationship-based practice (Featherstone et al., 2014). To a certain extent, there has always been an acknowledgement that relationships are central to good social work practice, whatever your theoretical standpoint (Ruch, 2010).

However, in recent years there has been a resurgence of interest in the professional and academic discourse of relationship-based practice (RBP) and its value for social work professionals as well as other disciplines. It has also been acknowledged that the task of adopting RBP is no longer straightforward in our bureaucratic, interdisciplinary and ever-changing world of social work. Notwithstanding, the conceptualisation of RBP has been developed, particularly from a person-centred point of view (Murphy et al., 2012), and this is reflected in the chapters contained within Part I.

Before going any further, it is useful to delineate our understanding of the term 'relationship-based practice' as this refers to a range of different ways of working. Indeed, existing literature explores a relational approach to 'people work' from many different theoretical bases (Trevithick, 2003), including the discipline of psychology (for example, in psychodynamic theory), to the person-centred approaches that have developed since the 1940s and 1950s from the work of counsellor Carl Rogers. In this book we employ the term RBP in its broadest sense and we are influenced by the person-centred ethos of Rogers (1965). We do, however, note the constraints and limitations of RBP, particularly in work that involves the highest level of risk and invokes safeguarding concerns. Notwithstanding, we adhere to a position that believes that RBP should be used where possible as it requires the application of some of the most fundamental values in social work, including respect and empathy.

The aim of Part I, then, is to give the reader a sense of the range of principles that are embedded within our relationship-based approach along with some more concrete ways to embed these into your work through skilful practice. Finally, as RBP is widely recognised as an approach that encourages reflexivity and the 'use of self' in the application of social work skills and knowledge, it is highly compatible with anti-oppressive practice and a commitment to social justice.

Person-Centred Communication
Dawn Whitaker

Links to the Professional Capabilities Framework

• Professionalism • Values and ethics • Diversity and equality • Knowledge • Critical reflection and analysis • Skills and interventions

Links to the Knowledge and Skills Statement for Child and Family Practitioners

• Child development • Communication • Adult mental ill-health, substance misuse, domestic violence, physical ill-health and disability • Abuse and neglect of children • Relationships and effective direct work • Child and family assessment • Analysis, decision-making, planning and review • The law and the family and youth justice systems • The role of supervision

Links to the Knowledge and Skills Statement for Social Workers in Adult Services

• The role of social workers working with adults • Person-centred practice • Safeguarding • Mental capacity • Effective assessments and outcome-based support planning • Direct work with individuals and families

Key messages

- Personalised practice means being led by the uniqueness of every individual, in everything you do, every day.
- Communication is a two-way, interactive process.
- Everyone communicates.
- Person-centred thinking is vital to person-centred communication.
- Person-centred communication is vital to achieving person-centred support.

INTRODUCTION

Much of our thinking about **person-centred** communication stems from the work of Carl Rogers relating to person-centred counselling. Although not a social work approach per se, its 'techniques for talking, listening and being with people' are influential to how we understand and engage in person-centred and relationship-based practice (Lomax and Jones, 2014: 46).

The ethos of being *person-centred* is firmly embedded in UK health and social care policy; indeed, it is now a legal right for adults and carers assessed as eligible for social care support under the Care Act 2014. This reflects what is often referred to as the **personalisation** agenda, specifically the transformation of public services, from the traditional *one size fits all* approach, to one in which care and support should be tailored to individual requirements.

However, critics argue that personalisation is too often reduced to narrow, tokenistic descriptions of 'increased choice and control' (Beresford et al., 2011: 24) as opposed to 'a completely different way of seeing and working with people' (Sanderson et al., 2007 cited in Parley, 2001: 301). Whilst a full appraisal of these debates is beyond the scope of this chapter, the fundamental message is that person-centredness is 'not another job – it's *the* job' (Glynn et al., 2008 cited in Carr, 2012: 80).

This chapter introduces the essential components of general communication skills, before explaining the importance of person-centred communication and illuminating different methods for achieving it in practice. Whilst the focus of the chapter relates to adults rather than children, much of the content is relevant to both adults and children. See Chapter 3, for a dedicated discussion on communicating with children.

Introducing communication

Communication theory explains the essence of communication as follows:

1. A means of conveying a message *(language, gesture, writing)*;
2. The decoding of the message by the recipient *(hearing, seeing reading)*;
3. Making a response on the basis of the interaction *(reply)*. (Randall and Parker, 2000 cited in Parker, 2010: 124)

This is illustrated by Collins's communication cycle: it acts as a helpful reminder to provide as many opportunities for communication as possible during the communication process:

Inform: Present the information to be conveyed (in whatever format works best for the person).

Invite: Wait for a response (allow as much time as the person needs, and provide whatever communication aids/resources the person needs to enable them to respond).

Listen: Listen to, and/or recognise the person's response, using whatever methods are appropriate to check you have heard what the person intended you to hear.

Acknowledge: Demonstrate that you have listened, heard and understood *before* moving on to another piece of communication. (Collins: 2009: 30)

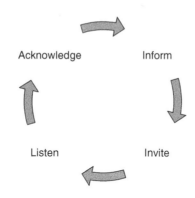

Figure 1.1   Collins's communication cycle (Collins, 2009: 30)

Source: Collins, Effective Communication A Workbook for Social Care Workers, 2009. Reproduced with permission of the Licensor through PLSclear.

Remember that as you work through the cycle above, the act of communication can take many forms (see Table 1.1).

Table 1.1   Different forms of communication

Language	The use of speech, which may be oral, written, electronic or sign language.
Paralanguage	The subtle signals that accompany the use of language, such as speech rate, pitch and tone. Everyday users of language become adept in how they practise these accompanying features of communication, so much so that they may not even be aware of it.
	In social work, however, it is important to remember that the features of paralanguage can be significant and highly meaningful in how they shape communication. In response, we must develop a level of sophistication in how we perceive and react to such signals.
Body Language	Essentially, this refers to all forms of non-verbal communication, such as eye contact, facial expression, gesture, touch, body movement and so on. Such communication is a powerful factor in shaping how people interact, and the meanings they attach to it. As with paralanguage, it is often done implicitly, without conscious awareness. Again, this requires the need to develop a level of sophistication in observing, reading and expressing non-verbal signals during our interactions with others.

Source: Adapted from Thompson (2010: 82–83). Reproduced with permission of Red Globe Press.

In practice, it is useful to tune in to each of these forms of communication simultaneously. Understanding a person's statement that they are angry will be more successful if you tune in to their pitch and tone of voice, paralanguage and associated non-verbal communication. This will better enable you to assess how to respond to the person, and adapt your speech, paralanguage and non-verbal expression accordingly.

LISTENING AS WELL AS TALKING

> It is imperative that we understand the point of view of the people we are working with. This is identified as a 'recurring theme in conversations about person-centred support' with people who use services. (Beresford et al., 2011: 249)

Silence is communication: Silence is not necessarily negative. Indeed, the *use* of silence offers space to think about and reflect on what has been communicated, as well as what is yet to be communicated. It is not always useful to fill the silence. Instead, use the time to ask yourself some reflective questions, such as:

Do you or the person feel awkward – if so, why might this be the case?

Have you posed a difficult or complex question, and does the person need time to think?

Is the person waiting for you to respond to something they have said?

You could acknowledge the silence by saying something like 'talking is difficult sometimes', or perhaps return to what was being said previously by summarising their last comment or stating 'you were saying …' (Koprowska, 2008: 78). Whichever approach you take, it is important to 'respect the silence' and 'remain engaged' with the person (Lishman, 2009: 106). For further information on active listening skills, see Chapter 2.

WHAT IS PERSON-CENTRED COMMUNICATION?

In essence, person-centred communication is the adaptation of the different forms of communication outlined above, to the uniqueness of the individual you are working with, and their particular communication style. By doing so, we should be better able to communicate with *all* people, regardless of their method of communication.

This is relevant to all of us, every day. For example, you may have had the experience of communicating with another person, and although they did listen, perhaps you did not feel heard. Whilst having our communication taken seriously is something we all value. It is particularly important to people receiving health and social care, as it often dictates the basis for subsequent **intervention**; that is, the identification of needs and associated responses.

All of us have preferred methods of communication, or communication comfort zones, and this is not particular to people with specific needs. However, as social workers, we do work with people that have identified communication needs; for example, people with some form of **cognitive impairment**, such as a **learning disability**, **brain injury** or **dementia**.

We also work alongside people who experience other forms of **neurodiversity** or **mental distress,** or some form of physical impairment that affects communication, such as a visual or hearing impairment.

It is important to remember, however, that regardless of the level of communication difficulty a person may experience, all people communicate in one way or another, including individuals who are non-verbal. This may include **pictorial communication, sign language, paralanguage,** the use of bespoke communication aids and/or behavioural communication through **body language** and so on. In essence then, 'We cannot not communicate, whatever we do, individually or collectively, gives off messages to other people, whether intentionally or not' (Thompson, 2010: 81). It is important to remember that lack of verbal skills does not amount to an inability to communicate. In such a circumstance, the onus is upon us as social workers to step outside of our communication comfort zone, in order to ascertain and work within the person's own communication style.

On this basis, it is imperative that we take *all action practicable* to enable the people we work with to communicate. Failure to do so can result in significant consequences for the individual; for example, not being able to:

- Have a conversation;
- Make choices about what they need and want;
- Exert **mental capacity** to make decisions;
- Express and fight for their **rights**;
- Access facilities and services as they would wish to;
- Achieve independence;
- Express themselves, which could lead to frustration, anger or behaviour that others find 'challenging'. (Collins, 2009: 23)

However, research tells us that people who 'communicate differently' are more likely to have other people speaking on their behalf:

> People with more problems, they tend not to listen to them. I think they can't be bothered to make the effort of sitting down with that person because it's going to take longer to talk to them. … It tends to take a long time to communicate and they end up making decisions for that person. (Beresford et al., 2011: 252)

Reflective activity

Consider this example: You are on a visit, and you witness a person being supported to choose their activity for that afternoon. The person is able to point at their chosen activity from a number of different photographs. The person then enters the dining room for lunch, and you observe them being given a sandwich and drink, without being asked what they want.

(Continued)

> You question this, but the member of staff states that the person is unable to speak, so they
> have made the decision for them.
>
> Reflect on the importance of your own decision-making. How would you feel if other people
> didn't understand what you communicated to them? How would you feel if people
> misunderstood you, or got it wrong? How might you feel if others made decisions on your
> behalf that you could make for yourself?
>
> The above exercise offers a powerful insight into the experience of being disempowered
> through failure to engage in person-centred communication.

Failure to engage in person-centred communication is incompatible with the legal and policy directives of person-centred support, as outlined in the introduction to this chapter. It is also in conflict with duties under the Care Act 2014, the Mental Capacity Act 2005 and the **United Nations Convention on the Rights of Persons with Disabilities (UNCRPD)**. For further information on these legal and policy documents visit the website https://study. sagepub.com/rogers2e.

So, how can we be person-centred in our communication? The answer is: preparation, preparation, preparation. This reflects what Koprowska refers to as second-order skills:

First-order skills are those required in direct communication itself, with service users, colleagues and others, including language, paralanguage and body language, as summarised in Table 1.1 above.

Second-order skills are those employed in *planning* our communication strategy, thinking about what we are doing, observing interactions, paying attention to feedback, reviewing what has happened, and modifying our next and future communications accordingly. (Koprowska, 2008: 8)

We know it is possible to better understand and respond to a person's communication needs by getting to know them (Espiner and Hartnett, 2011). In doing so, we are employing Koprowska's 'second-order' skills outlined above. The starting point must be to ascertain precise information about the person's specific communication style, then formulate an accessible, person-centred response.

The more we can understand the person's communication strengths and limitations the better. Useful **reflective questions** include:

- What is the nature of the person's communication difficulty? Do they have a cognitive and/or physical impairment, and what impact does this have on their communication strengths and limitations?
- Does the person require support with the format of how information is presented? For example, if the person is deaf, can they lip read or use **British Sign Language (BSL)**? If the person is non-verbal, might **Makaton, talking mats** or pictorial communication

aids be useful? Does the person prefer plain language, and short sentences and/or **easy-read materials**?

- Does the person require support to comprehend information? For example, abstract information about moving home. Might tangible or pictorial communication aids be useful, such as photographs of different housing options?
- Does the person require support to convey their communication to others? Are these methods the same or different from those used in how information is presented and comprehended, and if so how?
- Does the person have access to appropriate communication equipment, such as functioning hearing aids, glasses with a current prescription, false teeth (where appropriate)? Failure to provide these can have a deleterious effect on a person's ability to communicate.
- How does the person feel about using **assistive technology**? Might a sound amplifier be useful? A **minicom** machine that translates speech into text, or a computer program that translates text into speech? What about a visual smoke detector or doorbell? Is the person aware of speech and language therapy iPod apps that can aid communication and emotional expression? Has the person considered a memory app designed for people living with dementia?

Being led by the person

In addition to utilising the 'second-order skills' outlined above, it is important to recognise and value the expertise of the person you are working with. Essentially, this means engaging with the person in a manner that works for them. So rather than arranging a visit according to what is best for your diary, consider what day, or time might work best for the person. Some people communicate better in the morning rather than the afternoon, and vice versa. Similarly, it might not work for the person to be visited after taking powerful medication, as this can significantly affect a person's ability to communicate. Remember to take these matters into consideration when planning your person-centred communication.

In being led by the person, you are learning from their know-how of what does and does not work for them. In the rare circumstance that your ability to learn direct from the person is limited, endeavour to learn from other people who know the person better than you. This will likely be the person's family, friends and informal carers, as well as professionals who have experience of working closely with the person, such as a **keyworker** or **speech and language therapist**.

If possible, try to spend time with the person, and, if appropriate, with others who know them, and can assist you in learning their communication style. This will enable you to better understand the person's needs, and which communication aids work for them. Not only will this provide a sturdy foundation upon which to base your communication, it will also assist you to establish a rapport and build a positive working relationship.

Remember, since *all* communication should be person-centred, there is no *correct* method or *one size fits all* approach. Koprowska exemplifies this in her discussion of emotional communication and face-to-face contact:

It is especially important for people with hearing impairments, both to take in non-verbal information and to lip read, if they do so; they may also need to sit nearer than a hearing person and use touch. For other people, reading faces is difficult. People with varying degrees of visual impairment will take in only partial information, or none at all, and are more attuned to tone of voice, pace of speech, and larger body movements which can be seen, heard or felt. People with **autism** [may] find face-to-face contact disturbing or even painful, and have difficulty in recognising the expression of emotion. (2008: 38)

So, the basic principle of person-centred communication is to set aside your preferred method of communication and tune in to that of the person you are wanting to communicate with.

Reflective activity

Think of someone you have met either on placement or in practice who has a different communication style to you. Consider how that person's communication style is different to yours, and think through how you could use person-centred communication to maximise your ability to communicate with them.

PERSON-CENTRED PLANNING TOOLS

Person-centred planning tools are a communication method that encapsulates the principles set out above. While there is a general consensus that involving people in their own care and support is right and proper, such good intentions are insufficient without direct action. Person-centred planning tools aim to bridge this gap, and act as a conduit for achieving person-centred support in practice. There is a family of different person-centred communication tools available, which combine to form the basis of a person-centred care plan. All adhere to four key features: (1) they are orientated to the person's future; (2) they focus on strengths, not deficits; (3) they aim to illuminate the person's hopes and desires; and (4) they advocate creativity in planning and implementation (Stalker and Campbell, 1998 cited in Dowling et al., 2006: 7).

Another key feature of the method is that it should always be supported by a 'planning team' led by the person, including family members, friends, community advocates and professionals. The aim of the team is to assist in transforming the person's aims and aspirations into reality (O'Brien and O'Brien, 2002 cited in Taylor and Taylor, 2013: 217).

Pre-prepared person-centred communication tools

Whilst the tools outlined below originated from work with people with learning disability, they are also used with children with **special educational needs**; older adults, including people with dementia; people who experience mental distress; those living with substance use; and people living with cancer and other **long-term conditions**:

PATH (planning alternative tomorrows with hope): This approach begins by identifying the person's dream, then working back to ascertain the steps required to achieve it. It works particularly well with individuals who know what their dream is, but who feel stuck in working through how to make it a reality (developed by Jack Pearpoint, Marsha Forest and John O'Brien).

MAPS: This approach creates drawings that reflect a person's life. It describes their gifts and qualities, as well as their dream and nightmare. It learns from a person's past in order to shape their future, or in other words, it helps them move away from their nightmare towards their dream (developed by Judith Snow, Jack Pearpoint and Marsha Forest, in conjunction with John O'Brien and others).

Essential lifestyles planning: This involves using a collection of person-centred communication tools designed to get to know the person. Different tools are used to ascertain the most important things about a person's everyday life. Examples include:

- one-page profiles;
- what we like and admire about the person;
- what is working/not working;
- what is important to/for a person;
- what good support looks like;
- communication charts;
- decision-making agreements;
- relationship circles.

For further information about these person-centred planning tools and access to a 'How to …' guide on **one-page profiles**, visit the website (https://study.sagepub.com/rogers2e).

Whilst the value of pre-prepared person-centred tools is obvious. Critics argue that this reflects an encroaching 'industrialisation' of person-centred planning, as a once 'simple' person-centred exercise has now become 'a tool' that requires specialised training materials and accreditation (Kinsella, 2010). However, this does not have to be the case. While it does require time, space, a commitment to the person and person-centred thinking, it is an approach that is open and accessible to us all.

Indeed, for people with very particular communication needs, the best tools are often those designed with the uniqueness of that person in mind. This is particularly so in situations where you may wish to support a person to communicate their thinking on a specific matter, but no pre-prepared tool is appropriate. Do not worry if you are unable to locate the 'perfect' communication tool off the shelf. Instead, consider this an opportunity to engage in some one-to-one work with the individual, according to the person-centred communication principles outlined above. Utilise person-centred thinking to create some bespoke tools using whatever resources are likely to be successful for that person. This will likely involve the adaptation and amalgamation of some existing pre-prepared communication tools, alongside the expertise of the person and those who support them. Now visit the website (https://study.sagepub.com/rogers2e), and access some social work **case law** in which bespoke person-centred communication tools were used to good effect.

POTENTIAL BARRIERS TO PERSON-CENTRED COMMUNICATION AND APPROACHES

As much as the benefits of person-centred communication are well founded, the 'subjective, ambiguous and contingent nature of staff interpretation' is problematic (Phelvin, 2012: 32). This is not to deny the value of professional 'intuitive skills', but to acknowledge the 'dangers and limitations' associated with interpreting other people's communication (Phelvin, 2012: 34). As with any form of social work intervention, this necessitates the use of **critically reflective** and **reflexive** practice (see Chapter 6). We must be open to **disconfirming evidence** regarding competing interpretations of a person's communication, and not consider our understanding as the whole truth.

Furthermore, it is not always possible to achieve the conditions necessary for person-centred communication, as barriers can exist due to external variables, such as environmental distraction or interruption. Other difficulties may arise due to mistakes on our part, such as relationship difficulties, lack of rapport or misjudging the appropriate timeframe. Where possible, any such barriers should be anticipated, mitigated and resolved. Where this is not possible, and it is determined that person-centred communication is unlikely, we should reassess what needs to change in order to make it happen.

Notwithstanding these difficulties, person-centred communication/approaches can have a 'positive impact on the lives of people' across the whole of health and social care (Wigham et al., 2008: 143; Dowling et al., 2006; Riachi, 2017). Indeed, if used to good effect, person-centred approaches can (1) facilitate respectful interaction and trust; (2) provide direction by raising the question 'What matters to this person, now and in the future?'; (3) animate people so they try new things and increase their chances of discovering new opportunities and resources; and (4) create opportunities for updating the person's care plan, and encourage close attention to what is actually happening (O'Brien, 2004: 14). However, in acknowledging the benefits of this approach, we must recognise the '**implementation gap**' that exists in practice (Mansell and Beadle-Brown, 2004: 5). For example, research by National Voices, a coalition of charities that campaigns for people being in control of their care, found that progress remains patchy, despite improved access to person-centred communication across the health and social care landscape (2017: 4).

One way of achieving this is to encourage individuals' person-centred 'planning teams' to become 'circles of support' (COS). A COS is a group of friends, relatives and other invited non-professional people, who meet regularly to support the implementation of the plan (Stalker and Campbell, 1998 cited in Dowling et al., 2006: 7). This is illustrated by McIntosh and Sanderson's recommendation that: 'It requires persistence, patience, and great commitment from staff, families and people. ... Engaging families, working with them as colleagues and supporting them to lead in developing and implementing their relative's plan' (2006: 31). In doing so, we would be taking action to sustain the long-term success of the plan, as per the genuine ethos of person-centred care. This would be a valuable legacy of our involvement, conducive to honouring the person's voice and promoting 'a greater sense of ownership and control' over their lives (Espiner and Hartnett, 2011: 69).

CONCLUSION

This chapter introduced the personalisation agenda as the backdrop to person-centred communication and support before outlining the essential principles of person-centred communication, and how they can be used in practice. Effective communication also requires critical reflection, reflexivity, **empathy** and **anti-oppressive practice**, and you will be introduced to each of these subjects during the subsequent chapters of this book. For further information on how to apply your learning from this chapter in practice, see Chapter 27 on person-centred social work.

Having read this chapter, you should be able to:

- Use person-centred thinking to implement person-centred communication;
- Use person-centred communication to plan and deliver person-centred support;
- Overcome some of the common barriers to person-centred communication and practice.

RECOMMENDED READING

Bauby, J. (1998) *The Diving Bell and the Butterfly*. London: Fourth Estate.
Beresford, P. (2014) *Personalisation*. Bristol: Policy Press.
Carr, S. (2012) *Personalisation: A Rough Guide*. London: Social Care Institute of Excellence (SCIE).
Collins, S. (2009) *Effective Communication: Workbook for Social Care Workers*. London: Jessica Kingsley.
Helen Sanderson Associates Person-Centred Thinking Tools: www.helensandersonassociates.co.uk/
    person-centred-practice/person-centred-thinking-tools/

Active Listening Skills
Michaela Rogers

Links to the Professional Capabilities Framework

• Professionalism • Values and ethics • Diversity and equality • Rights, justice and economic wellbeing • Critical reflection and analysis • Skills and interventions

Links to the Knowledge and Skills Statement for Child and Family Practitioners

• Relationships and effective direct work • Communication

Links to the Knowledge and Skills Statement for Social Workers in Adult Services

• Person-centred practice • Effective assessments and outcome-based support planning
• Direct work with individuals and families

Key messages

- Active listening is a core skill which is central to relationship-building with service users and co-workers alike.
- You can demonstrate active listening through body language, verbal and non-verbal communication.
- Active listening ensures that a service user's views, wishes and feelings are understood and attended to wherever possible.

INTRODUCTION

A key component in relationship-building is the skill of **active listening** which Egan (2007: 78) calls 'the foundation of understanding'. It is a skill that holds the potential to convey respect, empathy and understanding. The ability to tune in and attend to service users is critical to social work interventions, especially work involving person-centred communication, as discussed in Chapter 1. This is because listening to a service user's views, needs, wishes and feelings enables you to build partnerships, to remain person-centred and to be responsive. When supporting others, the capacity for **cultural humility** is critical as this enables you to suspend what you know (or think you know) based on your cultural knowledge and to really listen to a service user without drawing on cultural stereotypes or norms that may have no foundation. In terms of working in multi-agency settings, hearing the voice of co-workers and allied professionals is also important as it enables more effective collaboration.

ACTIVE LISTENING

Active listening ensures that what a person is trying to say is fully communicated and accurately received and understood by the listener. Active listening, therefore, is a core skill for social work which relies on accurate information gathering and interpretation during the processes of communication, assessment and intervention. An effective listener is required to have a high degree of self-awareness and be attuned to the thoughts, feelings and responses of others within and across interpersonal and professional contexts. Active listening is a demanding task as you need to be aware of how *you* are communicating, whilst observing and listening to *others*, and whilst remaining alert to your internal voice as it responds to the communication of others. Coulshed and Orme comment that:

> Only by listening and observing the way that people seek help can there be an effective interpersonal exchange which correctly receives overt and covert messages, decodes them and responds to the various levels of communication therein. People may say one thing but their behaviour may indicate the opposite. (2012: 85)

Indeed, a person's thoughts and feelings might be conveyed more effectively by their **body language** as by the words that they use (Moss, 2012).

Chapter 12 explores the importance of interviewing skills along with some of the verbal responses that we can use to demonstrate that we are listening. These include the skills of paraphrasing, reflection and clarification (see Table 2.1 for examples of these and other active listening techniques). These skills are critical to 'accurate listening' (van Nieuwerburgh, 2014).

Table 2.1   Active listening skills

	Service user says...	Social Worker replies...
Paraphrasing	'I went on the programme at the Chestnut Centre. I've done everything and I'm ready.'	'Let me check I'm clear about this. You have completed the parenting programme at the Chestnut Centre and made the changes to your home that were detailed on the support plan?'
Clarification	'Someone comes in to sort mum out with meals and care. Clean her and make sure she gets up and dressed.'	'Can I just check, a carer makes sure your mother has all meals and ensures that she gets up and is mobile?'
Probing	'Matt has got a job now in the charity shop and gets a lift there whilst I'm on holiday from my work.'	'That's great, but what will happen when you go back to work?'
Reflection	'I worry about him going out on his own at night. He is growing up and a young man. I know that, but I don't want to let him grow up so quickly.'	'This sounds really difficult for you.'
Validation	'I know I have to get away from him and stop him, end the abuse, but I don't think I can face going leaving my home and going to a refuge.'	'I appreciate your honesty in describing the situation and your feelings. I understand how difficult it must be to talk about this.'
Summarising	'She doesn't listen to a word I say. It's like talking to a brick wall and I really I can't stand the sound of her voice, going on and on.'	'So it sounds to me like there has been a breakdown in communication between you both.'

Reflective activity

As well as being mindful about the way that you respond in terms of *what* you say, it is imperative to be careful about *how* you say it. Tone of voice is key in conveying the intended meaning of a word or phrase. See how many different tones of voice you can use in saying 'what is the problem?' You will note how using different tones of voice can completely change the meaning and intention.

Some of the most powerful forms of communication are present in our non-verbal communication and this is particularly true in relation to active listening. Some non-verbal communication includes: posture; nodding the head; eye contact; and gesturing. Barker (2003) describes this group of behaviours as showing 'attentiveness' (this is discussed further below) and it is important to show that you are attending to a service user from the start of any face-to-face contact in order to show that you are interested in what that person has to say. Some service users can feel nervous, angry or scared and it can be very encouraging, and empowering even, to know that you are being listened to.

> ### Reflective activity
>
> Next time you enter into a conversation with someone which centres on a controversial issue, or where you have opposing views, try to abstain from putting your view across. Instead, let the speaker tell you what they think. Ask questions and probe to elicit their thoughts and feelings on the issue. Use your body language and gesturing to show that you are attending and listening (even if you do not agree).
>
> Note how you feel, and what thoughts run through your mind as the other person speaks. This may be a challenging task; it is intended to help you to be mindful about the complexity of the skill of active listening (particularly if your own view or position does not accord with the speaker).

Another way to communicate that you are listening is to use **paralanguage**. This is defined as:

> The non-lexical component of communication by speech, for example intonation, pitch and speed of speaking, hesitation noises, gesture, and facial expression. (Lexico, 2019)

Paralanguage includes 'ah', 'hmm' and 'uh huh'. Lishman (2009) adds a note of caution by highlighting how such vocalisations can be misunderstood by service users who interpret them as showing agreement with their views, and in this way these vocalisations can act to reinforce unhealthy, risky or discriminatory attitudes or behaviours. Thus, the use of paralanguage and non-verbal communication relies heavily on timing and clarity. There must be congruence in terms of the message that these vocalisations convey in relation to the view that is held.

Case study: Marian I

Sam, a social worker, undertakes a visit to Marian, a 70-year-old woman who lives in a care home. At the visit, Marian's 50-year-old daughter Joyce is present. Joyce is very unhappy and wishes to speak to Sam about her mother's care.

Table 2.2 Case study: Marian I dialogue

	Dialogue
Joyce	Sam, I'm not happy with the care worker who looks after my mum.
Sam	OK, tell me what is your concern.

(Continued)

Table 2.2   (Continued)

	Dialogue
Joyce	Well, it's a man. A young man …
Sam	Ah [nods head].
Joyce	… yes. Yes, I know. It's not right, is it? A young man should not be cleaning an old lady, or toileting her. It's not right.
Sam	Hmmm. No, no I mean, OK. I understand your concern, but I'm not sure I share it with you.
Joyce	Well, she's an old lady. [Sam looks out of the window] Clearly you don't understand what I'm saying, or it's not important to you.
Sam	Sorry, no. I just heard a car and it's the activities person. Marian loves that. Shall we take her to join in and you and I can talk about this without her present?
Joyce	[In an irritated tone] I suppose so.

Reflective questions

- How do you think Joyce feels at this point in the conversation?
- How would you have communicated differently during this short exchange in order to build a relationship and rapport with Joyce?

ATTENDING AND TUNING IN

Visibly tuning in and attending to others demonstrates empathic communication (see Chapter 5 'Developing Empathic Skills'). Egan (2007: 76) suggests some general guidelines to display attentiveness, whilst noting that some minor modifications may be necessary in order to practise in a culturally competent manner. Egan proposes the mnemonic SOLER:

S = sit squarely;

O = adopt an open posture;

L = lean towards the other;

E = maintain good eye contact;

R = try to relax, and be natural.

Birkenmaier et al. (2014: 72) offer some additional suggestions:

- Sit with uncrossed arms and legs.
- Use facial expressions, smiling and head nodding for positive reinforcement.
- Adopt a warm tone of voice.

- Use brief, encouraging comments.
- Avoid the presence of any physical barrier between you and the service user (large object, or heavy furniture).

Visit the website to watch a video of someone displaying active listening skills. https://study.sagepub.com/rogers2e

. . . .

Case study: Marian II

Reimagine a more positive conversation between Joyce and Sam where Sam demonstrates good active listening skills and Joyce feels that she is listened to.

Table 2.3   Case study: Marian II dialogue

	Dialogue	**Non-verbal communication**
Joyce	Sam, I'm not happy with the care worker who looks after my mum.	Sam moves head to face Joyce and obtains eye contact.
Sam	OK, Joyce, tell me what is your concern?	Sam uses facial expression to show concern.
Joyce	Well, it's a man. A young man …	Sam maintains non-verbal communication.
Sam	Tell me what it is you're worried about.	Sam moves the chair so that Sam and Joyce are facing one another; Joyce has Sam's undivided attention.
Joyce	I'm worried about him respecting her dignity. You know, like when he feeds her, cleans her, takes her to the toilet. He's only young, she's an old lady …	Sam nods slowly.
Sam	Joyce, I understand your concern. I really do. I've met Dan, the carer, and he seems like a very nice young man. Shall we speak to Marie, the manager, together and we can discuss this some more?	Sam demonstrates empathy, respect and understanding through a warm tone of voice, open body posture and facial expression.

Reflective question

- How do you think Joyce feels at this point in the conversation (compare this with the first scenario)?

. . . .

SILENCE AS A FORM OF COMMUNICATION

Silence can generate uncomfortable feelings, and it can be tempting to fill a silence with talking. There are other assumptions about silence; such as silences indicate that you are not listening, or have poor communication skills, or silence can show a failure on the part of the practitioner to build rapport and engage with the service user. These assumptions are not necessarily true, although silences can indicate a negative component of a relationship, and they can even be used for unconstructive means, such as disapproval, resistance or rejection. Trevithick (2012: 215) distinguishes between these 'troubled silences', which also include those moments of embarrassment or anxiety, and 'creative silences'. Creative silences can be used for communicating something meaningful, such as empathy or sadness. Silences can give the speaker time to take a breath and gather their thoughts, particularly critical if they have been talking about a painful experience or situation. From the position of the practitioner, the ability to be calm and quiet during a difficult conversation is an important skill.

Reflections from a newly qualified social worker

One of the biggest challenges I have encountered as a NQSW is knowing what to do and how to react when someone is struggling to answer something you have asked them. Personally, I have found this most problematic in my work with a service user with bipolar disorder. This particular service user could range through a number of emotions in any one visit and knowing when to divert the conversation or allow them time to think and answer has been very challenging. It has only been through building up a relationship with the service user and observing their reactions with others and during my visits that I have learnt how to use silence as a powerful tool. There are certain areas that this service user does not like discussing so often will take a while to answer, or will totally divert the subject. Recognising when they are in a place where they can emotionally handle discussing certain things has been a challenge; however, allowing them the space to think, and learning myself to be, if not comfortable, at least able to handle silence without feeling the need to start talking, has really helped me to gain lots of information that does not appear to have been disclosed to previous workers. It can feel incredibly awkward sitting in silence with someone, especially when you are acutely aware you only have a limited amount of time, but it is definitely worth practising. I've even started using silences in meetings to gain further information from other professionals!

CULTURAL HUMILITY, CULTURAL COMPETENCE AND LISTENING

Birkenmaier et al. (2014) point out that effective listeners need to develop **cultural competence**. This means that you should consider the social characteristics and backgrounds of service users (for example, gender, ethnicity, language, (dis)ability and other aspects of social location). However, before you can do this, you need to practise **cultural humility**, which is the sustained willingness to suspend what you know, or what you think you know, about a person using generalisations and stereotypes which are based on their culture. Instead, what you learn about a service user and their culture or heritage evolves from what they express as being an important part of their sense of self and everyday life. The ability to practise both cultural humility and cultural competence adds another layer of complexity to the task of effective listening, but you should always strive to practise in a way that recognises cultural difference. In particular, it is good practice to enable a service user to speak in their own language and it may be that you need to work alongside a skilled interpreter or another practitioner who is competent in using sign language, for instance. There are additional important issues that you may need to consider in relation to intercultural awareness (Ryde, 2009). For example, when working with ethnic minority families, white social workers may (knowingly or not) give messages through verbal and non-verbal communication that may imply racist or stereotypical attitudes; hence, the central importance of cultural humility in everyday practice contexts.

Visit the website (https://study.sagepub.com/rogers2e) to access a 'How to …' guide on 'working with interpreters'.

Reflective activity

When you are with a service user whose background and experiences are very different from your own, consider the following:

- What are my attitudes towards the person?
- Am I attending and tuned in to them?
- What attitudes or values am I demonstrating in my verbal communication?
- What attitudes or values am I demonstrating in my non-verbal behaviour?
- To what degree is my non-verbal communication congruent with my internal thoughts and feelings?
- Do I need to moderate my verbal/non-verbal communication to attend more/be more 'present' with this service user?

BARRIERS TO LISTENING

A skilled practitioner understands that active listening is a conscious, not subconscious, activity. This is critical as Forrester et al. (2008) found in a study of 40 social workers that when presented with case studies, there was a tendency for the participants to adopt confrontational and aggressive interpersonal styles. Forrester et al. (2008) did note, however, that the lack of empathic listening was considered to be indicative of systemic, rather than personal, failings. Egan (2007: 94–96) describes how barriers can lead to various forms of distorted listening including:

- *Filtered listening* – personal, professional, sociological and cultural filters affect what we hear, and therefore introduce bias without us being aware of it.
- *Stereotype-based listening* – again, subconsciously, drawing on stereotypes to make sense of what we hear.
- *Fact-centred rather than person-centred listening* – focusing too much on collecting factual information, and therefore missing the person.
- *Sympathetic listening* – sympathy has a place in human relationships, but its presence can impact upon the ability to empower and remain focused on the task.

Accordingly, it is useful to identify the daily barriers to effective listening and these can be related to the setting, the speaker or the listener (Lishman, 2009). The multitude of barriers includes: the physical environment (noise distractions, other people present, lack of privacy); interruptions (by other people, your mobile phone); lack of empathy; personality clashes; communication problems (English is not your or the service user's first language, speech is impaired by physical ailment, speech is impaired by substance misuse); having preconceived ideas or stereotypes about the service user; being preoccupied with your last visit or work task; second guessing what the service user means; daydreaming; organisational demands and priorities; and so on.

Reflective activity

In your reflections on the discussion offered in this chapter, consider the barriers to active listening. How might your actions counter some of these? You might more consciously adopt some of the practices included in this chapter including SOLER and cultural humility. You might need to think about communication aids (use of interpreter, sign language/ Makaton) or practical concerns (the physical space, timing).

CONCLUSION

Active listening is a mode of listening and responding to another person which enhances mutual understanding. Listening skills are intrinsic to social work practice, but this demands more than just listening to a service user. Effective communicators will be able to regulate their emotional responses, moderate their non-verbal communication and hear what a service user is saying. All in all, this is a complex task and one that can be obscured by many barriers, as noted above. The penultimate section demonstrates the many inhibitors to active listening and this list is not exhaustive. Therefore, these skills should be worked at through self-awareness and a reflective stance.

Having read this chapter, you should be able to:

- Identify the ways that active listening is a core skill which is underpinned by a number of techniques;
- Consider the barriers and enablers to active listening;
- Acknowledge that good active listening relies on cultural humility.

RECOMMENDED READING

Egan, G. (2014) *The Skilled Helper: A Problem-Management and Opportunity-Development Approach to Helping* (10th edn). Stamford, CT: Cengage Learning Inc.

Howe, D. (2008) *The Emotionally Intelligent Social Worker.* Basingstoke: Palgrave Macmillan.

Koprowska, J. (2014) *Communication and Interpersonal Skills in Social Work* (4th edn). London: Sage Learning Matters.

Lishman, J. (2009) *Communication in Social Work* (2nd edn). Basingstoke: Palgrave Macmillan.

Moss, B. (2017) *Communication Skills in Health and Social Care* (4th edn). London: Sage.

Communicating with Children
Donna Peach

Links to the Professional Capabilities Framework

• Professionalism • Values and ethics • Diversity and equality • Knowledge • Rights, justice and economic wellbeing • Critical reflection and analysis • Skills and interventions

Links to the Knowledge and Skills Statement for Child and Family Practitioners

• Relationships and effective direct work • Communication • Child development

Key messages

- Enabling children to communicate is important.
- Children's early experiences can influence their ability to communicate their thoughts and feelings.
- Good communication requires us to reflectively listen and observe.
- Reflexivity requires a high degree of awareness of our self and others, which takes time, practice and patience to develop.

INTRODUCTION

The UN Convention on the Rights of the Child (UNCRC) (Articles 12 and 13) asserts that children should be free to express their views in all matters. It recognises that communication involves the right to seek, receive and share information. However, supporting children of all ages and abilities in this endeavour is a complex task, which requires knowledge and skills in the following areas:

- understanding yourself;
- child development;
- power dynamics;
- interpersonal skills;
- limitations of communication.

As social work practitioners, we want to ensure that judgements we are making are in a child's best interests. This is something readily said but we can forget that it is actually a skill to create spaces for children to be able to make sense of and then communicate their thoughts and feelings. In the process of eliciting children's views, we need to safeguard against simply following protocols and task-orientated completion of forms. Equally, we should not hide behind statements of children or young people not being able or willing to engage. Instead, we must be robust in examining our own efforts to build relationships with children and to facilitate different methods to enable them to feel safe in sharing their wishes. A critical understanding of the interpersonal and structural constraints that are intrinsic to this process is vital. Therefore, this chapter examines key issues which underpin the multifaceted skill of communicating with children.

UNDERSTANDING YOURSELF

All human interactions have the potential to be fulfilling, confusing or harmful. As social workers, we need to understand our self, if we are to comprehend and overcome the barriers to communication. It is important to ask yourself continually, if you are the right person to be communicating with the child. Take time to reflect critically on the child's perceptions of you and explore how that may influence what the child is able to share. Use supervision to explore these issues and to identify what expectations or assumptions you may have about what the child's views may be. It is easy to fall into a false premise that what a child communicates with us is superior to the messages the child shares with others. However, we have to balance this with the need to be alert to hidden or absent messages that a child may be relying on us to interpret.

CHILD DEVELOPMENT

Our understanding of others extends beyond language and includes how we say things and how we behave. Therefore, effective communication with children requires a good

Reflective activity

Communicating with someone in a position of authority, who has the power to make a difference to your life, is something we have all experienced. Think of two occasions, one when you felt heard, and one when you did not.

- What was different about your experience on each of these occasions?
- How might you use this reflective learning in your communication with children?

understanding of child development. During your social work studies you will be introduced to a range of developmental theorists such as Jean Piaget, Sigmund Freud and Lev Vygotsky. Despite the dominance of these theorists, it is important to reflect on the social construction of childhood, as this facilitates inclusion of difference constructed by race, gender, disability and culture. Thus, it is vital that your learning extends to diverse cultural aspects of development across different age ranges (Washbrook et al., 2012).

Social work practice is often dependent on knowledge emerging from developmental psychologists to inform us about children's ability to communicate. However, as research methods develop, so does our understanding of how babies and children are able to communicate. This is most important if we want to do all we can to support young children and those with learning or communication disabilities to share their views and wishes.

Visit the website to listen to Philip Heslop talk about communicating with children with autism. https://study.sagepub.com/rogers2e

It is easy to assume that infants are unable to communicate in a meaningful way and this can lead to reports of a child being too young to convey their wishes and feelings. However, a prominent psychologist, Professor Colwyn Trevarthen, has researched the musicality and coordination of infant movement and how we can understand this in their relationship with others. Although the underpinning psychology may be complex to understand, Trevarthen's research encourages us to reflect beyond our current understanding and to contemplate an infant's ability to communicate. Visit the website (https://study.sagepub.com/rogers2e) to hear Colwyn Trevarthen, Emeritus Professor of Child Psychology and Psychobiology at the University of Edinburgh, talk about communication with very young children.

While much is yet to be understood, Trevarthen's (2005) research supports the premise that from birth (and other evidence, for example from López-Teijón et al. [2015], would show even before birth) infants are actively engaging with the world around them. Thus, observing children's behaviour is a fundamental part of how we can begin to understand their experience of relationships and their self. Therefore, an important skill in communicating with children is to adapt to their level of cognitive, emotional and physical development. Responding to their attention span and language development while also reflecting on their social awareness helps to minimise misinterpretation.

PREVERBAL COMMUNICATION

It is important to understand that we can communicate with young children who have yet to develop language skills. From 12 months onwards, most infants can interact with others using both sounds and gestures (Vaiouli and Andreou, 2018). However, communication is also about behaviour, what we observe and how we make sense of what we see (Papoušek, 2007). Our adult communication with infants often adapts intuitively as we slow down and exaggerate our speech and facial expressions. We instinctively understand that communication is simultaneously a learning experience for children. Through these exchanges, children develop their ability to use sound and expression to intentionally convey their feelings. In research terms, the evidence of how we understand infant communication remains formative, but fascinating. Most studies focus on maternal–infant relationships, (Frizzo et al., 2013; Slaughter et al., 2009) but some include paternal–infant communication (Bronte-Tinkew et al., 2008; Fernald et al., 1989).

The use of pictures, games and play can help to create a means of communication that is more familiar to the child, allowing them to share and discuss complex ideas. You can draw on helpful publications such as *The Anti-Colouring Book* by Susan Striker and Edward Kimmel (2004) and *Direct Work with Vulnerable Children: Playful Activities and Strategies for Communication* by Audrey Tait (2012). Furthermore, as noted earlier, it is vital that your learning extends to diverse cultural aspects of development across different age ranges (Washbrook et al., 2012).

Many children, for multiple reasons, are not able to communicate verbally and you will need to develop a relationship so you understand how each child interacts with you and with others. This may take the form of playful interactions, or be more specific to eye contact or the sounds that a child emits to express their emotions. Taking time to contemplate not only what children share in that moment, but how their views may shift over time is essential to a holistic view of their needs and desires.

Visit the website (https://study.sagepub.com/rogers2e) to hear Colwyn Trevarthen describe the musicality of a 5-month-old infant who was born blind.

POWER DYNAMICS

We need to recognise the power dynamics underpinning communication between adults and children. Social work students need to develop their reflective skills to enable them to identify the structural powers and constraints that might influence their communication with a child. These may include social policies, resource issues or commonplace practices, which limit the weight given to the views of the child (McLeod, 2010). However, limiting the child's voice when determining what is in their best interests can also be detrimental to the child (Holt, 2011). Therefore, communicating with children has to navigate coexisting and, at times, conflicting duties of protecting and empowering a child. This again draws on not only how we perceive our professional duties but also the social construction of children.

In the previous section, we referred to young children, but age is also a factor in our perceptions of teenagers. This has become evident through inquiries into recent scandals of child sexual exploitation, such as the Jay (2014) inquiry in Rotherham, which found that some social workers viewed teenagers as culpable in their abuse. However, these incidents are not limited to sexual abuse or to certain geographic areas. A report entitled *Don't Make Assumptions: Children's and Young People's Views of the Child Protection System and Messages for Change*, published by the Office of the Children's Commissioner (Cossar et al., 2011), provides some key insights that we must heed in practice.

You will find a link to this report on the website (https://study.sagepub.com/rogers2e).

Positive messages include: 'A few children recalled being part of a child protection investigation. The sensitivity of the professionals involved made a difference to how difficult the experience was for the young people' (Cossar et al., 2011: 13). Negative messages include: 'Some of the children found it difficult to talk to their social workers because they felt pressured by the social worker asking questions, or said that the social worker twisted what they said' (Cossar et al., 2011: 12). Although we may be inclined to consider that as individuals we would never fall foul of such practice, it is vital to accept this is always a possibility. To safeguard against this, we need to ensure our practice remains critically reflective. Supervision is a key part of this process, but to be consistently effective we have to develop cultures of critical practice in our organisations. Furthermore, recognising the limits to the power of the social work practitioner to protect information the child shares with them adds to the complexity of this interpersonal exchange.

Visit the website to listen to Lisa Brett talk about communicating with young children in direct practice (https://study.sagepub.com/rogers2e).

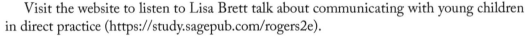

> ## Reflective activity
>
> - Think about how you would ascertain a child's understanding of your role with them as part of an assessment process.
> - Identify different children, by age, gender, race, class or ability/disability.
>
>   o What would you say or do?
>   o How would you do it?
>   o What communications might remain absent and how will you react to this uncertainty?
>   o How might this exercise influence reflective learning in your practice?

OBSERVATIONAL SKILLS

It can be easy to take observational skills for granted, but they have to be actively developed and practised. Our cognitive functioning is designed to take short cuts and to only process what is perceived to be relevant information. This is readily demonstrated by Daniel Simons' 'The Monkey Business Illusion'. You can find a link to this video on the website (https://study.sagepub.com/rogers2e). As you progress through your qualification and into social work practice, it is worthwhile creating opportunities to observe children of different ages and abilities, in different settings. Also, practise making notes while undertaking observations and on other occasions write up notes from memory to develop your recall skills. Make notes of what you saw and heard but also include reflective thoughts about how you drew on your own subjective experiences to make sense of what you observed. This aspect of learning is time intensive, but a worthwhile investment if you are to enhance awareness of your own skills and continuing learning needs.

- -

Case study: Andrew

Andrew is seven years old; he is subject to a care order and has been living with his foster family for 18 months. He has been having monthly contact with his mum, Becky, since the cessation of his care proceedings four months ago. Foster carer Sheila reports that Andrew's behaviour remains challenging especially after contact with his mum when he has difficulty sleeping for a few nights before and afterwards.

Reflective questions

- What information do you need to collate?
- How will you create a supportive environment to talk to Andrew?
- What information will you share with Andrew and when?
- What will be the key issues that you need to be mindful of?
- How would you communicate with Becky about the information she might want to share with Andrew?

- -

INTERPERSONAL SKILLS

Our own self-awareness can enhance our communication with children. As social workers, we often do not have control over the places within which we communicate with children. Therefore, the use of our embodied self is vital to creating a space in which meaningful communication can take place. An awareness of the memories that these communications may trigger for the child and indeed the memory making of these conversations is important. Thus, preparation for before, during and after your visit with the child is essential to support and empower the child. Allow the child to know that you are going to talk to them and consider how best to help them prepare, and plan to offer reassurance afterwards. This strategy should also be used with parents and carers, so that they and their relationship with the child are also supported, during what can be a lengthy and anxiety-provoking process.

The way in which we use touch to convey reassurance and empathy is a natural form of human communication. However, as a component of professional social work practice the use of touch in communicative practice is often constrained by concerns that it could be misinterpreted and thus cause harm to a child (Lynch and Garrett, 2010). Defining and making a commitment to child-centred communication remains a developing issue in social work, which relationship-based practice may assist with (Ruch, 2014). Understanding that communication is a dialogic process is the cornerstone of the National Children's Bureau's *Communicating with Children During Assessment: Training Pack* (Dalzell and Chamberlain, 2006). This is an open-access publication that you can link to via the website (https://study. sagepub.com/rogers2e).

CO-PRODUCING COMMUNICATION STRATEGIES

The Children Act 1989 requires us to include the wishes and feelings of the child when we are determining what decisions are in their best interests. The definition of what constitutes a child's best interests is multifaceted and therefore the meaningful inclusion of their views is vital to good decision-making. As stated above, the power dynamics between adults and children influence whether they feel heard. If we share power in decision-making with children and young people we recognise and support the integrity of their participation (Parnell and Patsarika, 2011). Increasingly, organisations such as the NHS recognise the valuable contribution of children and young people. We need to ensure that all children and young people have a consistent experience of inclusion throughout all aspects of their lives.

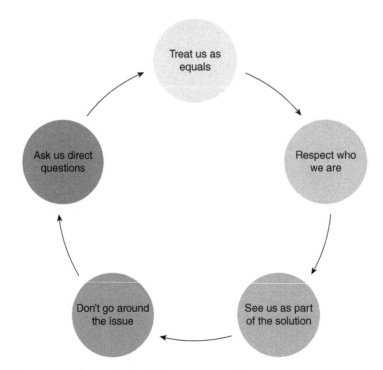

Figure 3.1   What young people say about starting a conversation

The NHS commissioned the 'Not Just A Thought …' (NJAT) project to co-produce a safeguarding model for children, young people and health professionals. Listen to the children and practitioners involved in the project (https://youtu.be/jSi5sAHSLsA) and hear how the key messages coming from the children and young people are about the need for good communication.

As shown in Figure 3.1, young people identified five key ingredients for starting a conversation. Being treated as equal and with respect is foundational to developing any relationship, but it is also an indication that we view young people as part of the solution. The NJAT contributors were also clear that in their experience adults can at times 'go around' an issue, perhaps because they are concerned not to upset the young people by asking the wrong question.

The clear message from young people is to ask direct questions. They even helped compile conversation-based questions which can be asked to explore the lives of children and young people. These questions and links to the other resources created by the project can be accessed on the project website www.notjustathought.org.uk and via the project report https://www.salford.ac.uk/__data/assets/pdf_file/0016/1532050/Not-Just-a-Thought-Report.pdf

Activity: Communication tool bag

Often as social workers, our discussions with children and young people can take place in a variety of settings, at their home, school, a playground or in your car. Everyday objects can be useful tools to assist communication, but it can also be helpful to have a supply of materials. These tips can also be shared with parents and carers to encourage them to identify accessible ways in which to communicate with children.

- Locate three everyday household items and write down how you could use these to communicate with a child. One example is the use of a washing-up sponge, using the soft side to talk about warm fuzzy feelings and the rougher scouring pad side to talk about cold prickly feelings. This can be done by letting the child rub each side of the sponge on her arm to sensitise her to the different touch experience.
- List 10 things that you will collect to form part of a communication tool bag that you can use when you visit a child.

Reflection from a newly qualified social worker

Undertaking direct work with children can be quite daunting, especially if you have not had a lot of experience of working with children and young people previously. I found that being prepared for direct work sessions, knowing what I would do during the session and what I

(Continued)

hoped to get out of it made me feel more relaxed, which helped the child relax and allow them to engage more effectively in the activities.

The local authority I work for has online resources and worksheets that can be really helpful in starting to undertake direct work with children. For example, during my student placement I was working with a child who we suspected was actually living with his grandparents but he and his parents always denied this. I used a 'Day in the life of …' worksheet with him that explored everything he did during the day and who he saw. As we went through the worksheet it became increasingly clear that he spent very little time at home, and even if he did actually sleep there, he was collected from school by his grandparents, did his homework there, ate his meals including breakfast and dinner there, bathed and got ready for bed there and was read his bedtime story there. This was very helpful as it allowed us to gain a better understanding of what daily life was actually like for him.

 Visit the website (https://study.sagepub.com/rogers2e) to access a practical guide: 'How to … Direct work with children'.

CONCLUSION

This chapter has demonstrated that communicating with children is complex and often undertaken at times when they might feel anxious and uncertain. Having an understanding of your own assumptions and the child's perceptions of you is vital. Any interactions are best when they take place within a secure relationship; however, sometimes social workers have to quickly develop rapport with children they do not know. As a social work student, it is good practice to begin to develop your observational and interpersonal skills. Find time to observe the behaviours of different children in order to better understand both verbal and non-verbal communication. Be creative in your approach and allow the child to guide you, at their own pace and in their own way. All our social interactions occur against a backdrop of social constructions, which influence the way we perceive others, and how they simultaneously view us. To navigate and appropriately encourage the inclusion of children's views and wishes, we need to be critically reflective of our engagement with them. Importantly, reflective practice is most consistent in an organisation committed to a culture of critical reflection. As students and in practice, we also need to be aware of how we contribute to the development and maintenance of our organisation's culture.

Having read this chapter, you should be able to:

- Understand the importance of enabling children to communicate, and create your own communication tool bag;
- Recognise the complex power dynamics that influence relationship-based practice;
- Examine how to support children to 'co-produce' the decisions that affect them.

RECOMMENDED READING

Frizzo, G., Vivian, B., Piccinini, A. and Lopes, G. (2013) Crying as a form of parent–infant communication in the context of maternal depression. *Journal of Child and Family Studies*, 22(4): 569–581.

Green, L. (2017) The trouble with touch? New insights and observations on touch for social work and social care. *The British Journal of Social Work*, 47(3): 773–792.

Lefevre, M. (2010) *Communicating with Children and Young People: Making a Difference*. Bristol: Policy Press.

Lefevre, M. (2015) Becoming effective communicators with children: developing practitioner capability through social work education. *British Journal of Social Work*, 45(1): 204–224.

Trevarthen, C. and Schore, A.N. (2001) Intrinsic motives for companionship in understanding: their origin, development, and significance for infant mental health. *Infant Mental Health Journal*, 22(1–2): 95–131.

Emotionally Intelligent Social Work
Donna Peach

Links to the Professional Capabilities Framework

• Professionalism   • Values and ethics   • Diversity and equality   • Critical reflection and analysis

Links to the Knowledge and Skills Statement for Child and Family Practitioners

• Relationships and effective direct work • Child and family assessment • Communication   • Analysis, decision-making, planning and review

Links to the Knowledge and Skills Statement for Social Workers in Adult Services

• Person-centred practice   • Effective assessments and outcome-based support planning • Direct work with individuals and families

Key messages

- Emotional intelligence is a complex and contentious concept.
- Emotions can arise from ourselves, those we work with and wider societal factors such as public awareness of the death of a child known to social services.
- To safeguard good practice, it is important to reflexively examine how emotions influence social work relationships.
- Nurturing your emotional wellness will benefit your social work practice.

INTRODUCTION

In its simplest form, emotional intelligence (EI) depicts our ability to recognise our own emotions and those of others. This process includes our ability to regulate our emotional responses and support others to do the same. As humans, we rely on our intuition when relating to others. However, in social work practice we need to demonstrate considered awareness of how our emotions affect others and vice versa. Often in practice, we are intervening at times of stress in people's lives. Indeed, it may be that our intervention, or lack of, is the cause of distress, anxiety or anger. Therefore, relational social work practice can require practitioners to psychologically 'hold' or 'contain' powerful emotions simultaneously held by themselves and others.

Good social work practice is emotionally intelligent; however, the research underpinning what EI is and how it is used in social work practice is highly complex. To unpack this, the chapter presents some models of EI and discusses our abilities and limitations in terms of transferring this knowledge into social work practice. Notably, it is common for social work students and even qualified practitioners to feel some anxiety when having to examine the complex theories that underpin our practice. In part, this is due to the realisation of the degree of uncertainty that can exist between research knowledge and professional practice. Arguably, we fill this gap with our reflexive self and use of supervision, which support a critical examination of our reasoned and intuitive responses.

In addition to this current chapter, there are several other chapters in this book which address the emotional and psychological impact of social work practice on both students and practitioners. Notably, the impact of vicarious trauma in crisis intervention (Chapter 31), developing an empathic practice (Chapter 5) and the importance of supervision in Chapter 20. As you read through all of the topics in this book, you will begin to realise the complexity of social work practice. The enormity of what we experience in our work is both stressful and anxiety-provoking, and hugely rewarding. The impact of our life and work experiences should not be considered a signifier of our abilities. Social work is made less stressful when the people we support have access to better public services, greater economic security, good education, decent housing, etc. Similarly, as students and practitioners, we also need to be well resourced and supported. That includes having adequate time, and access to resources to meet the needs of those with whom we work.

WHAT IS EMOTIONAL INTELLIGENCE?

Over the past 25 years, psychological research has aimed to define and understand **emotional intelligence** by examining the relationship between reasoned logic and emotions. This is a cyclical process: how we use logic to make sense of emotions and how our understanding of emotion can aid reasoned thought. Individually, the topics of intelligence and emotion are each extremely complex and subject to different interpretations.

Thus, to consider how they interrelate and how we can transfer that knowledge into social work practice is a huge challenge for two reasons. First, there are contrasting theoretical views of what it means to be human, which underpin research design, and the subsequent knowledge produced. Second, the integration of research knowledge into the development of social work skills is not an exact process and limitations of our understanding are therefore inevitable.

 Visit the website to listen to Andrew Whittaker talk about 'How Social Workers Make Decisions in Real Life Situations' (https://study.sagepub.com/rogers2e).

Several models of what constitutes EI form three broad categories, termed ability, trait and integrated (combining ability and trait models). Ability refers to our mental ability to determine feelings, such as how well you can judge the feelings of someone from a photograph of their face. Whereas trait models focus on how good we perceive ourselves to be at recognising and regulating emotion, and are often measured by the completion of self-reports. It is helpful to consider each of these terms as exploratory pathways to understanding, rather than the final answer to our understanding of EI. Indeed, while advances in neuroscience facilitate explorations of EI using measurements of brain activity (Killgore et al., 2012), we need to remain mindful of the social construction of emotion (Belli, 2010).

Ability

Mayer et al. (2012) developed an ability-based measure of personal intelligence. In order to test whether personal intelligence exists as a mental ability the researchers specified measurable items to demonstrate participants' understanding of emotional motivators and personality styles. If you read the paper, it will give you insight into the complexity of quantitative methodologies from which Mayer et al. relate what they term psychological mindedness to emotional intelligence. Although these concepts are complicated, they are important as they support the notion of our ability to interpret another person's behaviour.

Trait

Trait models explore characteristics such as empathy, stress management and adaptability (Bar-On, 2006). These traits are readily applicable to social work practice; for example, empathy is our ability to understand the feelings of another person. The development of empathic skills are discussed in more detail in Chapter 5.

Integrated/mixed

Some models integrate 'ability' and 'trait' based constructs. A seminal text from Goleman (1995) identified four main constructs: self-awareness, self-management, social awareness and relationship management. These integrated constructs of emotional intelligence suggest we need to understand both constructs of self and society. This enables us to look beyond ourselves as individuals and to examine how our emotions are interlinked with our social experiences.

Reflective activity

Type emotional intelligence test into any internet search engine and you will find a plethora of examples.

Visit the website (https://study.sagepub.com/rogers2e) to find a link to one measurement tool based on Goleman's (1995) seminal text. You *should not* use this to form any determinations about yourself or others, but this sample questionnaire can help illuminate the methodology of how EI is measured.

- What questions did you take longer to answer? Why do you think that was?
- Several questions ask about our reactions to being under pressure. Do you think you respond differently to different types or degrees of pressure?
- Did you find that you could choose either answer to some questions dependent upon the scenario you brought to mind?
- What view, if any, have you formed about the use of EI measurement tools?

EMOTIONAL INTELLIGENCE AS A SOCIAL WORK SKILL

By positioning emotion as central to the social work relationship, Ingram (2013a) builds on the work of Howe (2008) and Morrison (2007) linking EI to the expectations of service users and our professional core values. Ingram's (2013a) emotionally intelligent social work model (Figure 4.1) interweaves several theoretical strands of EI and aspects of relational

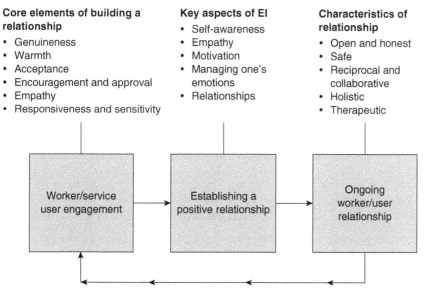

Figure 4.1 Ingram's intelligent social work model

Source: Taylor & Francis. *The British Journal of Social Work*, 43(5): 987–1004, July 2013.

social work practice. He uses connecting blocks to depict the stages of development of a practitioner and service user relationship. The core elements of building a relationship and ideal characteristics of a successful relationship will be readily identifiable to social work students. However, the model becomes complicated when we relate these to EI. We have seen the emergence of several tests for EI. One designed by Mayer et al. (2004) defined four branches of EI: perceiving emotion, facilitating thought, understanding emotion and managing emotion. Below we will discuss how these four branches relate to Ingram's intelligent social work model.

Perceiving emotion

Perceiving emotions is central to a social worker's ability to understand our self and others. Let us unpack what that actually means. Self-awareness requires a degree of consciousness about what we are thinking and feeling, which should extend to our understanding of the relationship between the two. Simultaneously, social work practitioners need to be able to perceive the emotional state of the person with whom they are communicating. In practice, we often have to assist people to reflect on and manage strong emotions that our actions may have precipitated. This can be further complicated if we are ourselves feeling frightened, aggrieved or confused.

As student social workers, it is natural for you to feel anxious and concerned, even frightened, as you undertake initial placement visits to meet service users. These feelings are perfectly natural and even helpful, providing we take time to recognise them and find ways to ensure that they do not overwhelm the purpose of your visit and the needs of the person you are meeting. Using a series of reflective activities allows us to walk through the following three branches of EI, and consider them as you prepare for or reflect on an initial placement visit to meet a service user.

Facilitating thought

One of the challenges of EI being constrained by a cognitive model is that it encourages us to contemplate thought as an individual activity. Whereas Morrison (2007) invites us to extend our worldview and to contemplate how our thoughts include those of others. These 'others' extend beyond those of the children, adults and families for whom we are the named social worker, and necessitate the inclusion of thoughts from our managers and other professionals who may have expectations of our practice.

Reflective activity

Use this reflective time to identify the thoughts and feelings you are having about your initial visit. It is important to remember that however long we are in practice we always still need to practise being self-aware in relation to the activities we are undertaking.

1   How are you feeling about your initial visit?
2   What thoughts do you have about the purpose of your visit?
3   How do you think you can demonstrate the core elements of wanting to build a relationship?
4   What thoughts do you have about how the service user(s) will present?
5   What do you think the person you are visiting is thinking about your visit?
6   Have you discussed your thoughts and feelings with your supervisor? If so, how did this influence your preparation?

Understanding emotion

Understanding emotion arises from the combined consciousness of how we perceive emotions and use our intellect to make sense of them. This process informs our decision-making. However, understanding emotions is complex, particularly within social work relationships, which often involve imbalanced power dynamics. Importantly, many failures in practice highlighted by serious case reviews (SCRs) are linked to situations when our understanding of emotional processes is incomplete (Ferguson, 2005; Munro, 2011). It is not difficult to imagine that a parent who is anxious that we may decide we want to remove their child could present as angry and frustrated. Equally, a social work practitioner who is anxious about asking difficult questions might falter and not make essential enquiries. As humans, these emotional responses are understandable; however, as professionals we need to develop the emotional intelligence that enables us to attend to these emotions.

Managing emotion

The term 'managing emotion' can disguise the real complexity of the emotions we experience as a social work practitioner. It is in our responses to the emotions of ourselves and others that our social work skills are most visible. This aspect of emotional intelligence extends beyond our internal thoughts and feelings and is expressed in all aspects of our behaviour. Thus, our interactions with others must be grounded in sincerity. In our practice, we bear witness to some of the worst and the best aspects of what it means to be human. Good social work recognises the emotional basis of our relationships, which includes experiencing the pain of our own mistakes and those of others. This demands resilience if we are to survive and help others survive stressful and challenging experiences. To sustain resilience in ourselves and others, we (and they) need to have robust and reliable support systems. Clearly, the supervisory relationship has a role to play in this, which is why reflective supervision is an essential component of social work practice (Ingram, 2013b).

EMOTIONAL COMPETENCE: STUDENT SOCIAL WORKER RESILIENCE

Broadly, emotional competencies can be understood as intrapersonal (inside our self) and interpersonal (relational with others) skills. The emotional competencies of EI include empathy, reflective ability and social competence, which are important to the resilience and wellbeing of social work students (Kinman and Grant, 2011). More specifically, from the findings of their study of 240 student social workers Kinman and Grant (2011) suggest emotional intelligence expands resilience which serves to promote psychological wellbeing. Their findings are important, particularly as their research found high levels of psychological distress with 46% of participants achieving scores which suggested some level of intervention. In particular, the researchers suggest student social workers would benefit from support that helped to develop emotional boundaries to reduce the incidence of empathic distress (Kinman and Grant, 2011).

Emotional wellness

Maintaining our emotional wellness is an important aspect of all our lives. It includes recognising and accepting how you are feeling. Emotional wellness has particular importance when our practice involves regularly empathising with people's traumatic experiences. The National Institutes of Health have a free online emotional wellness toolkit which includes six strategies for improving your emotional health:

- Brighten your outlook.
- Reduce stress.
- Get quality sleep.
- Cope with loss.
- Strengthen social connections.
- Be mindful.

You can find out more information about these strategies and locate other resources on the NIH website (www.nih.gov/health-information/emotional-wellness-toolkit).

When we are feeling stressed, it can be hard to engage in the strategies needed to feel emotionally well. Indeed, feeling emotionally unwell can lead us to seek comfort in activities that are unhelpful such as smoking and drinking. Below are some links to assist your awareness of and, if needed, engagement with strategies for good emotional health.

Brighten your outlook

Having a positive outlook can help to reframe situations that appear negative. However, moving from a negative to a positive outlook can be difficult and listening to upbeat music or finding a reason to laugh can help. In addition, the language we use to describe the situation is also powerful and changing how we describe issues and experiences can alter the way we think about it. Here is a link to a 10-minute TEDx talk from social psychologist Dr Alison Ledgerwood: https://youtu.be/7XFLTDQ4JMk

Reduce stress

Reducing stress is often related to lessening how anxious we feel. There is no single method that would suit everyone; some people like to write down their thoughts, others find exercise, cleaning or cooking are helpful activities. Use this link to see helpful tips from a range of psychologists: https://youtu.be/ENqcrQa5jno?t=3

Moodzone: Sleep problems

In this NHS podcast, Dr Chris Williams explains how we can address sleep problems that can at times last for several nights and weeks. These are important matters for students, who also have the extra pressures of studying demands in addition to those created by social work practice placements. Go to: www.nhs.uk/Video/Pages/sleep-problems-podcast.aspx

Cope with loss

Feelings of loss which can affect our health and wellbeing can occur as a result of multiple life events. Events such as coping with grief and bereavement can affect us all. At times, we can be misguided and think that our professional responsibilities mean we should not be emotionally affected. But emotions are part of who we are. Here is a link to a short NHS film about the experiences of a mountain rescue volunteer: https://youtu.be/qabCvFwmNyo

Strengthen social connections

Social connections with those we like and love are important to our wellbeing. This can be addressed by good organisations that facilitate social connections between colleagues. But outside of work it is also about time with friends and family, or even getting out and walking your dog. Take a look at this short animation: https://youtu.be/8az-gfljEbg

Be mindful

Mindfulness is a subjective psychological embodied experience as we take time to connect to our self-awareness and the world around us. Online you will find a range of mindfulness videos, and you may need to try several until you find one that suits you. You will find more information about mindfulness and good mental health on the mental health charity Mind's website: www.mind.org.uk/information-support/drugs-and-treatments/mindfulness/#.XEn7Klz7SUk

EMOTIONAL POLITICS

It is important to remind ourselves that we do not practise social work in isolation. In her recent text, Warner (2015) introduces the concept of emotional politics and situates this in the arena of social work and child protection. Not only does this serve to expand beyond the mainly attributable cognitive processes of individuals, but it enables a broader socio-logical view of factors that influence emotion. Her scope includes the role of the media and its relationship with politics when reporting and defining the role of social work(ers) following the death of a child. In practice, the publicised death of a child known to social services has a significant impact on child protection social workers and the families they work with. Amid the complex emotional politics described by Warner (2015), practitioners often need to navigate increased pressure to avoid risk. Unsurprisingly, both student and qualified social workers express concerns about their ability to practise effectively within a volatile socio-political environment. These dynamic social factors simultaneously increase the importance of EI in our practice while adding layers of complexity to the environments we work in. Warner (2015) demonstrates how events beyond individuals not only influence our understanding of self and others but also our interactions with them. Importantly, this complexity does not dismiss the usefulness of the above models, not least valuable concepts such as facilitating thought and managing emotion.

CONCLUSION

Emotion and our ability as practitioners to use it intelligently is a fundamental cor-nerstone of relational social work practice. However, the complexity of EI is evident theoretically and in our ability to integrate it consistently within our practice. Regrettably, a disruption in the consistency of EI is evident in SCRs following the death of children known to social services (Ferguson, 2005; Munro, 2011). Thus, the role and function of self-reflexivity and supervision are vital to maintaining the core elements of EI. This is especially true when we are aware of the social factors that influence the emotional landscape of social work practice. In particular, Warner (2015) provides a comprehensive debate that critically examines the interrelationship of the media and politics. This is important, as social work exists in a dynamic world where we are affected by discourses that surround and impinge on our practice. As such, there is a need to develop our critical understanding of the broader function of emotion in social work practice. To achieve this, we need to develop the debate about the role of social work in both child and adult protection. The responsibility for this lies with and beyond individual social workers; it is critical that politicians and the media consider their role in developing the emotional intelligence of our society.

Having read this chapter, you should be able to:

- Understand the multifaceted construct of emotional intelligence;
- Reflect on how your feelings interact with your practice experiences, and vice versa;
- Develop strategies to nurture your emotional wellness.

RECOMMENDED READING

Ferguson, H. (2005) Working with violence, the emotions and the psycho-social dynamics of child protection: reflections on the Victoria Climbié case. *Social Work Education*, 24(7): 781–795.

Howe, D. (2008) *The Emotionally Intelligent Social Worker*. Basingstoke: Palgrave Macmillan.

Ingram, R. (2013a) Locating emotional intelligence at the heart of social work practice. *British Journal of Social Work*, 43(5): 987–1004.

Morrison, T. (2007) Emotional intelligence, emotion and social work: context, characteristics, complications and contribution. *British Journal of Social Work*, 37(2): 245–263.

Warner, J. (2015) *The Emotional Politics of Social Work and Child Protection*. Bristol: Policy Press.

5

Developing Empathic Skills
Donna Peach

Links to the Professional Capabilities Framework

● Professionalism   ● Value and ethics   ● Diversity and equality   ● Rights, justice and economic wellbeing   ● Critical reflection and analysis

Links to the Knowledge and Skills Statement for Child and Family Practitioners

● Relationships and effective direct work   ● Communication   ● Child and family assessment
● Analysis, decision-making, planning and review

Links to the Knowledge and Skills Statement for Adult Practitioners

● Person-centred practice   ● Effective assessments and outcome-based support planning
● Direct work with individuals and families

Key messages

- There are diverse theories of empathy which reflect its complexity and what is yet to be understood.
- Practitioner to service user empathy is intrinsic to good social work practice.
- Empathy is a key element of emotional intelligent social work.
- The demands of multiple and competing needs can impact on our ability to work empathically.

INTRODUCTION

Empathy is intrinsic to good social work practice as it gets to the heart of the humanity of using our self to help others. However, social work students are often not provided with sufficient opportunities to understand and develop their empathic skills (Gerdes and Segal, 2009). This is, in part, because there is no consensus on how best to consistently teach empathy (Gerdes et al., 2011). Demonstrating empathy involves an ability to perceive the needs of others and to reflect on our understanding of their experiences. It is important that social workers situate the needs of the individual against the backdrop of socio-cultural factors. Empathic values should not be confined to service users and carers but are also integral to our inter-professional practice. However, there can be challenges when we are faced with the competing needs of ourselves, service users, carers and other professionals. Therefore, we need to use our moral and empathic compass to navigate these complexities and remain focused on the most vulnerable in our society.

How we make sense of what empathy is depends on how we understand what influences human behaviour. There are different theories of empathy that offer a variety of ways of understanding how people interact with one another. These different forms of knowledge (epistemologies) examine what we mean by empathy by exploring varied motivations underpinning how we behave. Historically, our knowledge of empathy has developed from two perspectives: the first is about our cognitive ability to understand what another person is feeling; and the second is how we are emotionally affected by someone else's feelings (Gladstein, 1984). The prominence of these models has developed in conjunction with the progression of psychological, sociological, **psychoanalytic** and more recently neurobiological theories. This complexity can leave student social workers perplexed when deciding how to ensure their practice is empathic. However, it is possible to identify empathic skills from the theoretical models and learn how to apply these within practice. This chapter will begin to guide you in how to achieve that.

Visit the website to listen to Juliet Koprowska talk about how social workers can apply interpersonal communication skills in their practice (https://study.sagepub.com/rogers2e).

EMPATHY OR SYMPATHY

There can be confusion about what the difference is between sympathy and empathy, this is often complicated by multiple definitions of both, which at times can appear to be the same (Eisenberg and Strayer, 1988; Trevithick, 2005). Both require an awareness of the needs of another; however, those who attempt to clarify their distinctiveness often attach the concept of 'emotional contagion' to a definition of empathy. Emotional contagion is a reflexive aspect of empathy which has been defined as 'the tendency to automatically mimic and synchronize facial expressions, vocalizations, postures, and movements with those of another person, and, consequently, to converge emotionally' (Hatfield et al., 1994: 153–154). This definition suggests that empathy involves a dynamic interaction between people that requires understanding across cellular, embodied, psychological and social paradigms.

However, it does not provide insight into whether, or to what extent, empathy is innate or learned. As a profession, it is important that we develop a detailed understanding of empathy, but in the meantime as a student social worker you need to have a pragmatic approach to being empathic. This will involve you taking steps to develop awareness of service users' experiences and convey that understanding to them.

Reflective activity

Watch this animation from the RSA where research professor Dr Brené Brown explains what is empathy: https://youtu.be/1Evwgu369Jw

---

A STAGED MODEL OF EMPATHY

In their process of reconceptualising empathy when exploring the behaviour of sex offenders, Marshall et al. (1995) proposed a four-stage model (see Table 5.1). This paradigm divides empathy into a series of staged responses.

Table 5.1   Marshall et al.'s (1995) four-stage model of empathy

Stage	Task
Stage one: Emotional recognition	This stage requires a person to recognise the emotion experienced by someone else.
Stage two: Perspective taking	This stage requires a person to perceive the world through the viewpoint of another.
Stage three: Emotion replication	This stage requires a person to reproduce the emotion that another is experiencing.
Stage four: Response decision	This final stage requires a person who has experienced the first three stages to make a decision on how they will or will not act as a result.

Source: Elsevier. *Clinical Psychology Review*, 15(2): 99–113, 1995.

Reflective activity

The following short videos will help explain some of the terms used in Marshall et al.'s model.

Emotional recognition: Is the process of identifying human emotion, most specifically from facial expressions: https://youtu.be/NnhKMUst4no

Perspective taking: Is the ability to understand how another person perceives an issue: https://youtu.be/DsSQtpCWPdg

---

Emotion replication: Is the ability to experience the emotion being experienced by another person. Some people who do not have this ability might have a psychopathic or sociopathic personality disorder: https://youtu.be/6dv8zJiggBs

Marshall et al. (1995) found some support for the usefulness of their model in understanding aspects of sex offenders' behaviour (Gery et al., 2009). However, the procedural structure of the model is also criticised for its inability to accommodate the speed of cognitive processes. For example, Pithers (1999) suggests that the speed of our compassionate responses means they could not be preceded by the earlier stages. In response to these views, Marshall and Marshall (2011) offered a revised model of empathy (see Figure 5.1) in which they suggest the lack of empathy demonstrated by people who commit sexual offences may be due to their inability to cope with the replication of the emotional distress that their victims experience. This has implications for the modes of intervention used with sexual offenders and others whose behaviour can cause harm and emotional distress. Importantly, more needs to be understood about the implications for social work practice when we engage with others who lack empathy.

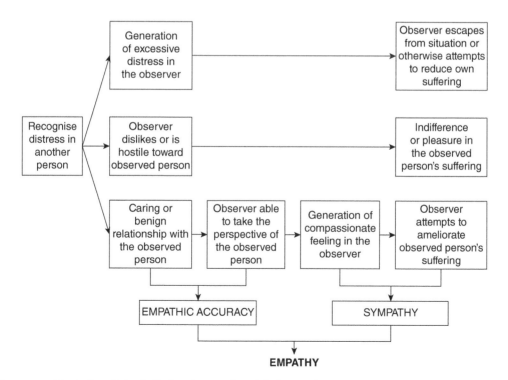

Figure 5.1 Marshall and Marshall's (2011) revised model of empathy

Source: Taylor & Francis. *Journal of Forensic Psychiatry and Psychology*, 22(5): 742–759, October 2011.

NEUROBIOLOGICAL MODELS OF EMPATHY

What is common to all theories is that empathy occurs in the interaction between people and our ability as humans to have understanding of another's experience. However, each theory takes a different approach to understanding this, which is often demonstrated in the weight each gives to the influence of cognitive and affective responses. Neurobiology is a sub-discipline of neuroscience and biology and it makes sense of human behaviour by exploring how our nervous system functions. As you would expect, neurobiology examines empathy at a cellular level, thus it observes and measure neuronal (nerve cell) activity and brain structures (see Figure 5.2) in order to make inferences about our capacity for empathy. The figure shows the frontoparietal mirror neuron system (MNS) (dark grey ovals) and visual input (lighter grey star shape) in the human brain. The anterior area of the MNS involves the posterior inferior frontal gyrus.

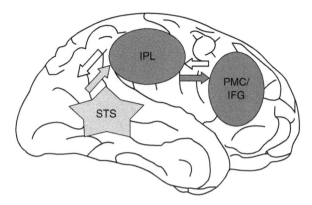

Figure 5.2   Neuronal basis of imitation (after Iacoboni and Dapretto, 2006, modified)

Source: After Iacoboni and Dapretto, 2006, modified. *Nature Reviews Neuroscience*, 7(12): 942–951, January 2007. Springer Nature. Reproduced with permission from Springer Nature.

Neurobiology is used to help us understand when our nervous system does not function as expected, often termed disorders. Neurobiological explanations of specific cell activity in particular areas of the brain proffer insights into 'disorders' such as autism (Wöhr and Scattoni, 2013). It is important to recognise that these explorations are in their infancy and that these cellular experiments are undertaken on rodents. Although this raises issues about the use of animals in research, it also indicates the distance between examining the activity of neurons (nerve cells) and the complex nature of human emotions.

Reflective activity

Gerdes et al. (2011) suggest that research into the function of mirror neurons can be used to examine how these influence interactions between people. The activity below is derived from some of their suggested activities:

1   Identify and watch an emotional scene between two to four characters in a film or programme. This could be a fictional account or you might want to use footage from programmes that depict actual situations, for example from reality television or those that reunite lost relatives.
2   After watching the clip:

    a   write down the feelings of each character/person;
    b   identify what you think motivated each character/person;
    c   write down what you think each of their intentions were.

3   Then watch the clip a second time; on this occasion make notes of the auditory and physical mimicry between the characters/people. What behaviours were empathic and why?

SELF TO OTHER MODEL OF EMPATHY (SOME)

Building on a neuroscience framework, Bird and Viding (2014) developed the 'self to other model' (Figure 5.3) in order to extend our understanding of how neuronal activity interacts with our cognitive representational systems. In essence, they are trying to explain the mechanistic cognitive structures that activate during our empathic encounters with others. Unsurprisingly, their model is a complex integration of psychological and neuronal concepts that individually endeavour to explain aspects of the way humans relate to and understand each other.

Figure 5.3 represents the input and representational systems involved in understanding one's own emotion. This model is difficult to interpret, which in itself demonstrates the social work challenge of applying theories such as theory of mind, which is a concept that depicts our ability to interpret another person's thoughts, emotions and beliefs. Note that although a representational system, the theory of mind system can also directly influence the affective representation system and therefore act as an input system. Empathy occurs via the action of the self/other switch which serves to bias input into the system so that it is appropriate for the other and assigns the resultant feeling state to the other. Conversely, emotion contagion can occur without the self/other switch and does not require the theory of mind system (Bird and Viding, 2014).

The field of neurobiology offers new and exciting modes of exploration, and it is important to understand these theoretical concepts and how they relate to other aspects of human development. However, it will always remain important to situate that knowledge in its social and cultural setting. The next section considers how Gerdes and Segal (2009) have adapted models of empathy and applied them to social work practice.

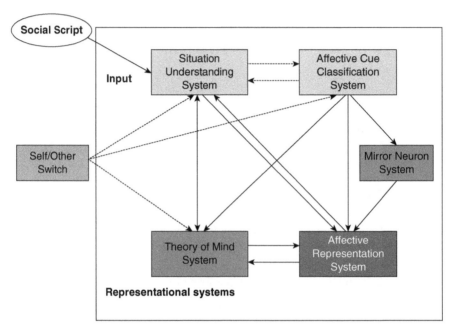

Figure 5.3   The input and representational systems involved in understanding one's own emotion

---

Reflective activity

Using your results from the previous activity, try to map the thoughts and emotional responses of each of your characters on Bird and Viding's (2014) model.

1   What are your thoughts and feelings about the potential interaction or separateness of our thoughts from our emotions?
2   Do you think there is greater reliability in how we interpret someone's thoughts and motivations or in our perception of their emotional state?
3   Reflect on how you might use the concept of mirroring in your social work placement.

A SOCIAL WORK MODEL OF EMPATHY

The Social Work Dictionary (Barker, 2003) defines empathy as 'the act of perceiving, understanding, experiencing, and responding to the emotional state and ideas of another person'.

This implies that in social work practice empathy is a means by which we can demonstrate how we value another person's view of the world. Importantly, empathy requires knowledge of ourselves and a willingness to critically explore our thoughts and feelings. As social workers, we share experiences with others that are often traumatic and emotionally charged.

To explain the cognitive and emotional experiences social workers have when engaging with others, Gerdes and Segal (2009) developed a social work model of empathy (see Table 5.2). Their model draws on a broad range of theoretical models of empathy applied to core components of social work practice, which reflect how social work is committed to social justice, and involves working with people in the social environment. Social workers are required to uphold principles of social justice supporting equality across economic, political and social spectrums. However, in practice, social workers can be challenged when the complex issues underpinning social justice conflict with the action or inaction of individuals.

Table 5.2 Social work model of empathy (Gerdes and Segal, 2009)

Component	Definition	Key aspects	Ways to develop
Affective response	Involuntary, physiological reaction to another's emotions and actions	Mirroring Mimicry Conditioning	Promote healthy neurological pathways
Cognitive processing	Voluntary mental thought processes used to interpret one's affective response; enables one to take the other person's perspective	Self-awareness Mental flexibility Role taking Emotion regulation Labelling Judgement Perspective taking Self-agency	Set boundaries Practise mindfulness Use role plays
Conscious decision-making	Voluntary choices for action made in response to cognitive processing	Empathic action Social empathy Morality Altruism	Helping Advocacy Organising Social action

Source: Gerdes and Segal (2009) *Advances in Social Work*, 10(2). Reproduced with kind permission of the authors.

EMPATHY IN SOCIAL WORK PRACTICE

There is a paucity of research into the use of empathy in social work practice. However, a recent study suggests social work communication in the area of child protection lacks a high level of empathy (Lynch et al., 2019). The methodological basis for their research is a mix of quantitative and qualitative data, from a source of audio recordings and applies a motivational interview definition of empathy. Lynch and colleagues had two research questions:

- What are the behavioural components of social worker communication of empathy?
- What are the qualitative features of social worker communication of empathy?

Their initial analysis explored four aspects of verbal behaviour which they associate with empathic skill: open questions, closed questions, simple reflections and complex reflections. The second stage of their analysis found that the length of the interaction correlated to the level of empathy demonstrated. The researchers admit their study has a number of limitations, but it is a useful read as we begin to make sense of what we think of as empathic social work practice. In particular, you may find the extracts of interviews useful to reflect on your own style of communication, particularly during conversations that have an assessment focus.

 Visit the website to listen to counselling scenarios focused on empathy (https://study. sagepub.com/rogers2e).

. . . .

Case study: Kathy

Kathy has mild learning difficulties. She is mother to four children: Simone, 14; Jack, 12; Ben, 6; and Thomas, 4 years old. Simone and Jack have the same biological father named Dave and a man named Phil fathered the younger two children. Dave's contact with the children is sporadic, but they talk fondly of him. Phil has been convicted of domestic violence towards Kathy; he has recently been released from prison and wants to continue a relationship with his children. The older children do not like Phil but his sons say they want to see their daddy. As a student social worker, you are asked to engage with Ben and Thomas to gain a greater understanding of their wish to see their father.

Using Gerdes and Segal's model, contemplate the affective responses that you might encounter when you meet with Kathy, Phil, Dave and each of the children.

Reflective questions

- What factors might be present that influence your motivations as you prepare to engage with the family?
- What empathy do you feel for each of the individuals involved? Do you feel more empathy for some members of the family; if so, what factors are influencing this?
- Did your empathy towards members of the family change as you considered each of their potential viewpoints?
- What are the cognitive processes that you can expect to navigate when considering each of their needs and abilities?
- What thoughts and feelings are you conscious of as you consider the decisions you might want individuals in the family to make or to agree to?
- How will you mediate any difference in your empathic understanding of their needs and what decisions you think are in their best interests?

. . . .

Although, the above models can support useful explanations of behaviour, as humans we are not consciously aware of our brain activity or of theoretical intricacies when relating to others. Thus, as social work practitioners we adopt a reflexive use of self to ensure that our social work practice accords with the needs of other people. This requires us to be critically aware of the influence of personal perceptions and social constructions when we are making determinations about the capabilities of others. Although we may all profess to have a universal ability to empathise, research evidence tells a different story. Pertinent for social work students and their educators is an Australian study which found that 23 of their 38 participants could not fully empathise with four emotive narrations, which included expressions of grief and loss (Gair, 2010). Other studies of professionals highlight their capacity for self-protection, such as medical professionals working with people in acute pain (Jankowiak-Siuda et al., 2011). This suggests there is a need for further research on the relationship between our personal and professional self and our use of empathy.

Reflective activity

- How do you know what someone else is feeling?
- Do you rely on what you think or how you feel when making decisions about someone else's experience?
- Do you think cognitive processes of professional rationalisation impact on our ability to empathise with service users and carers?
- Do you think that there are limitations in how much we can empathise with someone from a different class, gender, ability or culture?

CONCLUSION

Although we might think we know what empathy is, this chapter has demonstrated that it is a complex phenomenon which requires a multifaceted explanation. We have considered various models of empathy and highlighted their individual contribution to knowledge and limitations. Our understanding of what constitutes empathy includes cognitive, behavioural and emotional components. This chapter has highlighted recent research which is beginning to explore ways we can capture, analyse and understand how empathy is evidenced in practice. However, our understanding remains in its infancy and more research is needed to develop both our knowledge and practice.

The necessity of social workers to have empathy is without question and has implications for the individuals they work with. However, the application of empathy in social work practice is not straightforward, especially when we consider the multiple and complex needs of individual family members. The successful navigation of these issues is reliant upon our ability to reflect upon and understand the role of thought and emotion integral to empathic processes. Furthermore, we have demonstrated that empathy is integral to our profession's capacity to uphold wider principles of social justice. Thus, the way in which we practise empathy has implications not only in ensuring the wellbeing of others, but also in the maintenance of professional and social values of equality.

Having read this chapter, you should be able to:

- Understand the difference between sympathy and empathy;
- Identify the different theories of empathy and how they have been used to develop a social work model of empathy;
- Reflect on your own use of empathy and the impact it can have on the quality of your relationship-based practice.

RECOMMENDED READING

Gair, S. (2010) Social work students' thoughts on their (in)ability to empathise with a birth mother's story: pondering the need for a deeper focus on empathy. *Adoption and Fostering*, 34(4): 39–50.

Gerdes, K.E. and Segal, E.A. (2009) A social work model of empathy. *Advances in Social Work*, 1(2): 114–127.

Gerdes, K.E., Segal, E.A., Jackson, K.F. and Mullins, J.L. (2011) Teaching empathy: a framework rooted in social cognitive neuroscience and social justice. *Journal of Social Work Education*, 47(1): 109–131.

Lynch, A., Newlands, F. and Forrester, D. (2019) What does empathy sound like in social work communication? A mixed-methods study of empathy in child protection social work practice, *Child and Family Social Work*, 24(1): 139–147.

Reflection and Reflexivity

Michaela Rogers

Links to the Professional Capabilities Framework

- Professionalism   • Values and ethics   • Diversity and equality   • Skills and interventions
- Knowledge   • Critical reflection and analysis

Links to the Knowledge and Skills Statement for Child and Family Practitioners

- Communication   • The role of supervision

Links to the Knowledge and Skills Statement for Social Workers in Adult Services

- Person-centred practice   • Supervision, critical reflection and analysis

Key messages

- The art of critical reflection is a core skill for social work practice.
- There are several models of critical reflection.
- Critical thinking enables a reflexive approach; it requires an open mind as you need to adopt new ideas and perspectives.
- Reflexivity requires a high degree of awareness of self and others whilst being mindful of power relations and socio-cultural factors.

INTRODUCTION

In recent years there has been a mounting recognition that the social work profession has become constrained by the growth in managerialism and the preoccupation with risk (Featherstone et al., 2014; Munro, 2011). Unsurprisingly, there has been a renewed interest in **reflective practice** as this is said to help counter the dominance of bureaucratic processes, prescriptive legislation and policy frameworks (Ruch, 2005). The call for reflective practice has not only resulted from this recognition, but from an acknowledgement that reflection greatly helps practitioners to manage the challenges of working in a climate which is characterised by uncertainty, complexity, risk and constant flux (Fook and Gardner, 2007). Reflective practice offers the skilful practitioner a means to consider their use of self, their actions, thoughts and judgements as well as the actions of co-workers, the organisation and, of course, service users and carers in order to plan for future interventions.

MODELS FOR REFLECTION

Boud et al. (1983: 43) describe the act of reflection as 'an important human activity in which people recapture their experience think about it, mull it over and evaluate it'. Put simply, reflective practice is the ability to step back and think about your practice and the actions of others after, or during, an activity or intervention. Successful reflection emphasises the centrality of self-awareness and the capacity for analysis.

Reflective activity

Think about a recent event or exchange that you have had with another person in a professional context or another incident that is not personal to you. Think about your characteristics (imagine you are looking in a mirror) – what do you see? Do you think that any of your characteristics influenced the exchange? Have there been previous occasions when your characteristics have had an advantage, or disadvantaged you? Whilst you can identify these occasions, do you understand why your characteristics influenced what happened?

Most models of reflection have been influenced by the seminal work of Donald Schön (1983). Schön proffered the metaphor of the 'swampy lowlands' to describe the messy business of people-work, contrasting this with the 'high ground', which embeds theory and research, where problems are more easily resolved. Reflective practice integrates informal knowledge (intuition and tacit knowledge) and formal knowledge (theory, research and the evidence-base) in the process of making sense of situations and Schön linked reflection to the everyday knowledge that we bring to that process:

When we go about the spontaneous intuitive performance of the actions of everyday life, we show ourselves to be knowledgeable in a special way. Often, we cannot say what it is we know. … Our knowing is ordinarily tacit, implicit in our patterns of action and in our feel for the stuff with which we are dealing. It seems right to say that our knowing is in our action. (2002: 50)

This 'knowing-in-action' depicts the knowledge that you use and demonstrate in practice. Schön also identified distinct modes for reflection as a conscious activity:

- *Reflection-in-action*: the capability to reflect in the 'here and now' as something gives you a 'jolt', or having a 'feel' for something and practising according to this feeling;
- *Reflection-on-action*: the process of looking back to reflect on your actions or an event.

Most models of reflective practice are relationship-focused, **strengths-based** and, importantly, offer a counter-narrative to the pressures of the social work task (Featherstone et al., 2014; Ruch, 2005). Whilst there is a role for legally driven processes, there is also recognition of the need for practice that values creativity, professional judgement and **practice wisdom** (see Chapter 11 'Assessment Skills') (Munro, 2011). This position mirrors Schön's emphasis on the value of tacit and intuitive knowledge gained through experiences in the field. Moreover, the opportunity for regular reflection facilitates intuitive practice as it enables regular contemplation and evaluation of your practice, and, importantly, the opportunity to plan and identify training or development needs. This type of forward-thinking maps onto another reflective mode, reflection-for-practice, which encourages reflection on a topical issue or current case whilst planning for future interventions (Scragg, 2013; Thompson and Thompson, 2008).

The work of another influential theorist, Kolb (1984), resulted in the 'experiential learning cycle', a practical model that facilitates transformative learning. Kolb's model illuminates the iterative nature of reflective practice and contains four stages, which are:

- *Concrete experience*: being aware of an experience and attaching some value to it;
- *Reflective observation*: reviewing or reflecting on the experience;
- *Abstract conceptualisation*: moving to analysis, making links with theory and learning from the experience;
- *Active experimentation*: planning for future practice.

Kolb (1984) accepts that you may enter the reflective circle at any stage, but in order to ensure that links are made between each, he advocates that you should follow the stages in sequence. Reaching the 'active experimentation' stage does not necessarily mean the end of the process; another reflective cycle may begin. Building on Kolb's model, Graham Gibbs (1988) developed another model for practice, the 'reflective cycle', which offers a memorable format for the reflective process (see Figure 6.1).

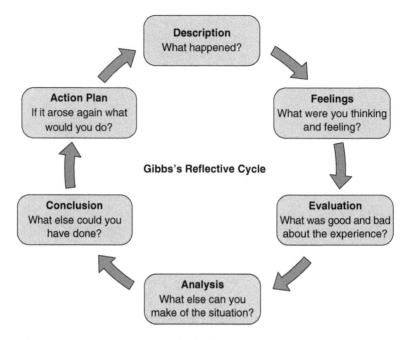

The reflective cycle was originally published in G. Gibbs (1988) *Learning by Doing: A Guide to Teaching and Learning Methods* (Further Education Unit. Oxford Polytechnic: Oxford). This book is now available to download as an ebook from the website of the Oxford Centre for Staff and Learning Development, Oxford Brookes University at http://www.brookes.ac.uk/ocsld/publications/

Figure 6.1　Gibbs's reflective cycle

Source: Reproduced with permission of the Research & Business Development Office, Oxford Brookes University.

This framework is helpful and popular with reflective practitioners as it reminds one to consider thoughts and feelings, as well as making an evaluation and constructing an analysis before reaching some kind of conclusion. If used on a regular basis, the reflective cycle can encourage 'thinking systematically and constructively' (Woolliams et al., 2011: 15).

Reflections from a child protection social worker (using Gibbs, 1988)

Description

Amy is 14 years old. Amy's parents admittedly had poor parenting skills and were struggling to provide effective guidance and boundaries. Amy would repeatedly be missing from school and was known to associate with older people. Discussing Amy with the team manager during supervision, she decided on a course of intervention for the parent. I felt the focus was on the parenting and not on the child. The risk was defined as 'bad parenting' and the team manager required me to encourage the parents to attend a parenting programme. However, through a relationship-based approach to direct work with Amy over a short period of time she disclosed that she was the victim of persistent attacks of emotional and physical abuse from two pupils at her school.

Feelings

Working with teenagers with complex emotional and behavioural difficulties have been the most rewarding and challenging experiences of my career so far. Intuitively, I felt that there was more to Amy's behaviour than just 'bad parenting'. I could sense the love that the parents had for their child, and vice versa. I knew that Amy's behaviour needed further exploration; however, time was not on my side as my assessment was given a tight timeframe by the team manager. I felt that I had to find time after my working day had finished in an attempt to get to know Amy better and to understand a day in her life.

Evaluation

It was a good feeling to have put the extra effort in with Amy on a one-to-one basis. This enabled her to open up and talk about what was causing her so much worry, hurt and anger. However, it wasn't good that from my manager's perspective it was the parents who were the focus and to ensure they attended a parenting class. As such, I chose to work extra hours to enable my one-to-one visits with Amy.

Analysis

A previous assessment had been completed on the family. That also focused on the parenting element: the lack of guidance and boundaries, as well as the lack of parents' engagement with services. The focus on parenting and parents' issues, rather than the child, is a common problem as social workers have been criticised in serious case reviews for losing sight of the child in this case. The requirement for Amy's parents to undertake a parenting programme needs further consideration as such interventions have been criticised and described as imposing of middle-class values on working-class families (Gillies, 2005). As such, this requirement can be experienced as shameful and stigmatising (Holt, 2010). Moreover, it has been highlighted that taking a capability approach, rather than one that pathologises, is a more humane and socially just social work practice (Gupta et al., 2016). However, a recent study has shown the benefits of parenting programmes when practitioners fully engage with attending parents (Symonds, 2018). In my direct work with Amy through a relationship-based approach I was able to build trust to the point that ensured a positive outcome and full disclosure of various underlying issues that were leading to her challenging behaviour. This direct work, rather than the attendance of Amy's parents on a parenting programme, helped us to move forward.

Conclusion

My lack of confidence within supervision meant that I didn't challenge the team manager's conclusion. In future, I will remain child-centred and advocate for what I feel is right for the child, and not their parents. This would help to ensure that the child's voice is heard.

CRITICAL INCIDENT ANALYSIS

A popular framework for reflection is entitled the 'critical incident analysis', which can be used when thinking about a specific incident. A critical incident is 'where an individual has taken some action and whatever he or she does has important consequences either for him or herself, the service user, others involved or all of the players' (Thomas, 2004: 104). A simple version of a critical incident analysis is offered by Beverley and Worsley (2007) which prompts you to analyse your feelings and actions in relation to a specific event:

1   Something surprises, confuses or disturbs you.
2   Recall the facts, thoughts and feelings.
3   Why did you do what you did?
4   What other ideas might help you understand and deal better with such a situation in the future?

Like many reflective models (some sketched out above), Beverley and Worsley's model is represented in a circular format, recognising that the process of reflection is ongoing, and not linear with a clear start and finish.

Reflective activity

Think about a recent event on placement or from practice where the outcome was unsuccessful or where there was an important consequence. Using Beverley and Worsley's questions prompts you to move around the cycle to reflect on the outcome and identify further learning needs, and/or plan for similar scenarios that may occur in the future.

ALTERNATIVE TOOLS

Borton's (1970) reflective model is very simple and encompasses just three question to be asked of the experience or intervention to be reflected on. These are:

1   What? (This is the description) – What is the incident, event or problem that you need to think about? What was your role? What happened and what did you do?
2   So what? (This is the analysis) – What was going through your mind? What thoughts, theory or research guided your actions and intervention? What were the consequences of your actions and intervention? What was so important about this experience? What did you learn?
3   Now what? (This is the synthesis) – Now what do I need to do? Are there further consequences of your actions and intervention? What could you do differently in the future?

Visit the website to listen to Siobhan Maclean talk about reflective practice (https://study. sagepub.com/rogers2e).

Another simple tip is to keep a reflective diary or log on a regular basis (daily or weekly). This is useful as it helps to structure your thinking, giving prompts for evaluative and analytical thinking. Examples for headings include:

- Brief description of the event.
- What was my reaction?
- What was I feeling at the time?
- What theory can I use to make sense of the event?
- What have I learned from the event?
- What might I do differently in future?
- Future learning needs.

EMBEDDING VALUES

Values are central to reflective practice (Parker, 2010). Integrating social work values (for example, respect, empathy, equity) helps to encourage open, honest and critical dialogue. This is critical as social work involves working with people from all sorts of backgrounds with a vast range of experiences, and skilful practice is flexible and responsive, and relies on continuous reflection. Ixer (2003) asserts that social constructs such as race, gender, sexuality and others should be continually explored within reflection. This helps to acknowledge the impact of social location and imbalances of power and privilege, contextualising these in relation to social work values. This also benefits personal insight as one's own values can be identified and sometimes challenged through this reflective, iterative process. The critical incident analysis can be a very useful tool in this respect and it has been successfully implemented in reflective work to look at diversity and oppression (Parker, 2010).

Reflective activity

- What values and cultural beliefs influence your actions and thinking?
- Which values and cultural beliefs influence the behaviour of others?
- Do you need to change your approach or language? Does your body language show empathy/trust/respect?
- Do you make assumptions? What are they founded upon? Are other people making assumptions; what are these based upon and how can you make sense of them?
- Are other people genuine and does their language/behaviour fit with your assumptions/understandings of their cultural beliefs and values?

DEVELOPING A CRITICAL AND REFLEXIVE APPROACH TO PRACTICE

Other writers have explored values and Fook (2002) points out that *critical reflection* can reveal the structural issues and power imbalances that impact on people's lives, helping to engender a broader understanding of socio-cultural, political contexts. Being 'critical' does not mean to adopt negativity, but to take an ever-questioning approach. Brookfield concludes that:

> … thinking critically involves our recognising the assumptions underlying our beliefs and behaviours. It means we can give justifications for our ideas and actions. Most important, perhaps, it means we try to judge the rationality of these justifications. We can do this by comparing them to a range of varying interpretations and perspectives. (1987: 13–14)

A critically reflective practitioner, then, can demonstrate a high degree of self-awareness as they understand their influence and use of self as central to skilful practice. Simultaneously, critically reflective practitioners will draw on and synthesise different types of knowledge: for example, relevant theories, the evidence-base, or consider the impact of social characteristics (socio-economic status, gender, age, ethnicity, etc.). The ability to critically reflect on practice, drawing on practice wisdom, theory or research to explain the behaviour or thought processes of ourselves or others, at a micro (individual) level, involves skill and regular practice.

As a social work student or newly qualified social worker you should be given ample opportunity to create reflective time and space, and you should aim to hone the skill of reflection to incorporate breadth and depth. Thompson and Thompson explain what this means:

- *Critical breadth*: Practitioners have the ability to recognise underpinning arguments and/or assumptions (these may be 'false, distorted or otherwise inappropriate' as well as positive and pertinent). Practitioners ensure that their thinking is not flawed (and potentially misleading, or even dangerous) and that they are not persuaded or carried away by the flawed thinking of others.
- *Critical depth*: Practitioners move from atomistic thinking to incorporate their reflections into the wider socio-politico-cultural context of practice and the lives and communities they serve. Thus, you should consider power dynamics, inequality, oppression and exclusion. (2008: 155)

If the ability to reflect can be mapped onto a continuum, a basic ability for reflection is at one end (for example, where you consider whether an intervention has had a successful outcome), while critical reflection and **reflexivity** is at the other (it is this critical end that you should be aiming for). Reflexivity involves the ability to 'reflect-in-action' whilst thinking critically. Put another way, being reflexive means:

… tak[ing] account of different perspectives, experiences and assumptions. … What is required increasingly is a capacity to handle uncertainty and change, as well as being able to operate in accordance with professional skills and knowledge … being continually aware of the discretionary and contextual basis of [our] practice. (Glaister, 2008: 8–9)

Engaging in this level of reflexivity, or critical practice, can be positively transformative. As Rutter and Brown (2012: 4) point out, thinking reflexively and critically can 'result in major shifts in our ways of thinking and the development of reflective scepticism, i.e. when nothing is regarded as a universal truth, or taken on trust anymore'.

Reflective activity

- What is your response to the statements made by Rutter and Brown?

Nothing is regarded as a universal truth: Rutter and Brown suggest that there is no single way to look at a situation, or to make sense of it, as we all draw from different perspectives, emotions and experiences when trying to evaluate and analyse a situation. *[Nothing is] taken on trust anymore:* remember that learning from public inquiries can help to enhance your practice. Following his inquiry into the death of Victoria Climbié, Lord Laming (2003) recommended that social workers adopt 'respectful uncertainty' in their work with service users. The notion of respectful uncertainty encourages you to consider that first appearances are not always as they seem and social workers should always adopt an inquisitive approach.

BARRIERS TO REFLECTIVE PRACTICE

For some people that art and skill of reflection comes easily. For others it does not, but it is something that can be learned. Either way, there are many obstacles that can impede reflective practice including:

- lack of personal insight and the belief that you've learned all there is to know;
- fear of opening up to others and the feeling or belief that evaluating your practice leaves you vulnerable;
- clashes of personality within the supervisory relationship;
- misuses of power within the supervisory relationship;
- lack of workplace support, or a culture that is not 'safe';
- belief that 'reflecting' is a waste of time;
- using reflection as therapy.

In addition, Parker (2010: 30) illustrates the complexity of the reflective task when noting 'it is not easy to develop reflective practice in our paradoxical assessment culture that emphasises both critical reflection and rather instrumental performance criteria'.

Whilst the benefits of reflective practice are clear, you should always acknowledge and respond to the potential barriers and attempt to manage the tensions inherent in the practice environment. There are strategies that you can employ to counter some of these; for example, get into the habit of having 20 minutes of reflective time at the end of the day, or use a reflective diary on a regular basis. If the supervisory relationship presents an obstacle (for any of the above reasons) be assertive and, using your skills as a social work practitioner, see if you can instigate an open and honest dialogue with your supervisor. Alternatively, seek to meet your needs to reflect on casework by having reflective discussions with co-workers.

CONCLUSION

Within this chapter we have provided you with different models and you can find extra proformas on the companion website (https://study.sagepub.com/rogers2e) for you to use in your reflective time at the end of each day.

We have considered what it means to be a critically reflective practitioner and the value of making time for reflection. Whilst most people are able to reflect to some degree, what we argue is that the ability to reflect at a deeper, more reflexive level is a key skill in social work practice and one that can be developed throughout your career.

Having read this chapter, you should be able to:

- Consider the ways that reflection and reflexivity underpin good ethical practice;
- Identify a number of different models for reflection;
- Consider the barriers and enablers to reflective practice.

RECOMMENDED READING

D'Cruz, H., Gillingham, P. and Melendez, S. (2007) Reflexivity, its meaning and relevance for social work: a critical review of the literature. *British Journal of Social Work*, 37(1): 73–90.

Fook, J. and Gardner, F. (2007) *Practising Critical Reflection: A Resource Handbook*. Maidenhead: Open University Press.

Knott, C. and Scragg, T. (2016) *Reflective Practice in Social Work* (4th edn). Exeter: Learning Matters.

Ruch, G. (2009) Identifying 'the critical' in a relationship-based model of reflection. *European Journal of Social Work*, 12(3): 349–362.

Thompson, N. and Pascal, J. (2012) Developing critically reflective practice. *Reflective Practice: International and Multidisciplinary Perspectives*, 13(2): 311–325.

The reflective cycle was originally published in Gibbs, G. (1988) *Learning by Doing: A Guide to Teaching and Learning Methods* (Further Education Unit. Oxford Polytechnic: Oxford). This book is now available to download as an ebook from the website of the Oxford Centre for Staff and Learning Development, Oxford Brookes University at www.brookes.ac.uk/ocsld/publications/

Understanding Values, Ethics and Human Rights

Dawn Whitaker

Links to the Professional Capabilities Framework

• Values and ethics   • Diversity and equality   • Rights, justice and economic wellbeing
• Knowledge   • Skills and interventions   • Contexts and organisations

Links to the Knowledge and Skills Statement for Child and Family Practitioners

• Relationships and effective direct work   • Communication   • Child development
• Adult mental ill health, substance use, domestic abuse, physical health and disability
• Abuse and neglect of children   • Child and family assessment   • Analysis, decision-making, planning and review   • The law and the family and youth justice systems   • The role of supervision   • Organisational context

Links to the Knowledge and Skills Statement for Social Workers in Adult Services

• The role of social workers working with adults   • Person-centred practice
• Safeguarding   • Mental capacity   • Effective assessments and outcome-based support planning   • Supervision, critical reflection and analysis   • Organisational context
• Professional ethics and leadership

Key messages

- Values, ethics and human rights are fundamental to social work practice.
- Values are personal, professional and political.
- Ethical practice must be situated and politicised.
- Rights-based practice necessitates critical reflection and reflexivity.
- The principles of anti-oppressive practice are embedded within social work education, research and practice.

INTRODUCTION

Values, ethics and human rights are fundamental to social work practice. Not least because social work is a complicated task that frequently involves us having to balance competing and conflicting rights and responsibilities. In this context, values, ethics and human rights help us navigate our way through uncertain and contradictory avenues of practice. Hence, though arguably it is a legal question whether to remove a child into care, the law does not dictate what ought to happen, just what is legally authorised (Banks, 1995). This illustrates how social work decision-making involves a complex interplay of value judgements, ethical considerations, and **socio-legal** and political issues that influence how we should interpret the law in practice.

THE TENSIONS OF SOCIAL WORK INTERVENTION

It is argued that the legitimacy of social work intervention stems from the privileges attached to the professional role. Indeed, Gewirth asserts that professionals, by virtue of their status, are *separatist* as they have rights and duties that are different and sometimes contrary to those of ordinary individuals (1986 cited in Clark, 2000). Conversely, Goldman argues that the moral obligations of professionals are no different from those of other members of society (1980 cited in Clark, 2000). Whilst this is a view that many in social work would find appealing, it fails to take account of the profession's **statutory responsibilities** that are separate from ordinary morality; for example, when social workers use their **statutory powers** to legally limit the self-determination of others, be that in regard to child protection, criminal justice, mental distress or **safeguarding adults**.

Whichever approach one adopts, the simple image of social work as a helping profession is clouded when interventions conflict with the expressed wish and preference of those who use services (particularly where individuals are non-voluntary service users). It is in situations like these that social workers must look to their values, ethics and codes of practice for guidance.

WHAT ARE VALUES AND ETHICS?

In the most basic and literal sense, values are valued *because* they reflect the things we value (Knowles and Lander, 2012 in Bassot, 2013: 74). Consequently, they usually mirror deep-rooted beliefs about ourselves, others and the world that reflect our personal, social and cultural context (Bassot, 2013: 74). In this sense, values are the 'elements of life' that people think should be 'cherished, preserved, promoted or respected' (Bell, 2018: 4). In social work, however, our values are personal *and* professional, meaning that in addition to our personal values, we must also subscribe to what are referred to as *social work values*. For Bell (2018: 7–8) these fall into two categories, 'traditional' and 'modern' or **'emancipatory'**, whereby traditional values emphasise the *rights of the individual,* such as the 'right to respect for persons', the right 'to self-determination', 'confidentiality' and so on. Whereas, modern or emancipatory values shift attention from the individual helping relationship, to the *broader structural factors* that impact people's lives, such as inequality, disadvantage, discrimination and oppression (Bell, 2018: 9–10).

However, whilst our personal and professional values might share certain core features, such as an intention to better understand the world and how we should act within it, they also differ from each other regarding personal and professional expectations and commitment. For example, though we may attach personal importance to individual liberty and self-determination, these values coexist alongside our professional values including safeguarding people from harm. This distinction is important, given that as social workers, we have a duty to adhere to the values of our profession, even where they may differ from our own: for example, restricting one person's right to liberty and self-determination in order to safeguard them and/or others from harm.

It is unsurprising, then, that whilst there is general agreement that social work is a **'values-based profession'** (Barnard, 2008: 6), there is a lack of consensus regarding how we understand the term. Critics argue that this is a deliberate strategy aimed at avoiding the need to address the messy complexity of values in practice. Indeed, it is said that the concept of values 'derives its popularity and legitimacy from the fact that it is an apparently simple, universally accessible concept ... delighting all and offending none because most people do not take the trouble to think about what it actually means in their own lives or those of others' (Pattison, 1998: 352).

Reflective activity

The following values have been regularly cited in stakeholder publications as those to be pursued in the provision of services: independence; citizenship; empowerment; social inclusion; respect for diversity; and care and protection for children and adults at risk (Waine et al., 2005: 7).

Consider the values that influenced your decision to become a social worker and to what extent they are compatible with those cited by the stakeholders above.

In practice, values and ethics combine to form a set of prescriptive rules or professional standards that instruct how we should act in uncertain or contested situations (Walz and Ritchie, 2000). A useful example is the Statement of Ethical Principles set out by the International Federation of Social Work, which focuses on:

- Recognition of the inherent dignity of humanity
- Promoting human rights
- Promoting social justice
- Promoting the right to self-determination

- Promoting the right to participation
- Respect for confidentiality and privacy
- Treating people as whole persons
- Ethical use of technology and social media
- Professional integrity (IFSW, 2018).

Additional guidance takes the form of professional **codes of practice**, such as those produced by the Health and Care Professions Council (HCPC) and British Association of Social Workers (BASW). Go to the website for this chapter, and familiarise yourself with the following codes of practice for social work (https://study.sagepub.com/rogers2e):

- HCPC Guidance on Conduct and Ethics for Students;
- HCPC Standards of Conduct, Performance and Ethics for Registrants;
- HCPC Standards of Proficiency for Social Work;
- BASW Code of Ethics.

Whilst formal codes of practice are considered by many to be 'a useful starting point', they 'cannot and should not be a substitute for practitioners engaging in ethical reflection' (Clifford and Burke, 2009: 56). Although regard for proceduralised, formal codes of practice may achieve conformity with prescribed rules and standards, this is unlikely, in isolation, to provide meaningful guidance for ethical action (Banks, 2014).

Situated and politicised ethics

In contrast to the procedural, formulaic approach to ethics, a new view has emerged founded upon professional autonomy and person-centred human relationships. Banks (2014: 18) outlines an approach termed 'situated ethics', within which people are valued according to the 'particularities' of their lives, in addition to 'the context of structures of power and oppression'. In this way of thinking, ethics are simultaneously person-centred *and* political, or as Banks declares 'a situated ethics of social justice':

> *Situated ethics* – ethics is not just about dilemmas and making difficult decisions about rights and resources by rational deduction from abstract principles. … Ethical being and ethical action require sensitivity to the particularities of situations and human relationships, and encompass emotion (empathy, care and compassion) as well as reason.

> *Politicised ethics* – if we regard social work as a movement as much as a profession or job, then we need to relate social work ethics explicitly to movements that promote practice that is variously categorised as anti-oppressive, critical, structural and radical. (Banks, 2014: 18)

Thus, the 'matter of ethics cannot be divorced' from our 'personal commitments and values' or from the 'wider political and social context' in which they exist (Banks, 2014: 18).

Anti-oppressive practice

As discussed above, anti-oppressive practice (AOP) is a component part of our journey towards achieving Banks's 'situated ethics of social justice' (Banks, 2014: 18). AOP is founded upon 'social work's historical concern with the underdog'; that is, people whose lives are affected by 'struggles against structural inequalities like poverty, racism and disablism' (Dominelli, 2009: 50). However, the nature of what constitutes anti-oppressive practice is contested due to the differing language used to describe the approach. Thompson (2012a) refers to anti-discriminatory practice (ADP) as an umbrella term that includes anti-oppressive action, whereas others separate out anti-discriminatory and anti-oppressive practice as having different, albeit related, intentions. For example, Clifford and Burke (2009: 2) view ADP as action to address individual or local discrimination, but AOP in terms of addressing wider structural and political issues.

Despite this definitional conflict, consensus exists regarding the need to challenge **discrimination** and **oppression** at both **micro** and **macro** levels. In doing so, AOP 'focusses on the use and abuse of power on and by various systems within society' (Teater, 2010: 11). This is demonstrated by Thompson's (2006) personal, cultural and social model of oppression (see Figure 7.1).

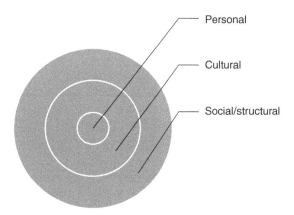

Personal

Cultural

Social/structural

Figure 7.1 Thompson's PCS model (2006)

Source: Republished with permission of Red Globe Press from Anti-discriminatory practice, Thompson, N., 6th edition, 2016; permission conveyed through Copyright Clearance Center, Inc.

Whilst acknowledging the individual experience of oppression as diverse, the model simultaneously identifies how oppression develops from interacting elements of social life, specifically **P**ersonal prejudices, **C**ultural beliefs, and wider **S**ocial and structural factors:

- Personal, or psychological – referring to individual thoughts, feelings and actions. The 'P' also represents practice (in terms of social work) and professional prejudice (in relation to inflexible attitudes and biases).
- Culture – 'shared ways of seeing, thinking and doing'. Culture refers to 'unwritten rules' and shared understandings, and, as such, it is influential in terms of setting out what is **'normative'**. The 'C' also denotes consensus and commonality.
- Social and structural – this refers to the dynamic network of structural relations and power. It prompts us to consider the institutionalised nature of inequality and discrimination and the socio-political dimension of power, privilege and influence. (Thompson, 2012a: 33–34)

Reflective activity

Reflect on a situation either on placement or in practice when Thompson's PCS model was or could have been applied. Try to map your answers against each of the three categories.

Comment:

- You should have identified some personal ways that people can contribute to or experience oppression, for example, the use of derogatory language, or an individual being treated negatively because of a personal characteristic.
- Cultural oppression can also include offensive language or jokes, as well as stigma and social exclusion.
- Structural analysis might involve the misuse of power in institutional systems, to create discrimination and inequality in wider society, i.e. education, employment or health and social care.

This analysis demonstrates the way in which personal, cultural and social aspects of life interact to create and reinforce discrimination and oppression. As social workers, it is important that we remain mindful of the way in which power is embedded within and across these systems, as this will help us remain anchored to anti-oppressive practice in our everyday work. You will return to this model in Chapter 8 regarding valuing difference and diversity.

 Visit the website to listen to why social justice and advocacy is important in social work (https://study.sagepub.com/rogers2e).

SOCIAL WORK AND HUMAN RIGHTS

Just as social work values and ethics should be situated and politicised, human rights can only be realised on a day-to-day basis if people show concern for each other *and* wider social factors. This is echoed in the global definition of social work approved by the International Federation of Social Work:

> Social work is a practice-based profession and an academic discipline that promotes social change and development, social cohesion, and the empowerment and liberation of people. Principles of social justice, human rights, collective responsibility and respect for diversities are central to social work. Underpinned by theories of social work, social sciences, humanities and indigenous knowledge, social work engages people and structures to address life challenges and enhance wellbeing. (IFSW, 2014)

Whilst the core concepts of this definition are open to debate, they do affirm the centrality of 'ethical and political concepts' such as human rights to the profession of social work (Clifford and Burke, 2009: 2). These reflect 'big picture values'; that is, the values that ought to underpin our day-to-day practice (Lomax and Jones, 2014: 53).

Reflective activity

- Think of an example where these 'big picture' values have been evident in your practice.
- How might ethical and political concepts like human rights drive your future practice?

WHAT ARE HUMAN RIGHTS?

In 2015, the UK marked the 800th anniversary of the sealing of the Magna Carta (or Great Charter), and the 15th anniversary of the implementation of the UK Human Rights Act (1998). Although separated in time by 785 years, these instruments represent a long-standing historical commitment to human rights in the UK. Modern human rights originate from the Universal Declaration of Human Rights (UDHR) in 1948, established in the aftermath of the Second World War. It was primarily intended to ensure that the atrocities committed during the war would never happen again. Whilst the Declaration is not, in itself, a legally binding instrument, it has spawned numerous national and international laws, treaties and institutions aimed at promoting and protecting human rights across the globe. The best known and most relevant to social work include the United Nations Conventions on the Rights of the Child (UNCRC), the Rights of Persons with Disabilities (UNCRPD) and the Elimination of All Forms of Discrimination against Women (UNCEDAW) (Johns, 2017).

The UDHR affirmed three types of rights: (1) 'civil and political rights', such as the right to a fair trial; (2) 'economic, social and cultural rights', such as those concerned with income, education and health; and (3) international 'cooperation' rights regarding economic development and the environment, and so on (Healy, 2008: 736). Prior to its enactment, 'there was almost no system that enabled criticism of – let alone action against – Government mistreatment of people within its borders' (Bowen, 2014). The UDHR also acted as a catalyst for European leaders to establish the regional European Convention on Human Rights (ECHR) in 1950. In contrast to the UDHR, the European Convention is a legally binding document, aimed at protecting certain fundamental rights; for example, the right to life, the prohibition of slavery and forced labour, and the right to liberty and security. In essence, modern human rights instruments decree that no government is above the law. They establish a 'set of minimum standards' that apply equally to everyone; and while they 'may be limited or restricted' in certain circumstances, they 'cannot be taken away' (British Institute of Human Rights, 2015).

The UK Human Rights Act 1998

The Human Rights Act (HRA, 1998) was intended to *bring rights home*, that is, embed the protections of the European Convention (ECHR) into UK domestic law. Essentially, it enabled UK citizens to bring human rights claims to national courts, rather than having to appeal to the European Court of Human Rights in Strasbourg.

The Act is fundamental to social work, given its 'desire to embed respect for human rights into the fabric of public services' provision (McDonald, 2007: 79). Consequently, social workers, as agents of **public authorities**, have an obligation to act in accordance with the Act, and take it into account during their day-to-day work.

Some rights under the HRA are *absolute*, and cannot be infringed, whereas others are *limited* (provided there is a proper basis in law), or *qualified* (where interference is lawful, legitimate, necessary and proportionate) (see Table 7.1).

Table 7.1   The Human Rights Act

Article	Absolute, Limited or Qualified
Article 2: Right to life	Absolute
Article 3: Prohibition from torture	Absolute
Article 4: Prohibition of slavery and forced labour	Absolute
Article 5: Right to liberty and security	Limited
Article 6: Right to a fair trial	Limited
Article 7: No punishment without law	Absolute
Article 8: Right to respect for private and family life	Qualified
Article 9: Freedom of thought, conscience and religion	Qualified
Article 10: Freedom of expression	Qualified
Article 11: Freedom of assembly and association	Qualified

Article

Article 12: The right to marry, does not fit into any of the categories of rights set out above. The detail and substance of this right should be decided according to national law. However, this must not be arbitrary or amount to an unnecessary interference.

Article 14: Prohibition of discrimination: There can be no discrimination in the application of human rights on any basis. This is described as a 'piggyback' right, in that rather than providing a standalone right to non-discrimination, it ensures that all other rights under the Act are secured without discrimination. Consequently, this right is only actionable where it is established that another right is also engaged under the Act.

Reflective activity

Identify and reflect on an event on placement or in practice where one or more of the Articles of the Human Rights Act (1998) might have been relevant. This may be in the context of safeguarding children or adults, the provision of residential or inpatient accommodation, or some other type of protective or restrictive intervention.

For social work, achieving human rights and social justice is a work in progress. While, 'the strong compatibility of the profession's mission and values' accords with human rights (Healy, 2008: 745), more needs to be done:

> We have not yet reached that state where dignity and justice for all people is either recognised or practiced. The fact that we have not yet achieved that state in our societies is the reason why many people become social workers – to work with people for positive change in their lives. … Where people are abused, harmed, discriminated against, commit violent acts against others; are confused, suffering from mental health issues; are deprived of basic life sources like food, water and shelter – you will find a role for social workers to help achieve social inclusion, social cohesion and social justice. (Stark, 2008)

Yet, as we celebrate the anniversaries of the Magna Carta and Human Rights Act, the current government is taking steps to reduce its commitment to human rights, through proposals to repeal the HRA, in favour of a British Bill of Rights. A Bill intended to 'limit the use of human rights laws to the most serious cases', depending on what is deemed to be an 'appropriate balance between individual rights and responsibilities to others' (Conservative Party, 2014: 4, 7).

Critics argue this is nothing more than a British Bill of Rights swindle:

> An attempted self-deception – a deception both of those who are for and against the notion of human rights. It is an attempt to pick and choose which and crucially whose freedoms are convenient for protection … potentially destructive to law, politics and the values that underpin democracy itself. (Chakrabarti, 2012: 454)

As social workers, we must remember that our profession grew out of 'humanitarian and democratic ideals'; therefore, practice must continue according to our core values of respect for the equality, worth and dignity of all people, regardless of the political climate that surrounds us (IFSW, 1992 cited in IFSW, 2002: 7).

· ·

Case study: Priya and Sunil

Priya and Sunil have two young children. As parents, they both have learning disabilities.

Social services wanted to ensure that the children were safe and well cared for. So, a decision was made to monitor the situation by staff arriving at the family's home every day without warning. Priya and Sunil found this very distressing, resulting in a constant state of anxiety and feeling frightened to open their door.

This had a real impact on their family time, and it was difficult for them to enjoy activities with their children.

Priya was in touch with an advocacy service who explained how the Human Rights Act protected the rights of family members to respect for private and family life (Article 8). With the advocate's support, Priya and Sunil explained to social services that they understood their right to respect for private and family life could be restricted to safeguard their children's right not to be harmed, but that such restrictions need to be lawful, legitimate, necessary and proportionate.

The couple felt that daily unannounced visits weren't proportionate, and that this had a negative impact on them and their children. In response, social services agreed that in the future, they would arrange their visits with Priya and Sunil in advance, so they could regain some control over their lives, unless there was an emergency. After which, Priya and Sunil felt like they had been able to regain their privacy and family time.

The above represents a real-life case, taken from the British Institute of Human Rights. You can find a link to this real-life case on the website (https://study.sagepub.com/rogers2e).

· ·

For further information on the Universal Declaration on Human Rights (UDHR), the European Convention on Human Rights (ECHR) and the UK Human Rights Act (HRA), visit the website (https://study.sagepub.com/rogers2e).

CONCLUSION

In this chapter we considered how values, ethics and human rights can help inform our practice. We also stressed the importance of understanding these concepts personally, professionally and politically, if we are to make anti-oppressive, **rights-based** social work a reality.

Having read this chapter, you should be able to:

- Reflect on the relationship between your personal and emerging professional values;
- Be familiar with core social work codes of practice and ethics;
- Understand the importance of situated and politicised ethics;
- Know how to engage in anti-oppressive practice;
- Understand the relevance of human rights to social work practice.

Visit the website to watch a video discussing the challenges that social workers have with diversity and equity (https://study.sagepub.com/rogers2e).

RECOMMENDED READING

Banks, S. (2014) *Ethics: Critical and Radical Debates in Social Work*. Bristol: Policy Press.

Barnard, A. (2008) Values, ethics and professionalization: a social work history. In A. Barnard, N. Horner and J. Wilde (eds), *The Value Base of Social Work and Social Care: An Active Learning Handbook*. Maidenhead: Open University Press, pp. 5–24.

Cemlyn, S. (2008) Human rights practice: possibilities and pitfalls for developing emancipatory social work. *Ethics and Social Welfare*, 2(3): 222–242.

Clifford, D. and Burke, B. (2009) *Anti-Oppressive Ethics and Values in Social Work*. Basingstoke: Palgrave Macmillan.

Healy, M.L. (2008) Exploring the history of social work as a human rights profession. *International Social Work*, 51(6): 735–748.

Johns, R. (2017) *Using the Law in Social Work* (7th edn). London: Sage.

8

Valuing Difference and Diversity
Michaela Rogers

Links to the Professional Capabilities Framework

• Professionalism • Values and ethics • Diversity and equality • Rights, justice and economic wellbeing • Knowledge • Critical reflection and analysis • Contexts and organisations

Links to the Knowledge and Skills Statement for Child and Family Practitioners

• Relationships and effective direct work • Communication • Child development • Adult mental ill-health, substance misuse, domestic abuse, physical ill-health and disability

Links to the Knowledge and Skills Statement for Social Workers in Adult Services

• Person-centred practice • Mental capacity • Direct work with individuals and families

Key messages

- Social identity is multidimensional and dynamic.
- Valuing difference and diversity underpins ethical social work.
- A skilled and reflexive practitioner will frequently review their practice to ensure that it reflects a commitment to valuing diversity and promoting equality.
- Valuing difference in social work practice is congruent with the principles of the Equality Act 2010.

INTRODUCTION

The composition of society is increasingly multicultural. This means that the social work profession requires reflexive practitioners who can respond to people's diverse identities, practices and needs. This is especially important for people who are socially excluded or experience marginalisation. In addition, the ethical foundation of social work requires practitioners to value difference: whether this is on the grounds of identity, background or experience. Indeed, the ability to be non-judgemental and respectful of difference is critical to reflexive *and* **anti-oppressive practice** (see Chapters 6 and 7).

This chapter introduces the notion that social identity is multidimensional and fluid to serve as a reminder that people are complex beings whose life experiences and social backgrounds are diverse. This is important as life events, social backgrounds and characteristics inevitably impact on wellbeing and how those individuals experience the world. The second half of the chapter considers practice implications and the importance of legislation, specifically the Equality Act 2010, which are constituent parts of the framework that underpins good, ethical practice.

SOCIAL IDENTITY AND INTERSECTIONALITY

It is generally acknowledged that our social identity is composite: it is made up of various characteristics and different aspects of social location. For instance, we belong to categories of gender, socio-economic status, ethnicity, age, sexual orientation, (dis)ability and so on. Our affiliation with various social categories can influence our life experiences and our unique identity provides us with a positive, or negative, 'sense of self'. Jenkins (2014) asserts that there are two interdependent processes which are integral to social identity: the processes of similarity and difference. Pointing to the interaction between the two, Jenkins (2014: 22) notes that 'neither makes sense without the other, and identification requires both'. Moreover, Jenkins offers a framework for understanding what he terms 'the internal and external moments of the dialectic of identification' (2000: 7). Put simply, this embeds an understanding of two iterative and dynamic practices: how we identify ourselves (internal identification – individually or in relation to group identification) and how others identify us (external social categorisation). It can be concluded, then, that identification is relational, intersubjective and constantly evolving.

The concept of intersectionality builds on the notion that identity is multidimensional. It emerged through Black feminist theory to explain how oppression is multilayered, but also how it is experienced by Black women in the context of other aspects of identity (see Crenshaw, 1991). As such, intersectionality can be drawn upon to understand how people's different social positions overlap. Intersectionality is also useful in helping to explore the connections and relations between different social categories (Anthias, 2008). It has, however, been criticised as rather 'mechanistic' and having 'rigidity' in the way that it theorises the operation of overlapping social identities (Ahmed, 2015; Ahmed and Rogers, 2017).

Case study: Jane

Born in the late 1950s, in her early childhood Jane was often clothed in beautiful dresses; she liked to play with her dolls and doing crafts with her mother. Thus, Jane's early childhood can be understood as being shaped by traditional, or normative, constructions of femininity. Jane's early experiences would have been different had she rejected those normative constructions, dressed as a boy and played with toys more typically associated with boys (such as soldiers, trains and so on).

Gender was not the only influence upon Jane's lived experience. As noted above, the concept of 'intersectionality' asserts that it is the interweaving of social characteristics that shape experience; we do not experience life solely as a female (or male), or as a child (or adult), but as a person with interconnecting and overlapping social characteristics (Crenshaw, 1991). So, in Jane's early childhood she lived with her family in a small mining village in Wales. The family was affluent as her father was employed as a senior manager at the local mine. This affluence meant that Jane led a comfortable life; she was able to enjoy her pastime of horse-riding and the family indulged in holidays abroad each year.

When the mines closed, Jane's family moved to England in order for her father to look for work. Newly located in a large English town, Jane experienced bullying as a result of 'being Welsh'. She became disengaged with education, leaving school at 15 years old without qualifications. Jane's father did not manage to find alternative employment and the family struggled financially. There were few apprenticeships for girls and Jane remained unemployed until she married and had her first child at 19.

Reflective questions

- Can you identify the processes of similarity and difference in the case study?
- What impact could you envisage these processes having on Jane's wellbeing or 'sense of self'?
- How does your social identity impact on others (service users, colleagues, other professionals)? Consider aspects such as socio-economic status, age, sexuality, ethnicity or (dis)ability and the intersections of these.
- Do people treat you differently in different contexts?
- Does this empower or put you/them at a disadvantage?

 Visit the website to listen to Dr Michaela Rogers talk about working with trans and non-binary people (https://study.sagepub.com/rogers2e).

HUMAN RIGHTS AND EQUALITY

The problems of service users are often seen as resulting from social inequality and disadvantage, rather than individual characteristics (Cowden and Singh, 2014). Inequality, then, is regarded as systemic (embedded within social systems and organisations) and resulting from dominant structures (the family, law, religion, binary gender) (see Chapter 7 for a discussion of Thompson's PCS model which helps to explain this further). Therefore, social factors (such as gender, ethnicity, age, socio-economic class and so on) are central to individual life chances.

Within this paradigm, certain groups can be seen as dominant whilst others have less power and are often denied a voice. Moreover, for marginalised communities, human rights are often discounted, and full citizenship is therefore denied. Consider the well-reported human rights infringements of refugees and asylum seekers. What is important to remember is that the concepts of intersectionality, in/equality and human rights help us to make sense of a person's experience of marginalisation or oppression, but this frequently this has multiple, not singular, dimensions; that is, people experience **multiple oppressions.** Consider an elderly person who is Black in a White dominated neighbourhood. They have a mental health diagnosis (schizophrenia, anxiety) and physical disabilities (arthritis and mobility problems due to childhood polio); these mean that they frequently need medical care and they have not been able to work for some years. Think about how they might experience inequality and discrimination on the grounds of race, age, economic status and health.

Visit the website to listen to Dr Dan Allen talk about his research on Gypsy, Roma and traveller communities (https://study.sagepub.com/rogers2e).

Key terms for understanding difference and diversity

Diversity: this can refer to many things in terms of everyday differences in hair colour, height, style of dress and so on. In social work, diversity refers to the differences between people that has *social* meaning as it influences people's lives in terms of experience, access and opportunities. This includes: gender, sexuality, ability/disability, race and ethnicity, employment status.

Empowerment: the process of becoming stronger and more confident particularly in taking control of your life, decision-making and claiming your rights.

Equality: the state of being equal in status, rights and/or opportunities.

Social exclusion: the ways in which particular groups lack the resources in life that inhibit their full participation in society.

Social inclusion: the ways in which particular groups have access to the resources they need in order to participate fully in social life.

Source: adapted from Ahmed and Rogers, 2016.

Reflective question

In 2019 do women enjoy the same level of power and privilege that men do; are women equal?

Five statistics and studies suggest otherwise:

1   The gender pay gap continues: in 2018 on average women earned 17.9% less than men (Equal Pay Portal, 2018).

(Continued)

2   Domestic violence and abuse (DVA) disproportionately affects more women than men. For example, two women are killed each week by a former or current partner (ONS, 2018).
3   A study of 900 people in Canada indicated that women still overwhelmingly do the majority of housework whatever age in the life course (Horne et al., 2017).
4   In 2018 of the top FTSE 100 and FTSE 250 companies just 7% and 2% respectively had women employed at the chief executive officer level (FTSE companies are those leading on the London Stock Exchange) (Statista, 2018).
5   After the 2017 General Election, there were 442 male Members of Parliament (MPs), but only 208 female MPs (House of Commons Library, 2018).

POWER/EMPOWERMENT

Whether individual, between one community and another, or between structures, relationships are imbued with various dimensions and dynamics of power. Who exercises power *intra*relationally and *inter*relationally (*within* and *across* those relationships) is subject to variation and can depend upon social processes and positioning. For example, in the doctor–patient relationship the doctor can exercise power in the process of diagnosis, and by prescribing treatment or referring to other health-based services. The patient, Al, is not able to do any of these things or access any medical intervention in this context without the facilitation of the doctor. However, in everyday life Al is in a position of power when performing his everyday role as a police chief inspector and he has the capacity to make important decisions affecting individuals, communities and the police force that he is responsible for. Mostly, however, powerlessness is not necessarily easy to identify; it is much more complex, diverse and even obscure. For example, as a minority community, lesbian, gay, bisexual, trans and queer (LGBTQ) people can be said to be marginalised at times (and there is an evidence-base to indicate ongoing discrimination against this community). Yet within this diverse population there are differences in terms of identity, lived experience, recognition and acceptance, with transgender/transsexual women experiencing the most in terms of marginalisation, discrimination and oppression (Serano, 2007). Therefore, it is more appropriate to talk of LGBTQ communities and people, not a singular community.

So far this chapter has argued that the problems that service users can experience often result from, or are inextricably interlocked with, some form of inequality. It is the task of the social worker to utilise an anti-discriminatory and anti-oppressive perspective (see Chapter 7). Adopting approaches to practice that help to cushion people from experiences of inequality and oppression is often called 'emancipatory' practice; a key objective of this is the **empowerment** of these individuals. There are various ways that you can be empowering in your practice and this concurrently helps to demonstrate that you value individuals and uniqueness (this also promotes difference and diversity). For example:

- by encouraging a child, whose family is being assessed and supported through child protection processes, to speak at a core group meeting or child protection conference you are demonstrating respect for a child's rights and ability to participate in the decision-making process that affects their life; or
- by arranging an independent advocate for a service user who has been detained under the Mental Health Act you are enabling someone to have an increased representation in processes which can be experienced as oppressive and punitive.

Both examples illustrate an empowerment model in practice, but it is also important to be mindful of collective empowerment that occurs at a group or community level. Dominelli (2002: 117) advocates for collective empowerment to mainstream 'the concerns of marginalised or dispossessed groups' and to provide a voice, raise awareness and enable groups or communities to take action. The work of Women's Aid Federation England (the national charity that works to end domestic violence and abuse) (WAFE, 2014) is a case in point. On a community level, the Women's Aid empowerment model seeks to produce greater gender equality and end violence against women, men and children by influencing policy and practice (collective empowerment), whilst local organisations work with individuals to help them get re-housed, take legal action and build a new life free from domestic violence and abuse (individual empowerment).

It is also important to consider celebrating difference and diversity. There are existing structures and events that occur in the UK and internationally that do this. For example, Black History Month takes place each year in the UK and around the world Pride events help to celebrate the richness and diversity of LGBTQ communities. On an individual level, as a social worker, you can do many things to indicate that you recognise and value difference and diversity – see the following activity for ideas. This can be experienced as incredibly empowering for a service user or carer.

Activity: Celebrating difference/Promoting empowerment

- Take an individual or group (for examples, a looked after child, or a group of people co-resident in a home for people with learning disabilities) to visit an exhibition or museum that illustrates aspects of their culture and heritage.
- Learn about a service user or carers' religion or ethnicity or learn a few words from a different language.
- Watch an international film or listen to music from a different culture.
- Celebrate a different culture's cuisine by cooking traditional food.

One way to embed good practice into social work is to embed cross-cultural practice principles (Tsang et al., 2011). Fundamentally, cross-cultural principles include cultural humility and cultural competence (see Chapter 2) along with being cognisant in communication of cultural difference between yourself (the social worker) and the service user, but with the goal of therapeutic alliance, constructive engagement and achieving positive change. It is important to remember that any reference to culture is not limited to particular influences (for example, ethnicity and religion); indeed there is an important body of work on cross-cultural practice and autism (Trembath et al., 2005).

Reflective activity

During your practice career, you may work with people who have committed abusive, violent or sexual acts that are particularly abhorrent (for example, sexual offences against young children). To what extent can you set aside any prejudice that you have and apply the values and principles of anti-oppressive practice?

You will also be tasked with working with people from different communities who have various different religious beliefs and norms to yours. To what extent can you set aside any stereotypes that you hold about this community and apply the values and principles of anti-oppressive practice?

In most circumstances, you should be guided by the remit of your role as well as professional standards: the Health and Care Professions Council's (HCPC) Standards of Conduct, Performance and Ethics (2018) and the British Association of Social Workers' (BASW) Code of Ethics (2014). However, there is often one individual where you will struggle to separate the person from their actions. Remember Rogers's (1965) three core conditions – empathy, **congruence**, unconditional positive regard – and try to remain anchored to a person-centred model (see Chapter 27). It is often helpful to consider the person who has committed an act of abuse or crime as a victim too. In the case of a person from a very different culture to your own, it is useful to remember that this person has been socialised in their culture's norms and beliefs; they may see your norms and beliefs as antithetical and difficult to embrace. In both cases, and in general, it is important to consider any **unconscious bias** which occurs when automatic, deeply engrained bias/es (for example, stereotyping) affects our cognitive process (thoughts and judgements) and actions (without us realising it).

THE LEGAL CONTEXT: EQUALITY ACT 2010

In addition to the requirement to embed good practice principles, as a social worker you have a *duty* to attend to difference in the context of service users' access to and interactions with formal processes and structures. The Equality Act 2010 is the key piece of legislation that provides protection from discrimination in the workplace and in wider society. The Equality Act 2010 outlines the different ways in which it is unlawful to treat somebody and incorporates nine distinct 'protected characteristics'. The protected characteristics are social categories with which people may identify and under which people may seek legal protection. The characteristics include: age; disability; gender reassignment; marriage and civil partnership; pregnancy and maternity; race; religion or belief; sex (gender); and sexual orientation. Whilst the Act represents some commitment to equality, it can be criticised for having rigid categories which do not always complement one another, but in individual cases, these can conflict and be incongruent with each other and other existing legislation (Ahmed and Rogers, 2016). For example, for a trans person who is in a heterosexual marriage at the start of their gender transitioning journey, there are other pieces of legislation relating to marriage that may conflict with or limit the protection offered under 'gender reassignment'.

The Public Sector Equality Duty was implemented following the introduction of the Equality Act 2010. The Equality Duty sets a standard for organisations who provide public services to treat everyone with dignity and respect. Organisations subject to the Equality Duty are required to comply with the three aims of the duty and must have due regard to:

1 eliminating unlawful discrimination, harassment and victimisation as well as other conduct prohibited by the EA;
2 advancing equality of opportunity between people who share a protected characteristic and those who do not;
3 fostering good relations between those who share a protected characteristic and those who do not. (EHRC, 2015)

Visit the website (https://study.sagepub.com/rogers2e) for information on the Equality Act and the Public Sector Equality Duty.

Reflective activity

In the first half of this chapter, the concept of intersectionality was introduced. This refers to the overlapping and multiple social locations that people can inhabit by identifying with different social categories. How does the notion of intersectionality challenge the differentiation of 'protected characteristics' as being discrete categories?

The Equality Act 2010 extended the various types of discrimination that can be drawn upon for legal redress. These are:

- *Direct discrimination*: This is where someone is treated less favourably than another person because of a protected characteristic.
- *Associative discrimination*: This is direct discrimination perpetrated against someone because they are associated with another person who possesses a protected characteristic; for example, the parent of a disabled child.
- *Discrimination based on perception*: This is direct discrimination against someone because others think that s/he possess a particular protected characteristic. They do not necessarily have to possess the characteristic, just be perceived to.
- *Indirect discrimination*: This can occur when there is a rule or policy that applies to everyone but disadvantages a person with a particular protected characteristic;

for example, the failure to provide religiously appropriate food (for instance, kosher or halal meat) when catering (indirect discrimination on grounds of religion or belief).

- *Harassment*: This is behaviour that is deemed offensive by the recipient. Employees can now complain of the behaviour they find offensive or humiliating even if it is not directed at them; for example, offensive jokes, comments, images or emails.
- *Victimisation*: This occurs when someone is treated badly because they have made or supported a complaint or grievance under this legislation. (EHRC, 2015)

• •

Case study: Kelsey

You have been working with 19-year-old Kelsey. She has a mild learning disability and a physical disability which necessitates the use of a wheelchair. She lives in local authority supported housing, but she is very independent, and she is doing well at college. Recently Kelsey has disclosed to you that she is a lesbian. She feels isolated as she has no gay friends at college or in the house where she lives. At college she has been teased because of her sexual orientation. In addition, Kelsey's parents refuse to acknowledge her sexuality and tend to be over-protective of her because of her perceived vulnerability as a disabled young person. The support workers in the home have not addressed any of these issues and on one occasion Kelsey complained about the other residents as they were making homophobic comments; this was not dealt with and now the other residents have stopped speaking to Kelsey.

Reflective questions

- Do you believe Kelsey has experienced discrimination?
- If so, identify (1) in what ways you think Kelsey has experienced discrimination, (2) any relevant protected characteristics and (3) the types of discrimination she may have encountered.
- Think of a family that you have recently worked with. Can you identify any ways that a single member or the family as a whole may have experienced discrimination because of individual or intersecting aspects of their social identity which constitute any of the protected characteristics of the Equality Act 2010?
- Could you have done anything to address this discrimination?

• •

THE PRACTICE CONTEXT: PRINCIPLES FOR SOCIAL WORK PRACTICE

As well as integrating the codes and requirements of the HCPC, BASW and the Equality Act 2010, it is important to develop skills that embed equality principles. These will reflect an acknowledgement of both positive and negative aspects of difference and diversity. Moreover, it is crucial that you are mindful to avoid stereotyping, tokenistic gestures, making assumptions and treating people differently (or negatively) purely based on their difference.

Comments from a social worker

Equality and diversity are terms with which we are all familiar, if only in terms of their definitions of creating a fairer society (equality) and recognising that everyone is different (diversity). What may be less obvious is the positive impact that embracing the concepts of equality, diversity and inclusion can have on an individual, the workplace and organisations. As a consultant who delivers workshops on equality, diversity and inclusion it has become evident over time that there is fear around the Equality Act 2010. The fear stems from the perspective that the Equality Act is about what one should not do rather than what one should do in order to be more inclusive. With this in mind I have moved from delivering training to facilitating workshops that focus on appreciating equality, diversity and inclusion – what works for success. The workshop employs appreciative enquiry, self-managed learning techniques and empowerment methodology to support relevant delivery and focus on compliance with the Equality Act 2010. We use a bi-cultural competence model to be curious about ourselves, perspectives and work environments, and to inspire participants to go beyond compliance to appreciate diversity and inclusion through action learning.

In addition to having a better understanding of the Equality Act 2010, participants begin to explore the significance of the Act within the organisation in which they work and whom they work with. Participants appreciate their values, qualities/skills and inspiration for growing equality, diversity and inclusion in organisations and communities, and begin to action plan what is needed for equality, diversity and inclusion to thrive in their organisations. What is reinforced is that everyone is a leader, and equality, diversity and inclusion is everyone's responsibility. In doing so, we can foster an atmosphere of inclusion and understanding that encourages everyone to participate.

The following list should be helpful in providing you with guiding principles and a framework for valuing difference and diversity. The list is by no means exhaustive and you should add your own ideas for achieving a high level of anti-oppressive practice (see also Chapter 7).

- Acknowledge and respond to service users and co-workers as individuals with unique social identities, needs and desires.
- Avoid stereotyping or making assumptions about people based on their social identity; for example, just because someone uses a wheelchair, do not make assumptions about their capabilities, needs or wishes.
- Acknowledge that an individual's understanding and feelings about aspects of their social identity may differ from yours.
- Recognise that treating people fairly does not mean treating people in the same way; we need to recognise difference and respond appropriately.
- Recognise that aspects of your social identity may impact upon others (service users, co-workers and other professionals) in different ways.
- Strive to increase your knowledge and understanding about aspects of social identity that may be different from your own; for example, use the website of the Equality and Human Rights Commission to research any of the nine protected characteristics of

the Equality Act 2010 and marginalised communities, for instance Gypsy Roma and Travellers.

- Strive to use appropriate language pertaining to social identity or social situations so that you convey respect and acceptance; for example, it is not acceptable to describe someone who has a mixed ethnic origin as 'half caste', this is out-of-date and offensive as it has negative connotations. You should refer to someone as having a 'mixed heritage'.
- Acknowledge that some organisational policy and procedures may not always recognise and attend to difference and diversity at an appropriate level.
- Recognise that organisational policy and procedure may impact negatively on some people more than others.
- Try to raise consciousness within your organisation so that there is an increased understanding and respect for difference; for example, on World Social Work Day organise a fundraising activity for your local charity.

CONCLUSION

In this chapter we have considered the importance of valuing difference and diversity in relation to both legal requirements and the principles of good practice. Whilst these provide a starting point, a high degree of reflexivity should also ensure your alignment with a relationship-based approach that reflects empathy, the value of respect and an acknowledgement of people's unique identity and lived experience.

Having read this chapter, you should be able to:

- Consider the ways that you can counter the negative experiences of difference and celebrate diversity in social work;
- Articulate the concepts of multiple oppressions, social exclusion and unconscious bias;
- Understand the importance of reflective practice in working with difference and diversity.

RECOMMENDED READING

Cocker, C. and Hafford-Letchfield, T. (eds) (2014) *Rethinking Anti-Discriminatory and Anti-Oppressive Theories for Social Work Practice*. Basingstoke: Palgrave Macmillan.

Gaine, C. (2010) *Equality and Diversity in Social Work Practice*. Exeter: Learning Matters.

Gast, L. and Patmore, A. (2012) *Mastering Approaches to Diversity in Social Work*. London: Jessica Kingsley.

Thompson, N. (2016) *Anti-Discriminatory Practice* (6th edn). Basingstoke: Palgrave Macmillan.

Resilience and Self-Care
Ciarán Murphy

Links to the Professionals Capabilities Framework

- Professionalism
- Critical reflection and analysis

Links to the Knowledge and Skills Statement for Child and Family Practitioners

- The role of supervision
- Organisational context

Links to the Knowledge and Skills Statement for Social Workers in Adult Services

- Supervision, critical reflection and analysis
- Organisational context

Key messages

- A commitment to developing resilience and promoting self-care will benefit you, your employer and your service users.
- 'Resilience' is not just a notion that is important to consider in working with service users, but is also important for you to develop as a practitioner.
- Building professional resilience allows us to overcome the challenges of practice and enjoy a long and satisfying career in social work.

INTRODUCTION

Through the course of your social work education, you will have had many opportunities to reflect on the challenges that accompany a career in social work. This will not just pertain to those encountered during the normal working day (e.g. high caseloads, limited time availability and the spectre of 'agile working'), but also the challenges that encroach into our personal lives (e.g. the need to work over contracted hours or to take administrative work home, and the worry about a case that can interrupt a family dinner or disturb an otherwise restful night's sleep).

Indeed, in the author's role as a practising social worker and then as a social work tutor, a recurring question posed by social work students (and indeed, some practising social workers) is how they can manage and overcome these challenges, so that they can enjoy a long and satisfying career in practice. The answer given is that practitioners should try to worry less about the features of practice which they cannot control (for example, high caseloads and limited time availability), and concentrate on developing strategies for managing themselves as practitioners.

Consider this comment from an experienced social worker:

> New social workers often ask me my secret … I mean, I have more than 10 years of practice experience working on various child protection teams, and I have never taken a day off (holidays aside). I tell them that my secret is that I know how to look after myself … and because of that, I have developed a resilience for those times when things can be really challenging at work.

These sentiments form the basis of this chapter – that is, how you as a practitioner can develop strategies for self-care and build professional **resilience**.

Reflective activity

Before we begin our discussion on your management of self, think about the challenges that you are worried about encountering/are encountering in your practice. How do these resonate with those identified in the introduction? What strategies do you already have for managing these challenges?

By taking some time to think about these questions, and by jotting down some answers, it will provide some context and help you get the most from the discussion that follows.

NOTIONS OF 'PROFESSIONAL RESILIENCE'

Elsewhere in this book it is noted that a clear and simple definition of 'resilience' remains somewhat elusive. However, we have asserted that resilience can:

- help individuals cope with, and adapt to adversity;
- be transformative and build inner strengths;
- help us overcome challenges in the present and the future;
- involve the navigation of internal and external resources to sustain and enhance wellbeing.

Whilst we have previously discussed how children can build resilience, we are equally concerned with how you as a professional practitioner can develop your own resilience, so that you can manage and overcome the challenges that you may well encounter in practice.

In this sense, we conceive 'professional resilience' as the worker's commitment to achieve a balance between occupational stressors and life challenges, while fostering professional values and career sustainability (Fink-Samnick, 2009). It is certainly a key concept for the 'helping' professionals who face highly challenging and complex situations on a daily basis (Grant and Kinman, 2012b), and moreover, it is essential for social workers if they are going to manage the demands of contemporary practice whilst avoiding burnout (Munro, 2011).

Research has shown that resilient professionals hold a number of particular qualities, including:

- a positive self-concept and a strong sense of identity;
- self-awareness and **emotional literacy**;
- **critical thinking** skills;
- the ability to set limits;
- well-developed social skills and social confidence to develop effective relationships;
- flexibility and adaptability, drawing on a wide range of coping strategies and creative problem-solving skills;
- the ability to identify and draw on internal and external resources;
- successful adaptation to change;
- persistence in the face of challenges, setbacks and adversity;
- a sense of purpose and the ability to derive a sense of meaning from difficulties and challenges; and
- the ability to learn from experience. (Grant and Kinman, 2012a)

Reflective activity

Which of these qualities do you think that you have? Would others agree with your assessment? Would they add or subtract other qualities from this list?

We know that resilience develops during times of stress, which can help us to understand why some social workers thrive in the face of particular challenges experienced at work. Rather than burnout, these practitioners develop strategies to overcome those current, but also future challenges more effectively.

As Grant and Kinman (2012a: 2) assert:

> It is not that resilient social workers lead a charmed existence. They face the same
> problems that other people encounter, but confront setbacks and persevere in the
> face of difficulties rather than giving in.

We should not conceive resilience as a personality trait ingrained in some but not others.
Resilience emerges from the experience of, and successful adaptation to, ordinary life
events.

Indeed, Masten (2009) argues that resilience does not require extraordinary resources
in most cases. Instead, it is the result of that which she describes as 'ordinary magic'
(p. 30): it results from a multiplicity of adaptive human systems which have evolved over
thousands of years, and align in certain ways and certain points to promote resilience in
individuals.

Thus, the implication – and good news for social workers – is that resilience is a
quality and a process that can be enhanced and developed (Kinman and Grant, 2011;
Masten, 2009).

For the remainder of this chapter, we will further consider some of the underlying competencies which have been associated with professional resilience, so as to set out how you
can develop these, before also identifying some of the specific strategies which may assist
you in this quest.

EMOTIONAL LITERACY

Emotional literacy (referred to elsewhere as '**emotional intelligence**') has interpersonal
(social intelligence) as well as intrapersonal (self-awareness) elements (Grant and Kinman,
2012a). We might conceive *interpersonal* emotional literacy as that which helps us to relate
effectively to others; whereas, *intrapersonal* literacy encompasses:

- the degree of attention we devote to our feelings;
- the clarity of these experiences; and
- our beliefs about repairing negative mood states or prolonging positive ones. (Grant
  and Kinman, 2012a)

In their research, Kinman and Grant (2011) found that social workers who

- are more adept at perceiving, appraising and expressing emotion;
- are able to understand, analyse and utilise emotional knowledge; and
- can regulate their emotions effectively …

… are not only more resilient to workplace stress and challenge, but are also more psychologically and physically healthy. Conversely, social workers whose emotional literacy skills
are underdeveloped may:

- have problems developing 'appropriate' empathy (see Chapter 5 'Developing Empathic Skills');
- escalate conflict by reciprocating in kind when faced with hostility and lack of cooperation;
- allow emotions to unconsciously influence decision-making; and
- attempt to 'repair' negative mood states by engaging in negative health behaviours (for example, comfort eating or excessive alcohol consumption). (Grant and Kinman, 2012b)

The implication is that to build professional resilience, we must develop both *inter-* and *intrapersonal* emotional literacy. Whilst the former is the focus of another chapter in this book, with the latter, this might entail taking time to reflect on our emotions during the working day, asking questions like:

- What are the negative emotions that I encounter?
- When and why do these occur?
- How do I overcome these emotions?

Social workers can then use forums like peer and manager supervision to discuss their emotions, identifying triggers, and strategies for overcoming negative emotions.

Activity: Emotional literacy self-assessment

Before continuing with the rest of the chapter, you may wish to take Louise Grant's Emotional Literacy Quiz (NB Grant uses the term 'resilience' rather than 'literacy', but her meaning is the same), which is available via the following link:

www.ccinform.co.uk/learning-tools/quiz-how-emotionally-resilient-are-you/

NB you will need a 'Community Care Inform' account to access the quiz, but most social work employers and higher education providers offer free access to this.

REFLECTIVE THINKING

We know that personal reflection on practice experience is important for professional development (see Chapter 6 'Reflection and Reflexivity'). Indeed, it can be used to enhance the service that we provide, whilst shaping our future approach to service users and their individual needs. The importance of reflective thinking lies in our ability to identify and learn from ourselves and our experiences of practice: for example, what we do well; what we do not do so well; what we can draw from our experiences of particular contexts to inform our future behaviour and choices.

Importantly though, reflective thinking also enables us to explore the dynamics of rational and irrational thoughts, emotions, doubts, assumptions and beliefs and the ways in which they impact on us as practitioners (Grant and Kinman, 2012a).

Kinman and Grant's (2010) research found this to be an important self-protective mechanism for social workers, building resilience through:

- Self-reflection ('Why do I do what I do, and how does this affect me?').
- Empathetic reflection ('Am I able to understand other people's positions?').
- Reflective communication ('Am I open to discussion and challenge about my opinions?'). (Grant and Kinman, 2012a)

Indeed, this links to the previous section on emotional literacy, as it is only by being aware of our irrational thoughts, emotions, doubts, assumptions and beliefs that we are able to challenge and develop strategies to overcome them. The implication again is that social workers who engage in regular reflective thinking are better able to develop professional resilience.

Reflective activity

How often do you reflect on your emotions at work? Can you find time to do this more often? What might you learn from such reflections?

PREPARING FOR CHALLENGING SOCIAL INTERACTIONS

We have already discussed how social workers require not only good communication skills, but also a level of comfort and confidence in social interactions, and an ability to be assertive and to challenge others when appropriate and necessary. Despite an emphasis on these elements appearing throughout documents such as the PCF and KSS, research indicates that they are often not a source of focus in social work education (Murphy, 2019).

Grant and Kinman (2012a) theorise that this might be explained by a general misconception that those who wish to train as social workers will have some innate ability in these areas. However, their research (Kinman and Grant, 2010) indicates that, actually, there is considerable variation in levels of social confidence amongst qualifying social workers – highlighting that some may require additional support to enhance this area of their practice.

Reflective activity

How comfortable are you in social interactions, especially those where you might have to be assertive and/or challenge, or perhaps those in which you are required to deliver bad news? Is this an area of your practice that you would like to develop?

Whilst there are various life coaching and training courses available which are designed to enhance our confidence and communication skills in interpersonal situations, one simple method – favoured by many social workers – is to engage in some form of preparation before an anticipated event. This might involve writing down, practising or even 'acting out' what you would say in a given scenario. It can be helpful in identifying, what would otherwise be, unforeseen difficulties. It can also help you refine the phrasing of the message(s) that you wish to deliver, and plan and prepare for a range of possible responses from a third party.

Consider this commentary from another experienced social worker:

> Something what has really benefitted me in practice is how I prepare for various social interactions. This usually involves me thinking about how an event might unfold, what I would want to say, and how I might respond to what others say. ... This has helped me in my personal life too, where in attending various medical appointments, I am much better at communicating with doctors and consultants ... being clear and concise but also assertive about my needs and those of my family.

Reflective activity

Preparing for a difficult social interaction

Think about a social interaction in your personal or professional life that you are worried about – for example, communicating to a medical professional some intimate health detail or telling a parent that you will seek the removal of their children.

Reflect on what exactly it is about this scenario that you are worried about, and think about how you might prepare yourself. Some questions for you to consider include:

- What are the important issues that I would want to communicate?
- How will I communicate them?
- What other issues might arise?
- What might the other party say?
- How will I respond?

In this way, you can practise preparing for a situation that you are apprehensive about and identify some strategies that might prove beneficial.

Oftentimes, social workers prepare for a particular interpersonal event by practising or role-playing with a colleague or manager (for example, during supervision). This can help ready them for unfamiliar or potentially difficult situations (for example, emotionally challenging conversations with service users or giving oral evidence in court).

This might be something that you wish to incorporate into your own practice, as whilst role-playing may cause some anxiety or embarrassment, the process of acting out a potentially difficult scenario in a safe environment with a familiar person can avoid a level of stress that might be otherwise encountered without adequate preparation. (It can also provide important information about how other people may respond to you and the strategies that may be most – and least – productive – Grant and Kinman, 2012a.)

Indeed, building in regular opportunities to prepare for interactions that we are worried about can enhance our feelings of self-confidence and our communication skills. Then, by successfully overcoming specific challenges or complex scenarios, we take away a knowledge of ourselves, and a confidence in our ability to overcome difficult professional situations – further informing our sense of professional resilience.

SOCIAL SUPPORT NETWORKS

Social support refers to positive psychosocial interactions with others with whom there is mutual trust and concern (Grant and Kinman, 2012a). Research tells us that people with a supportive social network tend to be more physically and psychologically healthy, and are more resilient as they are better able to manage times of stress – including workplace-induced stress (Kinman and Grant, 2010).

We can receive social support from many different sources including family, friends, colleagues and even pets. We can also receive support from our membership in associations (including recreational associations like gyms and tennis clubs, as well as professional associations and unions, for example, BASW and the Social Workers Union) or community groups (for example, church groups).

Reflective activity

What sources of social support do you have? How might this support help you deal with stressful times at work?

Social support can be more than providing a listening and empathetic ear, it can also include informational support (e.g. advice and feedback) and practical support (e.g. helping with physical tasks and offering monetary help).

As a social worker your relationships with friends and family will prove an important resource. You may choose to talk directly to them about any challenges/difficulties at work. Equally, you may see these relationships as a sanctuary from the workplace, and seek relief by choosing not to talk to them about any workplace issues. Ultimately, you will decide how to utilise this resource to best suit your needs. However, if you do choose to talk directly to family and friends about work, you should be mindful of the professional expectations placed on social workers pertaining to service users (and indeed, colleagues) and issues of confidentiality. Therefore, in talking to friends and family you may wish to reflect on:

- what you are able to say about others;
- what you should not say, so as to avoid breaching confidentiality;
- who you believe to be trustworthy as opposed to those who might repeat what you say to others.

It is also important for social workers to foster mutually supportive relationships from their wider personal and professional networks (Grant and Kinman, 2012b). This might entail a social group at your local gym; a running group hosted by your local church; or a five-aside football team organised by a colleague – here too it is also important to be mindful of issues of confidentiality. Equally, the group does not have to entail physical activity, but might constitute a reading group or a regular meet at the local pub after work on a Friday.

Visit the website to watch a video of current social workers discussing their social networks and the different ways that they choose to 'let off steam' (https://study.sagepub.com/rogers2e). Note how the social support networks mentioned consistute a mixture of personal and professional networks.

Ultimately, resilient social workers develop different social support networks away from work (the favourite of the author: a Friday night pizza group!). However, they also tend to have productive relationships with colleagues, especially those who understand the demands of being a social worker, and the value of the work that they do.

It is not unusual, therefore, to develop close relationships with your fellow social workers and colleagues that you see on a daily basis and with whom you share an office space. A supportive office environment to which you can return after a stressful visit or meeting, and a group that is willing to listen and provide a compassionate ear as you vent your frustrations, is worth its weight in gold. (This is also a reason why the authors do not favour the contemporary model of 'agile working' enforced by an increasing number of employers.) Whilst you will be/are surely very busy, it can be healthy to make the most of this resource, contributing to, and receiving from, a support network of fellow social workers/colleagues.

Finally, a point of emphasis is that a key skill of a resilient social worker is knowing what type of support they need at the time, and where it can best be found (Grant and Kinman, 2012b). Be wary of seeking support from areas of your network who might not be able to offer the type of support you need, as doing so could have a detrimental impact on your relationship with them. (For example, you would be ill advised to complain to a family support worker about how little social workers are paid; equally, there is little point in seeking advice on the intricacies of social work legislation from a family pet!)

TIPS FOR PROMOTING SELF-CARE AND BUILDING RESILIENCE

It is true that developing your professional resilience can take effort, but it is a necessary step in ensuring a long and satisfying career in practice. It involves:

- protecting your own physical and psychological health;
- managing stress effectively;
- maintaining your emotional equilibrium;
- fostering supportive relationships at home and work; and
- maintaining boundaries between home and work life.

Grant and Kinman (2012a: 8) draw from their research (Kinman and Grant, 2010) to offer 'top tips' to pre- and post-qualifying social workers, aimed at promoting self-care and building professional resilience.

Build a network of support

Resilient people tend to have strong social networks – family, friends and colleagues are great sources of support.

Manage time effectively

You should always use your diary effectively (Chapter 10 'Time Management' may help with this). Also, attempt to schedule work tasks to ensure that you aren't left feeling rushed or emotionally exhausted and build in adequate breaks. Ensure that you give yourself time to process your emotional reactions to one case before moving onto the next.

Develop achievable goals and take action to achieve them

Setting goals encourages a focus on the future rather than dwelling on past problems and present difficulties. Ensure that goals are achievable, and accept that setbacks are inevitable.

Be aware of your emotions

Regularly reflect on your workplace emotions. This allows valuable insight into why you feel as you do and helps to identify patterns in behaviour and reactions, ensuring that you can identify and challenge negative emotions and thoughts as they occur.

Prepare for, and make the most of, supervision

Supervision offers a forum in which to discuss stressors relating to your practice. Use it as an opportunity for critical reflection, self-evaluation and problem-solving, listening to (if not also accepting) the advice of the supervisor.

Prioritise work–life balance and maintain firm boundaries

It is crucial to establish firm boundaries between your working life and non-working life. This includes not working at a time where you need to be relaxing/recuperating (see Chapter 10 'Time Management'). If you find that you spend your personal time worrying about work, then set some time aside each day for worry, putting worries to the back of your mind the rest of the time (visualisation might help here). Remember that excessive worry causes stress and can mean suffering twice – firstly, whilst you are worrying, and secondly, when the event that you are worried about comes to pass (which it might not!).

Further, ensure that whenever possible you go home (or at least leave work) when you had planned to. Consider again the aforementioned experienced social worker:

> Another tip I give is to always go home at 5 o'clock, even if you have outstanding tasks – they will still be there tomorrow. For me, I am very strict – I work between 8.30 a.m. and 5 p.m. It's an important rule that I set myself. My manager approves, because she knows that by enforcing this rule, I stay well, and she can be sure therefore that I will be in again tomorrow!

Make time for relaxation

It is important to know your limits (which is why a work–life balance is crucial). By not giving some priority to your own needs and feelings, you risk burnout.

Try to incorporate into your weekly routine opportunities for relaxation. These might be hobbies or pastimes (painting, reading, exercise, etc.). They might be also social activities (pizza Friday!). They may be things that you can do at work to keep you calm (for example, breathing exercises).

It is also beneficial to book regular breaks from work (irrespective of whether you go away during these periods), and as you become an experienced practitioner, you will realise how often you require a scheduled break.

Reflect on experiences and adapt when necessary

Resilient practitioners learn lessons from setbacks and problems. You can reflect on how you have previously overcome adversity and employ similar strategies when problems arise at work.

Reframe stressful events as temporary and as learning opportunities

Resilient practitioners tend to frame stressful events as temporary and manageable, and as opportunities for learning and development. Do not get bogged down by problems at work, but stay focused on your reasons for becoming a social worker.

Be kind to yourself

Do not be overly critical of yourself – social work is a demanding and difficult job. Stay focused on doing your best and looking after yourself. Schedule regular treats, breaks and social interactions. Go home and relax. Give yourself permission to switch off, remembering that the social worker who is thinking about work even when at home is more likely to burn out.

CONCLUSION

We know that resilient social workers enjoy longer and more satisfying careers in practice; further, that resiliency can be developed. Through the course of this chapter, we have discussed different ways in which you can build your professional resilience and care for yourself as a practitioner.

Whilst this involves some time and commitment, the benefits are worthwhile. Whether you are at the beginning of your social work career or partway through it, there is always time to improve self-care and think about how you can develop your resilience. We hope that the suggestions in this chapter may help.

Having read this chapter, you should be able to:

- Better understand the different features of professional resilience and how these can be developed;
- Reflect on your own strategies for self-care and how these might be improved/developed; and in doing so, also improve/develop your own professional resilience.

RECOMMENDED READING

Howe, D. (2008) *The Emotionally Intelligent Social Worker*. Basingstoke: Palgrave Macmillan.
Neenan, M. (2009) *Developing Resilience: A Cognitive-Behavioural Approach.* New York: Routledge.
Thompson, N. and Thompson, S. (2008) *The Critically Reflective Practitioner*. Basingstoke: Palgrave Macmillan.

Time Management
Ciarán Murphy

Links to the Professionals Capabilities Framework

- Professionalism   • Critical reflection and analysis

Links to the Knowledge and Skills Statement for Child and Family Practitioners

- Child and family assessment   • Analysis, decision-making, planning and review
- Organisational context

Links to the Knowledge and Skills Statement for Social Workers in Adult Services

- Direct work with individuals and families   • Supervision, critical reflection and analysis
- Organisational context

Key messages

- Effective time management is a key skill in ensuring an appropriate approach to work and in achieving a work–life balance.
- Effective time management is important for enabling better service delivery.
- Time management involves strategies for time allocation, prioritisation and responding to the unplanned.
- Time management is an important exercise in the care of oneself.

INTRODUCTION

Elsewhere in this book we consider the notion of professional resilience and some of the strategies for self-care (see Chapter 9). In this chapter, we continue this theme, but focus on the practical task of time management as a strategy for achieving self-care and an appropriate work–life balance.

Consider these findings from a survey of practising social workers conducted by Unison and Community Care (2017):

- Almost half (47%) of workers finished the day with concerns about their cases; three-quarters (74%) of these said this was due to them being unable to get necessary paperwork completed.
- Two-thirds (67%) of those who completed the survey said they had not had a lunch break that day.
- An almost identical proportion (64%) said they 'almost never' took a break at work.
- The average number of hours worked on the day of the survey – including any time spent working at home – was 9.5 (as opposed to an average of 7.5 paid hours).

The implicit assertion here is that social workers have too little time in the day to complete their work. Whilst this is a long-standing concern – and is arguably increasing in the years of government austerity (as highlighted by the Unison and Community Care and survey) – our focus here is on how we can use what time we have available more effectively, so that we neither have to work over our contracted hours, nor take work home with us. Although implicit rather than explicit in the PCF and KSS, practising and non-practising social workers, researchers and academics agree that being an organised practitioner is central to a successful and a long career in social work.

Effective time management is the key means of achieving successful organisation – one which can offset/make the demands of practice more manageable.

 Visit our website to watch a video of social workers discussing what skills they find most valuable in negotiating a busy workload (https://study.sagepub.com/rogers2e).

PRINCIPLES OF EFFECTIVE TIME MANAGEMENT

Time management sounds simple, but for many it is a skill that they have not acquired before coming into practice. 'Time management' refers to how one organises and manages one's work time through the medium of a physical or virtual diary. It is something that requires ongoing attention and cultivation throughout our time in practice. Once mastered it can also prove beneficial to other parts of our life (for example, managing a busy home life, academic studies, familial or social responsibilities).

Most social workers choose either paper or electronic diaries, and it will be up to you to identify your preference. However, there are some points that you should consider in making your choice:

- As a social worker, you will be mobile, and your diary will need to be also.
- Will/do you have access to mobile electronic equipment on which you can access your diary?
- If yes, think carefully about using your personal (as opposed to employer issued) mobile electronic equipment, as to do so may breach data protection legislation.
- In addition, what does your employer require? (For example, some expect their social workers to record their whereabouts on their Microsoft 'Outlook' calendar, whilst simultaneously maintaining a paper diary for practical purposes.)

At the core of successful time management is organisation. An organised diary will record all of your tasks for the day/week/month/year(s) ahead. Diaries should be legible and easy to reorganise if needs be. You will often be compelled to add to, and remove from, your diary throughout the working day, and therefore there is a need to have access to your diary at all times. Time management allows you to plan ahead, strategise and ensure that you complete tasks and meet deadlines – it will also allow you to schedule the required (and surely deserved) lunch break!

DECIDING ON THE AMOUNT OF TIME TO BE ALLOCATED

One of the greatest challenges in time management is in deciding how much time to allocate to each work task, Rymell (2015) recommends the use of a 'time diary' in the early days/weeks/months of practice (although this task might still prove useful later on in practice). This simple self-evaluation tool can be used to understand how your time is really allocated, to become more aware and to learn how you use your time more effectively.

'But we just don't have the time to spare on a time diary!'

Rymell (2015) would argue that although a time diary does require an initial investment of time, effort and commitment, the dividends make this commitment worthwhile, and include:

- a more manageable work life;
- a better work–life balance;
- self-knowledge; and
- an insightful analysis that can be used in supervision for reflection and planning.

The time diary should be completed for one whole week in order to obtain the detail to analyse. Pre-arranged appointments and meeting times should be set out within it. It should also indicate where timings or indeed tasks change to reflect the reality of the week and changing demands.

Rymell (2015) recommends that when completing a time diary (see example in Table 10.1) the day should be divided into 15-minute segments (although you might prefer 30-minute or 1-hour segments). For each, a practitioner should list the time, identify the task and activity (or activities) being completed, and include all breaks and interruptions. In the third column, the practitioner writes their comments, which might include reflections such as:

- What was planned and what was unplanned?
- What took longer than anticipated?
- What might have been a better task to complete at this time?

Table 10.1   Example time diary

Time	Planned task	Actual task	Comments
09.15	Email catch-up	Gossip by the kettle	Unwelcome!
09.30	Email catch-up	Gossip by the kettle	
09.45	Email catch-up	Email catch-up	Running behind
10.00	Email catch-up	Email catch-up	Running behind
10.15	Case note writing	Email catch-up	
10.30	Case note writing	Email catch-up	
10.45	Case note writing	Case note writing	
11:00	Case note writing	Case note writing	Unfinished
11.15	Meeting	Meeting	Planned
11.30	Meeting	Meeting	Planned
11.45	Meeting	Meeting	Planned
12.00	Lunch time	Case note writing	Finish from earlier
12.15	Lunch time	Case note writing	
12.30	Lunch time	Lunch time	Less time than planned
12.45	Planned visit	Urgent paediatric medical	Unexpected emergency
...			
16.00	Planned visit	Urgent paediatric medical	Unexpected emergency
16.15	Planned visit	Urgent paediatric medical	Unexpected emergency
16.30	Planned visit	Urgent paediatric medical	Unexpected emergency
16.45	Final emails/paperwork	Urgent paediatric medical	Unexpected emergency
17.00	Home time	Urgent paediatric medical	Unexpected emergency
17.15	Home time	Urgent paediatric medical	Unexpected emergency
17.30	Home time	Urgent paediatric medical	Unexpected emergency
17.45	Home time	Case note writing	Following unexpected emergency
18.00	Home time	Home time	Well-deserved!

It is important to set some time aside to analyse the time diary after completion. Look at the activities and comments you have noted down and consider the following:

- What were the core/routine tasks (e.g. checking emails, case recording, attending meetings, etc.) as opposed to the unusual (e.g. emergency medicals)?
- What were the other activities which took up time (e.g. travel, talking to colleagues, lunch, etc.)?
- How long did you allocate to each task, and how long did each actually take?
- What are the lessons that you can take forward into your future diary planning?

Some learning points might include:

- How long you should allocate to 'routine' tasks.
- The best time of day for certain tasks (i.e. times where you are less likely to get distracted).
- The necessity to plan for 'unusual'/'unexpected' tasks (i.e. ensuring 'protected time' where you can catch up).
- The areas and times in which you tend to waste time, or tasks that take more time than you had expected.

By the end of this process, you should have a better sense of self-awareness, and how much time you should allocate to tasks in the future.

PRIORITISING BETWEEN TASKS

Social workers, like other professionals, often lament a lack of sufficient hours in the day to do the job 'effectively', and a typical complaint is that *'there is too much to do, but too little time to do it in!'* Whilst all develop their own strategies for managing this conflict, one usual course is to work over contracted hours (without additional pay) or to take work home. Whilst this is sometimes unavoidable (as with the emergency paediatric medical in the time diary above), it has been linked to burnout and staff leaving the profession and is therefore unsatisfactory (Munro, 2011). Moreover, this does not fit in with our model for self-care. Therefore, an alternative strategy is required, and often this lies in the underreported and indeed undervalued skill of *prioritisation*.

> ### Reflective activity
>
> What factors would inform how you would prioritise one work task over another?

If you have completed the reflective question above, then you might have included factors in your list such as:

- 'risk';
- service user 'need';
- organisational culture/expectations;
- statutory expectations; and/or
- a manager's request/direction.

Take a minute to jot down which of these would most influence how you choose to prioritise your social work tasks. Also, which would have the least influence?

In completing this task for a piece of research (Murphy, 2019) a group of social workers identified that before entering practice they ordered their influences on the prioritisation of work tasks as follows:

Risk (1); Need (2); Statutory expectations (3); Organisational expectations (4).

However, they also agreed that in practice they found that the order generally changed and was recorded as such:

Risk (1); Organisational (2); Statutory (3); Need (4).

Reflective activity

How do these lists compare with your own? Why do you think they are similar/different to your own?

Of course, how you choose to prioritise tasks is not necessarily fixed but can change on different days and in different contexts. The important issue is that you can reflect and identify those factors which are likely to influence how you prioritise your work tasks, so that when the time comes, you can make a decision quickly and are able to justify this decision afterwards.

Case scenario exercise

In this case example you are a social worker practising on a child protection team. You have a busy day ahead, and are faced with four 'important' tasks – each of which deserves some priority. However, each also needs completing before the end of the working day and you do not have the capacity to complete them all. Reflect on which of these you will prioritise and why.

1   A child has alleged an assault by his parent. He is due to return to the house tonight. The child needs visiting and interviewing before they return home so as to assess the veracity of the complaint and the suitability of a return home.

2   You have a professionals meeting scheduled for two days' time. You have not typed up, or sent out the minutes of the last meeting. This needs to be completed before the end of the day if attendees are to receive the last minutes in time for this meeting.

3   You completed a statutory home visit two days ago, but have not yet recorded this on the department's recording system. The local policy is that all visits need to be recorded on the system within 48 hours. You risk being reprimanded by a senior manager if this target is not met.

4   Your assessment is due to be submitted to the Family Court tomorrow. The whole Court timetable depends on it being received on time, however you have not completed it. You had planned to finish it this afternoon.

NB This exercise is not about you providing a 'right' answer, but is more to encourage you to think about the type of challenges that you might encounter in practice and to reflect on the factors which will influence your prioritisation of tasks. However, it is also useful in starting to think about how you might overcome competing demands, by, for example, asking colleagues to assist (which you might choose for Task 1); designating work to others (Task 2); and being confident when you feel that you have no other choice but to defer a task until a later time (as might be the case with Task 3).

Ultimately, how you choose to prioritise your work tasks will be a very personal choice, one that might also be informed by:

- your personal values and goals;
- a desire to achieve a certain outcome for a service user;
- pressure from management; Court; others;
- recent events – for example, a high-profile case in which a child was harmed.

Regardless, we have already established that on occasions you are unlikely to have enough time to complete all tasks, and so there will be a need to prioritise.

In deciding on the order of tasks, some of the questions you might ask yourself include:

- Which is most urgent versus important?
- Which will benefit the service user most?
- Which will benefit me the most?
- Which does my manager/organisation expect of me?
- What are my legal responsibilities?

(MOST) URGENT VERSUS IMPORTANT TASKS

Urgency infers negative consequences if a task is not completed within a limited period of time.

In terms of social work, urgency tends to be associated with risk and harm, for example:

- investigating an allegation of abuse;
- completing a paediatric medical;
- seeking treatment for a service user who is having suicidal thoughts.

Conversely, important tasks may not have immediate deadlines but have a strong impact on your work-related goals, for example,

- completing a referral for respite;
- undertaking a home visit;
- attending a panel to acquire funding.

Understanding the difference between urgent and important is crucial, and is a challenge to effective time management.

A further consideration is that effective time management should minimise the likelihood of pre-planned tasks becoming 'urgent' (although this is not always possible). Indeed, most 'urgency' appears as a result of the unplanned for/unexpected, as we discuss below.

Reflective activity

Differentiating between 'urgent' and 'important' tasks

Thinking back to your previous social work placement/practice experience, make a list of some of the different tasks that you encountered?

You might differentiate between:

- the daily or core tasks (e.g. emailing, phone calls, meetings, case recording);
- the more unusual tasks (e.g. painting and decorating, house moves, dressing up as Father – or Mrs – Christmas!);
- the more time-consuming tasks (e.g. Court paperwork, paediatric medicals, long-distance visits/meetings);
- the most challenging tasks (e.g. giving oral evidence in Court, removal of a child, advising family members of a negative assessment outcome).

Reviewing your list of tasks, sort them into the following categories:

1   Urgent;
2   Highly Important;
3   Fairly Important;
4   Not Very Important.

You may wish to simply place a number next to each to denote level of importance. (NB If you have multiple 'urgent' tasks, you might relabel one or two as 'most urgent'.)

Once finished, think again about the factors which influenced your decisions. This should provide further insight into how you choose to prioritise, as well as your reasoning for this.

As a final point on the issue of prioritisation, the benefit comes not only from being able to decide which tasks take precedence over others, but also in being able to explain how you came by this decision – justifying to yourself, and others, why some tasks should be left until another day and time (as opposed to working over contracted hours or taking work home with you).

NB You may note that in the example time diary above (see Table 10.1), the social worker worked over their contracted time so as to complete both the emergency paediatric medical and a written account of the task before going home. What this example shows is that in some situations, working over our contracted hours is unavoidable. However, these occasions should be *exceptions* to your normal routine, and should not become the norm (indeed, it remains to be seen whether the social worker in this example would have chosen to work over their contracted hours to complete other, less 'urgent', tasks) – this is where time management, prioritisation, but also setting boundaries for yourself and others is important. Indeed, the author strongly believes that a more suitable measure of work ethic is your ability to come to work every day (hopefully feeling relatively refreshed). This means that it is better to go home at 5 p.m. (or whenever your contracted hours expire), so that you can rest and recuperate, than work regularly into the night, risking fatigue, burnout, and ultimately a period of sickness (and therefore absence). Whilst we may, on occasions, feel under pressure to stay late so as to 'finish that last piece of work', the truth is that in a career like social work, there is *always* another piece of work to complete – thus, we must recognise our limits and learn to prioritise!

Reflective activity

Thinking about your approach to work, do you think that your service users (and for that matter your employer) would prefer you to go home every night (emergencies notwithstanding) at 5 p.m., with the knowledge that this will allow you to return to work feeling refreshed the next day, or for you to work into the evening, catching up on paperwork and admin, with the risk of burnout, and thus, a period of absence?

MANAGING THE UNEXPECTED (THE FUNDAMENTALS OF SOCIAL WORK)

Inherent within the task of social work, and a real challenge for time management, is encountering the unexpected. It is the unpredictable nature of people that leads to unexpected events occurring (Munro, 2011), and provides us with an inevitable discretionary space in our own time management (Murphy, 2019). Indeed, for many social workers, this is why social work cannot be conceived as a boring job!

However, these unexpected events often appear in the form of an emergency, and thus present some urgency (hence the term 'firefighting'). At these times, all the best-laid plans and meticulous diary management can become redundant as the social worker is expected to 'drop everything' and respond.

These situations can be frustrating for the social worker who had planned to get through that backlog of emails, or who had put some time aside to write that assessment – but they are nevertheless a normal part of social work practice.

When encountering the unexpected you may be required to cross out large parts of your planned activities for the day. Some of these may be easily jettisoned as they don't involve anyone else (i.e. the backlog of emails). For others, however, you may have to contact other parties (i.e. the attendees of a meeting, or the family you had made plans to visit), and here it is normal to ask for the assistance of a colleague or duty worker, whilst you prioritise the emergency/urgent task. (You might also ask a colleague or another professional to complete a task for you.)

However, some unexpected tasks may not fall into the category of 'urgent', and you will again be required to engage in the process of prioritisation. Furthermore, whilst some unexpected events may be perceived by others (service users, other professionals, your manager, etc.) as 'urgent', you might not agree on their assessment of 'urgency' when you consider the other pressing tasks in your diary. Where this is the case, you should not prioritise a less urgent task just to placate another party, but explain where necessary that whilst *important*, you have other *urgent* matters that must be resolved first, and that you will place this important task, on your 'to-do' list.

Reflective activity

Can you think of a time in your placement/practice where another person has asked you to complete a task that you thought was less important than the task that you had planned? How did you manage this situation?

Of course, when that other party is your manager or someone else who has some authority/seniority over you, saying 'no' to their request can be difficult. You can however make a case to say that whilst you cannot complete the task *now*, you will try and find time to do it *later*, explaining why other tasks should take priority.

Helpfully, Rymell (2015) makes the following recommendations to facilitate such a response:

- Being able to discuss/outline your current workload and priorities provides a good platform from which to negotiate.
- Having a clear set of goals and an associated diary of tasks can provide the foundation for a conversation that might otherwise be difficult.
- Engaging in ongoing communication about the realities and practicalities of your schedule is crucial to maintaining a productive manageable workload, and allows you to agree what can, and cannot, be accommodated into your work schedule.

CONCLUSION

In concluding this chapter, it is helpful to reflect on why you have chosen a career in social work. The answer to this question is surely not to work an 80-hour week, with little time for rest – never mind a personal life. If that were the case, then there are certainly other jobs which would facilitate such a lifestyle, but perhaps have less of an emotional impact – and be more financially rewarding – than a career in social work.

Invariably, you have chosen a career in social work as you have a desire to help, or make a difference to, other people. Further, you might have some excellent 'people skills' which you think make you ideally suited for social work.

On this basis it is important to remember that to be the best social worker you can be, means that you must stay energised (both physically and emotionally), and in order for this to be achieved, you must maintain some work–life balance in the interests of 'self-care'. Effective time management is one skill that can enable you to achieve this balance, and with some practice and application of the processes identified within this chapter, you can become a master of time management, for the benefit of not only yourself, but also your employer and your service users.

Having read this chapter you should be able to:

- Better understand the principles of effective time management;
- Understand that effective time management is not only important for your professional practice, but also in achieving a work–life balance;
- Be able to implement strategies to achieve effective time management - for example, using a time diary and prioritisation between tasks.

RECOMMENDED READING

Betts, Z. (2015) 'Clarity from the chaos': tips for time management in social work. Community Care. Available at: www.communitycare.co.uk/2015/07/28/clarity-chaos-tips-time-management-social-work/

Boylan, S. (2014) Time management tips for social workers struggling to maintain control. Community Care. Available at: www.communitycare.co.uk/2014/01/10/time-management-tips-social-workers-struggling-maintain-control/

SKILLS AND KNOWLEDGE
FOR ASSESSMENT AND
INTERVENTIONS

The second section of this book will develop the work covered in Part I, which outlined core skills for relationship-based practice. Part II focuses on key social work practice skills and knowledge and Carole Sutton's ASPIRE model as a template (Sutton, 1999). ASPIRE is a useful mnemonic and helps us remember, locate and order the stages of social work practice, commonly referred to as 'social work process'. ASPIRE features the following stages:

AS – assessment

P – planning

I – intervention

RE – review and evaluation

Social work is a complex business and so it is important we try to think about how to make sense of the day-to-day work we do and the different activities, processes and stages of the work we undertake. This helps us to understand *what* work we are doing and explain it to others (notably in working with service users and carers); it also helps us to begin to understand and think about how we may be doing certain things but also explain why (again this is really important in working with service users and carers).

As Edmondson (2014: 94) outlines:

Social work process has five distinct but interrelated and interdependent stages. These stages include:

1 *An initial referral* (a presenting difficulty or problem).
2 *An assessment* (collecting information and making sense of the resulting data).
3 *Planning and delivering a response* (producing a plan of care and delivering a social work intervention).
4 *Producing specific outputs* (e.g. practical services or equipment) *or other outcomes* (e.g. effective risk management, change and improvement).
5 *Review and evaluation.*

Assessment > **P**lanning > **I**ntervention > **R**eview & **E**valuation

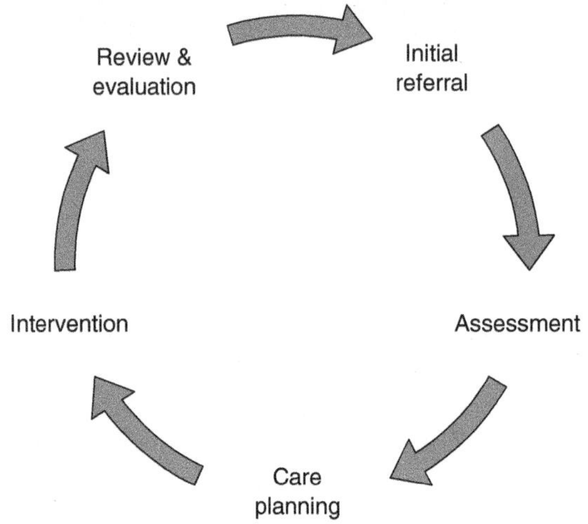

Figure II.1 Social work practice cycle

Although we often tend to think of a 'process' as linear and sequential – just as it is being described above – actually, it is much more useful in the context of social work to think of social work process as circular, cyclical and iterative in motion and action.

The cycle begins with the referral or presenting problem and concludes with a review and evaluation of the process. However, as frequently is the case in social work practice, the cycle needs to be flexible enough to enable any stage to be undertaken independently or for different stages to be revisited several times in order to accommodate and respond effectively to changes in circumstances, environments and risk issues (Edmondson, 2014). Becoming familiar with social work process and its constituent parts will assist you to develop your practice and manage your work more effectively.

Assessment Skills
Michaela Rogers

Links to the Professional Capabilities Framework

● Professionalism ● Values and ethics ● Knowledge ● Critical reflection and analysis ● Skills and interventions

Links to the Knowledge and Skills Statement for Child and Family Practitioners

● Relationships and effective direct work ● Communication ● Child development ● Adult mental ill-health, substance misuse, domestic abuse, physical ill-health and disability ● Abuse and neglect of children ● Child and family assessment ● Analysis, decision-making, planning and review ● The law and the family and youth justice systems ● The role of supervision ● Organisational context

Links to the Knowledge and Skills Statement for Social Workers in Adult Services

● Person-centred practice ● Safeguarding ● Mental capacity ● Effective assessments and outcome-based support planning ● Direct work with individuals and families ● Supervision, critical reflection and analysis ● Organisational context

Key messages

- Assessment is a continual process, not a singular event.
- Many assessment models and frameworks exist; there are, however, some core skills that underpin all assessments.
- Assessments involve collecting data, forming hypotheses and making professional judgements.
- Good assessments rely on systematic and analytical thinking.

INTRODUCTION

This chapter focuses on the '**assessment**' stage of Sutton's (1999, 2006) ASPIRE model, serving as an introduction to some common assessment models and core skills required in this process. Whatever the model or framework, assessments should be evidence-based (see Chapter 17 'Research-Informed Practice'), involve service users (see Chapter 14 'Working with Service User and Carers') and balance both risk and strengths (see Chapter 13 'A Positive Approach to Safeguarding' and Chapter 23 'Strengths-Based and Solution-Focused Approaches'). All social workers should be able to articulate the importance of assessment in terms of:

- enhancing the quality of information gathering;
- making the assessment process empowering;
- understanding the determination of eligibility to further support and resources;
- identifying and providing solutions;
- offering empathic and sensitive support at a time that is often stressful. (SCIE, 2007)

Clearly, a comprehensive skillset and the capacity to be flexible and responsive in utilising these skills is of upmost importance and fundamental to undertaking a good assessment.

WHAT IS ASSESSMENT?

In describing the function and boundaries of 'social work assessment', many definitions draw upon Coulshed and Orme's claim that:

> Assessment is not a singular event, it is an ongoing process in which the client participates, in order to assist the social worker in understanding people in relation to their environment. Assessment is also the basis for planning what needs to be done to maintain, improve or bring about change in the person, their environment or both. (2012: 22)

The process of assessment begins at the point of referral and only ends once an **intervention** is complete, or a case closes. As well as requiring numerous skills, there are various purposes of a social assessment (see Table 11.1).

Table 11.1   Five purposes of social work assessment (SCIE, 2007)

Purpose: interests or goals for which the assessor is agent	Assessor role
1. Individual and public protection	Risk assessor
2. Service user and carer needs	'Traditional' professional
3. Service user and carer representation	Advocate
4. Agency function, policy and priorities	Agency representative
5. Other professions or agencies	Proxy

Source: SCIE, 2007. Reproduced with permission of Social Care Institute for Excellence (SCIE).

These purposes are not always complementary and may conflict. It is the role of the social worker to negotiate and manage any contradictions.

Reflective activity

After a home visit you make a judgement that the carers (the parents) of the disabled young adult, Sam, who you visited, need a weekend of respite from their caring duties. Both parents are at the point of burnout. You know that Sam could attend a residential facility one weekend to give her parents a break (and you wish to advocate for the carers in this regard). Your manager tells you that you cannot apply for respite as the budget has been used for the financial year. In terms of the purposes of assessment and your role as an assessor; where is the conflict (review Table 11.1)?

MODELS FOR ASSESSMENT

There is no singular model that is the 'gold standard' in social work. However, research has shown that a systematic approach using a conceptual model is the best way to complete a rigorous, comprehensive assessment. In child and families social work the Assessment Framework (HM Government, 2018) (see Figure 11.1) is commonly used

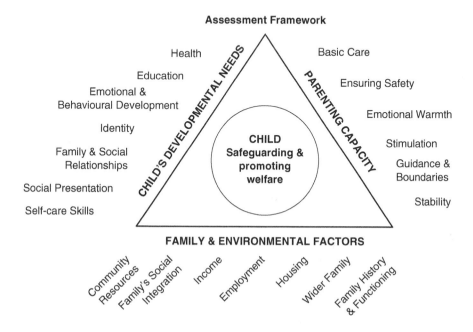

Figure 11.1 The Assessment Framework

Source: HM Government, 2018.

and this prompts the assessor to consider: the child's developmental needs; parenting capacity; and family functioning including the impact and influence of wider family, community and environmental factors. Increasingly, new models of assessment are being adopted in child and families social work: for example, Signs of Safety (Turnell, 2012; Turnell and Edwards, 1999) (see Chapter 23 'Strengths-Based and Solution-Focused Approaches').

In adults' social work, the Care Act 2014 stipulates that local authorities must carry out an assessment of anyone who appears to require care and support, regardless of their likely eligibility for state-funded care. In addition, there are specific assessments dependent on the presenting issue. For example, the Care Act 2014 also requires a carers assessment to be undertaken when needed and the Mental Capacity Act 2005 was implemented to support people who may lack capacity: that is, if they are unable to make specific decisions at a specific time because of an impairment in the functioning of the mind or brain. In these cases, a mental capacity assessment should be made using appropriate tools, and if a person does not have capacity then the social worker acts as a proxy in order to ensure that any decision-making is undertaken with the service user's best interests at the core. In addition, there are many specialised assessment tools to be found: for example, the DASH (domestic abuse, stalking and harassment) assessment tool helps to evaluate the risk in cases of domestic abuse (Safe Lives, 2014) and AIM2 assessments enable the assessment and intervention in cases of young people who present sexually harmful behaviour (Griffin and Vettor, 2012).

A helpful framework is offered by Smale et al. (1993), who propose three models of assessment:

- *The questioning model*: Where the social worker is concerned with a set format of questions, gathering data and making sense of it. In this way the social worker is seen as the expert, and problem solver.
- *The procedural model*: In which the social worker gathers information in order to see if agency criteria are met. This model is often associated with legislation and agency policy. A limitation is identified with this model as the social worker can become overly concerned with collecting data as per the relevant criteria, without probing further and paying little attention to the service user's strengths, abilities, rights, wishes and feelings.
- *The exchange model*: The service user is seen as an expert in their situation and needs and becomes empowered in this context. The social worker helps to provide resources and seeks to maximise the potential of the service user.

These models can guide an assessment in any area of practice, whether this is child and family safeguarding or in the field of social work with adults. These models do not need to be employed in isolation, but can be part of an eclectic approach which draws on various models and theories in the assessment process.

STAGES OF ASSESSMENT

Milner et al. (2015: 2) identify five stages of assessment:

1 *Preparation*: From the point of referral, or allocation of work, you make decisions about who to see or speak to; you may read existing files to gain an initial understanding; you will clarify the task at hand.
2 *Data collection*: You speak to other professionals and engage with service users; you should approach the task with 'respectful uncertainty' (Laming, 2003) and adopt an investigative approach; concurrently, be empowering and promote choice, but ensure that you collect the information that you need in order to identify needs, risks, strengths and gaps in your data.
3 *Applying professional knowledge*: This involves you using practice wisdom (see the section on practice wisdom below), theory or research to understand, interpret and/or analyse data.
4 *Making judgements*: About the needs, risks, strengths, relationships, standard of care, safety, levels of concern, capacity for people to change, how change will be measured.
5 *Making decisions or recommendations*: This is the stage at which judgements underpin interventions and a plan with a timeframe is drafted.

These stages are not discrete or necessarily linear; you may find yourself gathering data whilst you are analysing information gleaned from other professionals and collected at a home visit. It is fair to say that the task of assessment is a messy business! It is easy to fall into one of the many pitfalls of assessment. Go to the website (https://study.sagepub.com/rogers2e) and take a look at Broadhurst et al.'s (2010b) report 'Ten pitfalls and how to avoid them: what research tells us'.

> ## Reflective activity
>
> ### First encounters
>
> Take a moment to think about how you would approach the first meeting with a service user on a home visit. What would you need to do to prepare?
>
> Go to the website (https://study.sagepub.com/rogers2e) to access a 'How to ...' guide on 'Introductions'. This explores making initial contact, introducing yourself and building a professional relationship from the start. Another task early in the assessment process is collating information – as described above. A helpful way of doing this is to construct a chronology or a timeline; you will find 'How to ...' guides on the website for these activities too.

Before moving on, it is prudent to highlight the importance of analysis in the assessment process (particularly in light of previous criticisms about social workers' ability to gather data, but not analyse it). To analyse something is to break it down into its separate components, then to explore the relationship between the constituent parts. This helps to give you a better understanding of the case, as well as the ability to draw conclusions or shape hypotheses. Information can be complex, confusing and often incomplete. Just remember that a skilful practitioner will acknowledge the limitations of analysis whilst making the best use of the information and resources at hand.

Visit the website to think further about assessment as a process (https://study.sagepub.com/rogers2e).

INTEGRATING KNOWLEDGE

At each stage of an assessment you will need to draw from a wide range of knowledge to support your analysis and subsequent decision-making. Pawson et al. (2003) identify the following range of sources:

- *Practitioner knowledge*: Your own insight into a particular issue or about a service user, or knowledge gained through prior experience.
- *User knowledge*: Consider that the service user is the expert of their own situation and collect information from them directly.
- *Organisational knowledge*: Information that is collected by your employer about a particular service user group or locale. Alternatively, you could consult another local organisation for information relating to your task.
- *Research knowledge*: Draw from current research, the evidence-based literature and research reports from charities such as the NSPCC or Age UK.
- *Policy knowledge*: Refer to policy such as *Working Together to Safeguard Children* (HM Government, 2018), or *Valuing People Now* (DH, 2009).

You should also draw on formal theories and knowledge of the community where you are based (*theoretical knowledge, local knowledge*). Thinking about knowledge in this way can guide your assessment and help to identity gaps in evidence. To understand a particular issue, you may ask a colleague who has specialist knowledge of that issue (*practitioner knowledge*). To acquire the necessary user and carer knowledge, you may undertake a home visit and conduct interviews (see Chapter 12 'Interviewing Skills'). During a home visit you should rely on other sources of information, in addition to that gained through dialogue; this can be done through observations.

WHAT IS PRACTICE WISDOM?

Practice wisdom is the foundation for effective practice. It encompasses both the art and science of social work, and so bridges the gap between theory and practice. In terms of 'art', this can be thought of as the flexible, creative and intuitive elements of practice, whereas the 'science' is the component which embeds theory, research and the evidence-base (Samson, 2015). Litchfield (1999: 102) describes practice wisdom as 'a process of practice and reflexive development of theory within it; a form of **praxis**'. Rather than being static and stable, Litchfield conceptualised practice wisdom as a participatory process situated within a paradigm based on **constructivism**. Therefore, practice wisdom is fluid, co-constructed within and enhanced through the social worker–service user relationship. In this way, social workers develop their practice wisdom experientially. It is not easily defined or measured but is something of absolute value to each and every practitioner.

Reflective activity

Practice wisdom: Subjectivity versus objectivity

Consider the 'art' of practice, which is flexible, creative and intuitive. This can lend itself to taking a rather subjective approach to assessment. Relying on experiential or intuitive knowledge, as such, creates potential problems:

- There is no way of establishing reliability or validity. How then do you assure consistency in your analysis and decision-making?
- A lack of objectivity can mean a bias. For example, imagine a social worker who has strong anti-abortion beliefs and is tasked with supporting a young person who wishes to terminate a pregnancy.
- Practice wisdom is developmental in that it is developed over time and therefore a more experienced worker's practice wisdom will be much more developed than that of a newly qualified social worker.
- Human error is natural and cannot be anticipated in the present. (Calder and Hackett, 2013)

Consider how to counter these potential problems. Using intuition and experiential knowledge *in combination* with formal theory and the evidence-base adds an element of objectivity and provides a more substantial foundation for decision-making. Remember that you should always be able to provide evidence for your decision-making and professional judgements.

OBSERVATION SKILLS

Whilst dialogue is the most obvious means of gathering data, observation skills are crucial in different social work contexts and the places that practitioners find themselves; for example, during visits to residential accommodation or people's homes, or in school. Indeed, Fitzpatrick et al. (1995: 63) assert that 'assessment begins with observation'.

. . . .

Case study: Shelley

Three-year-old Shelley is living with foster carers, having been removed from her birth family due to concerns about poor home conditions (missing bedding, dirty floors, no toys and animal smells for example) as well as physical and emotional neglect. At the point of removal Shelley had experienced an accident; whilst unsupervised she had climbed up onto the kitchen worktop and fallen off, resulting in an injury to her leg. During weekly contact sessions in a local children's centre, Shelley's social worker, Al, was able to observe inter-actions between Shelley and her parents. Moreover, using attachment theory (theoretical knowledge – see Chapter 29 'Attachment Theory'), Al concluded that Shelley had an insecure attachment to both her parents.

During the fourth contact session Al watched Shelley's father, Rob, being affectionate with her, giving Shelley lots of cuddles and kisses. Al had not previously observed physical contact between father and daughter in this way. Although Shelley had mostly resisted Rob's efforts, at the end of the session Al spoke to Rob to provide some positive feedback about his efforts. During their conversation, Al detected the smell of alcohol. Al was aware that Rob had been treated for alcohol dependency in previous years and so a potentially new concern had presented – that of parental alcohol misuse.

. . . .

Considering the case study, it is evident that observational skills are not limited to what you hear, but includes what you see and smell. Yet, Ferguson (2011: 37) explores the move away from direct work with families towards, what he terms, 'the retreat from intimacy and face-to-face practice' as resulting from the way in which the profession has been driven to singularly focus on the management of risk, working to a prescriptive framework (including rigid timescales and unwieldy paperwork). These practices are rooted to the responses of consecutive governments following the public scrutiny of child deaths and other systemic failures (Ferguson, 2011). In actuality, what makes a good assessment is more time spent directly with families (Munro, 2011).

When visiting a service user in their home, school or residential accommodation, consider:

- *What can you smell?* Does the physical space have a smell? Does the service user? If appropriate, pick up the child, do they smell clean? What do your olfactory senses tell you?
- *What can you see?* Is the physical space clean and tidy? Are there signs of someone else living there (someone who you are unfamiliar with)? Are there toys and books? Is there appropriate clothing (including coats and shoes)? Is there food in the kitchen? Is the service user clean and tidy? What do your eyes tell you?
- *What can you feel?* If it is appropriate to pick up a child and put them on your knee: do they feel nourished, or underweight? If you shake the hand of a service user, how do they feel? How does the physical environment feel? Is it too cold, or too hot?

Ferguson (2011) argues for ethical, 'professional' touch, pointing to the way that social workers have become reluctant to use touch in their assessments. He explores well-known child deaths, such as Victoria Climbié and Peter Connelly (aka Baby P), to illustrate how professionals have tended to avoid children who, like Peter, are 'alive with nits and scabs from healing injuries' (BBC, 2008 cited in Ferguson, 2011: 100). In a study by Lynch and Garrett (2010) they found that the attitudes of social workers with regard to touch were underpinned by fear of misinterpretation, allegations and concern for harm to the child. However, Lynch and Garrett's study also showed how social workers recognise the benefits of touch in terms of communicating and conveying reassurance and empathy to a child. Finally, the practitioners in the study also acknowledged that touch occurs as a result of practicality and safety concerns for a child. The same principles apply in work with adults as touch conveys messages about acceptance, empathy and positive regard.

DEVELOPING HYPOTHESES AND MAKING JUDGEMENTS

Poor decision-making can have harmful results and even tragic consequences (Duffy and Collins, 2010). Making good decisions, however, is complex as the decision-making process can be affected by organisational policy, thresholds, statutory timescales, resource-led cultures, working with resistance and hostility, to name a few. Notwithstanding, sound decision-making can be achieved through inquisitive practice that takes a methodical approach to querying, evaluating and analysing data.

Sheppard (2007: 131) notes that 'generating **hypotheses** is a key element of the reflexive process of assessment'. A *singular hypothesis* is a tentative statement about the relationship between two or more variables. Put another way, a hypothesis is a proposition made on the basis of limited evidence as a starting point for further investigation. *Whole case hypotheses* are propositions that sum up a case as a whole. Whether singular, or a whole case, hypotheses are only as good as the information held at the time and, as such, they are (and should be) subject to scrutiny and revision (Sheppard, 2007).

Reflective activity

Reconsider the case study above and the end point which suggests Rob's alcohol use. Al, the social worker, generates a *partial case hypothesis* (rather than making a general summation of a case) that focuses on one particular aspect:

> Rob has a history of alcohol misuse and dependency and he has resorted to this past behaviour.

(Continued)

However, questions to ask are:

- Why does Rob smell of alcohol on this occasion (at the contact session)? This may be a one-off incident. Rob may have bumped into a long-lost friend and had one drink before coming to contact. He may have been to a family gathering and enjoyed one celebratory drink.
- Why would Rob drink alcohol as he knows the risks that this poses in relation to his contact arrangement? Perhaps Rob finds contact to be very stressful and it makes him anxious; he may have had a drink to try to steady his nerves in order that he can appear 'normal' in front of Al, the social worker. Perhaps Rob finds the setting (which is run down and stark) to be superficial and very difficult to manage (particularly as it brings back unhappy memories of being in care homes as a child).

Developing hypotheses and making good decisions are important as they guide interventions. Moreover, it has been noted that *professional judgement*, supported by practice wisdom, should take more precedence in assessments in order to move away from bureaucratic, less creative and intuitive practice (Munro, 2011). Munro's (2011) review of child protection illustrated this point well by noting how organisational procedures did not allow for the use of the more tacit skills and knowledge that constitute professional judgement and expertise. Furthermore, professional judgement is connected with accountable decision-making and underpins each of the five stages of assessment (Milner et al., 2015). There are some dangers with judgement making and you should be aware not to fall into these common traps (see Table 11.2).

In reality, time will not always be on your side and you may be asked to make quick judgements, or brief statements, about a case. Rutter and Brown (2012) explore how to use different types of judgement statements to establish your professional authority and credibility. These different judgement statements are:

- *Value statement*, e.g. Rob and Jane do not provide the right type of environment for Shelley. Values are different for everyone and so what constitutes the 'right type of environment' needs to be clarified and critically examined.
- *Empirical statement*, e.g. Shelley was injured. The injuries were evidenced and therefore verifiable.
- *Conceptual statement*, e.g. Rob is anxious. More empirical evidence is needed to make a statement that is underpinned by a particular concept or set of ideas.
- *Causal statement*, e.g. Shelley will sustain more injuries if she does not go to other carers. This statement assumes that one thing affects another. The detail of the specific cause or connection is not evident, however. (Rutter and Brown, 2012: 19)

Table 11.2 Professional judgements and danger zones

Anchoring	The tendency to rely too heavily, or 'anchor', on one piece of information when reaching a judgement (usually the first piece of information acquired).
Confirmation bias	The tendency to search for, interpret and stick to information that supports your existing hypothesis.
Continued influence effect	The tendency to believe wrong information even after it has been corrected and the misinformation continues to influence views and judgements.
Courtesy bias	The inclination to project an opinion that is more socially acceptable than your real opinion to avoid offending anyone.
Empathy gap	The tendency to underestimate the strength or influence of emotions in oneself (or others.)
Focusing effect	The tendency to incorrectly overly emphasise one aspect of an event.
Groupthink	The desire to avoid conflict by being compliant, or 'going with the flow', also known as the 'bandwagon effect'.
Hindsight bias	The proclivity to see past events as being predictable at the time those events happened, also known as the 'I knew it all along!' effect.
Information bias	The tendency to seek information even when it cannot affect your decision-making or actions.
Optimism bias	The tendency to be over-optimistic, overestimating favourable and positive outcomes.

CONCLUSION

The continuous process of assessment requires a complex amalgam of skills in order to effectively gather data, by whatever means you can, and make sense of it before moving to the processes of planning and intervening. This chapter discusses only a few areas of the skills necessary to this process. Other chapters in this book guide you through some of the additional core skills (interviewing, active listening) to give you a more comprehensive sense of the complexity of the task. Reading these chapters will provide you with a head start in the task of completing assessments, but remember that assessment skills are honed through experience and you should never be complacent about developing your craft as a skilful practitioner.

Having read this chapter, you should be able to:

- Consider a variety of models for social work assessment;
- Value the import of observational skills during the assessment process;
- Articulate some of the biases that can occur in making decisions and professional judgements.

RECOMMENDED READING

Broadhurst, K., White, S., Fish, S., Munro, E., Fletcher, K. and Lincoln, H. (2010b) *Ten Pitfalls and How to Avoid Them: What Research Tells Us*. London: NSPCC.

Milner, J., Myers, S. and O'Byrne, P. (2015) *Assessment in Social Work* (4th edn). London: Palgrave Macmillan.

Taylor, B.J. (2012) Models for professional judgement in social work. *European Journal of Social Work*, 15(4): 546–562.

Taylor, B.J. (2017) *Decision Making, Assessment and Risk in Social Work* (3rd edn). London: Learning Matters.

Interviewing Skills
Michaela Rogers

Links to the Professional Capabilities Framework

- Professionalism   • Values and ethics   • Knowledge   • Critical reflection and analysis
- Skills and interventions

Links to the Knowledge and Skills Statement for Child and Family Practitioners

- Relationships and effective direct work   • Communication   • Child and family assessment

Links to the Knowledge and Skills Statement for Social Workers in Adult Services

- Person-centred practice   • Effective assessments and outcome-based support planning
- Direct work with individuals and families

Key messages

- An interview is a conversation that has a purpose.
- Interviewing skills are intrinsic to social work assessments.
- Being aware of the many barriers to interviewing is important in order to counter these and facilitate effective communication.

INTRODUCTION

Put simply, an interview can be described as a conversation that is held, or designed, to meet a specific purpose (Barker, 2003). As such, interviewing constitutes a key skill that is essential to information gathering as part of a social work **assessment** (Trevithick, 2012). There are some core principles to good practice in interviewing which include:

- Always prepare and plan for an interview.
- Ensure that you are clear on your focus or goal.
- Aim to build rapport and adopt a relationship-based approach (this can be achieved in one visit, or during one contact).
- Aim to work in partnership and empower people where possible.
- Avoid jargon and use appropriate language in order that your role, remit and any plan or actions are understood.

In terms of the communication and person-centred skills that are essential to successful interviewing, many of these are explored in Part I. This chapter will focus on the art of questioning to elicit information (and this chapter should be considered in tandem with Chapter 2 'Active Listening Skills' in Part I). The chapter will also introduce the reader to motivational interviewing as this provides a very useful framework for structuring a number of sessions.

QUESTIONING

The importance of information gathering is central to the social work task and due to the nature of the social work role and remit, it is often undertaken in sensitive and challenging circumstances. Thus, at times it will take courage and determination to ask the right questions and, sometimes, to assume a position of 'respectful uncertainty' and to probe further (Laming, 2003). An effective communicator will have the ability to use a range of questions and techniques to engender a positive working relationship, to evoke a sense of trust, to elicit key information and/or to complete a thorough investigation. An effective communicator will not get drawn into delivering an interrogation, or simply completing a 'question-and-answer' style session (return to Chapter 11 'Assessment Skills' and review Smale et al.'s (1993) model of assessment).

TYPES OF QUESTIONS

Open questions

An open-ended question is very useful as it is designed to enable the responder to express their thoughts and feelings in their own words. Examples of an open-ended question are:

- What is your view of the concerns raised?
- What is your experience of living with this issue?
- How could we work together to find a solution?

In relationship-based practice, open questions help a service user to feel that they are being listened to, that their thoughts and feelings are valued and taken into account and that they have a say about any future actions or plan. During an **intervention**, using any social work model, open questions should form the majority of those asked as they help to elicit full and detailed responses. Nonetheless, a more hesitant approach to questioning should be taken if interviewing younger children, adults who lack **mental capacity** or with those children or adults who may find it hard to respond verbally in any kind of detailed way (Trevithick, 2012). Hence, it is important for you to be alert, flexible and reflexive to ensure that you use open questions when appropriate.

Closed questions

Closed questions can be used to gather answers that require a yes/no response or when only a short answer is required: for example, a person's name, address, age and so on. Factual information can be gathered in this way. Closed questions can also be used when working with the types of service users referred to above: children, or adults with impaired cognition, or limited mental capacity. In addition, closed questions are less threatening if you are working with someone who finds it difficult to speak up for themselves or formulate their thoughts and feelings.

Indirect questions

Indirect questions are questions phrased as sentences, rather than questions (Birkenmaier et al., 2014). They allow service users the choice of whether to respond or not, as well as providing flexibility in the type or length of response. For example:

Jamie:	My foster carer is awful. She hates me. She's always telling me off for things I don't do and the other kids are doing.
Worker:	That sounds really upsetting. It must be horrid to feel that your foster carer doesn't like you.

Probing questions

Egan (2007) describes probes and prompts as 'verbal tactics' for helping people to talk about themselves more concretely or in greater detail. Probes can be direct or indirect questions. For example, 'You sound very angry, but I'm not sure what about' (indirect), or 'You say that Jill upset you yesterday. Can you tell me what happened?' (direct).

Hypothetical questions

Hypothetical questions can be very useful when trying to engage service users to think positively and be future-oriented (see Chapter 23 'Strengths-Based and Solution-Focused Approaches'). Some examples of hypothetical questions include:

Worker 1:   Can you imagine how it would be if you did not live with the worry of violence every day?

Worker 2:   What would you like to be doing in a couple of years' time when you leave school? Where would you like to be?

Worker 3:   Can you imagine how you might deal with the situation that your sister is in? What would you do?

Case study: Joshua

A social worker undertakes a visit to 12-year-old Joshua. Joshua lives with his mother, Sharron. Sharron has low level mental health problems and a long-term problem linked to alcohol use (although she has abstained in the past). Joshua is considered to be a 'child in need'.

Table 12.1   Case study: Joshua dialogue

	Dialogue	Type of question
Worker	Josh, how are you today?	Closed question
Joshua	Good.	
Worker	Great. So, you wanted me to come over to talk about the school incident yesterday. It must be awful to be called names like that.	Indirect question
Joshua	Yes, I can't stand them. Always picking on me and calling my mum and me. Saying I'm this and that. Next time I'm gonna smack them.	
Worker	Could you find another way? Think about the trouble you'd get in at school.	Closed question Indirect question
Joshua	Yeah, suppose.	
Worker	How could we find a solution together, Josh?	Open question

PARAPHRASING, REFLECTION AND CLARIFICATION

The art of reflection enables you to demonstrate to a service user that you are listening, hearing and understanding them. We do this by reflecting back what we have heard in terms of what the service user has just stated. This can be done in different ways and may simply be a case of repeating what you have heard: 'you say you were angry …'. Alternatively, you may wish to paraphrase; this is the skill of repeating back to someone your understanding of what you have heard, but in your own words. For example:

> Amina: I miss my house. I can't stand living in this hostel away from everyone. I know I'm safe and he can't hit me, hurt me, but he's still there. I miss it. The other people here are doing my head in. It's noisy, kids are noisy.

Amina refers to several issues here, but the clear message is that she is feeling lonely and isolated; the fact that she has left her home and is living in refuge accommodation away from her violent partner, and that the other residents upset her only add to these feelings. An effective communicator would be able to pick out the most significant issue for Amina and show empathy and understanding by reflecting: 'Amina, clearly you are feeling isolated and alone …'. An additional benefit of paraphrasing is that this can assist service users to clarify their own thoughts (Birkenmaier et al., 2014). To avoid repetition, there are a number of ways to paraphrase or reflect, such as: 'As I understand it …'; 'It sounds like …'; 'I'm building a picture of …'; and 'It seems to me …'.

Clearly, it is important to use active listening in order to select the most pertinent issue to reflect or clarify in terms of what the service user has said. Try to do this rather than pick out what you think is the most important issue; this way your practice will be congruent with relationship-based practice (RBP). Indeed, paraphrasing is a very useful tool to help you to check the accuracy of your understanding and interpretation.

MOTIVATIONAL INTERVIEWING

Motivational interviewing (MI) was developed as a model for facilitating behaviour change (Miller and Rollnick, 1991). Miller and Rollnick (2002: 25) define MI as 'a client centered, directive method for enhancing intrinsic motivation to change by exploring and resolving ambivalence'. MI has various theoretical influences incorporating some features of **psychosocial** and **cognitive behavioural approaches** but it is strongly welded to the transtheoretical model (Prochaska and DiClemente, 1983). Briefly, this conceptualises behaviour transformation as achieved through a series of stages of change. Each stage represents a distinct category along a continuum of readiness and level of motivation towards change. These categories include:

- *Precontemplation*: The state in which an individual is not yet considering the possibility of change.
- *Contemplation*: This stage is characterised by the ambivalence that is held by an individual in relation to the possibility of changing or initiating new behaviour.
- *Preparation*: This is the stage where an individual is preparing for upcoming change.
- *Action*: The point at which an individual takes action to achieve a behaviour change.

- *Maintenance*: The next stage where the individual seeks to maintain or fully integrate the behaviour change.
- *Relapse*: The point at which an individual reverts to previous problematic behaviour. (Prochaska and DiClemente, 1983)

MI can be empowering as it avoids taking a deficit approach to someone's problems. It avoids labelling, stereotyping or pathologising. In addition, MI places responsibility for change with the individual, rather than the social worker, but relies upon the skills of the practitioner to help facilitate the behaviour change. Lastly, MI can be adapted to be used with a range of problems, which can involve denial and resistance, and requires skilled communication and interview skills.

Reflective activity

Return to our case study. The next thing you do is visit Joshua's mum, Sharron. You know that in the past Sharron, with the appropriate professional support, has stopped drinking and maintained a lengthy period of abstinence. Consider how you might initiate a conversation with Sharron at that *precomtemplation* stage. What type of information might you need to gather? What type of information might you need to be equipped with to give to Sharron? What type of questions might you ask?

BARRIERS TO AN EFFECTIVE INTERVIEW

As a skilful practitioner you will be able to identify and be responsive to any pre-existing conditions that can block effective communication. You will also develop the skill to respond to newly presenting barriers. Furthermore, a reflexive practitioner should be able to identify blocks that result from their own actions and/or presence. Barriers come in many forms, including:

- *Symbolic communication*: for example, a notepad on your knee conveys a sense that you are there to complete a task, and this does not promote RBP.
- *Environment*: Rooms that are too hot or too cold can impact upon communication. Internal (television) or external (traffic) noise can have an effect too.
- *Interruptions*: Make sure your phone is on silent. The slightest interruption can impede the flow of communication.
- *Assumptions and stereotypes*: These lead to misunderstandings, errors, distorted judgements and poor decision-making.
- *Technical language*: Use of jargon or acronyms; even the word 'assessment' can be intimidating, or not understood by service users.

In addition, there are some common pitfalls to effective questioning. Gambrill (2006: 143) identified seven common errors specific to questioning:

1   Asking leading questions;
2   Poor timing (questions asked at the wrong time are distracting, or interrupt the flow of the conversation);
3   Asking closed questions, which call for a yes/no answer, where more information is required;
4   Asking irrelevant questions;
5   Asking multiple questions all at once (this can be confusing and counter-productive);
6   Asking complicated questions (the question can be unclear);
7   Asking a service user why something occurs and thereby assuming that s/he knows the answer.

In our increasingly multicultural society, another consideration may be that in order to communicate effectively, the use of interpreters is required; this can be an aid or a hindrance. Working with interpreters requires skilled management of the task at hand.

On the website (https://study.sagepub.com/rogers2e) you will find a 'How to …' guide on working with interpreters.

Reflective activity

Think about a recent meeting with a service user that, on reflection, was not productive. Can you identify any of the barriers, or pitfalls, described above? Think about how the conversation went, reflect on the environment and try to be reflexive (consider how the service user's presentation and expression impacted on you, as well as how you and your practice have impacted on the service user).

Using techniques that do not rely on a mere 'question and answer' model can be very useful and can counter some of the difficulties in engaging people in the process of attempting to elicit information. See the website (https://study.sagepub.com/rogers2e) for several helpful 'How to …' practice guides on using genograms, ecomaps and one-page profiles.

Top 10 cognitive distortions

Cognitive distortions are biased ideas and thoughts that we adopt. These are irrational thoughts and beliefs, but over time, we can unknowingly reinforce them as they become a feature of our daily thinking. They become negative automatic thoughts which can be very difficult to identify. Often, they are subtle but damaging. As social workers we need to recognise the ways in which the people that we work with think. This includes identifying the cognitive distortions that people have, recognising how these affect their daily lives (and often their mental health) and influence their capacity for change.

(Continued)

Cognitive distortions come in various guises and here are the top 10:

1 *All-or-nothing (polarised) thinking*: thinking in absolutes (there are no shades, or grey areas). This is characterised by the tendency to use 'never', 'always', 'every'.
2 *Over-generalisation*: this is the tendency to exaggerate from one experience or one example of something (whether positive or negative) and make sweeping generalisations about it as representing an overall pattern.
3 *Mental filter*: the inclination to focus on a single negative and exclude all the positives.
4 *Discounting the positive*: in contrast, you acknowledge the positives, but discount them without reason.
5 *Mind reading*: without evidence, or checking your thinking, you arbitrarily surmise that someone is reacting negatively to you.
6 *Fortune-telling*: again, based on no evidence you predict that things will turn out badly.
7 *Emotional reasoning*: this is a common cognitive distortion which is rooted in the tendency to assume that your emotions are fact. For example, thinking 'I feel it, so I know its true ...' or 'I feel guilty. I must be an awful person.'
8 *Magnification or minimisation*: the tendency to exaggerate or minimise the impact of something without foundation.
9 *Labelling/mislabelling*: both are extreme forms of over-generalisation and can be damaging whether applied to yourself or to others.
10 *Personalisation and blame*: the inclination to take everything personally and assume blame without any logical basis to believe that you are to blame.

Positive reframing

As part of your skillset, it is not enough to recognise the tendency for cognitive distortions in the people that we work with (or indeed, ourselves or our colleagues), we need a counter. Encouraging someone to engage in 'positive reframing' can help. This is when you look at a situation and try to see positives. Here are some tips:

- Encourage the person to explore the problem or situation and to view the situation through a positive lens.
- Encourage a person to consider what aspects of their situation or the problem that they would like to change and to think about the ways that this could be achieved. With positive reframing this may help a person to identify possibilities that they were not aware of or could not recognise due to the tendency for cognitive distorted thinking.
- Ask the person to identify the ways in which they have made a positive difference to the problem or situation or to explain how they have coped with it (see Chapter 23 on strengths-based practice).
- Use humour: try to break the pattern of negative thinking by finding aspects of the situation that are so ridiculous that you cannot help but see the funny side. This is not a common occurrence in social work, but humour can be a powerful tool.

Reflective activity

Return to think about your conversation with Sharron (Table 12.2).

Table 12.2 Cognitive distortions

You say:	Sharron replies:	
'You have been successful before and given up drinking...'	'I fail at everything. I'll never give up. I'm a failure.'	
'With proper support, you can do it again ...'	'I'd get support at first and then I'd fail. I'd go back to drinking as soon as things get a bit hard or Joshua played me up. I know it.'	
'Joshua has been having some issues in school. He seems very angry ... you have been doing a good job on your own as school say Josh has good attendance, always in his uniform and has a go at the work.'	'He is angry. He's angry at me. I make him angry. I know I'm a mess, and he's angry because I'm a rubbish mum'.	Can you spot the cognitive distortions? How could you help Sharron to positively reframe?
'The impact of your daily drinking is affecting Joshua in a number of ways ...'	'Joshua is fine. He doesn't even notice. He's too busy on his X-Box.'	

ENDING AN INTERVIEW

Try to draw a timely end to an interview without the need for hastening or leaving insufficient time to review what has been covered as it is particularly important to summarise any agreed action or further intervention. Trevethick (2012: 219) describes one pitfall as the danger of the 'doorknob revelation', where significant or sensitive information is disclosed to you just as you are about to leave. There is no easy solution to this type of dilemma, but a good habit to get into is to mark a boundary by stating 'OK, we've got five minutes, is there anything else you wish to talk about?'

CONCLUSION

As with other chapters of the book, this chapter should be read in unison with others (particularly Chapter 2) as here we have focused on the art of questioning as an intrinsic aspect of successful interviewing, whilst acknowledging that there are other skills necessary too. The value of effective questioning can be uncovered during reflective discussions when you explore what worked well, or less well, with service users. Consider how you approached the interview and what types of questions you used; how did you build rapport and implement a relationship-based approach?

Having read this chapter, you should be able to:

- Identify a number of different questioning techniques and consider the ways that these are helpful in different circumstances;
- Consider the barriers and enablers to effective interviewing skills;
- Articulate a recognised model for interviewing: MI.

RECOMMENDED READING

Dunhill, A., Elliott, B. and Shaw, A. (2009) *Effective Communication and Engagement with Children and Young People, their Families and Carers*. London: Learning Matters.

Lishman, J. (2009) *Communication in Social Work* (2nd edn). Basingstoke: Palgrave Macmillan.

Miller, R.W. and Rollnick, S. (2012) *Motivational Interviewing: Helping People Change* (3rd edn). New York: Guilford Press.

A Positive Approach to Safeguarding: Risk in Humane Social Work

Donna Peach

Links to the Professional Capabilities Framework

● Professionalism   ● Values and ethics   ● Diversity and equality   ● Knowledge   ● Critical reflection and analysis   ● Skills and interventions

Links to the Knowledge and Skills Statement for Child and Family Practitioners

● Relationships and effective direct work   ● Communication   ● Child and family assessment

Links to the Knowledge and Skills Statement for Adult Practitioners

● Person-centred practice   ● Effective assessments and outcome-based support planning
● Direct work with individuals and families   ● Supervision, critical reflection and analysis

Key messages

- Risk is a multifaceted and ever-changing concept.
- Decisions made by social workers can both increase and decrease risk.
- Humane social work practice requires us to practise while experiencing a degree of uncertainty.
- Reflexive supervision is fundamental to retaining our consciousness of risk.
- We need to counter the cultures of blame that arise when risk becomes exposed.

INTRODUCTION

The concept of risk in social work practice is limited as a means of exploring the complex decisions and professional judgements social workers make every day. It draws a spotlight on the responsibility of the decisions that we take and their potential intended or unintended consequences. Importantly, the notion of risk carries a host of negative connotations and can lead to employing a microscopic lens that searches for who to blame when outcomes are not as hoped for, or expected. However, we need to be clear, children in our society experience abuse every day and often that abuse remains hidden. Conversely, too many risk assessments are undertaken where no 'risk' is found to be present. Thus, there is a need to review the complex relationship between mitigating risk and a humane approach to social work.

In social work practice, we know both adults and children we work with die every week. This is always devastating and should always be subject to critical interrogation so we can learn from events. As practitioners we should be held to account, if our practice is determined to be harmful. However, a mature and reflective process is the opposite from one that is anchored in a spiral of fear and blame. We need to accommodate the presence of 'risk', while co-producing more meaningful, strength-based discourses with those whose lives are affected by our intervention.

 Visit the website to listen to Ray Jones talk about child neglect and protection (https://study.sagepub.com/rogers2e).

THE COMPLEX LANDSCAPE OF RISK

It is important to recognise that what constitutes risk changes over time and place. The construction of risk is influenced by legislation, social policy and economic factors. For many social work students and newly qualified social workers, the advent of the Children Act 1989 seems a long time ago. The 1989 Act replaced what was commonly referred to as the 'orange book', entitled *Protecting Children: A Guide for Social Workers Undertaking a Comprehensive Assessment* (Department of Health [DH], 1988) and which formed the basis of a nationally adopted standardised risk assessment tool (Littlechild, 2008). It was replaced with what was initially referred to as the lilac book, formally entitled *Framework for the Assessment of Children in Need and their Families* (DH, 2000). This assessment pack included questionnaires that social workers could give to parents so they could identify their own strengths and areas they were having difficulty with. The social work profession no longer resides within the DH; indeed the last 16 years have seen huge changes in social policy that effect social work as a profession, and the lives of those we work with.

Importantly, several factors can influence the balance of strengths and risk. These can emanate from both individual and social factors. A parent's misuse of heroin could have consequences on their capacity to parent their child. However, while there has to be a degree of individual accountability, we also need to be mindful of the responsibility of government to prevent the availability of illicit substances and to provide support to enable people to stop the misuse of drugs and alcohol. For those working with children and families, central to all of those considerations has to remain the needs of the child. Focusing on the child should include recognising the strengths of the relationship they have with their parents, but equally any strengths should not blinker concerns. As such, social work students need to learn how to simultaneously identify both strengths and concerns in order to determine the best means of supporting those within the family.

Social work practice does not exist in isolation and both social workers and the families we work with are impacted by publicised events such as the death of a child. There have been numerous public inquiries following the tragic deaths of children, including:

Dennis O'Neill (1945)

Maria Colwell (1973)

Jasmine Beckford (1984)

Victoria Climbié (2000)

Peter Connelly (2007)

Daniel Pelka (2012)

Visit the website (https://study.sagepub.com/rogers2e) to read about each of these public inquiries in more detail.

In 2003, following Lord Laming's inquiry into the death of Victoria Climbié, a thrust to invest in every child via the Every Child Matters policies saw significant investment in welfare provision. A decade later we are constrained by austerity, with more children being looked after by the state than ever before. As a profession, we are now having to contemplate the impact of economic austerity on the incidence of child neglect and mediate the responsibilities of parents and the state. The rise in children's needs is situated against growing concerns about the capacity of local authorities to provide adequate services. Worryingly, in December 2015, Ofsted reported that 77% of councils were not doing enough to protect children, and a quarter were found to be inadequate. Thus, the concept of risk is arguably more complex than ever before.

Visit the website (https://study.sagepub.com/rogers2e) to access more details on Lord Laming's inquiry and Every Child Matters.

THE ROLE OF THE MEDIA

Recent years have witnessed significant media interest in social work practice. This is against a broader and complex socio-political climate. Jones (2012) offers some insights into the significant media coverage of child protection events that became the subject of high-profile media attention between 2008 and 2010. He highlights the negative portrayal of individual social workers, which, he argues, could serve to negate the value of social work as a profession with the general public. Furthermore, he suggests such limited coverage not only fails to present the complexity of social work practice, but discourages discussion about the ethical dilemmas faced by social workers every day. Visit the website to listen to Ray Jones talk about personalisation and social work.

Reflective activity

So far this chapter has outlined the complexity of risk that is inherent in social work practice. Importantly, much of the risk identified is situated at macro and meso levels of practice. Thus, our concept of risk is anchored in legislation, social policy and the cultural landscape we practise within.

1 How do you make sense of this landscape and how does it influence your perceptions of the social worker you want to become?
2 What strategies could you adopt to identify and manage any rise in anxiety associated with risk-related practice in your placements?
3 Can you distinguish between policy-driven strategies to manage risk and the relationships you hope to develop with your service users and carers?

FROM COMPLIANCE TO LEARNING: MESSAGES FROM MUNRO

In a desire to control and contain risk, social work practice developed bureaucratic methods that aim to improve efficiency and specify accountability. In an interesting ethnographic study, Broadhurst et al. (2010a) highlight the importance of understanding the nuanced relational aspect of social work practice in negating or contributing to risk. Importantly, this nuanced relationship can be affected when social work practice comes under public scrutiny, raising individual and organisational anxiety (Munro, 2011). The conclusion is that risk is mediated when social workers are supported in the development of their relationships with the children, adults and families with whom they work. However, the current social work landscape suggests that the practice climate is austere, with unprecedented levels of increased need and a reduction in the availability and quality of resources.

 Visit the website (https://study.sagepub.com/rogers2e) to listen to Ray Jones talk about successful and resilient social work organisations.

As a social work student, you might feel anxious about your positioning within this austere landscape and it is easy to become despondent about the future. In practice, we have to be aware of the intricacy and emotional investment in each decision we make (O'Connor and Leonard, 2014). However, even though as a profession we have challenges ahead of us, the necessity of our survival, of our availability, is more important than ever. It may seem an onerous task but as a student you are part of creating the future of social work. The voices of all practitioners working with children and adults are essential if we are to collectively advocate the importance of our relationships. But that collective voice has to be heard and our role as agents of the state is vital to the success of humane social work (Figure 13.1).

You can find a link to Parton's journal article 'Child protection and safeguarding in England' (2011) on the website (https://study.sagepub.com/rogers2e).

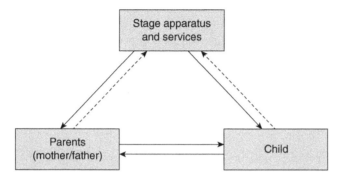

Figure 13.1   The triangular relationship of state–child–parents

Source: adapted from Dencik (1989) Growing up in the post-modern age: on the child's situation in the modern family, and on the position of the family in the modern welfare state. *Acta Sociologica*, 32(2): 155–180.

Case study: Jessica

A nursery worker contacts social services at 4 p.m. to report bruising on the bottom of a 14-month-old child, Jessica. The bruising was observed while the nursery worker was changing Jessica's nappy earlier that day. There have been no previous concerns and no bruising seen on Jessica. The nursery report good attendance and observations of a good relationship between Jessica and her mother. The nursery allowed Jessica to return home with her mother and did not mention their concerns. You are unable to contact the family's health visitor. You phone Jessica's mum, Lisa, and arrange for you and a colleague to conduct a home visit. It's winter and by the time you arrive at the family home it's 5.30 p.m. The house is clean, tidy and warm, Jessica is in her pyjamas and playing happily with toys on the floor of the lounge, both parents are present and seem anxious about your presence. They explain that Jessica is learning to walk and they are toilet training her so often she is walking without a nappy on and will fall down and land on her toys, and that this is the cause of her bruising.

Reflective questions

- What is your initial view on the potential strengths and risks?
- What courses of action/inaction are available to you?
- What are the potential implications of your actions for all concerned?
- What policies and theories underpin the actions available to you?

FROM RISK-FOCUSED TO HUMANE SOCIAL WORK

One of the challenges in social work practice is our capacity to adapt to newly identified risks as they become visible. One example of this are risk factors associated with developing digital technologies (Reamer, 2013). These risks originate in different areas of concern to social work practice such as the sexual abuse of children and women (Hughes, 2004). Other challenges include how we empathically respond and adapt to the role of social media in creating opportunities for adopted children and their birth families to re-establish relationships that would have been improbable a generation ago (MacDonald and McSherry, 2013). However, we must remember that technology can also provide us with useful solutions in locating and supporting victims and survivors (Sarkar, 2015). Usefully, Broadhurst et al. (2010a) position moral rationalities, care and respect at the heart of humane social work practice. Their paper highlights the sensitivity needed to carefully examine multiple and complex needs rather than responding with a systemic and managerial approach. Humane practice is absolutely what we should strive to deliver; however, it also needs to be adequately resourced and social work practitioners need to be well supported. Broadhurst et al. (2010a: 1052) suggest three key elements underpin a risk-management approach:

1   The logics of risk-management strategies are emergent/contingent; they arise in relation to particular cases as reflexive, individualised and tailored responses.
2   Risk-assessment practices are embedded in social relations – team culture, client–worker relationships that create unique contingencies, but also habitual responses.
3   A multiplicity of rationalities operate, concerning not just instrumental matters, but human virtues of compassion, empathy and a sense of moral responsibility for others.

The following case study describes a situation where an adopted child has unexpected contact with his birth family. Read the case study then complete the activity below.

. . . .

Case study: Sam

Sam is 14 years old and has lived with his adopted parents since the age of two. He knows that he was adopted and that he has an older half-sister, Fran, who lives with their dad. Sam has had regular letterbox contact from his biological dad twice a year. He has had no contact with his biological mum since she stopped sending letters when Sam was six years old. Sam's adoptive parents, John and Liz, know that Sam has a Facebook account and Liz is friends with him so she can monitor his social media activity. Looking through Sam's list of friends Liz is shocked to see that he is friends with Fran. When she speaks to Sam he admits that he has been talking to his biological dad and Fran through private messaging and that he has also been searching for his mum. Liz is very upset and tells Sam that he is banned from using Facebook. She talks to John and they worry that Sam will feel compelled to explore the potential of having direct contact with or even living with one of his biological parents.

During the night Liz reads all of Sam's messages and is concerned that Fran has told him that their father had always wanted to keep him. Fran states that their father was never given the chance to care for him and that she misses not having her baby brother with her. Liz phones you in a very distressed state the following morning.

Reflective activity

Using the above case study design a plan of action and reflect on the relationship between procedural and humane approaches. Featherstone et al. (2014) argue for family-minded social work practice. In the above scenario, how, and by whom, is 'family' determined?

- Identify the different needs of each of those represented in the case study?
- What are the underpinning issues that form the foundations of your response?
- How might your response differ, or not, for different people in the scenario?
- What are the biggest challenges you face when deciding how to proceed?

MOVING AWAY FROM THE BLAME GAME – LEARNING FROM THOSE WITH LIVED EXPERIENCE

There is a lot of pressure on student social workers and those in practice to consistently perform well. Indeed, we should have high standards, as our intervention often has a huge impact on people's lives. An insightful autoethnographical account comes from Dr Jadwiga Leigh's (2016: 418) previous social work practice on a duty team. Although, initially rejecting the risk-averse social work culture she had encountered, Dr Leigh found her identity synonymous with the Police Protection Orders (PPO) used in emergency situations. She reflects:

> In this instance, the term 'PPO queen' immediately enabled me to see that I had become a fully integrated member of a culture I had initially rejected. The signs had been there all along, I had just refused to acknowledge that, which I now was. In cases where I had doubted my own decision-making, I had opted for the decision that was the safest and chosen to remove any child I visited who was in a risky situation. Therefore, rather than taking informed risks, I had preferred to not take any risks at all and instead moved the child to what I considered to be a safer place for their own good.

In addition to her academic career, Dr Leigh has founded the New Beginnings project which works to empower parents to help keep families together (www.newbeginningsgm.com/)

When our practice involves decisions about children, they can have a lifetime effect. The autobiography *Hackney Child: A True Story of Surviving Poverty and the Care System* provides a perfect example. The author, now known publicly as Dr h.c. Jenny Molloy (https://twitter.com/HackneyChild), is an inspiration who continues to work tirelessly to facilitate the improvement of our profession. Her story draws attention to how our practice, decision-making processes, verbal and written communication are so important to get right, not only at the time when they are delivered but also years later when as adults those children build the courage to access their case files.

Another prominent care leaver who continues to campaign for the rights of children in care is Ben Ashcroft (https://twitter.com/AshcroftBen). His autobiography, *Fifty-One Moves*, depicts a catalogue of loss and rejection which ultimately led to a custodial sentence. Shockingly, at least 24% of our prison population has been a looked after child, a statistic that has to be considered by our profession if we are to have a comprehensive review of what constitute humane outcomes from our practice. Evidence about young adults in the criminal justice system was provided to the Justice Committee in November 2017, which you can watch using the link www.parliamentlive.tv/Event/Index/49fa4ae1-e865-4d14-a3ba-605d1fb3f12b#player-tabs

CONCLUSION

This chapter has explored how the concept of risk is ever-changing and subject to influence from the media and technology, and how we as humans respond, or not, to our ever-changing environment. The concept of humane social work is at one level easy to conceive; however, when applying this in practice it highlights numerous issues that need further contemplation. What is risk, and the managerial or humane responses to it, extends beyond a social worker's interactions with families; it exists in the fabric of our laws and social policies and in the cultural norms that permeate through each of our communities.

In Britain, children die every week as a result of abuse or neglect. It is absolutely correct that these tragic events should be critically examined and understood. However, the scope for learning how we can best keep children and adults safe in our society has to be everybody's business. Importantly, social workers are tasked with a particular role alongside other safeguarding services such as the police, education and health. It is crucial to acknowledge that at times individually and collectively these services have failed to adequately protect some children. Importantly, we also need to recognise that many children are alive and happy today because of the intervention of social work practitioners. However, we need to continue to progress and social work has to be able to adapt to the ever-changing needs of families. To do so effectively, the social work profession needs society to support and adapt to the ethical dilemmas that social work practitioners face every day.

Having read this chapter, you should be able to:

- Understand the complexity of what constitutes a risk;
- Recognise that the decisions made by social workers and others can both increase and decrease risk, across a child's life;
- Appreciate that learning from the experiences of those who have been subject to social work intervention is vital to the future wellbeing of the children and families we work with.

RECOMMENDED READING

Ashcroft, B. (2013) *Fifty-One Moves.* Hook: Waterside Press.

Broadhurst, K., Hall, C., Wastell, D., White, S. and Pithouse, A. (2010a) Risk, instrumentalism and the humane project in social work: identifying the informal logics of risk management in children's statutory services. *British Journal of Social Work*, 40(4): 1046–1064.

Daniels, H. and Livingstone, M. (2014) *Hackney Child: A True Story of Surviving Poverty and the Care System.* London: Simon and Schuster.

Featherstone, B., White, S. and Morris, K. (2014) *Re-Imagining Child Protection: Towards Humane Social Work with Families.* Bristol: Policy Press.

Leigh, J. (2016) The story of the PPO queen: the development and acceptance of a spoiled identity in child protection social work. *Child and Family Social Work*, 21(4): 412–420.

Parton, N. (2014) Social work, child protection and politics: some critical and constructive reflections. *British Journal of Social Work,* 44(7): 2042–2056.

Webb, S. (2006) *Social Work in a Risk Society: Social and Political Perspectives.* Basingstoke: Palgrave Macmillan.

14

Working with Service Users and Carers

David Edmondson

Links to the Professional Capabilities Framework

- Values and ethics • Knowledge • Skills and interventions

Links to the Knowledge and Skills Statement for Child and Family Practitioners

- Relationships and effective direct work   • Communication

Links to the Knowledge and Skills Statement for Social Workers in Adult Services

- Person-centred practice   • Direct work with individuals and families

Key messages

- Including and involving service users and carers is essential for value-led, ethical social work practice.
- It supports genuine partnership working and positive models of change.

INTRODUCTION

Service user and carer inclusion and involvement in social work practice are essential to ensure the planning and production of value-led, ethical services and effective outcomes. This approach is driven in part by early principles and ideas developed from within the social work profession itself, but also clearly by external rights-based movements and human rights. These elements are important to note if we are to understand not only how social workers are expected to behave and what they ought to do, but just as crucially, why. If we are not working with service users and carers, we may well find we are working against them. Your decision is what sort of social work you intend to practise.

COLLABORATION AND FORGING ALLIANCES WITH SERVICE USERS AND CARERS: PRINCIPLES AND VALUES

The social work profession seeks to promote the fundamental rights of individuals, groups and communities, in particular those who are marginalised, excluded and ignored, to be heard and supported in order to improve their situations and lives. Social work emphasises working together and collaboratively with service users and carers to achieve these ends. This is in part a practical response to addressing complex social problems, as working *with* people as much as possible is more likely to develop positive working relationships and outcomes. However, perhaps more importantly, it is also a moral and essentially political position, derived from recognition of the rights of all individuals to have as much choice and control as possible over their own lives.

Within the social work profession, these ideas and principles are well established in standard social work texts and have been given shape and direction through a succession of social work professional bodies relevant to our discussion here, most notably: the National Institute for Social Work (1961–2003), the Central Council for Social Work Education and Training (1970–2001), the General Social Care Council (2010–2012) and more recently, until its early demise, The College of Social Work (2012–2015). Within contemporary social work, these principles are reflected in the requirements set out in the Professional Capabilities Framework for Social Workers (2018), the Knowledge Skills Statements relating to adults (2015) and also children and families workers (2018). They are fundamental to models of health and social care such as 'person-centred practice', 'partnership working' and 'co-production'. As individual professional social workers, it is important to remain vigilant in defending and promoting our core values as the foundation of our work and practice. How we work with others, and particularly with service users and carers, is central to showing policy makers, commissioners and the public that sound, ethical and effective social work is achievable and worth the investment. How we work with service users and carers, often meeting them during some of the most difficult, stressful and challenging moments in their lives, is perhaps the most obvious and tangible demonstration of the application of our foundations, values and ethics. It is also where, when done well, social work does make a difference. The chapter here refers to work with both children and families and also adults. However, it should be noted that the core principles, values and behaviours being suggested here overlap and can be duplicated for each.

The British Association of Social Workers (BASW), founded in 1970, first produced a Code of Ethics in 1975 and in their updated 2014 code state in plain, unambiguous terms: 'Professional social work is focused on problem solving and change. As such, social workers are change agents in society and in the lives of the individuals, families and communities they serve' (BASW, 2014: 5). Helping people with problems, assisting them to address these and achieve change, whether with individuals, families or communities, is in essence what social work is about. David Howe (2009) and Sarah Banks (2012) describe how values and ethics are central in social work as they help guide the actions of social workers. The BASW Code of Ethics for Social Workers (2014) identifies human rights, social justice and professional integrity as central drivers for social work practice and locate these directly within the pivotal relationship between social worker, service user and carers:

> Since its beginnings over a century ago, social work practice has focused on meeting human needs and developing human potential. Human rights and social justice serve as the motivation and justification for social work action. In solidarity with those who are dis-advantaged, the profession strives to alleviate poverty and to work with vulnerable and oppressed people in order to promote social inclusion. (BASW, 2014: 4)

We can identify the following as key basic values for social workers to recognise, uphold and practise in their work with service users, families, carers and communities:

- respect;
- acceptance;
- individuality;
- honesty and integrity;
- equality.

These values relate in part to those personal and professional values considered important for social workers to hold firmly and which in turn should guide the way we think and act.

Reflective activity

In relation to the above social work values, make some brief notes about how you demonstrate these in your daily work with service users or carers you have been working with.

Just to note, we all have good and bad days influenced by a number of factors. However, if your values are sound, we would suggest that more days than not you are likely to be able to demonstrate these positively in your practice. Trying to be reflective as much as you can *in* the moment as well as *on* the moment (after the event) you will be more capable of being in touch with your own values, testing and maintaining these, keeping them at the centre of your practice. Consider the following questions:

Respect for others: When you meet a service user or carer, are you always polite and courteous? Are you warm and approachable? Do you pay attention to them and give people an opportunity to speak, offer a point of view or disagree with you? Do you consider their views worth listening to and always take these into account even where you do not agree with them?

Acceptance of others: How well do you accept people who may hold beliefs and attitudes you do not share or which are contrary to your own values?

Treat each person as an individual: Do you try to get to know more about a person and their history? Are you interested in their personal story? Do you make an effort to remember individuals' names and spell these properly in reports?

Demonstrate honesty and integrity in your work: Maintaining a professional approach and within the bounds of confidentiality, are you always fully honest and open with people? Do you sometimes withhold or manipulate information to unduly influence or coerce a person?

Treat each person equally: Do you give people equal time and fair access to your resources? Do you give more time to some people than to others, but perhaps without a clear rationale? Do you speak to some people differently and more or less warmly and welcoming than to others? Do you *really* work openly, collaboratively and in partnership with service users and carers?

In the section below, a social worker comments on how and why working with service users and carers is so important in professional practice.

An example from practice of direct social work with children and families

Sarah, a child and families social worker, comments:

My experience of practising social work has raised my awareness of the ease at which we as practitioners can lose sight of what is arguably the most important part our work, engaging with service users and their families. Within a child protection context, social workers are faced with competing demands and the well-known pressures of procedure, high workloads and diminishing resources, all of which impact upon a practitioner's ability to engage fully in the role and with families.

I have witnessed and participated in decision making for and with families, where families have been able to actively participate in their own plans. However, I have also seen situations where involvement and inclusion is discouraged and has been met with great resistance and challenge within a multi-agency arena.

As a social worker, this can make you feel uneasy and isolated. Including such experiences and feelings as a regular feature of reflective supervision can help develop your confidence in this area and can act as a useful check when making decisions in respect of promoting the safety of children. I often ask myself the question, who is to benefit and be protected by the recommendation that I am about to make? Although such a question can at first glance appear simplistic, it is significant in aiding reflection, self-challenge and the understanding of the behaviour of others. This again is an example of the importance of keeping not only the child but the whole family central when undertaking social work as they can easily become lost when practitioners feel the need to self-protect because of the blame culture that social care functions within.

Reflective activity

The BASW Code of Ethics for Social Work (2014) outlines five key values and ethics principles of social work:

1 Upholding and promoting human dignity and well-being;
2 Respecting the right to self-determination;
3 Promoting the right to participation;
4 Treating each person as a whole;
5 Identifying and developing strengths.

Make notes with examples to evidence how you demonstrate you meet BASW principle 3 in your daily work and interactions with service users and carers.

Principle 3 states:

> Social workers should promote the full involvement and participation of people using their services in ways that enable them to be empowered in all aspects of decisions and actions affecting their lives. (BASW, 2014: 7)

 A full copy of the Code of Ethics for Social Work can be found at the BASW website www.basw.co.uk/resources/basw-code-ethics-social-work, also accessible via the website (https://study.sagepub.com/rogers2e).

PRINCIPLES OF WORKING WITH SERVICE USERS AND CARERS

As social workers, it is accepted that you have a job to do and tasks to complete that may be heavily directed by statutory duties and responsibilities and agency functions and goals. Some of these may bring you into conflict with service users and carers, having to make decisions that are unwelcome and run contrary to their views and wishes. This is inevitable. However, it is important to commit to continuing to seek to work with individuals, families and communities who are in crisis, or in conflict with us.

Managing difficult conversations – An example from practice in children and families social work

Sarah, a child and families social worker, comments:

> By the very nature of child protection work, it frequently requires social workers to have very difficult conversations with service users. It means that at times you are required to challenge views and offer opinion which differs to the opinion of others and which quite often can have significant implications for the person involved. From my observations, this element of the role can be challenging to the most experienced of practitioners and for those who chose to come into the profession to help others, such challenging situations can be difficult to manage. Whilst of course there is a requirement to be professional, that does not mean that you stop being a person who feels and who can empathise with service users. It is my experience that such feelings can result in the avoidance of such conversations and the first time families become aware of particularly difficult information is when they are in formal meetings as part of the child protection process. Although I do not believe that such occurrences are motivated by malice or a lack of care for families, it quite often results in an adversarial environment which limits family's ability to engage fully in important processes.

> I still, at times, find the delivery of difficult information challenging but have found several practice skills ease the process.

> I have received a lot of feedback that I am direct in communication, this is definitely a skill which has developed during my social work career but being direct does not mean being rude or mean to families but rather that I am clear with them about what has happened and what needs to happen next. Families often tell me that they appreciate my honesty and this is really important when working with families as honesty can grow into trust, something which is a beneficial element of any relationship which supports change in behaviour. It is important to keep the following in mind when working with others:

> - Respect the individuality of the people we work with and the assertion that all individuals are capable of change.
> - Seek to make positive changes in people's lives by helping them to solve problems.
> - Empower people by helping them learn how to address similar problems for themselves in the future.

- Identify and support people's strengths, both actual and potential. Build on rather than discounting or ignoring individual strengths, resources, skills and knowledge.
- Help people towards independence.
- Acknowledge and support the resilience of others.

Managing difficult conversations – An example from practice in adult social work

David, a former social worker with adults, comments:

> Very early in my career I remember sometimes being quite intimidated and unnerved when talking to older adults about the prospect of them moving into permanent residential care if when despite the best efforts of everyone involved they were no longer able to cope at home. As a relatively inexperienced worker, the sense of genuine sadness and loss this often generated for people made me feel uncomfortable. Despite being able to rationalise the decision, I knew I sometimes found ways to delay and evade these conversations. I recall raising this in supervision with my manager and being reminded that this was part of the sometimes uncomfortable job of being a social worker. On reflection, this reticence was really about my own insecurity and needs. I learned that whatever the context, if I was to discuss things that were likely to cause distress, break bad news or make decisions that were to impact on peoples lives – which is often the lot of the social worker – then I needed to do this as well as I could and with honesty, respect and care. In this sense, the core humane values and ethics of social work are the drivers of good practice. By periodically revisiting this in my work throughout my career I came to understand:
>
> - *how* you do your job is immensely important and something you had a professional and ethical duty to do to the best of your ability;
> - you do exercise control and choice over *what* you do and whether you do this to the best of your ability;
> - being vigilant and keeping these elements at the forefront of your practice is the key to doing things better;
> - good practice, takes practice!
>
> As time went on, I observed and listened closely to how social workers I admired and respected approached such tasks, what they said, the way they said it, how they gave people a chance to talk, to express their views and feelings. I quickly began to see that discussing difficult matters required you to think before you speak, to speak honestly to people, to say what you think needed saying in a clear unambiguous way and to try to say things with respect, care and consideration. I learned to listen better and to give people room and time to talk. I think all these actions made me a better worker, but it was the values and ethics underpinning them that made the real difference.

Personalisation and co-production in social work

Visit the website (https://study.sagepub.com/rogers2e) to watch a video on personalisation and social work.

Visit the website to watch a video on co-production in social work.

Reflective activity: points of initial contact, interventions

First contacts, in the form of home visits, meeting people in your place of work or telephone calls, are important as they are the first time worker and service user or carer will meet each other and communicate. This is also likely to be the first interaction as part of trying to understand what are the presenting difficulties and problems a person or family may be facing, considering what if anything needs to be done and when, and formulating a plan based on a detailed assessment. As we have suggested earlier, doing things with people rather than to or for people is meant to be an important principle of our practice.

The exchange model

Smale et al. (2000) identified three distinct models of assessment in social work: the questioning model (where the worker is the 'expert'); the administrative or procedural model (typified by a rigid system of assessment, prescribed forms and process); and the exchange model. Smale et al. recommend this last model as it facilitates an approach that encourages working together, working out an agreed plan and order of work to be undertaken, and builds on strengths and mutual actions. In the exchange model:

- Both worker and service user construct their own agenda and priorities.
- Information sharing and exchange are important to both building mutual knowledge, and identifying resources and opportunities.
- Participation in the decision-making process is important to develop engagement, trust and an informal contract of commitment.
- Exploration of problems and differing perceptions are valued and seen as potentially creative, more open and as helping to build relationships.
- The individual is respected as being an expert – and therefore knowledgeable and skilled – about their own situation and perhaps in terms of problem-solving.

Reflect on your recent contact or work with a service user and carers. Consider the following:

- How well did your contact work reflect an exchange model? Rate yourself out of 10!
- In what ways did the purpose, circumstances and environment of your contact or work impact on the quality of your work here?
- Overall, how could you perhaps do things better next time?

DIRECT WORK AND COMMUNICATION WITH CHILDREN AND FAMILIES

It is important that when working with families – both the children and the adults – you are consciously aware of the difference between fact and opinion and are able to communicate this with families. When I discuss information with families, I am always conscious to encourage them to offer their opinion in responses as service user participation is a crucial element of social work. Families respond well to the acknowledgement that their opinion matters, is heard and is included equally alongside the opinions of professionals. This is something which is quite fundamental when working with children and their parents and evidences respect, something which can be overlooked within the reactive nature of child protection social work. Obtaining the views of service users is so very important in assessing a family situation; it not only encourages mutual respect and reduces conflict but usefully provides real insight into the functioning of a family unit. When assessing a situation which is potentially harmful to a family I am always keen to establish how family members attribute responsibility of a situation as it provides insight into their understanding of a situation as well as providing an indication of their readiness to engage in discussions about plans to address behaviour and achieve change in order to reduce risk.

Social workers often worry about causing distress to children by discussing the concerns regarding their life with them. However, whilst well intentioned, this fails to acknowledge that children are living within an environment of the concerns and that they are quite often that child's norm. Choosing not to discuss the concerns or explain the actions that you as a professional are taking in response, does not lesson the trauma of that child's experience, but it does ease the difficulty that the practitioner will experience in relation to having to talk about something which may be uncomfortable. Children can be very observant and will in many cases sense when you are avoiding something; it is important that you provide children with a space to share their concerns whether this be verbally or non-verbally and that you share information with them in an age-appropriate way – doing so often acts as a method by which children feel that they are given the permission by an adult to speak about difficult subjects. When sitting in child protection conferences, there is little which rivals the gravity of children's wishes and feelings when shared with parents and professionals as it brings to life their experiences and provides actual evidence of the effect that their environment has upon them.

THE EXPECTATIONS OF YOUNG PEOPLE

User movements frequently comment on the experiences and quality of their contacts and relationships with health and social care services and professionals. This is important as feedback but also as a critical commentary on how we choose to work with service users and carers.

Here are some social work dos and don'ts from a conversation, specifically for this book, with Maya and Jo, a young person and youth and community worker from 42nd Street in Manchester.

Perceptions and concerns about social workers:

Young people often feel petrified of social workers ... worried what they will tell their parents and pass on when sharing information.

A common perception of social work influences me to think:

... you might take me away from my family.

One of the things young people really struggle with is that they have often had so many social workers along the way, they often feel let down and disappointed when a worker they have got to know and begun to trust has to change.

Some key don'ts for social workers:

Don't make promises you can't keep.

Don't only contact or visit me when there is something wrong ... giving me a ring every couple of weeks or so would only take a minute but it shows you care.

Don't compare me or where and how I live with other people ... this happens quite a lot in my experience and it's not fair on me or the people you are comparing me with ...

Some key dos for social workers:

Trust is really important.

It is important for social workers to:

... talk with the person you are working with, put them at their ease ... try to make sure I can feel safe with you.

I want a social worker to be genuine with me and want to work with me.

Social workers should take time to introduce themselves properly and say who they are and what they are doing here today.

It's really important for social workers to be realistic and honest in the way they work with young people ... and to not give false hope by promising too much or making commitments they cannot make or keep.

Be reliable.

We can all accept there have to be professional boundaries and these are generally good things, but: It's good if I can know something about you, or you can share some of your own experiences … it helps to break down barriers if I feel I'm talking to a real person … [and if] I can feel you are exchanging things with me and not just taking down information on a form.

If you need to record things, try to talk to me as well …

Get to know me as a person, not just as a child or young person, I'm me.

Comment: These views seem to offer lessons for social workers in any area of practice or setting.

MESSAGES FROM RESEARCH: THE VIEWS OF CHILDREN AND YOUNG PEOPLE ON WHAT THEY VALUE IN THEIR SOCIAL WORKER

Helen Mayall and Teresa O'Neill (2014) are social work academics and researchers who worked with groups of young people to identify how social workers should try to work with them. They identify three reasons why social work relationships with young people are important:

First, social workers do make a difference to children's lives. Young people want good relationships with their social worker and some remember their social workers for a long time.

Second, relationships with young people are central to safeguarding their welfare.

Third, successive government policy emphasises the importance of maintaining a focus on the child. (Mayall and O'Neill, 2014: 78)

The views of young people on what they value in their social worker

Young people's own reflections on best social work practice:

Empathy is important, remember you were a child or a young person once yourself. The best way to make a difference is to treat people with respect and encourage a friendly dialogue in the social work process.

Remember that what you're communicating to a young person may sound different to them, so be sure to repeat what it is you have said and clarify that they understand.

You have to be a good listener as well as communicator, it's not just all about the talking.

Try to understand what the child has been through, and be sensitive/cautious about what words you use when talking to them.

Be reliable and just show them that you care and are there to help. Social workers go that extra mile.

My ideal social worker would be calm and cool. They would be understanding, patient, caring and have a passion to help me repair my family.

They would treat those they worked with as human beings, and understand that each person is different. They'd work with their co-workers, children and young people in a considerate manner. One cannot call oneself a social worker if they are not truly social. (Mayall and O'Neill, 2014: 88)

You should read Helen Mayall and Teresa O'Neill's full chapter in *Social Work Practice Learning: A Student Guide*.

Christine Oliver has commented that overall:

… studies show that the key characteristics that children look for in a social worker are: a willingness to listen and show empathy; reliability; taking action; respecting confidences, and viewing the child or young person as a whole person and not overly identifying a child with a particular problem. (2010: 8)

Oliver (2010: 8) commented in her review that children want social work support that is:

- flexible;
- responsive;
- individualised/personalised;
- respectful of children's views and wishes;
- participative.

You'll find a helpful link to Christine Oliver's full report on the website (https://study.sagepub.com/rogers2e).

THE EXPECTATIONS OF ADULT SERVICE USERS

Just as social work has given primary importance to building and maintaining collaborative and genuine working relationships with service users and carers, so user and carer movements have made a critical and important contribution to this debate. Beresford (2002) has suggested the service user involvement has emerged out of two differing rationales for participation, one emphasising the importance of political rights and self-advocacy alongside demands for democratic participation and citizenship. The other is relocating service users as no longer passive recipients of prescribed services, but much more as active consumers of services, where the expectation and demand is for services to be responsive and flexible and to act on feedback and comments in order to improve service delivery and outcomes. This has now developed further, notably in adult services, with personalisation as the approach for social care provision linked particularly to direct payments and personal and individualised budgets that seek to increase more individual choice and control for users.

Beresford (2012) suggests the following features are what service users want from their social workers:

- the importance of a relationship with a social worker, working *with* rather than *on* people;
- seeing the social as important and seeing the person in the round, building on their strengths and the things they can do;
- someone who offers both practical *and* emotional support;
- someone who listens and recognises its importance as a foundation for 'co-production';
- someone who delivers what service users want as well as providing advocacy when it is needed and who will encourage community support for individuals and groups.

Reflective activity

How would you rate your own work against the criteria Beresford sets out?

How might you improve on this?

On your next visit to see someone, ask them what they would like from their social worker. What do they say? How might this inform your practice?

MESSAGES FROM RESEARCH: THE VIEWS OF ADULT SERVICE USERS ON WHAT THEY VALUE IN THEIR SOCIAL WORKER

Whittington (2007) has summarised research undertaken for the Social Care Institute for Excellence (SCIE). This outlined what service users felt was important to them in terms of social work relating to assessment. Service users were asked for their views about what they wanted from a social worker:

- dependability;
- a desire for strong advocacy on the service user's behalf;
- clarity about the social work role;
- the need for plain English to be used in assessments.

THE EXPECTATIONS OF CARERS

Carers are a key part of the social care system. It would collapse without the commitment of the estimated 6.5 million carers in the UK, which equates to 1 in 8 of the population. By 2037 it is estimated the figure will rise to 9 million people (Carers UK, 2019).

However, people providing high levels of care are said to be twice as likely to be permanently sick or disabled, socially isolated and living in poverty. How can social workers help? Surveys identify a number of recurrent themes that carers feel are important to them:

Part 1

- Recognition, acknowledgment and respect for them as carers
- Carers are experts in care
- Carers ought to be treated with dignity and compassion
- Carers need to have help in maintaining their own health and well-being through the provision of reliable and flexible care and support services

Part 2

- Information is properly and fully shared with them and other professionals
- Social workers should help signpost carers to local resources and support
- Social workers should link services and professionals together
- Social workers should advocate for carers
- Services should think about the whole family, including young and young adult carers

---

Reflective activity

Look through both parts of the above list.

In relation to Part 1, how well do your attitudes and behaviours reflect these statements? What might you do to build or improve on this?

In relation to Part 2, how well does your practice meet the criteria set out here? What might you do to build or improve on this?

CONCLUSION

Whatever the future of social work as a profession, perhaps the central task for social workers is to ensure we seek to work *with* service users and carers, work collaboratively *with* individuals, families and communities, forge alliances to help people in practical and tangible ways, and advocate to promote the rights and needs of the most vulnerable in our society.

Having read this chapter, you should be able to:

- Identify the views of service users and carers about what they want from their social workers;
- Identify practical ways to promote and deliver humane and improved services.

RECOMMENDED READING

Beresford, P., Croft, S. and Adshead, L. (2008) 'We don't see her as a social worker': a service user case study of the importance of the social worker's relationship and humanity. *British Journal of Social Work*, 38(7): 1388–1407.

Mayall, H. and O'Neill, T. (2014) Translating values and ethics into practice. In D. Edmondson (ed.), *Social Work Practice Learning: A Student Guide*. London: Sage.

Oliver, C. (2010) *Children's Views and Experiences of their Contact with Social Workers: A Focused Review of the Evidence*. Leeds: Children's Workforce Development Council (CWDC).

SCIE (Social Care Institute for Excellence) (2015) *Partnership Working in Child Protection: Cardiff Case Study*. Available at: www.scie.org.uk/socialcaretv/video-player.asp?v=partnership-working-in-child-protection-cardiff

Warner, L., Mariathasan, J., Lawton-Smith, S. and Samele, C. (2006) *Choice Literature Review: A Review of the Literature and Consultation on Choice and Decision-Making for Users and Carers of Mental Health and Social Care Services*. Briefing Paper 31. Centre for Mental Health.

Whittington, C. (2007) *Assessment in Social Work: A Guide for Learning and Teaching*. London: SCIE.

Building Resilience in Others
Michaela Rogers

Links to the Professional Capabilities Framework

- Professionalism   • Values and ethics   • Critical reflection and analysis   • Knowledge
- Skills and interventions

Links to the Knowledge and Skills Statement for Child and Family Practitioners

- Relationships and effective direct work   • Child development   • Adult mental ill-health, substance misuse, domestic abuse, physical ill-health and disability   • Abuse and neglect of children

Links to the Knowledge and Skills Statement for Social Workers in Adult Services

- The role of social workers working with adults   • Effective assessments and outcome-based support planning   • Direct work with individuals and families

Key messages

- Resilience is a process rather than a static aspect of an individual's character.
- Frameworks for understanding resilience utilise theories of human development including attachment and ecological models.
- The complex interplay of risk and protective factors impacts upon resilience at individual, family and community levels.
- Building resilience is a core task of social work intervention and helps to equip service users to deal with future adversity.

INTRODUCTION

Theories of child development, human growth, trauma and resilience are core to both understanding and responding to the conditions and problems faced by service users and carers. As such, theoretical insight can inform planning and interventions in order to centre on the individual, helping that individual to reach their potential. This is particularly important for children and vulnerable adults who may have faced adversity and who may need help to build **resilience**. This chapter focuses on childhood and clarifies what is meant by 'resilience', making links with key theories such as attachment (see Chapter 29) and systems theory (see Chapter 24). However, many of the concepts and much of the discussion can be applied to adults too. Finally, the chapter explores the ways in which social workers can work with children, young people and their carers to build resilience.

WHAT IS RESILIENCE?

A clear, simple definition of resilience can be rather elusive as the terminology employed in definitions mostly conveys the meaning and operation of resilience. Newman (2004: 1) describes resilience as 'positive adaptation in the face of severe adversities'. The significance of resilience is widely acknowledged as being critical as an element of human capacity in relation to facing and overcoming adversity, or being transformed by and building strength as a result of difficult life experiences (Grotberg, 1995).

Thus, we can conceptualise resilience as doing more than helping an individual to cope or adapt to adversity (or indeed adapt to constructive change); resilience can be positively transformative and help to build inner strengths. In this way, resilience has a benefit for challenges in the present, but additionally there is a future advantage too. This discourse encourages us to move beyond an understanding of resilience as a character trait to one that views it as fluid and as a dynamic process: 'resilience is not something an individual "has" – it is a multiply determined developmental process that is not fixed or immutable' (Cicchetti, 2010: 146).

Reflective activity

Think of a difficult life experience that you have survived. This might be a bereavement, challenging relationship, house move, illness or any other event that was meaningful to you. Think about the personal qualities and assets that you hold that helped you to cope with the situation and move forward. These might include: patience; loyalty; honesty; self-awareness; the ability to remain calm; kindness; a helpful disposition; humour; close relationships; a friendship group.

Reflect on what you learned from going through this difficult event or period in your life. Are there qualities and assets that you developed as a result? Could you draw on these again should you need to? (This type of thinking underpins crisis intervention, see Chapter 31).

Resilience is a complex concept that involves access to and navigation of internal and external resources (pertaining to psychological, physical, social and cultural resources) to sustain or enhance wellbeing. As such, it can be articulated and interpreted as a social construct; specifically, it is a concept that is socially produced, socially situated and understood differently in various socio-cultural contexts. Therefore, children growing up in quite diverse circumstances will have different levels of resilience.

Reflective activity

Think about how these three 18-year-olds may respond to being at university and away from home for the first time:

- Ben comes from a one-parent family as his father died when he was just a baby. He has a younger brother, Tommy, but Tommy's father is not around either. Ben's mother works full-time as a supermarket supervisor and so Ben used to get home from school and get tea ready for himself and his younger brother. He also took a great deal of responsibility for babysitting, cleaning and helping out generally. He had not been away from the family home before, but Ben looked forward to getting his own space and having some freedom away from his caring duties.
- Charlotte enjoyed lots of time away from her family in her teenage years as each year her private school offered students the wonderful opportunity of long cultural trips abroad. Charlotte had never wanted for anything; she was lucky that she was from an affluent background (her parents were both medical consultants and her mother had a Harley Street office for her private practice work). However, Charlotte was a little nervous about having to manage on her own at university and make new friends.
- Raza's parents are migrants from Pakistan. His father is a successful local businessman and Raza had worked in his father's business since he was a little boy. As the eldest son Raza was expected to do well in his studies in order that he would eventually take over the running of the family business. Therefore, he had the benefit of extra tuition in his studies and he was good at managing lots of demands (studies, working in the business). He was, however, a bit young for his age and he had never held any other responsibility (or made a meal, or picked his dirty clothes up off his bedroom floor).

Do you think Ben, Charlotte and Raza will have good levels of resilience; in what areas and why? What aspects of their childhoods will have helped develop their levels of resilience? What aspects of their new life (living away from home for the first time) might be more challenging and why?

ASSOCIATED CONCEPTS

Understanding resilience necessitates an exploration of three interrelated factors: risk, vulnerability and protective factors. **Risk** can be thought of as any factor, or combination of factors, that increases the chance of an undesirable outcome affecting a person. In addition, it is important to consider that adversity and risk have various dimensions in terms of:

- common/everyday and severe/exceptional adversity;
- material/non-material adversity;
- single and multiple risks;
- presenting within families or being embedded in communities and society;
- single presentation or accumulation;
- timing. (Mitchell, 2011)

Vulnerability is a feature that renders a person more susceptible to a threat, adversity or risk, whereas **protective factors** are the circumstances that moderate or lessen the effects of risk (Newman, 2004). These, too, are cumulative and subject to timing (Mitchell, 2011). An intrinsic (internal) protective factor may be a high level of intelligence whereas an extrinsic (external) protective factor might be represented by a positive relationship with a family member or support worker. Bronfenbrenner's ecological systems theory (see Chapter 24) provides a frame against which to map risk and protective factors in an individual's life at individual, family, community and societal levels. Resilience is said to be built upon the complex interplay and operation of risk and protective factors at these different levels (Mitchell, 2011).

Reflective activity

Think of a service user whom you have supported, or reflect on a difficult personal experience. In either situation can you identity each of these:

- resilience factors;
- risks;
- vulnerabilities;
- protective factors?

Can you map these to the different aspects of the individual, the family and/or community?

FACTORS ASSOCIATED WITH RESILIENCE

Research into factors associated with resilience show them to be diverse and as varying in relation to different stages of the life course. For example, in infancy being female, first born and having been born at full term with no birth defects will increase levels of resilience (Daniel and Wassell, 2002a). In resilience theory, factors associated with childhood have been broken down into different stages. Table 15.1 shows some of the individual characteristics associated with good levels of resilience; note how there are some differences in terms of gender.

Table 15.1 Characteristics associated with good levels of resilience (from Mitchell, 2011)

Infancy	School years	Adolescence
• Female	• Female	• Male
• First born	• Sense of competence and self-efficacy	• Takes responsibility
• No birth complications	• Internal locus of control	• Empathy with others
• Full term	• Empathy with others	• Internal locus of control
• Easy sleeping and feeding	• Skills in problem-solving	• Social maturity
• Affectionate	• Communication skills	• Positive self-concept
• Socially responsive	• Sociable	• Achievement orientation
• Secure attachment	• Independent	• Gentleness, nurturance
• Advanced in communication	• Reflective (not impulsive)	• Social perceptiveness
• Alert and cheerful	• Good concentration	• Preference for structure
• Adaptable	• Autonomy (girls)	• A set of values
• Fearless	• Emotionally expressive (boys)	• Intelligence
• Seeks out new experiences	• Sense of humour	• Willingness and capacity to plan

Source: Mitchell, 2011. Reproduced with kind permission of the author.

Resilience is not entirely dependent on personal traits and capacities, however. It is also affected by factors associated with an individual's family and environment. For instance, protective factors can be found in having close bonds with family members, and resilience can be enhanced when children live with harmonious family conditions, where parental and sibling attachments are secure. In terms of the gender differences noted in the 'school years' column in Table 15.1, relationships with family and others also have a part to play in helping to build resilience. For example, a positive factor for girls is when they are located in families who encourage them to be autonomous and independent. Similarly, a positive factor for boys is when they have relationships with people who encourage them to have good emotional intelligence and this includes being able to express a spectrum of emotions. Good school experiences are also important, and hobbies, peer relationships and having positive role models outside of the family all help children to develop resilience (Daniel and Wassell, 2002b, 2002c).

Life course transitions (for example, the movement from infancy to school, or into adolescence) present both threats and opportunities for resilience. As do other transition points: for example, consider the impact to a child who is removed from their family of origin and placed with foster carers. Life events (death, births, one-off events – such as an assault) also offer positives and negatives as individuals can learn and grow from such events; for example, developing new coping mechanisms. Or they can experience fear, physical injury and trauma which is unresolved and long-lasting. Often when risks and adversities are experienced over time and the impact is cumulative, when the chain is broken, most children are able to recover from even the most severe exposure to adversities in early life (Newman, 2004). Acute episodes of abuse or adversity are less likely to have long-lasting impacts on children's development and wellbeing.

BUILDING RESILIENCE

Research into factors associated with resilience has led to the development of a range of frameworks for practice. Whilst there are differences between these frameworks, there is some consensus in terms of what should be focused upon and this includes:

- altering or reducing a child's exposure to risk;
- reducing the 'chain reaction' or 'pile up' of risk exposures;
- creating opportunities or increasing resources available to children;
- (focusing upon) processes, for example, in improving attachment, self-efficacy or self-esteem, or 'resilience strings' that can have a knock on effect. (Mitchell, 2011: n.p.)

It has been argued that resilience must be understood from a developmental perspective as indicators and expectations in relation to outcomes change with age (Yates and Masten, 2004). Thus, any intervention must consider appropriate expectations based on age and capacity, but also remain alert to the changing nature of these. Age-appropriate interventions should be developed whilst bearing in mind that chronological age does not always correlate with a child's emotional age and adaptive capacity. The presence and enhancement of assets, rather than the mere absence of risk, is one way in which resilience may be increased (Yates and Masten, 2004). Yet, any approach that does not attend to risk, as well as strengthening protective factors, has been described as 'an incomplete strategy' (Pollard et al., 1999). The most effective intervention, then, will be multidimensional in nature addressing or, where possible, attempting to reduce risk, increasing and strengthening assets and protective factors. In relation to this, Daniel et al. (2010) identify three building blocks of resilience:

1 A *secure base*: this enables a child to experience a sense of belonging and to feel secure.
2 Good *self-esteem*: this incorporates an internal sense of worth and competence.
3 A sense of *self-efficacy*: in other words, a sense of mastery and control over one's life along with a good sense of one's individual strengths and limitations.

Daniel et al. (2010) suggest that people who work with children can focus on these aspects of a child's life and help to strengthen each, which will result in greater resilience. As a social worker you can help children to develop resilience through activities (which centre around the three building blocks) and through the relationship that is formed when you are working to care for and safeguard children. Moreover, you can help parents and carers to learn the importance of nurturing and good communication along with other qualitative aspects of their relationships with children such as dependability, honesty and consistency. It is useful to think of areas to focus on in terms of 'domains'. In their model for resilience-building, Daniel and Wassell (2002a, 2002b, 2002c) identify six domains of resilience: a secure base; education; social competencies; friendships; talent and interests; and positive values. These domains easily map onto the different elements of child health and development (health, education, emotional and behavioural development, family and peer relationships, self-care and competence, identity, social presentation) which are identified in the Assessment Framework (AF), the main assessment model utilised by child and family social workers (DH, 2000). The AF also requires practitioners to identify risks and vulnerabilities as well as strengths and protective factors (all associated with resilience). However, it is also important to acknowledge that resilience is a heterogeneous and dynamic concept that must be understood within the cultural context of a child, their family and community. The notion of resilience cannot be uniformly and uncritically applied in different cultural settings.

KEY QUESTIONS TO EXPLORE A CHILD'S RESILIENCE AND VULNERABILITIES

The International Resilience Project developed an interview guide to support the development of a Child and Youth Resilience Measure (CYRM-28, now the CYRM-12) (Liebenberg et al., 2013). Questions included in the guide can be used or adapted in your work to explore resilience and concerns for children or vulnerable adults:

1 Why are you worried?
2 What sort of behaviour is causing the problem?
3 Who is being affected, how, when and where?
4 When did it start?
5 What factors are present in the child's (adult's) background (e.g. divorce/illness)?
6 What are the present and past risks and protective factors?
7 Which risk factors can be decreased?
8 Which protective factors can be increased?
9 What are the strengths in the child, family, community, school and how can they be built on?
10 What is the worst thing that could happen?

CHALLENGES FOR PRACTICE

Despite good intentions, it is not always easy to help children (and indeed vulnerable adults) to build resilience, and there are various tensions and challenges that can arise. As noted above, aspects of identity (such as cultural identity and belonging) can impede social work interventions, particularly if there are aspects of difference and marginalisation.

Other individualised tensions can be present such as low self-esteem, and feelings of incompetence and blame can prevent children and adults from moving forward and developing the aspects of self that build resilience.

Access to material resources is an obvious challenge as, at the time of writing this book, in the UK we are living in a period of austerity where cuts to finances and services abound. There are also interpersonal tensions that can form as part of any social work intervention, as personality clashes, resistance, anger and fear can impede the development of trusting, caring and honest relationships with practitioners, parents, siblings and significant others.

CONCLUSION

There are some essential factors that help children to achieve wellbeing and aid resilience-building. These include: a good education; love and a sense of belonging; decent standard of living; good parenting; intelligence; and opportunities to contribute to their communities. These are common protective factors for children and young people, but they are also important for vulnerable adults' continued resilience as they transition into adulthood. However, undoubtedly resilience is a complex and dynamic concept and it is one that is positively and negatively affected by a great many variables. This recognition is needed in the social work task to ensure that interventions are appropriate, holistic and regularly reviewed. This will help the work that is undertaken to enhance resilience to adapt in correlation with the change in resilience levels.

Having read this chapter, you should be able to:

- Recognise that resilience is a dynamic process that is affected by various factors;
- Articulate the ways that social workers can help to build resilience;
- Acknowledge that resilience is undermined by adversity and as such it can be lowered for anyone experiencing stress and difficulty whatever their age, ethnicity, ability, gender, sexuality or religion.

RECOMMENDED READING

Daniel, B., Wassell, S. and Gilligan, R. (2010) *Child Development for Child Care and Protection Workers*. London: Jessica Kingsley.

Grant, L. and Kinman, G. (eds) (2014) *Developing Resilience for Social Work Practice*. London: Palgrave.

Harms, L. (2015) *Understanding Trauma and Resilience*. London: Palgrave.

Newman, T. (2004) *What Works in Building Resilience*. London: Barnado's.

Conflict Management and Resolution
David Edmondson and Charlotte Ashworth

Links to the Professional Capabilities Framework

- Professionalism   • Skills and interventions   • Values and ethics

Links to the Knowledge and Skills Statement for Child and Family Practitioners

- Relationships and effective direct work   • Communication   • Analysis, decision-making, planning and review   • Organisational context

Links to the Knowledge and Skills Statement for Social Workers in Adult Services

- Person-centred practice   • Direct work with individuals and families   • Organisational context   • Professional ethics and leadership

Key messages

- Conflict is part of everyday life and a common feature of all work, notably social work.
- Conflicts can arise at any time and workers need to be alert and as prepared as they can to face and address them effectively.
- Social workers need to be aware of the context and nature of conflict and be able to develop positive responses towards resolution and change.

INTRODUCTION

Conflict is a part of everyday life and within the field of social work is almost unavoidable. As Allan Barsky, a social work academic and practitioner and an expert in conflict resolution, notes:

> Helping professions deal with conflict in virtually all aspects of their life – with supervisors, co-workers, clients, families, social systems and other community members. In order to deal effectively with conflict, helping professionals need to understand the nature of conflict and the range of approaches for dealing with it. (2015: xii)

Conflict theory is relevant in helping to inform and support social work practice (Goroff, 2014). Hutchinson and Oltedal (2014) argue that social systems and structures impose limits on individuals, groups and social classes which produce differences and inequalities. Social work practice intersects at the point between the individual and society. Principles of social justice, rights and equality of opportunity and access to goods and services inevitably bring social workers into practice situations where conflict exists and is likely to occur. Inequality in power and choice is key here and for social work achieving real social change inevitably involves encountering and addressing conflict at some level. Models in social work of anti-oppressive practice, community social work and critical social work each acknowledge and involve analysis of social inequality, imbalance of power and social conflicts. Such models emphasise the necessary commitment to strive for egalitarian principles that all people deserve equal rights and opportunities.

In the context of social work practice, conflict may manifest itself in a number of direct ways, for example arguments and criticism, unwelcome and unwanted demands, challenges, hostility and aggression (passive or active, physical or verbal).

As skills, conflict resolution and problem-solving skills take time to develop. This short guide offers a brief summary and you are encouraged to draw on the resources we include at the end of this chapter to develop your knowledge and skills. You are also encouraged to link your reading to other chapters in the book, particularly those on reflection and reflexivity, review and evaluation, and supervision.

Conflicts and problems in social work can arise for a variety of reasons, including agency role and having to exercise legal duties and powers; encountering resistance to change; differences in service cultures, criteria and goals; tensions between different professions and agencies; advocacy work and having to compete for rationed and scarce resources (De Dreu, 2007; Edmondson, 2014).

AGENCY ROLE AND LEGAL DUTIES

In relation to the protection and safeguarding of children and adults considered most vulnerable and at risk, social workers in England have specific powers, duties and legal responsibilities. Frequently, these interactions to address risk take place within the private and public spheres of people's lives, in their homes and in the heart of their local communities. This often causes the immediate environment within which social workers have to operate on a day-to-day basis to be, understandably, viewed as confrontational, hostile and deeply personal.

It is important to acknowledge that irrespective of the level of professionalism and understanding exercised by workers, decisions to intervene in individual and family life, or to remove a child or vulnerable adult from their family home are likely to cause conflict and result in tension, anger and hostility. How we respond and learn from this is a professional responsibility.

In the section below, a social worker comments on conflicts that can arise in direct work with individuals, families and others in practice.

CONFLICTS THAT CAN ARISE IN DIRECT WORK WITH INDIVIDUALS, FAMILIES AND OTHERS IN RELATION TO CHILD PROTECTION

Ian, a children and families social worker, comments:

> As a social worker in child protection, I recognise that my primary role is to identify risks to children and to ensure that the child is safeguarded against these risks as far as possible; considering thresholds, parenting capacity and parental ability and motivation to change. Identifying risks often results in areas of conflict being uncovered in the systems around the child. My conjecture is that it is within conflict and the way that it is handled, where a lot of the work of social work is completed; to whatever has happened by the time case files are closed. From the narrow stance of workers avoiding conflict with parents, the avoidance of this conflict may have contributed to the ongoing systematic abuse suffered by children like Peter Connelly, Victoria Climbié and Daniel Pelka.

> Conflicts are often best overcome by communication. Encouraging or facilitating communication between conflicting elements of the system are good skills for social workers, and I have found that face-to-face communication is more effective than telephone in trying to address conflict. I've had the phone put down on me by parents several times, but I've not yet been threatened in or asked to leave a home.

Reflective activity

Think of a situation which involved some conflict and where you feel you managed this well. Note down what you did. What were you thinking and how did you feel at the time? What did you do and say? How did you 'manage' yourself? How was the conflict managed or resolved? Being aware of the thoughts, actions and skills you identify may help you next time.

Read through the rest of the chapter and then revisit the notes you have made.

TENSIONS BETWEEN PROFESSIONALS AND SERVICES

The interdisciplinary and inter-agency expectations and requirements of many aspects of social work mean workers also come into contact with a range of different professionals and services during the course of their work. This work can be positive and rewarding. However, differences in service cultures, criteria and goals, as well as tensions between professions and agencies, can lead to disagreements and conflicts.

In the section below, a social worker comments on their work and the conflicts that can arise with other disciplines and agencies.

REFLECTIONS AND RESPONSES TO CONFLICT WITH OTHER PROFESSIONALS AND SERVICES

Charlotte, a child and families social worker, comments:

> In my experience, conflicts with other professionals fall into three categories – disagreement regarding thresholds in child protection (either perceived as too low or too high); disagreements regarding case planning; and disagreements as to whether things have improved and the case can be closed.

> I have found that the most helpful strategy is to try to understand the root of the conflict. Anxiety around child protection can lead to professionals over-reacting and sometimes reassurance and advice will resolve conflict around thresholds. It can be more difficult to resolve conflict when it stems from prejudice of social workers and individual families and is based on assumptions and value judgements, rather than evidence. A lot of professional resistance I have met is when trying to close a case following intervention – there does seem to be a systemic problem where some professionals seem to prefer cases to be kept open to social workers indefinitely 'in case something happens' when this is neither practicable nor in the best interests of the child. I suspect this has something to do with the deeply ingrained blame culture.

> When conflict with other professionals arises, I always try to see if I can sort it out by speaking to the individual(s) involved in the first instance. When doing this, it is important to be as clear as possible and ensure you are linking it to how it is impacting on the child and family.

> It is easy to underestimate how parents and carers can feel intimidated by multi-agency working and hostility and disagreements between professionals can be very noticeable in multi-agency meetings. It is important to chair meetings professionally, have a clear agenda and indicate when professionals and the family can bring up any further issues.

> I would also recommend knowing what advocacy services are out there for families and enlisting support from people within your local authority – contacts in housing,

LAC education, school health, etc. can be really helpful when you are in conflict with other professionals.

Remember that most situations will get better and can be resolved.

This honest account of day-to-day social work identifies a number of common features present in trying to work together with professionals and others, notably dynamics arising from misunderstanding and ignorance (of an incident, situation or person), intimidation and anxiety (arising from a perceived risky situation or the burden of professional responsibility). It also points to possible responses which you as the reader can think about, notably: open and speedy communication, trying to understand the position of others, other resources you might draw on to use or assist you where conflict arises. Studies on task-related conflict have suggested that moderate levels of conflict can actually stimulate innovation and creativity in terms of achieving better quality decisions (De Drue, 2007). Social work, advocacy and managing resources

Social work can be linked to advocacy work, typically promoting rights, challenging decisions or oppressive and discriminatory behaviour. Dalrymple and Boylan (2013: 3) identify different forms of advocacy in relation to *external advocacy* (which 'refers to advocates working outside a system') and (2013: 6) *internal advocacy* (which 'relates to advocacy by social workers and other professionals working within a system'), and dynamically in terms of *active* and *passive* advocacy.

Reflective activity

Read Chapter 1, 'What is Advocacy and How Do We Use it in Social Work?', of Dalrymple and Boylan's excellent book *Effective Advocacy in Social Work* (2013). You can find a link on the website (https://study.sagepub.com/rogers2e).

Identify examples of advocacy from your own practice that featured some degree of conflict. Note down what you did. What were you thinking and how did you feel at the time? What did you do and say? How did you 'manage' yourself? How was the conflict resolved? Being aware of the thoughts, actions and skills you identify may help you next time.

It is important to recognise the importance of valuing and being valued in social work. A key part of value-led and ethical social work is a commitment to anti-discriminatory and anti-oppressive practice. It would be naïve and flawed to suppose that social work, social workers and settings for the provision of social work and social care are free from discrimination and oppression. However, anti-oppressive practice recognises the existence of social divisions in terms of race, age, gender, sexuality, disability and social class; of societal and structural inequality and of imbalances of rights and power. Social work as an activity is tasked to challenge discrimination and oppression and, in doing so, promote justice and rights. This can and should involve some element of challenge and with this, disagreement or conflict.

APPROACHES TO CONFLICT MANAGEMENT AND RESOLUTION

As we have mentioned elsewhere, social work makes claims to a philosophical tradition of egalitarianism and a belief in and commitment to social justice, humane values and principles. Promoting positive social change, personal development, community and social cohesion are central tenets of social work practice (Edmondson, 2014). Social workers have the key challenge of trying to combine managing risk effectively with the humane project of social work (Broadhurst et al., 2010a).

A key part of professional practice should be anticipating conflict, with the goal of not just resolution but also achieving positive change and development. If we are committed to promoting positive change, then we should accept the presence of conflict and disagreement as a 'normal' part of helping others. Keefe and Koch (1999) assert that there are two important principles that should be kept at the forefront of social work practice and interventions where conflict occurs. These are to seek to promote a 'cooperative motivational orientation' and 'by engaging in constructive conflict management, participants identify not only their own needs and interests, but also the needs and interests of others' (Keefe and Koch, 1999: 36). Thus, for example, in relation to child protection work, it may be necessary to remove a child for their safety, but it is also part of our professional duty to aim where possible to ensure the child maintains contact with their family.

Within child protection services, the increased use of family group conferencing and promotion of family network meetings in practice models such as Signs of Safety promotes the family's role in managing and resolving conflict. This puts the emphasis on helping and supporting the family to seek resolutions to conflict and in arriving at acceptable solutions where there are child protection concerns.

SELF-AWARENESS

Awareness of personal feelings and beliefs, recognising how as an individual we respond to conflict and disagreement, and understanding your own needs as a practitioner are all key issues in preparing for practice. This is an important aspect of being a professional worker.

Barsky (2015: 46) identifies different 'conflict styles' of practitioners within helping professions. These are: avoiders, accommodators, competitors, compromisers and collaborators. Each style is different although some features overlap across styles.

Responses to conflict can be influenced by how we feel at a particular time. Stress, tiredness, ill-health and events inside/outside work may all impact on how we are likely to act and respond in our day-to-day practice.

In the section below, social workers reflect and comment on their personal and professional responses to conflict.

Managing conflict

Charlotte, a child and families social worker, comments:

> Managing conflict is a necessary skill to be an effective child protection social worker. I remember being a student and a newly qualified social worker and, at first, really struggling to manage conflict with families and professionals. I would feel intimidated by professionals with more experience than me, even when I was making valid points.
>
> After a certain amount of 'toughing up', I also realised the importance of maintaining focus on how the conflict is impacting on the family and child and framing things in this way is really helpful when discussing these issues. Being clear and direct is very important when dealing with conflict and ensuring that you are calm, even if you are witnessing unprofessional behaviour. Always consider what will happen if you do escalate issues and what will happen if you don't.
>
> Most things can be sorted out in a couple of phone calls and sometimes you might just be getting the brunt of someone's bad day. We all have them!

Shani, a mental health social worker, comments:

> Working in adult mental health I reflected on a conflict arising with a service user and her family following a decision to make a referral to children's services due to concerns about a child's welfare in the context of drug misuse and domestic violence. Needless to say the family were less than impressed and it seemed that our working relationship was well and truly over. I had really struggled and wanted to have the case transferred to someone else. I thought about it constantly, wondering if I had done the right thing. Procedurally I knew I had, but it still all felt wrong. The family demanded a change of worker. I welcomed this news, but something in me knew this was not the answer.
>
> I discussed the matter in supervision. My supervisor and I agreed that this would be the easy option, but would simply reinforce this pattern of behaviour in the service user and her family, which would be detrimental to her in the long-term. We agreed that I would continue but with firm boundaries.
>
> Initially the service user was unwilling to work with me and felt that I was using my power against her, i.e. things not being on her terms. However, taking a gentle, consistent approach eventually broke her resolve and she began to meet. She had stopped using substances and was getting on better with her family. We discussed what had happened and I shared my reasons for it, without judgement. On one occasion she thanked me for making the referral, saying it 'made me open my eyes'.
>
> Soon after the service user wrote a letter to the service, thanking us for our input and advising that she had decided to take early discharge. Whilst this could be seen

as negative, it was actually a positive step. The service user had made a decision for herself and ended on a positive note.

Looking back, I'm not sure I would have done much differently. However, I think having clear discussions at the start about consequences and the possibility of child safeguarding referrals having to be made in certain instances might help. Conflict will always occur, but remember good things can come of it if dealt with in the right way.

Whether our responses to conflict are influenced by our personality, 'conflict style' or external/environmental factors, it is important to try to be aware of each element, its impact and more importantly how it has impacted on our actions and responses to conflict. We cannot remove our feelings, but being aware of them does give us an opportunity to try to manage how these features may impact on our work and minimise their negative impact.

It is important to remember that as a professional worker you must take responsibility for your practice and behaviour. A frequently used practice approach recommended in social work relates to what is generally termed the 'problem-solving' (or similarly, 'crisis-intervention', 'solution-focused') approach to social work practice. The value of 'problem-solving' as an approach is that it is positive in its outlook and seeks to build on strengths and assets to solve problems; it asserts that positive change is possible and is a worthy goal of social work. Problem-solving also implicitly accepts and acknowledges that in the course of our day-to-day work, problems and conflicts will arise and are likely to be of sufficient number and significance to merit a strategy to address and challenge this.

PROBLEM-SOLVING AND CONFLICT

A problem-solving approach in the context of managing and resolving conflict is useful and you may find considering the following steps helpful when dealing with conflict:

- identifying the problem and arising areas of conflict and the obstacles to resolving these (including yourself);
- commitment to learn from difficulties, challenges and problems as well as successes;
- willingness to engage with conflict and disagreement and be committed to resolving these in a professional manner;
- acknowledgement of how your own feelings or behaviour may be blocking resolution of a problem (e.g. feelings of anger, hurt or upset and actions which are defensive, resistant or distancing);
- commitment to act on fresh approaches that contribute to positive change (e.g. being willing to listen, making your own points without becoming personal, acknowledging the feelings and views of others, genuinely seeking a resolution to the problem).

PRACTICAL APPROACHES TO CONFLICT MANAGEMENT AND RESOLUTION

This final section of the chapter provides a brief checklist of practical approaches and strategies to use in situations where conflict arises and where you want to offer a positive response and show a commitment to its management and resolution.

Safety

Safety is a primary concern. Where conflict arises, you should decide whether it is safe and if it is desirable to stop, adjourn, or continue. Be prepared and willing to do this. This is not avoidance it is about being responsible. If someone – including you – is very angry or upset then it may be better to take a break or stop an interview in order to help calm things down, seek further advice or obtain additional support.

Setting and timing

If you know you are going to have to address a difficult matter with someone or a group then some attention should be given to trying to identify a preferred setting and time for this. Of course, this level of planning and the setting is not always possible and may not suit every occasion or problem. However, planning and preparation can effectively manage potential conflict, help facilitate discussion and support the process of resolution. On a practical level, access to a meeting room that you can book for sufficient time, which is quiet and where additional support and advice is on hand, can be very beneficial.

The Checklist

Listen before you talk:

- Do listen to what the other person is saying.
- Do show in your body language and non-verbal communication you are paying attention.
- Don't interrupt the person when they are speaking.
- Don't show disapproval of the person's right to have their say.

Talk to the other person/s:

- Decide what you want to say, how much you need to say in this meeting and the way you want to say it.
- Do talk calmly and quietly.
- Don't raise your voice or shout over other people.

Check and clarify areas of agreement and disagreement:

- Summarise the areas of agreement and disagreement.
- Ask the other person if he or she agrees with your assessment.
- Modify your assessment until both of you agree on the areas of conflict.

Identify any areas of mutual interest or shared outcomes:

- Start with the most important conflict and seek to resolve this.
- If there are limited areas of agreement, try to identify some common desired outcomes, e.g. discussion has helped to 'clear the air'.

Be goal-oriented:

- Maintain a collaborative approach that seeks to accommodate potential future disagreements and manage/resolve conflicts.
- Point out areas of progress and use these to build on areas of success.
- Set up further meeting times to continue your discussions, acknowledge and accommodate issues.

Be clear about boundaries and information sharing:

- You need to be aware of your professional and your personal boundaries.
- Try to not 'spill' your personal feelings into your professional practice.

CONCLUSION

This is a very brief introduction to managing and resolving conflict in social work. Like most challenging things in work and life it needs effort and commitment if you are to get better at it. However, with careful thought and an honest genuine approach you will find you can improve your professional practice and in turn your personal wellbeing and health. This is good for you, the colleagues around you and perhaps most importantly the people on the receiving end of our services.

Having read this chapter, you should be able to:

- Better understand the context and nature of conflict in social work;
- Identify some practical ways to plan for and address conflict and in doing so promote better working together.

RECOMMENDED READING

Barsky, A. (2015) *Conflict Resolution for the Helping Professions* (3rd edn). New York: Oxford University Press.

Chetkow-Yanoov, B.H. (1996) *Social Work Approaches to Conflict Resolution: Making Fighting Obsolete* (Haworth Social Work Practice). Abingdon: Routledge.

Conflict Resolution Information. Available at: http://crinfo.org

Dalrymple, J. and Boylan, J. (2013) *Effective Advocacy in Social Work*. London: Sage.

De Dreu, C. (2007) The virtue and vice of workplace conflict: food for (pessimistic) thought. *Journal of Organizational Behavior*, 29(1): 5–18.

Goroff, N.N. (2014) Conflict theories and social work education. *Journal of Sociology and Social Welfare*, 5(4): Article 5.

Roche, W., Teague, P. and Colvin, A. (eds) (2014) *The Oxford Handbook of Conflict Management in Organizations*. New York: Oxford University Press.

Research-Informed Practice
Donna Peach

Links to the Professional Capabilities Framework

• Professionalism   • Skills and interventions   • Knowledge   • Critical reflection and analysis

Links to the Knowledge and Skills Statement for Child and Family Practitioners

• Relationships and effective direct work   • Child development   • Communication
• Child and family assessment

Links to the Knowledge and Skills Statement for Adult Practitioners

• Person-centred practice   • Effective assessments and outcome-based support planning
• Direct work with individuals and families   • Supervision, critical reflection and analysis

Key messages

• Social work practice is underpinned by a range of research knowledge.
• Research can aid our understanding of complex individual needs.
• Research can demonstrate the impact of societal behaviour on the individual.
• Research knowledge always has limitations.
• Transferring research knowledge into practice can be challenging.

INTRODUCTION

Research knowledge is vital to the development of our social work practice. It facilitates our understanding of complex individual needs and the impact of social policies and practices on each of us. The extent of understanding required, the necessity to critique research knowledge, and the complexity of transferring that awareness to practice present a challenge to our profession. Thus, it is unsurprising that student social workers and those newly qualified can feel anxious about drawing links between research evidence and social work practice.

This chapter examines the complexity of research knowledge in social work practice, while also demystifying some of the challenges. It is important to remember that we live in a scientific age that encourages a desire for certainty. Social work is pioneering as it is situated on the frontline of simultaneously understanding and meeting complex human needs. However, the research knowledge we have to draw on is incomplete and ever expanding, leaving social workers having to practise amid multifaceted uncertainty.

SOCIAL WORK: THEORY OR PRACTICE?

If we accept social work is an activity that uses knowledge from a range of theoretical disciplines, then we have to query the existence of 'social work theory'. Arguably, this is an important distinction that serves to position us as information channels between research theory and practice. However, social work as a profession and the education of student social workers are also themselves important areas of research. Thus, if we are research conductors and conduits this is not a passive and linear process but one which is forever cyclical and dynamic (Montaño, 2012).

Social work practice is underpinned by a wide range of theoretical paradigms, including **anthropology, psychology, sociology, biology** and **neurology**. You will see evidence of each of these disciplines throughout this book. Student social workers are often faced with theoretical models which themselves can coexist, complement or conflict with power dynamics between the state, social worker and service user. It is the complexity of the interaction between theory, knowledge and practice that can make us feel overwhelmed (Parker, 2006). Unfortunately, when we feel overwhelmed it can affect how competent we feel, which in turn might reduce our motivation. Student social workers can lack self-efficacy and feel unable to manage the challenges we each face in practice (Collins, 2015).

EVIDENCED-BASED PRACTICE AND PRACTICE-BASED RESEARCH

Usefully, when exploring the use of research evidence in social work practice, Roberts and Yeager (2006) discuss the concept of evidence-based practice (EBP) in relation to practice-based research (PBR). The terminology of 'evidence-based practice' originated in health care settings which are reflected in definitions that triangulate research

evidence, clinical expertise and patient values (Mullen et al., 2008). Rosen (2003) proposed five categories which he suggests can hamper EBP in social work:

1   Characteristics of the knowledge to be used;
2   Characteristics of the practice situation and setting;
3   Characteristics of the practitioner;
4   Attributes of the medium through which knowledge is communicated;
5   The socio-cultural context in which utilisation takes place.

Rosen (2003) suggests many of the obstacles of EBP lie in the practitioner's failure to
adhere to what he terms rational decision-making. Rosen examined the complexity of
decision-making, which involves emotion, experience and intuition. Notably, a scientific
view would (and Rosen does) herald these attributes as fallible and thereby promotes a
systemic systems approach (SSP) to 'rational decision-making'. You will see in Figure 17.1
that Rosen couples SSP with a process of single-system design (SSD), with the aim of
facilitating the ongoing evaluation of the SSP approach. Rosen suggests that these twin
processes support the maintenance of practice guidelines for intervention (PGI).

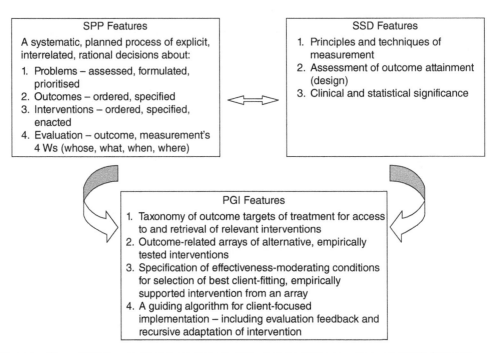

In his paper Rosen (2003) recognised the limitations of his model and the gaps that can remain between
research knowledge and a person's needs.

Figure 17.1   Features of systemic planned practice and single system designs relating to the use of
practice guidelines for intervention (Rosen, 2003: 202)

Source: Rosen, Evidence-based social work practice: Challenges and promise, Social Work Research (2002), 27 (4), 202.
Reproduced with permission from Oxford University Press

In view of the dilemma of applying empirical generalizations to an individual, it is important for the practitioner to realize that because the intervention chosen may still not fit their client's needs optimally, it should be viewed only as the best empirically supported approximation to the optimal. (Rosen, 2003: 202)

Rosen's approach to EBP could be viewed as 'top-down', whereas Jaynes (2014) suggests practice-based research is 'bottom up' as it starts with the needs of the practitioner rather than those of the researcher. McMillen et al. (2009) identified four characteristics of PBR:

1   Data collected reflects service provision needs, not academic focus.
2   The potential for long-term practice-based research networks.
3   Partnerships with academic institutions can share research workload.
4   Practitioners retain greater power over the development of a research focus.

Any model that serves to share power is positive, and PBR could assist you as a student social worker or NQSW, to see a greater connection between knowledge and practice. However, neither approach integrates service users and their carers, which requires a further sharing of power, especially if the knowledge we construct is to be co-produced. Morley (2012) discusses how the process of critical reflection can create new understanding and inform future practice. Her analysis of the narrative of a participating social worker examined the complexity of practising when there are gaps in the application of knowledge. Morley demonstrates the usefulness of critical reflection as an interrogative tool necessary to unpick assumptions and perceptions that can unduly influence our decision-making. You might find it useful to read Morley's paper before undertaking the case study and reflective exercises in the chapter.

. . . .

Case study: Tom

The following case study provides a scenario that has themes common to a lot of social work practice with children and families. Read the scenario and write down as many theories as you can identify that would inform a social worker's perspective.

Tom, aged 15 years, has been known to social services since the age of three; there were a number of referrals relating to concerns of neglect and of Tom experiencing domestic abuse perpetrated by several of his mother's partners. At times of crisis Tom's maternal grandmother would intervene, and issues of concern were never raised above Tom being a child in need. Tom lived at home with his mother until the age of 13, when she found his behaviour too challenging to manage. He then went to live full-time with his grandmother, who died unexpectedly last week. Tom's mother, Linda, aged 31, works part-time in a local store, and has a methadone prescription. Linda is refusing to have Tom home to live with her. Tom tells you he has been staying alone in his grandmother's council flat.

(Continued)

Reflective questions

- What are your initial thoughts about the needs of Tom and Linda?
- What theories are associated with the needs you have identified?
- How could those theories influence your intervention with Tom and Linda?

• •

We will now explore some of the theories and research studies that provide insights into the needs and abilities of the individuals and the functioning of their relationships. One of the dominant themes within the case study is that of parenting and the impact this can have on the way a child develops. At a societal level we need to be mindful of how mothers and fathers are constructed in twenty-first-century British society. Importantly, these are not homogeneous groups and the construction of their identities intersect with other concepts such as class, race and sexuality. For centuries, parenthood has been more synonymous with motherhood, and developing ideologies of motherhood have influenced social work practice (Leskošek, 2011). Importantly, Fisher's (2005) exploration of the interwar 'Fathercraft' movement demonstrates the capacity of and limitations upon men to actively engage in the welfare of children.

Reflective activity

Return to the above case study and summarise what your expectations are of Linda. Then critically review these. A key social work skill is being able to have awareness of our own bias and prejudice; we are human too and just as influenced by social discourses.

1   Do you think there is a difference in how we expect mothers and fathers to behave?
2   If you think there are no differences in expectations then take time to think reflexively about the discourses and research evidence that contribute to the construction of each.
3   How might age impact on our expectations and explanations of parental behaviour?
4   Tom is 15 years old – how might that influence what state provision is available for him and how long the state might consider itself responsible for his parental care?

ATTACHMENT THEORY

In terms of research, a dominant theory that underpins concepts of motherhood is Bowlby's attachment theory (Bretherton, 1997). This enduring theory remains a cornerstone of contemporary social work. However, there is a void between the theoretical concept of attachment and how we seek to understand the strength of relationships between children and their families, or to be more precise children and their mothers, which highlights one of the fundamental limitations to what we conceive as attachment.

You will find Chapter 29 useful as it examines the use of maternal sensitivity scales in the construct of attachment theory.

Reflective activity

Now take time to contemplate what you might expect Tom's attachment style to be. The questions below will encourage you to explore the assumptions that we all make in our understanding of attachment. In part, how we as humans make sense of relationships becomes entwined with what we regard as accepted knowledge. This, however, can be different from the specificity of research knowledge.

1   What information about Tom and Linda's early childhood would you want to know, and how would you gather this information?
2   Are there events that have happened to Tom and Linda post infancy that you think would contribute to their attachment style?
3   How would you assess the attachment between Linda and Tom?
4   Is it possible to support the development of a secure attachment between Linda and Tom? If so, how could you achieve this?

CHILD DEVELOPMENTAL THEORIES

The case study reports that Linda has found Tom's behaviour challenging at times. There are several theories that could provide an explanation for these behaviours. In addition to attachment theory, it is useful to explore theoretical concepts about how children learn. Theories that support the notion that children learn how to behave from their social environment are underpinned by developmental theorists such as Jean Piaget's stages of cognitive development and Lev Vygotsky's social development theory. In 1961, Albert Bandura conducted an experiment that sought to understand if aggressive behaviour could be a result of observing others behaving in an aggressive manner. Findings from his famous Bobo doll experiment suggest children are more likely to act aggressively if they observe others doing the same. Contemporary research (Callaghan et al., 2016) extends our comprehension of the impact of domestic violence and leads us to perceive children as experiencing rather than simply witnessing domestic violence.

You can find out more about Jean Piaget's stages of cognitive development, Lev Vygotsky's social development theory and Albert Bandura's Bobo doll experiment by watching the helpful videos on the website (https://study.sagepub.com/rogers2e).

THEORIES OF LOSS AND BEREAVEMENT

The model by which we understand relationships can also inform how we perceive and respond to the impact of loss and separation. Many theories promote the notion of a staged process that can include a sense of denial leading to acceptance.

Kübler-Ross (1969) provides us with a five-stage linear model, which you are likely to be familiar with:

1   *Denial*: a temporary mechanism, denial is often the earliest stage of grief and can include thoughts and feelings that 'this isn't happening to me'.
2   *Anger*: a dying person, or someone close to them, might question why they are facing death. They may look for someone or something to blame.
3   *Bargaining*: a reluctance to accept that death is inevitable may lead a person to bargain with themselves, or with God.
4   *Depression*: as we begin to accept the inevitability of death, we may experience overwhelming depression, sadness or hopelessness.
5   *Acceptance*: at this stage, a person accepts the inevitability of death. Although they may find some peace with this resolution they may continue to grieve.

Reflective activity

Using the information in the case study:

1   What factors do you think influence Tom's reported challenging behaviour?
2   What enquiries would you make in order to assess this?
3   How might your conclusions influence modes of intervention?

ROLE OF THE SOCIAL WORKER AS A RESEARCH CONDUIT

We should not underestimate the complex challenge of managing the divide between research knowledge and social work practice. As a student social worker, it might feel easier to focus on practical processes as we engage with children, adults and families, rather than navigate the uncertainty of research knowledge. However, we have a responsibility to bridge that gap and to engage service users, members of the public, policy makers and other professionals in the conversation. Accepting the limits to our knowledge and reflecting on how we use our 'self' to make sense of the voids in our understanding contributes to good practice.

 Visit the website to listen to The SHARE Model with Siobhan Maclean and Paul Yusuf McCormack (https://study.sagepub.com/rogers2e).

CONCLUSION

The chapter has highlighted some of the complexity of the origins of research knowledge. Although research is crucial to the development of our understanding, it also remains limited.

These limitations are multiple and include an awareness of the theoretical constraints within which a study was designed. Importantly, we have learned that the design of any research has a subsequent influence on the knowledge produced. The case study and reflective activities provide a means by which you can begin to safely explore how you as a student social worker will develop awareness of how you make sense of (assess) the behaviour of others. The information provided in this chapter should help you to navigate that understanding and aid you to reflect on how you fill the research knowledge gaps when you apply reasoned knowledge.

   You will have identified numerous research topic areas from the case study that we have been unable to explore. However, you now have the tools to draw on research from each of the areas identified and begin to develop a more sophisticated application of research knowledge to practice. Throughout this book, numerous examples of research are discussed to assist your development as a social work practitioner. This supports a cyclical development of your skills and the knowledge base that supports them. Finally, recognising that marrying research and practice is a complex task should not be underestimated. It is important to stay informed, to be reflective, and to use supervision and further training to ensure that you are best placed to provide consistently good social work provision to the people who rely on you to do so.

Having read this chapter, you should be able to:

- Understand the relationship between evidence-based practice and practice-based research;
- Recognise that systemic approaches to practice have benefits but are also limited in their application to meet individual need;
- Develop your understanding of critical reflection as a research method to construct emancipatory change.

RECOMMENDED READING

Hester, R. and Taylor, W. (2011) Responding to bereavement, grief and loss: charting the troubled relationship between research and practice in youth offending services. *Mortality*, 16(3): 191–203.

Montaño, C. (2012) Social work theory-practice relationship: challenges to overcoming positivist and postmodern fragmentation. *International Social Work*, 55(3): 306–319.

Roberts, A. and Yeager, K. (2006) *Foundations of Evidence-Based Social Work Practice.* Oxford: Oxford University Press.

Rosen, A. (2003) Evidence-based social work. *Social Work Research*, 27(4): 197–208.

18

Writing Skills for Practice
Michaela Rogers

Links to the Professional Capabilities Framework

• Professionalism   • Critical reflection and analysis   • Skills and interventions   • Contexts and organisations

Links to the Knowledge and Skills Statement for Child and Family Practitioners

• Communication   • Child and family assessment   • Analysis, decision-making, planning and review   • Organisational context

Links to the Knowledge and Skills Statement for Social Workers in Adult Services

• Effective assessments and outcome-based support planning   • Organisational context

Key messages

- A good level of writing skill is necessary for a range of writing tasks including case recording and the production of formal reports.
- Case records should be up-to-date, accurate, relevant and concise.
- Well-written reports will have analysis integrated throughout.
- Social work ethics should underpin all activities in producing written records and should be person-centred (include the service user's voice), needs and strengths focused, and accessible (written in a style that is clear and easy to understand).

INTRODUCTION

This chapter focuses on a range of contexts in which competent writing skills are essential and could be called upon during various stages in the ASPIRE model (during assessments, for planning and following interventions). Two common writing tasks are report writing and case recording. Each form of written communication has a different purpose and audience as well as requiring a different technique and style. So, whilst much of this book so far has been centred around relationship-based practice and face-to-face skills, this chapter turns its attention to what is considered to be one of the more mundane tasks of social work practice, but one that is important in terms of reflection, clarification, accountability and professional responsibility (Jones, 2016). A good standard of written communication skills is important in terms of social work as a professional activity, but also for the people who use social work services (Constable, 2013).

THE PURPOSE OF WRITING

Pieces of writing can be extremely powerful; as Thompson (2005: 88) states, 'a great deal depends on the written word'. Think about the impact of legislation, the protocols in your workplace, and consider the power of the media (newspapers, or the internet). Even think about the experience of walking or driving down the road and the ways in which you respond to pedestrian and road signs. Clearly, writing is a powerful form of communication. Look at the activity below which explores this point through some examples of email communication. In social work, we use written documents in our everyday practice to fulfil several functions, including:

- to record referral information and transfer this to others;
- by reading existing documents we gain further knowledge of the people that we are working with;
- to act as a record of our actions;
- to record our decision-making;
- to pass information and insights between co-workers;
- to make arrangements with others for meetings or home visits;
- to produce formal reports in court-mandated work.

These are just a few examples of the ways in which writing is central to our work. Moon (2004) considers that any exercise in writing is beneficial in that it creates the space for developing reflection and **critical thinking** skills. This is because the process of writing slows down our thinking and enables our brain to organise our thoughts and emotions, giving us structure and control so that key issues can be identified and responded to. This enhances our understanding as well as our problem-solving capacity. Finally, critical and reflective thinking time also enables us to make connections between old and new information, using theory and knowledge to make sense of the current circumstance.

Email communication: Examples of 'what to do' and 'what not to do'

Can you identify what is wrong in these examples of poor communication from a student to his tutor?

Table 18.1   Examples of poor communication

Poor communication	Good communication
I CANT ACCESS BB. When is teh lecture on w riting skills?!?	Dear Michaela
	I hope that this email finds you well. Could you please let me know when the seminar on writing skills is taking place as I can't access that Blackboard site at the moment due to an IT problem?
	Many thanks
	Dave
Michaela	Dear Michaela
I'm writing to you as tutor for the course, Skills Development. You said that the extra assignment information would be on the Blackboard site on Monday. It's not. Why is it not there and when will it be there? I'm going to work on my assignment today and I need it now.	I'm writing to you as tutor for the course, Skills Development. It would be very helpful if you could let me know when the assignment information will be on the Blackboard site because I'm a part-time student and I'm currently planning my shifts at work with my academic deadlines.
	Much appreciated.
	Best wishes
	Dave
Hi Michaela	[*There is no example here because as a student on the social work programme, Dave should be able to use his initiative to find any tutors' contact information as it will be provided in the programme handbook, it will be found online in the University's staff profile webpages, and in the virtual learning environment, Blackboard, on module and programme webpages!*]
What is Dawn's email, please?	
Dave, 2nd year BA	
Hi Michla, I'm gonna b l8 today. tell Lucy 4 me? can u give me a ring? ☺	Hi Michaela
	Sorry to bother you. I'd really like your help as my personal tutor. I have a personal problem that is affecting my ability to attend on time, and regularly. I'm worried that this will affect my place on the programme. Please could you ring me to discuss?
	Many thanks
	Dave

In the box above you should be able to identify some very poor writing styles and habits such as: lack of proper salutation (greeting) and use of name; text speak and use of emojis; use of capitals; confrontational tone; spelling errors; lack of appropriate content; to name a few. Remember that in emails the person receiving the communication misses other useful forms of communication such as body language, facial gestures, intonation and paralanguage.

CASE RECORDS

Case recording is a core activity in social work practice. Records can include: telephone messages; case notes; emails; safeguarding referrals and investigations; assessments; care/support plans; risk assessments; case reviews; referrals to other organisations; staff handover documents; supervision and training records; complaints. Poor record-keeping is essentially poor communication and can put both workers and service users at risk. It can lead to inactivity or ill-informed decision-making. Effective recording is central to tracking and making sense of the experiences of service users (Constable, 2013). As such, good records will also integrate the voice of the service user. A framework for good record-keeping involves:

1   having an organised approach;
2   sharing information appropriately;
3   being able to locate and retrieve records when required;
4   providing evidence of activities, decisions and actions;
5   providing evidence of adherence to relevant legislation and policy;
6   keeping what you need only for as long as is required (depending on administrative, legal or statutory requirements).

. . . .

Case study: Example of a case note following a telephone call

12.12.2015 Tel/call from Len Bowler (support worker) re: Jimmy Jones DOB: 2.3.1988 (resident at supported housing unit, White Lodge). Jimmy has requested a visit from his social worker (Nadine Moore) to review his support package. Jimmy reports that he is unhappy with transport arrangements as he often arrives late to his independent living skills class and is getting in trouble at college. Jimmy is very upset as he has no control over the transport. Len reports a deterioration in Jimmy's mental health over the past week.

Action: email sent to Nadine Moore (Learning Disabilities Social Worker) including the above information 12.12.2015.

Kelly Quigley, social worker, Adult Social Care Duty Team

. . . .

CASE RECORDS: CONTENT AND STYLE

There are several factors that contribute to high-quality and effective record-keeping. Records should:

- be factual, concise, consistent and accurate;
- be written as soon as possible after an event has occurred, providing current information on the safety and wellbeing of the service user;
- be written clearly and in such a manner that the text cannot be erased;
- be written in such a manner that any alterations or additions are dated, timed and signed in such a way that the original entry can still be read clearly;
- be accurately dated, timed and signed, with the signature printed alongside the first entry if relevant;
- not include abbreviations, jargon, meaningless phrases, irrelevant speculation and offensive subjective statements.

In addition, records should be written, wherever possible, with the involvement of the service user or their carer; be written in terms that the service user can understand; identify problems that have arisen and the action taken to rectify them; provide clear evidence of the care or actions planned, the decisions made, the intervention that was delivered and the information shared.

. . . .

Case study: Eve Taylor

Eve is almost 18 years old and has been living with a foster family for two years. As a very young child Eve spent a few years living in foster care as her parents were heroin users who were unable to care for their children. Eve and her siblings returned home once her mother achieved abstinence following her divorce from Eve's father. Eve became a 'looked after child' again when social care services grew concerned as Eve's mother was reported to have lapsed and was back using heroin and neglecting the children. In addition, there were indications that Eve and her younger sister, May, were being sexually abused by their mother's new partner (a known violent offender). You are new in post as a social worker and visit Eve for the first time. Eve is just beginning to show that she is pregnant; but the case notes that you read did not hold any information about this.

Reflection

You need to have a conversation about Eve's pregnancy. How would you feel if you were Eve, knowing that this new social worker is not aware of the most important event for you right now even though the intimate details of this had been shared with your previous social worker? If you were Eve you might think that social workers do not care, and that you were not important. Imagine that Eve and the baby's father had a rocky relationship and this is now over. You may have to dredge up raw emotions for Eve as she tells you her story; a story that has already been told.

. . . .

As noted above, case recording is a form of communication. The activity of recording information can also be undertaken using diagrammatic tools and techniques, such as an ecomap or genogram, or by creating a historical record (a chronology). You will find 'How to …' guides on the website (https://study.sagepub.com/rogers2e) for each of these tools.

FORMAL REPORTS

Formal reports are produced for **child protection conferences**; in support of applications for families to foster or adopt; after a **mental capacity** assessment has been undertaken; or in the case of **mental health review tribunal**. Reports can be produced to support applications for resources (for example, in the case of housing, furniture grants from charities, or for respite care when parents or carers need a break). Despite the diversity of contexts and requirements, there are some core ethics connected to report writing as these should be constructed whilst integrating anti-discriminatory and non-judgemental approaches (Thompson, 2005). The report should include factual accounts of background information in order to inform evidenced-based planning, decision-making and future action (Bogg, 2012). Bogg identifies some key guidelines to bear in mind:

1   The purpose of the report is clear.
2   All information provided is based on evidence.
3   All sources of information are clearly identified.
4   Any opinions or third party information are identified.
5   Appropriate language is used for the report's purpose.
6   The report is an appropriate length and is concise.
7   The report is proofread for errors.
8   The report is signed and dated.
9   The report lists the names of the people copied into it. (2012: 3)

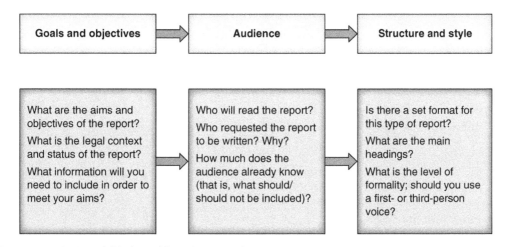

Figure 18.1   GAS model (adapted from Bogg, 2012)

Source: Adapted from Bogg (2012). Reproduced with permission of Open University Press/McGraw-Hill Education

Keeping these principles in mind will help you to produce good, professional reports that are fit for purpose. In terms of structure and format, these will differ according to the task, audience and agency protocols; many organisations will have their own specific format.

Bogg (2012: 6) advocates the use of the GAS model of report writing which shows how the goals/objectives (G) and audience (A) as well as structure and style (S) should be applied (see Figure 18.1). Bogg argues that each element is an important consideration and will help ensure that your reports are appropriate and focused.

· ·

Case study: Report for Eve Taylor

Let's return to Eve Taylor (see box above). When you visited Eve for the first time you were mindful that a looked-after-child's review meeting (LAC review) was imminent, for which you will need to prepare a report. The LAC review is a multi-professional meeting that is held on a regular basis in order to review Eve's care plan. An independent reviewing officer (IRO) is allocated to Eve and the main job of the IRO is to oversee Eve's safety, health and wellbeing in order to ensure that the local authority, who has a statutory duty to care for Eve, is meeting her needs. The report should give adequate attention to Eve's pregnancy and the wellbeing of her unborn child. The report will help those in attendance at the LAC review to assess Eve's needs and make decisions about any changes to her care plan and about any interventions that might be needed in light of her pregnancy.

Applying the GAS model

Goals and objectives:

- The main aim of the report is to present a view of the risks, needs and strengths in Eve's case.
- The report aims to produce an objective, factual and up-to-date picture of Eve's situation in order that her care plan is fit for purpose and meets her needs (as well as those of her unborn baby).
- As Eve is the subject of a care order under section 31 of the Children Act 1989, the report is being presented within the context of her legal status and in order to comply with the statutory duties of the local authority, which has responsibilities in relation to Eve's care and wellbeing as set out in the Children Act 1989.

Audience:

- The report will be read by the IRO, other LAC review attendees (including the foster carers) as well as by Eve.
- There is a statutory requirement for the report to cover different elements of Eve's safety, health and wellbeing and to be produced within a certain timeframe; this is set out in legislation and policy.
- The report should include information about any decisions regarding Eve's care plans and interventions that may be needed.

Structure and style:

- The local authority (the corporate parent) has a template, or set structure, for reports of this kind and this should be used.

- Again, the main headings are fairly standard and include: background information; care arrangements; education; health; contact with birth family; Eve's views and so on.
- The report is intended for an LAC review which is a formal process and it may be later used in any legal proceedings that may arise. Therefore, the report should adopt a formal style.

Reflection

On 5 August 2015 Community Care Online reported on a case where a social worker was 'strongly criticised for "opaque" language in a court report that the family involved would struggle to understand' and that the report 'might just as well have been written in a foreign language' according to the judge. You can read this article in full by following the link on the website (https://study.sagepub.com/rogers2e).

An example of the 'opaque' language used by the social worker was given when s/he described a couple's relationship as being 'imbued with ambivalence'. It is easy to see why the judge made the comments that he did. There is, however, a great deal of complexity involved in the skill of professional report writing where social workers are required to have a good standard of grammar, wide vocabulary and skills in articulation. There is not always clear direction or training in report writing. Jones (2016: 26) highlights the value of KISS: Keep It Simple Stupid.

INTEGRATING ANALYSIS

Criticisms about social work reports have been made about length (too little or too much), ambiguity and lack of analysis (Lishman, 2009). The first two can be addressed by using a model such as GAS, and it is agreed that reports must integrate analysis. In fact, reports should integrate plenty of analytical content alongside description and contextual information (Rogers and Allen, 2019). You should aim to: identify the significance of the information that you have gathered, for example, by highlighting impacts or emerging patterns in the life of the service user; make evaluations (judge the value of strengths and weaknesses, assess credibility); weigh up one piece of information against another. Ensure that you accurately credit sources of evidence so as to differentiate between fact and opinion. Use 'connectives' to establish cause and effect (as a result, because, since, therefore, so) and for contrast/comparison (whereas, though, while, unless, similarly, however, equally, on the other hand). See Rogers and Allen (2019) for a detailed discussion of integrating critical thinking and analysis into social work practice.

By integrating these practices into your reports, you can build arguments according to the available information and, in turn, this can enhance defensible and evidence-based decision-making. You will be able to make reasoned professional judgements which are substantiated by gathered information and supported by the evidence-base and/or theory. To support your analysis, you should identify gaps, where further information or action is required. This demonstrates that you have analysed the information to hand, but also situated it within the broader context of what is known about the particular issue, family or community. Finally, when proposing recommendations, you should not just describe what should happen next, but provide evidence or explain why something is appropriate and will work best. Resources and timing might be important, and influential, and you should consider the whole picture before making a range of recommendations that may not be achievable.

Visit the website to listen to Dr Lucy Rai, who offers a useful perspective when thinking about professional and academic writing (https://study.sagepub.com/rogers2e).

CONCLUSION

This chapter has explored the practicalities of writing for social work and, in turn, this has reinforced the messages contained within the PCF about the need to be skilled in writing. Using two everyday activities (case recording and report writing), a range of guidance has been included to help your skill development in this integral area of practice. Finally, whatever the format of your written work, Birkenmaier et al. (2014: 225) remind us to maintain an ethical approach, as we should:

> Keep the values and ethics of the social work professional at the forefront of your writing. Just as with your practice, your commitment to client self-determination, strengths, empowerment, and cultural competence must be ever present as you write about clients in any form of documentation.

Having read this chapter, you should be able to:

- Identify the 'dos' and 'don'ts' of written communication;
- Consider the ways to structure a formal report;
- Identify best practice in record-keeping.

RECOMMENDED READING

Bogg, D. (2012) *Report Writing*. Maidenhead: Open University Press.
Healy, K. and Mulholland, J. (2019) *Writing Skills for Social Workers* (3rd edn). London: Sage.
Koprowska, J. (2019) *Communication and Interpersonal Skills in Social Work* (5th edn). Exeter: Learning Matters.
Lishman, J. (2009) *Communication in Social Work* (2nd edn). Basingstoke: Palgrave Macmillan.
Rogers, M. and Allen, D. (2019) *Applying Critical Thinking and Analysis in Social Work*. London: Sage.

Inter-Professional Practice and Working Together

David Edmondson and Charlotte Ashworth

Links to the Professional Capabilities Framework

• Professionalism • Context and organisations • Professional leadership

Links to the Knowledge and Skills Statement for Child and Family Practitioners

• Relationships and effective direct work • Communication • Analysis, decision-making, planning and review • Organisational context

Links to the Knowledge and Skills Statement for Social Workers in Adult Services

• Person-centred practice • Safeguarding • Effective assessments and outcome-based support planning • Direct work with individuals and families • Organisational context • Professional ethics and leadership

Key messages

• Working collaboratively is a positive thing and done properly is additive to the quality of delivery and standard of services we seek to achieve in our work.
• Although the evidence-base for inter-professional practice is mixed and its development and practice has challenges, a commitment to learning to work together is an essential part of contemporary social work practice.

INTRODUCTION

Inter-professional practice and joint working is an accepted part of social work practice in the twenty-first century and social workers should develop skills and knowledge that support effective working and productive outcomes (Thomas et al., 2014). There is a plethora of terms used to describe and characterise different forms of collaboration and joint working, such as inter-professional practice, interdisciplinary working, multidisciplinary working, collaborative practice and partnership working. These terms are often used interchangeably or conflated sometimes without consideration of their differences, features and requirements. The recommended reading included with this chapter offers the reader the opportunity to explore terminology in more detail.

This chapter will focus on social work inter-professional practice, noting that principles of 'working together' (Leathard, 2003) extend not only to other approaches to work between professionals but importantly in turn to how to work collaboratively alongside individuals, families and carers (Sharland et al., 2007; Whittington et al., 2009). This chapter will use the definition of inter-professional practice to mean: 'two or more professions working together as a team with a common purpose, commitment and mutual respect' (Freeth et al., 2005 cited in Dunstan et al., 2009: 6). This definition seems fairly straightforward at first glance. However, each element underlines that inter-professional practice requires much more than simply the moving and merging of staff groups into a 'new team' on the assumption this will somehow produce better services and results. For inter-professional practice to be effective, professionals brought together or collaborating require clarity and some common agreement about the collective purpose of their work. This chapter will focus on the knowledge and skills required to promote better working together.

The advantages of inter-professional practice and collaboration has been endorsed by several writers (Barrett et al., 2005; Dalrymple and Boylan, 2013; Quinney and Hafford-Letchfield, 2012). In the general literature there is an underlying assumption and orthodoxy that close-working and shared goals are central to delivering safer and effective services and that such services should be by design integrated and coordinated (Banks, 2012; Dunstan et al., 2009). Policy in health and social care has over many years promoted a commitment to 'joined-up' working and the development of 'seamless services'.

The Care Quality Commission (CQC) in commenting on the legal framework in relation to safeguarding children and adults emphasises multi-agency working and reaffirms the importance of clarity and purpose in respect of organisational responsibilities and roles:

> ... the overarching objective for both is to enable children and adults to live a life free from abuse or neglect. This cannot be achieved by any single agency. Every organisation and person who comes into contact with a child or adult has a responsibility and a role to play to help keep children and adults safe. (CQC, 2015: 3)

Within social work education there is a clear acknowledgement that:

> Contemporary Social Work increasingly takes place in an inter-agency context, and social workers work collaboratively with others towards interdisciplinary and cross-professional objectives. (QAA, 2016: 7)

Following on from this, social work training should therefore prepare students:

> … to work as part of the social care workforce, working increasingly in integrated teams across and within specialist settings in adult health, mental health and children's services; interprofessionally alongside professionals in the National Health Service, schools, police, criminal justice and housing, and in partnership with service users and carers. (QAA, 2016: 9)

This approach is also reflected in the revised requirements set out in the Professional Capabilities Framework for Social Workers (2018) and in the Health Care Profession Councils Standards of Proficiency for Social Workers in England (2017). The inclusion of individuals, families and carers in these guidelines is an essential part of genuinely working together. This links to core social work values ('working with and not doing to others') and to the importance we attach to behaviours that promote inclusive, anti-discriminatory and anti-oppressive practice (Dominelli, 2002; Thompson, 2012a).

Although the establishment of inter-professional and multi-professional teams has become the accepted orthodoxy, the evidence-base for inter-professional practice presents a more mixed picture of success and is not without its challenges (McLaughlin, 2013). From their systematic review of 46 papers, reporting 30 separate studies, Cameron et al. (2012) conclude: 'The evidence base underpinning joint and integrated working remains less than compelling' (2012: 1). However, given the clear direction of service models and team configurations in the field, you will find yourself engaging with just such issues.

In the quote below, Sarah, a child and families social worker, comments on the importance and value of inter-professional practice:

> When thinking about inter-professional working, difference is something which is a reoccurring theme and one which needs to be both celebrated but challenged at the same time. By this, I mean that one of the key benefits of multi-agency working is the specialisms that it can bring to the table. When working effectively it promotes the sharing of a wide variety of knowledge and skills to help service users and it is this difference which should truly be celebrated. However, the difference between practitioners and agencies can also be the source of conflict and this, in my experience, has often been based upon a lack of understanding of the roles and responsibilities of agencies.

Sharing information and formulating a coordinated multi-agency response is likely to improve the prospect that a child and family would receive the best available services whilst also relieving some pressure from one agency attempting to respond to every need alone, particularly when the need lies outside of their area of expertise.

Reflective activity

Read the SCIE systematic review *Factors that Promote and Hinder Joint and Integrated Working between Health and Social Care Services* by Ailsa Cameron, Rachel Lart, Lisa Bostock and Caroline Coomber (Cameron et al., 2012). Consider the findings from the report and the views of the social workers in relation to your own team experiences.

Key points from the report:

- It demonstrates some positive outcomes of such an approach for people who use services, carers and organisations delivering services.
- Three broad themes are used to organise the factors that support or hinder joint or integrated working: organisational issues; cultural and professional issues; and contextual issues.
- There is significant overlap between positive and negative factors, with many of the organisational factors identified in research as promoting joint working also being identified as hindering collaboration when insufficient attention is paid to their importance.
- Securing the understanding and commitment of staff to the aims and desired outcomes of new partnerships is crucial to the success of joint working, particularly among health professionals.
- Defining outcomes that matter to service users and carers is important. Outcomes defined by service users may differ from policy and practice imperatives but are a crucial aspect of understanding the effectiveness of joint or integrated services.
- Although most service users and carers report high levels of satisfaction, more can be done to involve them in care planning and influencing future care options. Joint and integrated services work best when they promote increased user involvement, choice and control.
- The evidence-base underpinning joint and integrated working remains less than compelling. It largely consists of small-scale evaluations of local initiatives which are often of poor quality and poorly reported. No evaluation studied for the purpose of this briefing included an analysis of cost-effectiveness.
- There is an urgent need to develop high-quality, large-scale research studies that can test the underpinning assumptions of joint and integrated working in a more robust manner and assess the process from the perspective of service users and carers as well as from an economic perspective. (Cameron et al., 2012: 1)

FACTORS IMPACTING ON INTER-PROFESSIONAL PRACTICE AND WORKING TOGETHER

As Cameron et al. (2012) suggest, the same factors overlap in terms of features that can either help or hinder positive inter-professional practice. This is also present in other writing on the subject (CAIPE, 2007; Dalrymple and Boylan, 2013) and suggests such factors and features are not only important in their own right but pivotal as to whether inter-professional working is likely to: make a positive contribution; provide a rewarding and fulfilling environment for professionals to work in; and encourage and support models of service that seek to offer people genuine choice and control in their lives. A key factor in making any model function effectively is genuine 'buy-in' in terms of commitment and participation (McLaughlin, 2013). The exercise below invites you to consider factors and features that have helped or hindered inter-professional practice and collaborative working together in your own team and service. This exercise will help inform the final section of this chapter about developing practical approaches to better working together.

Reflective activity

Assess your own experience of inter-professional practice and collaboration using the questions and template form on the website.

Examine your own experience of inter-professional practice and its contribution towards partnership working using the 'Cause and Effect Diagram of Common Barriers to Partnership' (Joint Improvement Team Scotland, 2009: 4). Links to the full diagram and report can be found on the website (https://study.sagepub.com/rogers2e).

SERVICE DESIGN AND WORKING COLLABORATIVELY WITH OTHER PROFESSIONALS IN TEAMS

This chapter asserts working collaboratively is a positive thing. On a practical level, no single worker or service for that matter can or ought to deliver services in isolation to others. Working together, done well, is additive and given how stretched are resources in contemporary practice it should also promote an efficient and cost-effective model of working. Further, by working together and in close collaboration, workers can draw on each other's respective expertise, knowledge and skills to inform their own work, and with careful planning ensure they do not duplicate, inadvertently contradict or undermine the efforts of each other.

Reflective activity

How well do I work with others?

    A. Give three examples from your own practice, where you have sought out the knowledge, skills or views of a professional colleague or those of another sort of expert:

(Continued)

1

2

3

If you cannot think of any, how might you change this? What are the gains of seeking out the views of others?

B. Reflecting on your work in your own team or placement identify one example where another professional has sought your advice:

1

If you cannot think of any, how might you change this?

Service design in recent years has keenly adopted the idea that different professions are at their most effective when they are co-located and have a shared working environment. The assumption seems to be that if people are made to sit together in the same room they will by default communicate and work better together. In addition, in co-locating teams the sharing of certain activities across professional groups promotes unity and efficiency. Typically, this might include:

- tasks that are now common and shared within multi-professional teams, e.g. initial assessments, care planning, ongoing coordination of care, office duty;
- the increased use of common assessment forms, uniform care plan forms, linked reporting systems across services and within teams;
- pooled budgets and resources with common application systems for access and distribution;
- leadership and management which is not profession specific.

Within inter-professional co-located teams the sharing out of such tasks is perhaps inevitable from an agency-workload perspective. However, the desirability of moving beyond this and towards a more generic hybrid form of worker needs to be carefully considered. In the context of health and social care, individuals frequently present with a range of complex problems and multiple difficulties that are likely to require help from experts with a range of skills and knowledge. However, McGrath believes that a balance can be found:

> Interprofessional working is not about fudging the boundaries between the professions and trying to create a generic care worker. It is instead about developing professionals who are confident in their own core skills and expertise, who are fully aware and confident in the skills and expertise of fellow health and care

professionals, and who conduct their own practice in a non-hierarchical and collegiate way with other members of the working team, so as to continuously improve the health of their communities and to meet the real care needs of individual patients and clients. (McGrath, 1991 in CAIPE, 2007: 8)

POSITIVE ACTIVITIES THAT SUPPORT BETTER INTER-PROFESSIONAL WORKING

Meads and Ashcroft (2005) argue that inter-professional practice and working can enhance profession-specific identity rather than erode it. Barrett and Keeping (2005), Thomas et al. (2014), Dalrymple and Boylan (2013), Davies and Jones (2015) offer the following as examples of good practice in developing inter-professional collaboration:

- clarity of the purpose of the intended collaboration, team or service;
- commitment to goals and outcomes that focus on better service delivery and outcomes for individuals, families, carers and the wider community;
- management support at all levels and consistently over time;
- acceptance that effective inter-professional working may be achievable but requires ongoing support and adequate resources if it is to be sustained;
- a personal and professional willingness and commitment to work together;
- clarity and appreciation of team and professional roles, skills and knowledge;
- power differences are acknowledged; lines of decision-making, responsibility and accountability are clear;
- there is open and honest communication between workers;
- there is interest in and better understanding of different professional roles, skills and knowledge;
- there is trust and mutual respect for each other; ranking and values attached to different professions are acknowledged and managed;
- an acceptance that professional differences are inevitable and can be positive; that there is a mechanism and professional culture to deal with disagreements and conflict.

In the section below, a social worker comments on effective collaboration in the context of inter-professional practice.

Social work perspectives on effective collaboration

Sarah, a child and families social worker, gives an example from practice:

Prior to entering a statutory social work role, I made a referral to social care as a partner agency. Having made the referral, I arranged with the social worker to meet with her at the young person's college that day and support the young person in discussing the concerns. This occurred at the end of the college day. Having heard the young person's disclosures the social worker agreed that it was not safe for her to return home. The accommodation of a child is not a simple task; it requires complex social care deliberations with senior management, in this case consent from parents, the sourcing of an appropriate placement and managing a child's emotional presentation in respect of what is happening to them. In this case, the college staff remained at college until 7 p.m. at night with the young person as they had the best relationship with the child whilst I accompanied the social worker to visit the family. Together, we then placed the child at 11 p.m. that night. The following day there was correspondence between the social care manager and my manager discussing how effectively the agencies worked together and how refreshing it was that resources were used to ensure the best outcome for the young person.

Good social worker practitioners can do a number of things to promote effective collaboration and inter-professional working:

- Explain your roles, responsibilities and duties to others, acknowledging the dilemmas, challenges and opportunities of the work.
- Explain the purpose of social work to others, linking this to its core values and principles.
- Define and explain your particular skills and knowledge; what you bring to the service and work.
- Retain and develop links with other social workers in your agency and service to provide mutual support and advocacy for each other.
- Be prepared to take a lead in strategic work and direct casework.
- Be a resource.
- Be positive about your own contribution to working with others.
- Work hard and be professional – you represent the profession, not just yourself.

Professional identity and effective working

Sarah, comments:

> A crucial function of the role of a social worker is being able to articulate the role and its responsibilities to others. This can often be challenging, particularly when your explanation contravenes others' understanding. When I started practising in frontline child and family social work, I would carry a copy of the local authority's policy regarding roles and thresholds to use as a tool to discuss with agencies in order to support the ideas that I attempted to articulate to them. Whilst this approach is still useful in some contexts, as I have become more experienced the relational component to multi-agency working has become of greater use to me.

> I have found that the most influential element of multi-agency working has been to consciously make an effort to invest in developing a relationship with other practitioners outside of my immediate team. Whilst to some this may not initially appear to be a particular challenge, it does require that you make a real effort with others

and undertake tasks which for some practitioners may not be considered an absolute necessity to ensure the safety of children. Examples of such practices are to:

- Visit another agency's office to discuss a referral rather than doing so over the phone. This tells other agencies that you take their concerns seriously, helps humanise you and your decision-making process and quite often results in agencies providing more detailed information than they may well have done via the phone or email.
- Call people to provide updates after meetings or decisions have been made and in doing so acknowledging their contributions and thanking them.

Actions such as these do support the development of relationships with practitioners within other agencies which is the foundation upon which trust and mutual respect can be developed. It is necessary to be able to achieve trust and mutual respect as it increases transparency and reduces the conflict which can occur within inter-professional working whilst also encouraging positive modelling for service users.

CONCLUSION

Inter-professional working is a key feature of contemporary social work and mandatory in child protection. However, it requires effort to make it work and as professionals committed to promoting positive change through partnership working, we should be willing not only to contribute to this but to lead by good example.

Having read this chapter, you should be able to:

- Better understand the link between inter-professional practice and social work values and ethics;
- Identify knowledge and skills which you can use and which will promote better collaboration and working together.

RECOMMENDED READING

Bailey, D. (2012) *Interdisciplinary Working in Mental Health*. Basingstoke: Palgrave Macmillan

Cameron, A., Lart, R., Bostock, L. and Coomber, C. (2012) *Research Briefing 41: Factors that Promote and Hinder Joint and Integrated Working between Health and Social Care Services*. London: SCIE. Available at: www.scie.org.uk/publications/briefings/files/briefing41.pdf (accessed 13 March 2016).

Davies, K. and Jones, R. (eds) (2015) *Skills for Social Work Practice*. Basingstoke: Palgrave Macmillan.

Edmondson, D. (2014) *Social Work Practice Learning: A Student Guide*. London: Sage.

Hammick, M., Freeth, D., Copperman, J. and Goodsman, D. (2009) *Being Interprofessional*. Cambridge: Polity Press.

Littlechild, B. and Smith, R. (eds) (2012) *A Handbook for Interprofessional Practice in the Human Services: Learning to Work Together*. Harlow: Pearson.

Maximising Supervision
Michaela Rogers

Links to the Professional Capabilities Framework

- Professionalism   • Knowledge   • Critical reflection and analysis

Links to the Knowledge and Skills Statement for Child and Family Practitioners

- The role of supervision   • Organisational context

Links to the Knowledge and Skills Statement for Social Workers in Adult Services

- Supervision, critical reflection and analysis   • Organisational context

Key messages

- Quality supervision is at the heart of social work practice.
- Supervision provides an important space for reflection.
- Supervision should be regular, planned for and a protected, undisturbed time.
- Reflective supervision leads to continuous professional development.

INTRODUCTION

Throughout your social work career, supervision should take a central role and is of value at any stage of the ASPIRE model. Indeed, good-quality, reflective supervision is the bedrock of practice and will enable you to develop a person-centred, value-based approach to working with vulnerable individuals and families. SfC/CWDC (2007: 4) suggest that:

> [Supervision is] an accountable process which supports, assesses and develops the knowledge, skills and values of an individual, group or team. The purpose is to improve the quality of [your] work to achieve agreed objectives and outcomes. In [social care and social work services] this should optimise the capacity of people who use services to lead independent and fulfilling lives.

This definition is congruent with the **paradigm** that underpins this book as we wish you to consider your developing practice and skills as imperative in the pursuit of relationship-based practice (RBP). RBP values the contribution of you (the practitioner) and the people that you work with (the service users, co-workers and other professionals). Moreover, through **serious case reviews** it has been highlighted that a lack of supervision can be a factor in cases where there has been a practice failing resulting in harmful outcomes.

FUNCTIONS OF SUPERVISION

Edmondson and Rogers highlight the value of supervision in terms of past, present and future practice:

> Done well, supervision offers an opportunity to think not just about what you have been doing, but also how and why you have been practising the way you have, and perhaps most importantly how, as active learners, we can develop to become better practitioners. (2014: 139)

Whilst this view is generally accepted, supervision is not always prioritised as high caseloads and other pressing demands can get in the way. However, supervision should be regular, planned and offer a safe space within which you are able to have a constructive dialogue in order to develop your *professional knowledge* and *practice* (Doel, 2010).

Supervision has several functions, including:

- *Case management and administration*: This function ensures social work interventions are appropriate, ethical and timely, in order that your practice is compliant with agency protocols and meets professional standards, such as the UK's Health and Care Professions Council's (HCPC) Standards of Proficiency. There is also an opportunity to review the work plan for each case and plan for further intervention or inter-agency involvement. Cases can be closed, and/or new work can be negotiated.

Other administrative demands can be discussed in relation to, for example, health and safety or employment issues.

- *Learning and development*: Supervision encapsulates reflective practice so that you (the supervisee) can consider in full your practice and decision-making, whilst engaging in theoretical discussions or considering the legislative underpinning or implications of your work. Reflective practice should result in a plan or agreed action that enables you to learn and develop skills. This is the place for you to agree a training programme or a plan for your continuing professional development (CPD).
- *Support*: The landscape of social work is complex, ambiguous and subject to continuous change. Thus, daily service provision is never easy and the work can become very stressful at times. Support to all practitioners should be offered when appropriate and when needed. A competent supervisor will be skilled at identifying these times, and a responsible practitioner should be able to ask for help (although sometimes this is easier said than done when feeling under pressure). Having the ability to 'offload' enables you to remain focused, and to maintain motivation and commitment to the individuals and families that you work with. Parker (2010: 77) describes this function of supervision as 'restorative'.
- *Exploration*: Both individual and group supervision can be used to develop knowledge by using hypothetical case studies to elicit discussion. These exploratory discussions can evaluate theory, new initiatives and case law as well as current issues (for example, child sexual exploitation [CSE], or radicalisation). 'Eureka' moments can occur during these exploratory discussions which potentially lead to self-discovery (in terms of revealing new knowledge or skills gained).
- *Assessment*: Social work students or practitioners who are newly qualified, in their 'assessed and supported year in employment' (ASYE), may also find that supervision forms part of their course assessment.

Whilst all these functions form important elements of supervision, during different times one may take precedence over another as a particular function needs to take priority. For instance, if you have a personal difficulty that means that you need to be away from the office for a week or two, supervision quite rightly may focus on the management of your allocated cases. You are then assured that you can leave knowing that your work is covered and individuals or families are not left without support. As such, this type of discussion can be understood as a 'joint activity' which highlights how supervision 'gives expression to the central tenet of people-work, that it is a shared responsibility, you do not have to soldier on alone or in isolation' (Moss, 2012: 203).

Beddoe (2010) has commented on the growing realisation of the value of supervision in contemporary practice, whilst noting its correlation with quality and accountability. In order to elucidate the weight given to different functions, Beddoe asked important questions to experienced supervisors about whether supervision is seen as a necessary reflective space or whether it is simply a means of surveillance, or 'snoopervision' (Thompson, 2006: 75). Beddoe noted some of the ambiguity and tensions in the supervisee–supervisor relationship but, overall, she found that supervision was viewed as a conduit for reflection. In turn, this was seen as fundamental to effective practice and respondents rejected the surveillance role.

Commentary from a social work student

During my final placement I had an on-site Practice Supervisor (PS) and an off-site Practice Educator (PE); whilst this met the needs of the placement provider, I felt at times that my needs were not always met in terms of providing me with an effective space to explore my thoughts and feelings around interventions and use these reflections to influence my future practice. There was a distinct split between the case management supervision with my PS and the more reflective supervision with my PE and I found it difficult to bring the two together. Fox (2011) expects supervision to 'facilitate the supervisee to explore their feelings about the work and the family' (p. 7) they are dealing with and 'ensure that practitioners fully understand their roles, responsibilities and the scope of their professional discretion and authority' (p. 8). For me, this was not always achieved within placement and I did not feel able to express this to my PS which has, I feel, hindered my ability to engage as effectively as I would have liked to in subsequent supervision sessions.

This experience has helped me to clarify what I want and need from supervision and I will use this knowledge and experience to feed into my future supervision agreements. The British Association of Social Workers (BASW, 2011) recommends that as part of encouraging a 'supervision culture' agencies should use supervision agreements and encourage discussion of supervision history to maximise the effectiveness of the supervisory relationship. Had I not had such a mixed experience with supervision during placement I do not believe I would have developed as strong a sense of what works for me and what does not in terms of supervision style; so although I have struggled with this area during placement, I believe it has helped me to understand myself more and this can only be of benefit when advancing into practice.

MODELS OF SUPERVISION

Different models of supervision are appropriate for different service settings. For example, in a large agency in addition to formal one-to-one supervision sessions, it may be beneficial to have group supervision as this is a helpful format for sharing information that needs to be distributed across a sizeable department. The most common types of supervision are:

Formal one-to-one supervision: This should take place on a regular and planned basis in a safe, reflective space. Formal supervision should be built on and structured around an agenda and provide opportunities for both parties to raise agenda items; it is the type of supervision that covers all four of the functions described above (and assessment too for students).

Group or peer supervision: This can be formal or informal and may take place between a group of co-workers, a mix of practitioners and students, or students only. Personal issues, however, should be kept for discussion in one-to-one supervision sessions.

Informal supervision: Potentially this may take place at any time, in any setting. This includes, for instance, a discussion held with a senior staff member during a car journey following a home visit (reflection-on-action), or seeking advice when in the midst of a telephone duty call (reflection-in-action) (see Chapter 6 'Reflection and Reflexivity'). Whilst conversations might be informal, it may be necessary to properly record, or log, the details and any decisions made.

Reflective activity

Consider the functions and models of supervision; what conditions, or prerequisites, do you think are essential for formal supervision:

- on a one-to-one basis?
- and within a peer group?

Think about space, place, time, interactions, relationships and practical concerns.

Go to the website (https://study.sagepub.com/rogers2e) to access a 'How to …' guide on 'Preparing for Supervision'.

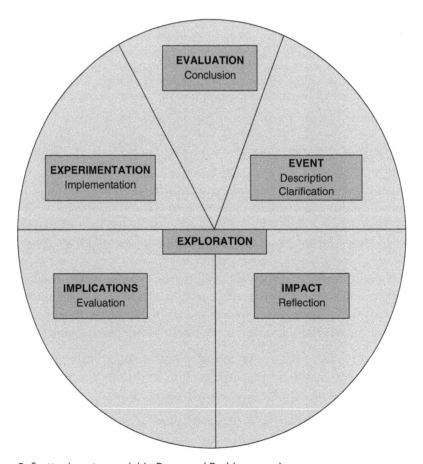

Figure 20.1   Reflective learning model (© Davys and Beddoe, 2009)

Source: Davys and Beddoe (2009) The reflective learning model: supervision of social work students. *Social Work Education*, 28(8): 919–933.

THE REFLECTIVE LEARNING MODEL

A helpful way of integrating reflection into the functions of supervision is through the reflective learning model created by Davys and Beddoe (2009) (see Figure 20.1). The model was constructed with students in mind, but it can be effectively utilised within other supervisory environments. The reflective learning model focuses on the processes of supervision to describe a staged approach to reflection mirroring Kolb's (1984) cycle of experiential learning (see Chapter 6 'Reflection and Reflexivity').

· ·

Case study using the reflective learning model: Niall

Niall is a newly qualified social worker, in his ASYE year. He arrived at supervision and was flustered and clearly feeling under some pressure.

The event: The supervisor, Naseem, encouraged Niall to explain how he was feeling and why. Niall disclosed that a visit with a family, the Smiths, had not gone well that morning. Then on arrival at his desk he read an email allocating more work with a family, the Johnsons, a family well known to services. Niall felt that whilst his caseload was no higher than his co-workers', his cases were more complex.

Impact: Niall was worried that he was not doing his best by the Smiths and others that he was supporting. He felt that he couldn't give enough time to those families that needed him at the moment in time. On reflection, Niall felt that he was letting them all down. Niall also admitted that he felt that he was not experienced enough to engage the Johnsons into working with him.

Implications: Naseem encouraged Niall to evaluate the work he had done so far with the Smith family. Niall admitted that he had developed positive relationships with the young parents and agreed a care plan that safeguarded the baby, Summer. Summer's parents had also re-engaged with their substance misuse workers with Niall's encouragement. Niall then was able to contextualise his feelings at the start of supervision and admitted that he felt a little overwhelmed with the newly allocated case. Through an honest discussion, with Naseem's support Niall was able to agree a plan on how to approach the new case.

Experimentation: Naseem and Niall discussed possible scenarios in his work with the new family, the Johnsons. Mr Johnson was known to be involved with local criminal gangs and Mrs Johnson had been in and out of drug rehabilitation services through the years. Their previous social worker had encountered difficulties in getting the Johnsons to engage with them. Both agreed that Niall should attend some upcoming training on 'Working with Resistance' and that he should work with Mr Johnson's probation officer to understand the family dynamics and the best way to approach working in partnership with them.

Evaluation: Naseem and Niall agreed timescales, and revisited the plan to ensure that Niall felt adequately equipped to move forward. They moved to discuss the next case, beginning the reflective learning cycle once more.

· ·

MAXIMISING SUPERVISION

There are some fundamental principles for effective supervision. These include:

- regular meetings with adequate time set aside;
- a venue that is safe and free from interruptions;
- a supervision contract with agreed arrangements;
- preparation and planning;
- a record, or minutes, of the supervision;
- a focus on professional development;
- a consideration of learning needs and learning styles;
- awareness of authority and accountability;
- mutual trust and respect;
- support through an open and honest relationship;
- and, importantly, a celebration of strengths and achievements.

Moss (2012) asserts that for supervision to be effective, you should be (1) assertive, (2) open, (3) reflective, (4) responsive and (5) accurate in your communication. This is sound advice particularly in the context of the inherent hierarchy and power dynamics within the supervisory relationship. There may also be issues around gender, ethnicity, sexuality, age and (dis)ability that impact on these power dynamics and Lishman (2007) asserts that effective supervision must embed anti-oppressive and anti-discriminatory principles.

Visit the website (https://study.sagepub.com/rogers2e) to listen to more about the value of supervision.

> ### Reflective activity
>
> - What might you need to do to prepare for supervision?
> - Consider that all the elements for maximising supervision are present (including a well-prepared supervisor and supervisee/peer group), so what are the benefits of formal supervision on (a) a one-to-one basis, and (b) within a group?

BARRIERS TO EFFECTIVE SUPERVISION

Notwithstanding the above principles for maximising supervision, there are many barriers, including:

- lack of regular supervision;
- lack of adequate time given;

- lack of personal insight and the belief that you are able to manage all the demands of your caseload alone;
- the belief that you've learned all there is to know – you've 'been there, done that';
- lack of trust in the supervisory relationship;
- a fear of being honest and open and the feeling that evaluating your practice will render you vulnerable in your position in the agency;
- personality clashes between the supervisor and supervisee;
- an imbalance and misuses of power within supervision sessions;
- 'unfinished business' – matters discussed in the last supervision that remain unresolved or unaddressed;
- lack of agency resources to meet any identified learning needs;
- imbalance in focus (too much time spent on case management, and no time for learning, or support);
- stress or 'burnout'.

Reflective activity

- What strategies or actions might you take to address some of the above barriers?

A skilful practitioner will always approach supervision as a means for reflection, learning and growth, and if there are barriers to effective supervision or to implement the plan that you co-produce with your supervisor, a solution should be sought. This might mean tackling the problem head on (initiating a frank discussion with your supervisor), but it may also mean looking to other sources of supervision (for instance, through peer support). On a practical basis, you may need to be proactive to seek out and secure a more suitable space, or you may need to revisit the supervision contract to review the agreed principles. If your agency does not have the financial resources to meet training needs, see if you can negotiate with colleagues in an external agency to 'swap' training with you and your team.

CONCLUSION

This chapter has set out the underpinning framework for effective supervision which incorporates several functions (management, support, development, exploration and, for students, assessment). There has also been some consideration of 'enablers' and 'barriers' with suggestions on how to circumnavigate some of the latter to increase the efficacy of supervision. The message is that supervision should be a central element of professional practice throughout your career, not just during training or in your early years of employment. As Field et al. (2014: 76) note, supervision is 'where [your] professional identity as a social worker matures'.

Having read this chapter, you should be able to:

- Articulate the different functions of supervision;
- Identify the different models for supervision;
- Consider the barriers and enablers to effective supervision.

RECOMMENDED READING

Beddoe, L. (2010) Surveillance or reflection: professional supervision in 'the risk society'. *British Journal of Social Work*, 40(4): 1279–1296.

Davys, A. and Beddoe, L. (2009) The reflective learning model: supervision of social work students. *Social Work Education: The International Journal*, 28(8): 919–933. Available at: http://web.a.ebscohost.com/ehost/pdfviewer/pdfviewer?vid=8&sid=0a88a7f5-e83e-45b6-b89f-b2f9f0f8ca8d%-40sessionmgr4005&hid=4106

Hawkins, P. and Shohet, R. (2012) *Supervision in the Helping Professions: Supervision in Context* (4th edn). Buckingham: Open University Press.

Thompson, N. and Gilbert, P. (2011) *Supervision Skills: A Learning and Development Manual*. Lyme Regis: Russell House Publishing.

Wonnacott, J. (2012) *Mastering Social Work Supervision*. London: Jessica Kingsley.

Review and Evaluation
David Edmondson

Links to the Professional Capabilities Framework

• Critical reflection and analysis • Professionalism • Skills and interventions • Values and ethics

Links to the Knowledge and Skills Statement for Child and Family Practitioners

• Relationships and effective direct work • Analysis, decision-making, planning and review • Organisational context

Links to the Knowledge and Skills Statement for Social Workers in Adult Services

• Person-centred practice • Direct work with individuals and families • Organisational context • Professional ethics and leadership

Key message

• Review and evaluation is key to understanding past practice and behaviour, and to improving your future work.

INTRODUCTION

Review and evaluation is identified as the final strand of the cycle that represents social work process. In terms of our individual casework, it follows Assessment, Planning and Intervention in Sutton's ASPIRE model (1999, 2006), which is outlined in the Introduction to Part II of this book.

For our purposes here, review is taken to involve looking back on your work or practice, over a set period, in order to identify what has been done, think about how well your interventions and actions have worked and identify what needs to be done in order to introduce change and improvement. Evaluation here is distinctly different from audit or output and is taken to be the use of a structured approach to judge the amount, quality and value of your work, linking this to your professional role. It is also being used here to promote a model of practice which is not inward looking or inert, but designed to help you think about your professional practice in a way which supports learning, improvement and development. In this regard, review and evaluation is linked here to use of supervision in professional practice and also critical reflective practice, both of which are covered in this book (see Chapter 20 and Chapter 6).

Most, if not all, organisations include some form of in-service professional development review process. You will have already encountered a form of this during your professional training and quite likely in your post-qualifying employment. Ideas in this chapter are offered to complement these processes. Done in an open and receptive way, review and evaluation will: help you make sense of your day-to-day actions and decisions; help you to better appraise the work you do; contribute to informing your future work and interventions; promote more effective and efficient practice and service delivery.

The section below begins by looking at reviews of individual casework, and building on this to review and evaluate your caseload of work and broader professional practice.

PRACTICAL APPROACHES TO REVIEWING AND EVALUATING YOUR INDIVIDUAL CASEWORK

Reviewing work can be done in a number of ways but accurately measuring change and improvement is not easy or obvious. Many factors can contribute to change. Some may be known to us, but others may be hidden from view or simply unknown. Similarly, we cannot control all the variables or environmental factors within which social work practice takes place. By its nature social work takes place within contexts and situations which can change and fluctuate relatively quickly. This can make it difficult to confidently claim that it is our specific intervention at this moment in time that has been the key change factor. This also makes appraising our personal contribution as 'change agents' difficult to definitively prove, even if we feel confident our efforts have been a contributing factor to something being improved. However, this is not to say we should not attempt to review or evaluate social work process and casework, and that we cannot produce credible or trustworthy accounts to appraise the work we have done, identify what we have achieved and done well, and think about ways of doing things better next time.

ESSENTIAL FEATURES AND CONSIDERATIONS WHEN PREPARING TO REVIEW YOUR WORK

In order to evaluate your individual casework, it is useful to begin by considering what factors we need to consider in planning any review of practice. Table 21.1 sets out some features to be considered.

Table 21.1   Features to consider when preparing to review your work

Essential features of tasks and activities	Comment
They must be achievable.	An obvious point but worth remembering.
They must be capable of measure, scaling and rating, or at least amenable to some form of assessment or interpretation.	Routine and procedural tasks can be measured fairly straightforwardly, e.g. completing an assessment form on time or writing up records.
	Other tasks can be much more complex and difficult to measure, e.g. measuring a change in a person's mental health.
	However, some features, e.g. wellbeing and quality of life, are not at all easy to quantify or measure. These may require more interpretation. In situations where 'proof' of change is less easy to ascertain you may need to draw on a range of different views and perspectives from others to identify changes.
	You will also need to consider how you might rank or rate change:
	• Number ratings from 1 to 10 with set criteria • Banded ratings: completed/incomplete/uncompleted, or successful/partially successful/unsuccessful
They ought to be capable of being set within realistic and viable timescales.	Timescales are important in terms of service quality assurance. However, they also need to be achievable within your own and the agency's resources.
You should be able to distinguish between practical and immediate actions with short-term goals and achievements and more aspirational outcomes, which may require a concerted set of activities that take place over time and have longer-term outcomes.	Some work may be considered more urgent than others, e.g. the threat of eviction. However, these can often rely on third parties and access to other services outside your control.
	More aspirational or longer-terms goals need to be acknowledged as harder to achieve, e.g. reducing self-harming, introducing anger management and reducing substance misuse.

SOME PRACTICAL MODELS – BEFORE AND AFTER REVIEW AND EVALUATION

Post-intervention reviews

Simple *post-intervention* models of review and evaluation can be used to review and reflect on an intervention after it has occurred. Here, no prior views are available or have been taken from people involved in the intervention, primarily the person receiving the service. This approach gives no information about what things were like prior to the intervention and tends to rely on memory.

Before and after reviews

An alternative model is to use a *before–after* comparison model that may give us more useful information from which to identify some relationships between our intervention(s) and change. This model is commonly used in evaluation work. By undertaking a detailed assessment of the situation of the case *before* your intervention (sometimes referred to as making a baseline assessment) and then comparing this to how things are *after* your intervention we can judge whether there seems to have been any improvements in the immediate or particular circumstances of the case through specific interventions (e.g. financial worries or pressures being reduced by welfare benefits support and advice) and if there have been any broader changes brought about by your whole intervention over time (e.g. anxiety has been reduced by a combination of interventions such as money advice, rehousing support and stress management techniques). The model does require some pre-planning in that times need to be set in order to assess the impact of an intervention (as in Table 21.2).

Table 21.2   Intervention impacts

Time 1	Intervention – e.g. six-week task-centred social work	Time 2
Assess the situation before the intervention	The intervention is introduced and completed	Reassess the situation after the intervention

Variations on the *before–after* model include adding additional time points before, during and after the intervention(s) to provide more detail and observation in order to appraise what other additional or external factors may be influencing the changes and outcomes.

Comparison work can be used to further assess the efficacy of an intervention by comparing similar individuals or groups who get the intervention with those who have not received it as yet.

Reviewing interventions and practice

Charlotte, a children and families social worker, comments:

> Reviewing intervention taking place with a family and your own practice is the only way you will know whether things are improving for the children you are working with. It is important to be really honest and try to evaluate whether the intervention has actually improved things for that child. And if so, how? It is very easy to get caught up in identifying actions and tasks (particularly at meetings and Child Protection Conferences) and thinking that the plan is being progressed because things have been achieved (such as attending a parenting course, etc.).
>
> Good plans will detail why things are being done and how this is positively impacting on the family and child(ren). I find it is often my colleagues who will critique my practice the most and we often take the opportunity on duty to go out in pairs. I will receive suggestions for case planning or have a different perspective put to me regarding an issue or family. This can be challenging, but ultimately helps me to grow as a practitioner.

USING INTERNAL AND EXTERNAL REVIEW FOR VERIFICATION

In addition to using *post-intervention* or *before–after* models to measure change, we can also use internal and external verification techniques to assess the impact of an intervention or service. An obvious start is to ask the service user themselves whether they feel any change or improvement has occurred as a result of an intervention or over a period of time, and what they feel contributed most significantly to this. A formal review (e.g. Care Programme Approach mental health care review, Looked-After-Children [LAC] review) may be a helpful forum for this, or a questionnaire or survey may be appropriate.

Similarly, it is often helpful to also ask people involved with the person concerned (e.g. family members, carers, professionals) whether they see improvements, what they think has contributed to this, to rank significant factors (positive and negative).

Check out the website (https://study.sagepub.com/rogers2e) to access resources to help with internal and external review.

CASE STUDY APPROACHES

The case study can be a valuable way of analysing your work, demonstrating your practice to others and evidencing your learning and development. It offers an opportunity to review and critically analyse in some depth the complexity of your social work casework and your practice. The case study is sometimes called 'an authentic anecdote'. Using case studies can also bring to life casework as a narrative, enabling you also to interweave a case with the complexity of 'real life' and both explain and assess how social work interventions can often be better understood as a suite of actions and activities designed to respond to immediate crises but also interventions that perhaps require longer-term engagement.

Simons (2009) has suggested that a common theme of case study research approaches is a commitment to study the complexity and uniqueness of 'a particular project, policy, institution, program or system in a "real life" context' (2009: 21). Stake (1995) argues that the goals of case study work should centre on producing intuitive and 'naturalistic' conclusions that resonate with the experiences of its intended readers and audience (e.g. colleagues, service users and others).

Approaches, methods and techniques of 'case study' work vary considerably. Yin (1994, 2009) has described three different types of case study work: descriptive, exploratory and explanatory. He suggests case studies have at least four applications and tasks, to:

- describe the real-life context within which an intervention has occurred;
- describe the intervention itself;
- try to explain complex causal links between features and interventions described in the case study;
- explore and better understand the situations in which the intervention being evaluated has no clear set of outcomes.

Edmondson (2014) suggests that social work case study reports will be likely to include elements of:

- the brief context and background to the case;
- an analysis and report on the services and interventions involved in the case;
- the case as seen from the view of the recipients of your services;
- consideration of safeguarding and risk;
- critical self-reflection – what 'I' did and how and why I did it;
- critical analysis of social work values, theories and approaches;
- assessment of principles such as co-production, choice and control;
- assessment of a commitment to anti-oppressive practice.

Victoria, a children and families social worker, shares an approach to review she uses in her work:

> This is a case that I reviewed regularly, as it was the first assessment I completed as a newly qualified social worker.
>
> The most useful approach I used to review my practice was informal supervision. Having a manager or colleague that is also a 'critical friend' enabled me to reflect on my practice. It took another person to say 'do you notice that you sigh and roll your eyes every time you talk about this case?' for me to start to recognise my own emotional responses and how this was impacting on tasks I had to complete.

I had started to become over-critical of my approach which was affecting my self-confidence. Asking a colleague to attend a visit with me, meant that the family and I both had the chance of experiencing another person's approach. This also meant that I could ask for critical feedback, and would have the opportunity to learn from another colleague's set of skills.

CASELOAD AUDIT AND REVIEW

Most workers have to undertake some form of annual professional performance review. In relation to your caseload and casework, this provides an opportunity to take an overview of your work over the year. Bringing together learning from your individual casework can be very revealing about the scale of work you have undertaken over the year, but also to identify areas of strength in your practice as well as areas for development.

It is important to remember that you also represent a financial asset to your employer and as such it is worthwhile making an effort to quantify your work by breaking it down into meaningful constituent parts. Computerised databases facilitate this more easily and efficiently in today's services and so it is possible to calculate caseload numbers, numbers of open/closed cases, visits made, attendance at coordination meetings, liaison work, as well as assess income generation (e.g. benefits, money from charity applications, additional financial support) and even cost–benefit analysis (e.g. projecting the reduction of days in institutionalised care × cost per day).

Visit the website (https://study.sagepub.com/rogers2e) to view evaluations of community health and social care programmes, which include cost–benefit analysis.

LINKING REVIEW AND EVALUATION OF YOUR SOCIAL WORK PRACTICE TO WIDER PROFESSIONAL SOCIAL WORK PRINCIPLES

Increasingly, social work practice is being undertaken within multidisciplinary services and within agencies where social work is not the lead agency. This means you cannot assume the agency you work in and the professionals you work alongside will always know what a professional social worker does or is supposed to do. Part of your professional role is to help others – service users, carers and other professionals – to understand your work, to make a case for the contribution you can make in relation to complex and challenging areas of work, to offer a range of specialist skills and knowledge to the area of work you are practising in. This can easily get lost within formalised, competency and audit-led reviews, particularly given the rush and pressure of day-to-day work, the frequent change and reorganisation of public services. Refuge is taken in looking at what is immediately in front of us, typically the immediate daily jobs and bureaucracy of the job (e.g. getting the agency's assessment forms completed, getting tasks done on time, keeping our records up to date, doing all our visits). These are relevant tasks, but the expectations of professional social work require more than this and you need to not lose sight of this in your work. In essence, you need to be constantly thinking about not just what you do, but also how and why.

PROFESSIONAL PURPOSE AND VALUES: OUR ETHICAL COMPASS

The IFSW agreed a new Global Definition of Social Work in 2014, which states that, 'Social work is a practice-based profession … that promotes social change and development, social cohesion, and the empowerment and liberation of people' (IFSW, 2014). In its history, social work has made claims to a philosophical tradition of egalitarianism and a belief and commitment to social justice, humane values and principles. Promoting positive social change, personal development, community and social cohesion are central tenets of social work practice (Edmondson, 2014). We need to keep these principles and features in mind in both planning and justifying our work (at the front end of social work process) and in turn to be able to better appraise what we do and how well we do it (at the end of the cycle).

LINKING YOUR SOCIAL WORK PRACTICE TO THE GOALS AND REVIEW PROCESSES OF YOUR SERVICE

The IFSW definition of social work emphasises the importance of social workers as practical and active professionals located within communities and operating through a range of welfare settings and services. Social workers can be found in a range of services and settings (e.g. local and national government agencies, voluntary, charitable and religious organisations). Working in such organisations brings with it specific actions and tasks expected of you as an employee, typically identified in your job description and role specification, in turn linked to the ethos and mission statements of the service.

Good learning organisations – hopefully one like yours – encourage their staff to: adopt the ethos of their service and understand how each worker fits into delivering its goals; contribute to improving the service and its delivery; identify new and emerging problems and help set new goals for the service. Irrespective of the organisation you work in, this is an important critical reflection and investigation for you to undertake, for the people you work alongside and, perhaps most importantly, the people you directly work with. Review and evaluation of your own work and the work of the organisation should be part of your annual formal professional development review.

CONCLUSION

Social work is complex and challenging work, often undertaken in contexts where the people we work with frequently feel marginalised, excluded and targeted; services are stretched and underresourced; workers are frequently stressed and working in cultures of blame. The opportunity to review and evaluate social work should be seen as an important opportunity to stop, think and learn. Done properly, it can audit work and output, but much more importantly, it can be used to understand and learn from our past actions and behaviour towards becoming better professionals with better skills and knowledge, which in turn produces better experiences and opportunities for the people we work with in the future.

Having read this chapter, you should be able to:

- Better understand the importance of review and evaluation in improving professional practice and development;
- Identify features to consider when preparing to review your work;
- Identify some basic models and approaches which you can use in practice.

RECOMMENDED READING

Moriarty, J. and Manthorpe, J. (2016) *The Effectiveness of Social Work with Adults: A Systematic Scoping Review.* London: Social Care Workforce Research Unit, King's College London. Available at: www.ripfa.org.uk/latest-news/news-scwru-effectiveness-of-social-work-mar2016/ (accessed 3 March 2019).

Quincy, R., Lu, S. and Huang, C.-C. (2012) *SWOT Analysis: Raising Capacity of Your Organization in Relation to Social Work.* Beijing: China Philanthropy Research Institute

Simons, H. (2009) *Case Study Research in Practice.* London: Sage.

Sutton, C. (2006) *Helping Families with Troubled Children: A Preventative Approach* (2nd edn). Chichester: Wiley-Blackwell.

22

Court Skills
Dawn Whitaker

Links to the Professional Capabilities Framework

● Professionalism   ● Knowledge   ● Rights, justice and economic wellbeing   ● Critical reflection and analysis   ● Skills and interventions   ● Contexts and organisations

Links to the Knowledge and Skills Statement for Child and Family Social Workers

● Relationships and effective direct work   ● Communication   ● Adult mental ill-health, substance misuse, domestic violence, physical ill-health and disability   ● Abuse and neglect of children   ● Child and family assessment   ● Analysis, decision-making, planning and review   ● The law and the family and youth justice systems   ● The role of supervision ● Organisational context

Links to the Knowledge and Skills Statement for Social Workers in Adult Services

● The role of social workers working with adults   ● Person centred practice   ● Safeguarding ● Mental capacity   ● Effective assessments and outcome-based support planning ● Supervision, critical reflection and analysis   ● Organisational context   ● Professional ethics and leadership

Key messages

- Court work is central to social work practice.
- Good court work is founded upon everyday social work skills.
- Court skills can bridge the gap between law in theory and law in practice.
- Court and legal skills are fundamental to legitimate, defensible and professional decision-making and practice.

INTRODUCTION

As part of the early assessment or at the end of the ASPIRE process it may be that the evaluation of the situation, and subsequent intervention perhaps, is not favourable. At this stage it may be that more formal processes are called for. This chapter, therefore, considers the role of court work as fundamental to social work processes. Indeed, research raises a number of issues regarding social work practice in the courts. Of particular concern is the rising number of applications for court orders, a mixed response to social work evidence in court, and issues relating to social workers' confidence and preparedness for undertaking court work (Lewis and Erlen, 2012: 3). Given the centrality of court work to social work practice, and the far-reaching consequences for individuals and families subjected to it, it is imperative that we take action to develop our professional practice in this regard:

> By learning the 'rules of the game' and developing the skills required, you are not compromising the values of your profession; rather, you are establishing yourself as an equal partner in the court setting, which provides the opportunity to influence events and potentially make a difference to the experience of service users. (Seymour and Seymour, 2011: 3)

SOCIAL WORK AND COURT

Whilst the two main areas of practice for which practitioners give evidence in court are **youth justice** and *children and families* social work, instances of court-related intervention in other areas of practice are growing (Johns, 2017). This may be as part of:

- **domestic violence** proceedings;
- giving evidence at a **public inquiry** about the death of a child;
- giving evidence in the **Coroner's Court**;
- a tribunal regarding mental health, asylum, employment or education;
- in safeguarding adult or **judicial review** proceedings in the **High Court** or **Court of Protection**;
- in **best interests** and/or **deprivation of liberty** disputes under the Mental Capacity Act 2005 and/or Liberty Protection Safeguards (Cooper, 2014; Johns, 2017).

Although some of the cases that reach court reflect examples of less than good practice, we must remind ourselves that a significant amount of good practice goes 'unnoticed', and that the courts and **ombudsman** have also found social work to be 'lawful, rational and reasonable' (Cooper, 2014: 4; Preston-Shoot, 2014: 14).

Reflective activity

- Can it ever be beneficial for social work decisions to be scrutinised by a court?
- Consider this question both from the perspective of people who use social work services as well that of professional social workers.

Activity comment

Points for consideration:

- The court is a powerful arbiter between the rights of individuals and the state.
- The court can provide an independent means of challenge for individuals and families who disagree with social work decisions and actions.
- The court can provide individuals and families with **legal advocacy** and redress where local authorities have acted unlawfully.
- The court can be helpful in clarifying social work's professional understanding and application of the law in practice.

Yet, despite these benefits, it is not unusual for social workers to be defensive about being in court, especially when traditionally it was seen as a last resort or even punishment: 'It's a parade of all your failures' (Parker, 1979: 110). This statement typifies how many social workers feel about court work: that is, as 'an encroachment upon, if not a reproach' of their own practice (Parker, 1979: 110). This defensiveness originates from the 1970s, when legislative changes brought local authorities into closer alignment with the courts, giving rise to negative criticism (Fishwick, 1989: 146) which continues to this day. Indeed, more recent research examining **legal literacy** within the profession, found that social workers struggle with 'critical analysis of the legal rules, and applying skills and reasoning to practice' (RiPfA, 2015).

In response, we must hone the skills required to counter the difficulties outlined above and present a positive and proficient image of social work in the courts. After all, it must be expected that 'in an increasingly sophisticated and rights-conscious society, the professional competence of social work practitioners will be increasingly tested' (Fishwick, 1989: 148). This is echoed by a growing move towards increased transparency and **open justice** across the English court system (Series et al., 2015).

THE ROLE OF SOCIAL WORK IN COURT

Social workers usually undertake one of two main roles in court work:

A professional witness: usually a local authority social worker, called to provide evidence on a matter for the court, related to a case in which they have direct involvement.

An independent social worker: this may be as a **children's guardian,** or independent social work witness.

Whichever role you undertake, expect to be asked to explain your professional qualifications, experience and specialist knowledge of the matter before the court, and be prepared to be questioned and challenged on this.

Whilst it is natural to experience anxiety when undertaking court work, especially for the first time, 'appearing in court can be fun' (Johns, 2017: 146). For some, there are benefits associated with being challenged and having their knowledge and practice scrutinised. This can aid clarity of thought, build competence and confidence, and lead to improved practice outcomes. For others, even those who are less eager at the prospect, it can be a cathartic experience, as it enables them to test out hypotheses and assessments, evidence recommendations and/or justify their actions (Johns, 2017).

Reflective activity

What actions could you take that might alleviate, mitigate or resolve any fears or anxieties you might experience about giving evidence in court?

Be assured that if you work in a local authority and are acting in court on their behalf, you will be supported in your preparation by your agency's legal advisors, who will also be present if you are called to give evidence during the proceedings.

Remember that whilst solicitors and barristers are subjective in their representations on behalf of their client, that is, they aim to make the best of his or her case, and diminish that of their opponent's, the opposite is true in social work (Fishwick, 1989: 40). As social workers, our primary duty is to the court, not the individual we are providing evidence about or our employer. It is the legal advocate's responsibility to make their case, not yours. The court is the final arbiter of all evidence presented to it.

It is important to note that the image of social work and social work evidence has improved over time. This is illustrated in this statement by Sir James Munby, a retired English judge who was president of the **Family Division of the High Court** of England and Wales:

> Social workers are experts. In just the same way, I might add, CAFCASS [**Children and Family Court Advisory and Support Service**] officers are experts. In every care case we have at least two experts – a social worker and a guardian – yet we have grown up in a culture of believing that they are not really experts and that we therefore need experts with a capital E. The plain fact is that much of the time we do not. (Sir James Munby P, 2013 in Ruck Keene et al., 2014: 333)

However, this does not negate our duty to maintain professional standards or relieve us of ensuring that our work stands up to appropriate scrutiny. Failure to do so will continue to result in criticism, as highlighted in this recent case:

I was somewhat critical, and unapologetically so, of the way in which the report … was written. Reports by experts are not written solely for the benefit of other professionals, the advocates and the Judge. The parents and other litigants need to understand what is being said and why. … Otherwise there may not be a fair hearing. … There were passages in the report which were written in language which made their meaning quite opaque. I suspect as far as P was concerned, these passages might just as well have been written in a foreign language. (*Derbyshire County Council* v. *SH* [2015] EWFC B102: Paragraphs 34, 35, 38)

Disheartening as such criticism is, it is nonetheless 'instructive' in learning the dos and don'ts of court work (Preston-Shoot, 2014: 14). For additional information on these and other cases regarding the role of social work in the courts, visit the website (https://study.sagepub.com/rogers2e).

COURT SKILLS

> ### Reflective activity
>
> Based on what you have read so far, what social work skills do you think are important to court work?

Rather than develop *specific* court skills, we must hone everyday social work skills to be effective in the court context. On this basis, it is important that you read and understand this chapter in union with the other chapters of this book.

Beyond the court room

When we think of court skills, we tend to focus on the physical act of being in court, for example giving witness evidence. However, the practice reality is that court work involves a range of skills and activities that actually take place away from the location of the court itself. This includes record keeping, undertaking interviews and assessments, writing reports and witness statements, and consulting other professionals – most of which take place before we give direct witness evidence.

Administration

Whilst this might seem obvious, good professional practice requires good administration. Whilst all court work is administratively burdensome at times, lack of care in this regard can result in unnecessary delay, disappointment, breach of confidentiality and even injustice (Fishwick, 1989: 154). As Cooper puts it 'records can make or break a case', as they are often used to establish a case history and judge the quality of practice (2014: 20).

Preparation

One of the best ways to prepare for court work is to shadow a more experienced colleague. Where possible, do so from the point at which a court hearing is indicated. This way you will be able to shadow your colleague throughout their out-of-court preparation, as well as during their time in court. If you can, include any court-related assessments or interviews in the shadowing process, as well as the preparation of reports and witness statements. In doing so, you will gain invaluable insight into how the preliminary court-related tasks form the basis of the in-court action. This is vital, both in terms of learning how to translate your assessments, hypotheses and recommendations into evidence, and the ability to explain and justify this under cross-examination.

Furthermore, the act of shadowing provides for more than just the nuts and bolts of gathering and preparing evidence as outlined above. It also affords an opportunity to get to know the practicalities of the court's processes, for example the layout of the court, how witnesses are dealt with, how to address the different parties, what to wear and so on.

The importance of good preparation cannot be overstated, it will help you feel in command of your evidence and assist you to reduce and manage any anxiety or nervousness that you might experience during the process (Fishwick, 1989: 45).

WHAT COUNTS AS EVIDENCE?

This varies according to the category of law and the court; for example, it is different in criminal and **civil proceedings**. However, your evidence is likely to start out as a written report or witness statement, leading to a recommendation to the court, followed by direct evidence, and possible cross-examination.

Written evidence

When asked to provide written evidence you are usually directed by the court regarding what is expected; for example, the nature, format, scope, length and so on. In the majority of cases this takes the form of a report or witness statement, but it may also include risk assessments or care planning documentation. Whatever form the written work takes, it is expected to conform to certain key principles (see Tables 22.1 and 22.2).

Table 22.1 Key principles for the format of written work

The format:

- It adheres to the appropriate template/format (where one exists).
- It should be relevant and concise, with an absence of extraneous information.
- It is clearly written in plain, neutral, non-emotional language, and avoids jargon.
- Pages and paragraphs are numbered, and section headings are visible to aid easy navigation.

(Continued)

Table 22.1   (Continued)

- It is proofread and contains no spelling and grammatical errors.
- It is made available for the agreed deadline set by the court.
- A name, date and signature are usually required, and some courts also request a short professional profile as an addendum.
- Some courts also require a professional declaration, but they will advise where this is the case.

Table 22.2   Key principles for the content of written work

The content:

- It reflects the court's instructions.
- It clearly establishes the general 'facts' of the case, as well as 'threshold' evidence (e.g. of significant harm under the Children Act).
- It cites *all* sources that are relied upon in the text, even if **'hearsay'**.
- It distinguishes between fact, interpretation and professional opinion.
- It is research-informed, and draws upon theory, research, policy and legislation.
- It usually contains some appropriate background, a case chronology and social context, including cultural and religious factors where relevant.
- It may contain or refer to needs and risk assessment documentation.
- It should be balanced and contain information about strengths as well as difficulties (as appropriate).
- It clearly sets out the author's reasoning, and preferably contains a weighing and balancing *analysis* of the different options available to the court (not just description).
- It contains clear, well-founded recommendations that are lawful, available and fit for purpose (if applicable).
- Where there is a conflict of opinion, this is fully and impartially discussed to avoid accusations of bias.
- It states any unforeseen limitations, e.g. lack of access to appropriate records or information (Cooper, 2014; Fishwick, 1989; Johns, 2017).

For further information on honing your social work written skills see Chapter 18.

Direct evidence

The skills related to providing direct evidence in court are similar to those required for good writing. It is important to follow the court's instructions, be clear and concise in your verbal communication, and be able to substantiate your evidence and recommendations.

Protocol and practicalities

Arrive in good time. This is important in order to find the appropriate court room, but also in ensuring that you have time to access refreshments and so on. On arrival, make yourself known to the appropriate usher or clerk of the court, and compose yourself ahead of the proceedings commencing. It is important to seek guidance regarding the specific protocol of the court you are going to attend. Table 22.3 details the etiquette that exists within some of the more formal courts, and the different forms of address used in each.

Table 22.3 Formal court etiquette

Court	Form of address	Physical movement
In all courts	You should address the magistrate or judge, *not* the person that asks you the questions.	Ask the usher or clerk of the court where to sit – this will depend on your specific role, and may alter as you undertake different roles in the proceedings.
		Always stand when the magistrate or judge enters, rises or leaves the court room.
		In more formal courts, you will be asked to give an oath (*swear on a holy text*) or affirmation (*make a solemn promise*) that you will be truthful.
		Witnesses often stand when giving evidence (unless it is in the family court).
	Form of address	
Magistrates' Court	Collectively as 'Your Worships' or as 'Sir' or 'Madam' individually	
High Court	'My Lord' or 'My Lady'	
Family Court/ County Court	'Your Honour' in the County Court or 'Sir' or 'Madam' (unless it is the Family Division of the High Court)	
Tribunals		
Crown Court	'Your Honour' unless in the Old Bailey, then 'My Lord'	
In all courts	Solicitors and barristers refer to each other as 'learned friends'. Other professionals refer to barristers as 'counsel'.	
	The clerk to the court is usually referred to as the 'the learned clerk'.	
	All other participants in the court process should be afforded the courtesy of Mr, Mrs, Miss or Ms followed by their surname.	

In the witness box

Communication and confidence are key. Listen very carefully to what you are asked, and ensure you fully understand before responding. If you are unclear about what is being asked, or are not sure how to respond, seek clarification. Do not rush your responses, and make sure you articulate yourself clearly, using notes where appropriate (however, be mindful that these can be shared with all parties). If interrupted by a barrister, ask the magistrate or judge if you can be allowed to continue with your explanation, but don't speak over others. Be honest, concise and to the point in your responses, taking care not to go off topic. Accept where you may have made a mistake and move on. Stay calm, neutral and non-defensive. Only comment on matters within your direct knowledge or area of expertise.

Cooper (2014: 63) outlines three cross-examination techniques to be aware of when giving evidence:

1   The use of leading questions: questions that suggest a preferred answer.
2   Attempts to control the witness: the advocate knows the answer before asking it.
3   The 'tell – don't ask' technique: action to prevent the witness's explanation.

As previously discussed, preparation is key to giving good evidence in court. Go through your evidence in advance of the hearing with a colleague, taking time to check your argument. In doing so, make use of prediction; that is, try to anticipate the types of questions you might be asked (Johns, 2017). Useful tips include thinking about what you would want to know if you were the judge. What is the individual's and family's view, and how does this differ from your own and other professional perspectives (Johns, 2017)?

Role-play activity

Taking into account the guidance above on providing written and direct evidence:

1   Write a short statement about a piece of practice.
2   Using the guidance on providing written evidence, write a 150-word explanation to justify the initial statement.
3   Share the statement and explanation with a peer, and using the guidance on giving direct evidence, role play being cross-examined on it.
4   Swap roles and repeat the exercise.
5   Provide some reflective feedback to each other about the experience.

Professionalism

Whilst this is usually assessed in accordance with our written and oral evidence, it is also determined by our professional demeanour. Key features include:

- *Professional identity*: This means being able to clearly articulate the remit of your role and function to the court. This should entail a sense of competence in analysing and interpreting evidence. As Fishwick puts it, 'it is an unwise practitioner who either draws those boundaries so narrowly as to appear uninformed and incompetent in areas where his or her expertise can reasonably be expected, or draws them so widely as to appear to stray arrogantly into areas more properly covered by others' (1989: 152). For example, a child and family social worker *is* qualified to provide an opinion on the best interests of a child they are working with, but they are *not* qualified to provide an opinion on how an injury might have occurred based on hospital records (Cooper, 2014: 45).

- *What to wear?* Rightly or wrongly, 'cues' as to individual and professional character and reliability are often taken from 'demeanour and dress' (Parker, 1979: 112). Even in modern-day courts, conservative attire dominates the court room. There is an expectation on all parties of deference to the court. Whilst bearing the above formalities in mind, it is important to dress in a manner that enables you to feel comfortable, professional and confident.
- *Humanity and aftercare*: It is important to remember that court can be a very stressful experience for non-professionals. This is reiterated by research examining the experiential accounts of people involved in legal proceedings (Johns, 2017). Whilst it is not our role to 'humanise the legal process', our skills can be helpful to others who are less familiar with it (Fishwick, 1989: 155). Our role in this context is to listen, observe and respond appropriately to each person or family.
- *Final tips*: Maintaining a professional demeanour is particularly important in the moment when the court either accepts or rejects your professional recommendations. Remember not to take this personally, as professional challenge is inevitable, and practice doesn't always work out the way we expect. Avoid outward celebration or disappointment whatever the outcome and make use of supervision to manage your inward sentiments. Your actions at this time could have a significant impact on any ongoing work with that individual or family.

Remember to maintain critical reflexivity in all aspects of your court work. Be aware of the power imbalance involved in the court's processes and try to mitigate this through anti-oppressive practice. Revisit Chapters 7 and 8 for more information in this regard.

CONCLUSION

This chapter introduced the role of social work in the courts, before illustrating how everyday social work skills can be used to good effect in court work. It emphasised the role of courts as something we should value not fear, asserting it as an opportunity to celebrate good practice and advance the future of the profession. We recommend you read this chapter in conjunction with those outlined above.

Having read this chapter, you should be able to:

- Understand the relationship between social work and the court;
- Be clear about your role in the court process;
- Begin to hone your court skills;
- Know how to demonstrate professionalism in court.

Visit the website to watch videos on court room advocacy and skills, and preparing a young person for court (https://study.sagepub.com/rogers2e).

RECOMMENDED READING

Cooper, P. (2014) *Court and Legal Skills*. Basingstoke: Palgrave Macmillan.

Fishwick, C. (1989) *Court Work* (2nd edn). Birmingham: PEPAR Publications.

Johns, R. (2017) *Using the Law in Social Work* (7th edn). London: Sage.

Lewis, J. and Erlen, N. (2012) *Resource Pack: Evidence Matters in Family Justice*. Totnes: Research in Practice.

Seymour, C. and Seymour, R. (2011) *Courtroom and Report Writing Skills for Social Workers* (2nd edn). Exeter: Learning Matters.

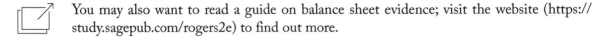 You may also want to read a guide on balance sheet evidence; visit the website (https://study.sagepub.com/rogers2e) to find out more.

KEY SOCIAL WORK
THEORIES AND METHODS

The final section of this book will provide a critical backdrop to Part I and Part II by introducing some of the theories and models that are dominant in social work. Barker (2003: 434) offers a definition of theory as 'a group of related **hypotheses**, concepts, and constructs, based on facts and observations, that attempts to explain a particular phenomenon'. The importance of **theory**, as well as other forms of knowledge (for instance, experiential knowledge), cannot be underestimated in the complex activity that constitutes social work as theory represents an explanatory framework (Oko, 2008). Each day, practitioners are required to work with people who experience multiple forms of adversity, discrimination and deprivation, and social workers are tasked with making sense of perplexing and conflicting information that is often incomplete and contradictory. Sometimes this information is modest and at other times you may feel swamped by the amount of paperwork that has been produced in relation to one individual. Applying theory can help you to make sense of this information. It can help you to understand a problem and make predictions about future behaviour or risks and, as such, it can also guide decision-making and inform interventions. Indeed, theory helps us to 'make judgements about: what we think is going on; what can done to help, and why' (Oko, 2008: 17). Part III will present some of the established theories and **paradigms** that are acknowledged to be helpful in these processes.

Parts I and II have demonstrated how social work requires practitioners to employ a range of skills from communication to assessment to working with other professionals and within organisational structures. In addition, these require cognitive processes such as the engagement with reflective practice as well as self and intersubjective awareness. An essential aspect of social work, then, is the ability to move from micro-relations (the daily interactions with service users) to consider meso-level influences (the boundaries of organisational policy, or the engagement with communities). Social work also relies on you having an ever-evolving sophisticated and nuanced understanding of the structural factors that impact on everyday life (political decisions, legislation, ideology, and structures such as gender, ethnicity and class to name a few). It is easy to see how formal theories would enhance these processes and interactions at each level (micro, meso and macro) by offering a means of making sense of our experiences and those of others.

As well as theory, Part III introduces particular methods and models for social work practice that we consider to be congruent with relationship-based and person-centred work. We made the decision to locate this section last as we wanted to emphasise the centrality of skills and practice, before moving the reader to consider the theoretical underpinning of the wide array of skills that are previously discussed in this book, whilst also pointing out that theory is referred to throughout; indeed, RBP and person-centred work both offer approaches that are underpinned by theories for practice.

Strengths-Based and Solution-Focused Approaches

Michaela Rogers

Links to the Professional Capabilities Framework

• Values and ethics • Diversity and equality • Knowledge • Critical reflection and analysis • Skills and interventions

Links to the Knowledge and Skills Statement for Child and Family Practitioners

• Relationships and effective direct work • Communication • Child and family assessment

Links to the Knowledge and Skills Statement for Social Workers in Adult Services

• Person-centred practice • Mental capacity • Effective assessments and outcome-based support planning • Direct work with individuals and families

Key messages

- Focusing on strengths helps to move away from a preoccupation with risk and risk management.
- Working in a strengths-based and solution-focused way helps to develop partnerships with service users and recognises their uniqueness.
- Strengths-based and solution-focused work allows service users to build skills and resources for the future.

INTRODUCTION

Social work has been identified with a deficit approach to working with people, where 'clients become clients because they have deficits, problems, pathologies and diseases ... they are, in some critical way, flawed and weak' (Saleebey, 1997: 15). In this **paradigm** for practice, social work is viewed as an activity characterised by the need to assess, manage and diminish problems and deficits. More recently, this approach to social work has been criticised for being prescriptive, bureaucratic and preoccupied with the task of managing risk. Therefore, it is important that attempts are made to identify the positives: for example, the strengths in a service user's capabilities and circumstances, as well as other resources and support systems.

Dennis Saleebey's (1997) influential text on strengths-based approaches has helped to move beyond such a negative paradigm of service users' lives to one that promotes a strengths perspective. This approach argues that building on people's strengths is of greater value than focusing on their deficits as the latter serves to negate a person's capabilities or pre-existing coping mechanisms which can contribute to finding solutions. Furthermore, a strengths perspective 'acknowledges the inherent capacity to adapt, learn, grow, change, and use ... inner resources to confront and respond to daily challenges' (Trevithick, 2012: 349). This approach has been critiqued, however, and described as part of the neoliberal agenda serving to reduce the role and expenditure of government, placing further burden on ordinary people in their time of need. Notwithstanding, the strengths perspective has garnered considerable interest over the last couple of decades and support with many other social work models clearly influenced by the philosophy of the strengths perspective, including the solution-focused approach.

THE PRINCIPLES OF A STRENGTHS-BASED PERSPECTIVE

Saleebey (2013) argues that a strengths-based approach is a perspective, or lens, rather than a **theory** or model. It offers a way of viewing service users' lives recognising an understanding of the world that is ever evolving and this can be employed alongside other complementary approaches or models for social work practice (for instance, **task-centred** work). Saleebey (2013: 17–21) outlines some underlying principles of strengths-based practice:

- Every individual, group, family and community has strengths.
- Trauma, abuse and adversity may be harmful, but they may also be sources of strength and opportunity.
- Do not assume to know the limits of a person, group or community's ability to change and grow.
- Best practice should be collaborative practice.
- Every environment (family, or community) will be abundant with resources.
- Social work is about care, care-taking and hope.

A strengths perspective helps to address the power imbalances that are inherent within the relationship between a social worker and service user. It does so by incorporating an element of empowering practice that situates the service user as the 'problem solver' (rather than as the cause of the problem). Another way that strengths-based work addresses power imbalances is through its integration of a partnership approach to working *with* individuals and communities.

Strengths-based work is effective when the social work practitioner asks 'good questions' (Trevithick, 2012: 350), but these are of a particular nature and include the following:

Survival questions: What has worked in the past? How have you previously coped? In the past how did you manage this problem/challenge/situation?

Support questions: Who helps you and gives you support and guidance? Where are these people? Are they still around to support and offer understanding?

Esteem questions: When people say nice things about you, how do you feel? What are these things? What have you accomplished in your life that you are proud of?

Perspective questions: What thoughts and ideas do you have about the problem/challenge/situation?

Change questions: What would you like to change the most in your life, and how can I help you?

Meaning questions: What do you value most in life? What gives your life meaning?

A SOLUTION-FOCUSED APPROACH

Solution-focused brief therapy (SFBT) derives from a strengths perspective and was developed by Steve de Shazer and colleagues in a therapeutic setting during the 1980s (O'Connell and Palmer, 2005). O'Connell offers a definition: 'The Solution Focused approach builds upon clients' resources. It aims to help clients achieve their preferred outcomes by evoking and co-constructing solutions to their problems' (2001: 1). SFBT is a brief intervention intended to help individuals to identify past behaviours that produced positive results with the hope that these actions can be repeated to build further success. Shennan (2014: 2) describes solution-focused practice as a 'talking-based activity … and one of the main activities of a solution-focused practitioner is to ask questions, intended to help the talking go in such a way that it does become useful'. The specific solution-focused techniques of talking with people (detailed below) enables an individual to explore the behaviours and attitudes about a problem to identify an 'exception': this is an exception in the past when behaviours and attitudes have produced a desired change or outcome. In this way, people identify their own solutions and are able to see that change is possible.

. . . .

Case study: Signs of Safety

During the 1990s Turnell and Edwards (1999) drew from strengths-based and solution-focused approaches to develop their model Signs of Safety (SoS), in their quest to reform child protection practice in Western Australia. Turnell (2012) claims that SoS is constantly evolving as a response to its international growth; SoS is used in countries including Australia, the USA, Canada, the UK, Denmark, Sweden, Finland and Japan.

The SoS model is designed to create a shared focus among all stakeholders involved in child protection work. This includes families as well as all relevant agencies. Essentially, the SoS framework involves 'creating a map of the circumstances surrounding a vulnerable child' with three underpinning principles to this process (Turnell, 2012: 8). These are:

- The development of constructive working relationships between families and professionals should be at the heart of child protection work.
- The core professional stance should be to foster a questioning approach, or a spirit of enquiry.
- Approaches to child protection practice should move away from paternalism and be developed hand-in-hand with practitioners to effect more rigour, skilfulness and greater depth of thinking in daily complex and challenging work.

In essence, the primary focus is on developing and increasing levels of safety for children and therefore parents are required to demonstrate behaviour that is 'measurably safe' (Milner et al., 2015). The SoS Assessment and Planning Framework offers a set of tools for practitioners to use in the line of enquiry by asking: what are we worried about? (considers past harm, future danger and complicating factors); what's working well? (identifies existing strengths and safety); what needs to happen? (this is oriented to future safety). Safety planning is undertaken with families to offer a genuine opportunity for their participation in an approach designed to be proactive, structured and monitored.

Visit the website (https://study.sagepub.com/rogers2e) to find out further information about SoS.

. . . .

APPLYING THEORY IN PRACTICE: A SOLUTION-FOCUSED INTERVENTION

Whilst the SFBT model offers a specific approach, the range of techniques contained within the solution-focused practitioner's toolkit has much to offer social work practice. These are identified below:

Problem-free talk

Whilst it is useful to implement problem-free talk throughout much of an intervention, visit or session, there are times when this is difficult and, sometimes, not possible. Nevertheless, at the start of an intervention, try to use problem-free talk as this conveys an important message that the person is more than the sum of their difficulties.

Exception seeking

When discussing a problem, active listening will help you to identify a time when the service user has managed the problem better or times when the problem has not been present. You may also be able to identify transferable skills, abilities or strategies from other parts of the individual's experiences. There are always exceptions waiting to be found (O'Connell and Palmer, 2005). You can elicit this type of information through *coping questions* (Shennan, 2014) which seek to identify a time when a service user has coped with a problem, or uncover how a service user manages with a continuing issue.

Competence seeking

Useful in the pursuit of emancipatory practice, this technique encourages people to acknowledge their own resources, strengths and qualities. This is particularly meaningful if people are entrenched in their problems or have been immersed in social work interventions for so long they have lost sight of their personal capabilities or any of the positives about their circumstances.

Scaling questions

Scaling is a very practical and versatile tool as scaling questions can be used in almost any situation. The purpose of scaling is to help the service user to 'set small identifiable goals; measure progress and establish priorities for action' (O'Connell and Palmer, 2005: 9). In this sense, it can also be used with lots of other social work methods, such as task-centred practice (see Chapter 26). Ask service users to consider feelings, thoughts, general circumstances or specific issues and rate them; use a scale of 0 to 10, where 10 represents no problem and 0 the worst.

The miracle question

This is a key technique found in the toolkit of a solution-focused practitioner. The miracle question invites people to imagine a future where a solution to their problem has been found and it no longer dominates their lives. The miracle question:

> Imagine when you go to sleep one night, a miracle happens and the problems we've been talking about disappear. As you were asleep, you did not know that a miracle had happened. When you wake up what will be the first signs for you that a miracle has happened? (de Shazer, 1988 cited in O'Connell and Palmer, 2005: 8)

You can rephrase the question however you like. The importance of the miracle question is that using the imagination in this way encourages people to think positively and imagine a brighter future.

   Visit the website to listen to Guy Shennan talk about the first part of the process in solution-focused work (https://study.sagepub.com/rogers2e).

. . . .

Case study: Len

You have just begun work with Len, an elderly man who has recently lost his wife, Lucy. Len found himself living alone for the first time in 40 years. He has depression and has been misusing alcohol; Len says it helps him to cope with loneliness. However, with your support, Len has been encouraged to join a local social group at his community centre and he has made a great many new friends. You call Len one morning to see how he is as his daughter, Louise, has telephoned to say that she is worried about him and that she cannot cope with him as well as her own grief.

Worker: Hello, Len. How are you today?

Len: Don't know. No good. What do you want?

Worker: Just ringing to see how you are, Len. Are you not feeling great?

Len: I feel terrible. I don't know why I got up. I miss Lucy. Don't know what to do now she's not here. What's the point ...

Worker: Aw, Len. Don't think like that. Your children and grandchildren need you to be there for them. Louise has been on the phone and she's worried about you. She's visiting on Friday with the grandchildren and they'll be looking forward to seeing you. It won't do them any good to see you sad.

Len: So, what do you want? What are you phoning for – just to give me a hard time?

Worker: No, of course not. I'm not trying to give you a hard time.

(*Len hangs up.*)

Alternatively, a solution-focused dialogue:

Worker: Hello, Len. How are you today?

Len: Don't know. No good. What do you want?

Worker: Just ringing to see how you are, Len, because you've been doing so well and it's the social club today.

Len: I feel terrible. I don't know why I got up. I miss Lucy. Don't know what to do now she's not here. What's the point ...

Worker: Len, you still have an amazing family, who care for you very much and I know they are really looking forward to seeing you on Friday. I can imagine you'll have a wonderful time at the social club today, just as you did last week.

Len: Not going, don't feel like it.

Worker: I think you said it was wonderful to be there. What helped you to get there last time as I recall that you said you didn't feel like it much then?

Len: Don't know ... went with Arthur next door.

Worker: Oh yes. Is he calling for you again? I remember now that Arthur told me that he really values your friendship and your support to him since his wife died. You seem to be supporting each other.

Len: Suppose so.

Worker: So, you'll go today?

Len: Suppose so. Yes.

Worker: Brilliant, Len. I'm so proud of you, and Louise will be too. Speak to you next week.

Reflective question

- Which solution-focused techniques can you spot in this dialogue?

• •

Table 23.1   Benefits and limitations of strengths-based and solution-focused work

Benefits
The strengths perspective represents the catalyst for an important paradigm shift in social work and moves practitioners away from a preoccupation with risk.
It prompts you to consider risks and strengths, and thus it is empowering as individuals are encouraged to identify positives and find their own solutions.
A strengths-based approach enables people to consolidate strengths and build resilience through an anti-oppressive, emancipatory and culturally sensitive approach to practice (Trevithick, 2012).
Solution-focused work is empowering as people come to see themselves as 'enablers' and 'problem solvers'.

Limitations
It is not always possible to promote strengths and work in partnership if safeguarding and other protective work is to be undertaken.
Drawing on strengths and using a solution-focused approach requires skill and if not undertaken well and practised appropriately, it can attract criticism particularly for not addressing concerns well or taking matters seriously.
Highlighting someone's strengths too soon within the social worker/service user relationship can make people feel that there are great expectations on their capacity to effect change. This can actually be experienced as disempowering and invalidating.
The resources required to work towards a solution are not always available (Jack and Gill, 2003).

CONCLUSION

This chapter has explored the benefits and techniques that a strengths-based and solution-focused framework can offer from the position that a positive lens can be applied to the scrutiny of people's lives whilst simultaneously acknowledging the presenting risks. These approaches offer flexible choices and can also be implemented alongside other methods of working; for example, a task-centred approach (see Chapter 26).

Having read this chapter, you should be able to:

- Outline some of the underlying principles of a strengths-based model;
- Identify a number of questioning techniques associated with both approaches;
- Acknowledge that strengths-based working and solution-focused approaches have both benefits and limitations.

RECOMMENDED READING

Milner, J. and Myers, S. (2017) *Creative Ideas for Solution Focused Practice: Inspiring Guidance, Ideas and Activities*. London: Jessica Kingsley.

Saleebey, D. (2013) *The Strengths Perspective in Social Work Practice* (6th edn). London: Pearson.

Shennan, G. (2019) *Solution-Focused Practice: Effective Communication to Facilitate Change* (2nd edn). Basingstoke: Palgrave Macmillan.

Turnell, A. (2017) *The Signs of Safety: Comprehensive Briefing Paper*. Perth, Australia: Resolutions Consultancy.

Systems Theory and an Ecological Approach

Michaela Rogers and Jennifer Cooper

Links to the Professional Capabilities Framework

● Professionalism   ● Values and ethics   ● Knowledge   ● Critical reflection and analysis
● Skills and interventions

Links to the Knowledge and Skills Statement for Child and Family Practitioners

● Relationships and effective direct work   ● Communication   ● Child and family assessment

Links to the Knowledge and Skills Statement for Social Workers in Adult Services

● Effective assessments and outcome-based support planning   ● Direct work with individuals and families

Key messages

- An ecological perspective prompts us to consider an individual *and* their environment.
- Systems theory considers an individual to be a system in their own right, but they are also parts of other subsystems (such as the family).
- Working systemically allows input from multiple professionals with varied experiences, skills and knowledge that can create better hypotheses and more effective intervention planning.

INTRODUCTION

An ecological approach orients us towards 'understanding people and their environment and the nature of their transactions' (Barker, 2003: 136). Ecological approaches draw substantially from systems theory. Systems theory emerged from scientific disciplines, biology in particular. However, systems theory lends itself to practice with people as it prompts us to consider human beings as systems in their own right, but also as members of subsystems (for example, family, school, church) and of a larger system (a super-system such as society). Howe describes the basic premise of systems theory:

> Complex systems are made up of many parts. It is not possible to understand the whole without recognising how the component parts interact, affect and change each other. As the parts interact, they create the character and function of the whole. (2009: 109)

Munro (2011: 1137) illustrates this further when she notes how 'systems have inputs, processes, outputs and outcomes, with ongoing feedback among these various parts'. Consider a local football team set up to offer local young people a regular, positive activity as a subsystem of a community (the system); the 'parts' can be said to be constituted by individuals of that football team. Each individual contributes to change, whilst they are affected by others within the system. For example, if two members of the football team argue and one leaves taking his three friends with him, inevitably this disrupts the team. It may also impact on the wider community if those four boys start hanging out around the local shops as they have nothing else to do. The concept of **homeostasis** (or balance) helps to conceptualise these changes.

Through the interaction of a system's constituent parts, homeostasis is naturally reached. In other words, the system is balanced and harmonious. If there is a negative or positive change in the behaviour, status or functioning of one part, then homeostasis is destabilised until the system adapts and a new balance is reached. Thus, how a system maintains its homeostasis is critical. The theory that changes in one part of the system inevitably impacts on the system as a whole, has clear implications for application in social work practice and can be seen to have influence in generic practice as well as in relation to specific interventions, such as family therapy. In social work practice the family is seen as a system in its own right which has subsystems (individuals, sibling groups, parents and so on). As such, social work can help by intervening when homeostasis is out of balance; for example, when a member becomes unwell, involved in deviant behaviour or any other change or event that will cause disruption and imbalance to the other subsystems or parts. The objective for the social worker, therefore, is to empower the family to restore homeostasis.

ECOLOGICAL SYSTEMS THEORY

Ecological approaches view society as a network; imagine the individual at the middle of layers of concentric circles with society as the outer ring (see Figure 24.1).

The layers, or rings in between, represent different structural levels: family, community, society. The ecological model proposed by Bronfenbrenner in 1979 has been highly influential in social work policy and practice, as well as other fields pertaining to human development.

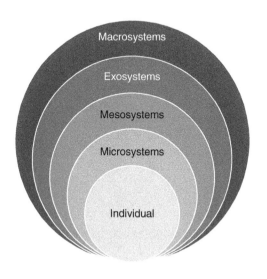

Macrosystems
Structural systems that impact on a child's life, including: the state; gender; values; norms; law.
Exosystems
Secondary systems that impact on a child's life, including: parental workplace; family social networks; neighbourhood & community.
Mesosystems
Child's interactions with community & surroundings that impact on their life, for example: school; extra-curricular activities; community events.
Microsystems
For example: nuclear family; sibling group; friends; playground; swimming class.

Figure 24.1   The ecological model

Source: Bronfenbrenner, 1979.

Gordon Jack (2000) has drawn from ecological theory to explore the complex interactions of different aspects of a child's life to demonstrate how these impact on development and life chances. Jack has promoted a discourse that identifies risk factors (influences that negatively affect the child's development) and protective factors (influences that positively affect a child's development and can neutralise more negative influences).

An example of the influence of Bronfenbrenner's model is provided by the *Framework for the Assessment of Children in Need and their Families* (DH, 2000) (the Assessment Framework). The Assessment Framework's theoretical underpinning is reflected in the diagram in Figure 11.1 (see Chapter 11), known as the triangle, as the main focus of any assessment should be a child's needs and the formal and informal sources of support, whether via family, school, other groups or community.

SYSTEMIC PRACTICE

The adoption of systems theory in practice has grown in the UK, but how it is incorporated into everyday social work practice varies from one local authority to another.

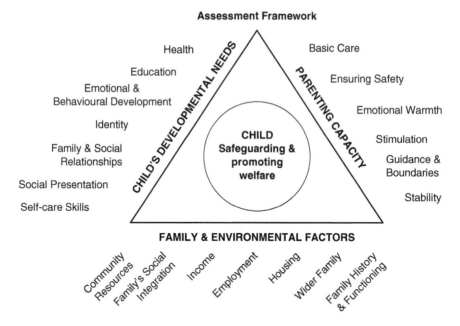

Figure 24.2   The Assessment Framework

Source: HM Government, 2018.

Many local authorities using systemic practice base their vision on the 'Hackney Model', aka the 'Reclaiming Social Work' model (Goodman and Trowler, 2011). The original model used small pods of workers consisting of: a consultant social worker who was the case holder for all cases in the pod; a social worker; a child care coordinator (often a newly qualified social worker or unqualified worker with relevant experience); a family therapist; and a pod coordinator (an administrative role). The team was supported by a clinical psychologist with whom regular clinical supervision was undertaken in a group format.

This model, however, is interpreted differently in different areas, an issue which has raised concern amongst some professionals (see Pemberton, 2013). Notwithstanding, the idea of small 'teams within teams' that hold cases collectively and work with families in teams, rather than as individual social workers, appears to be consistent in the implementation of systemic practice. There are several benefits of this approach:

- It allows for input from individuals which focuses on their various strengths.
- It provides a forum to discuss cases as a group, develop multiple hypotheses and test these over time.
- The burden of administrative tasks on social workers decreases over time.

The benefits of systemic thinking in this collaborative format include allowing the broadest range of possibilities to emerge whilst uncovering wisdom held within a group.

Reflections of a newly qualified social worker

As a newly qualified social worker the thought of holding my own caseload was quite daunting having undertaken my final placement in a team that did not work systemically. On commencing my first social work job I was in a team that was just developing systemic working and this was a very beneficial experience for me because I felt a lot more supported by my pod, was able to seek their advice and run ideas past them in clinical supervision on a weekly basis – as they were also able to do. This meant I was able to see multiple points of view and hypotheses from the start of working with a family that, as a newly qualified social worker, I might not have picked up on myself.

The clinical supervision sessions helped build my confidence as I could also contribute ideas, theories and research to case discussions; in addition they provided me a safe space to ask what I felt were 'simple' questions but which often would not have been asked by more experienced workers, which led to additional discussion, challenging of assumptions and the development of competing hypotheses.

APPLYING THEORY IN PRACTICE

You can incorporate a systemic approach into your daily practice at the start of your intervention with any individual or family. Completing a **genogram** (diagram of a family structure) enables you to convey the message that you appreciate that an individual is part of a family system (within which people can represent risk, or be a source of protection and support), and to enable you to respond appropriately, you need to understand the family system. The task of understanding and assessing family dynamics, family history and family functioning can be challenging, yet essential to your work. Using a tool, like a genogram or an **ecomap** (pictorial representation of a social network), can be an aid for talking about the family system, which in turn helps you to develop rapport and helps to shape your hypotheses about the situation.

Visit the website (https://study.sagepub.com/rogers2e) to access the 'How to …' guides for using genograms and ecomaps.

· ·

Case study: Applying systems thinking

Thirteen-year-old Tenneh was the eldest child in the Sesay family. Tenneh's mother, Adama, was a single mother with three younger children. The family had recently arrived in the UK from Sierra Leone and were seeking asylum. Tenneh was referred to children's social care as school held concerns about her increasingly challenging behaviour and disengagement from school life. Tenneh had not settled or built any friendships. School knew that Tenneh's family were seeking asylum and had limited resources, but Tenneh had been seen with an expensive new phone and money. In addition, there were concerns about the possibility of child sexual

(Continued)

exploitation as Tenneh had been seen getting into the car of a man known to school, police and social care. On the first home visit, May, the social worker, completed a genogram with Adama (Tenneh refused to speak to her). In the process of collecting information and plotting out the family tree, May learnt that the family had previously lived with Eustace (Adama's brother and Tenneh's maternal uncle) before coming to the UK. Eustace had died only three weeks before the family had left for the UK. He was their only protection from the threats of violence that Adama was receiving from her ex-partner, a criminal gang member and perpetrator of considerable violence and abuse towards Adama and the children.

Whilst completing the genogram, Adama was open and answered May's questions about the family relationships and functioning. Tenneh had been very close to Eustace and she had closed herself off emotionally after his death. Soon after arriving in the UK, Adama began a relationship with a new partner, Des, and Adama admitted that she had little time for Tenneh in between looking after the younger children and putting time into a new relationship. After completing the genogram with Adama, May felt that she had gained a better understanding of the support and difficulties that the family had faced in the UK. More importantly, May felt that she could understand some of the difficult issues that Tenneh was dealing with. May had several concerns, which included:

- Tenneh had unresolved feelings of grief, loss and separation.
- Tenneh was emotionally and socially isolated, lacking peer relationships and peer support.
- Tenneh lacked an inconsistent and readily available caregiver (when she needed her mother, she was not there). Adama did her best but Tenneh was not her only child. As the eldest Adama expected Tenneh to fend for herself.

May felt that the concerns about child sexual exploitation needed to be fully investigated in light of Tenneh's vulnerabilities and limited **protective factors**. Thinking systemically and using a tool to gather data about the family helped May to begin to understand Tenneh's family system, the dynamics of her closest family relationships and her recent risk-taking behaviours in the context of these. May ended the first visit feeling satisfied that she had gained a clearer picture of Tenneh's microsystems.

Reflective activity

Can you consider the ways in which aspects of Tenneh's macrosystem would affect her daily life? Think about her family's status as an asylum-seeking family. Consider wider influences (social norms, values, the media, the legal system, welfare benefits and so on) and how these would affect everyday life for the Sesay family.

. . . .

Other tools that can be very useful in systemic practice include working with families to create vision statements and circular questioning techniques.

Vision statement

Creating a vision statement with a family can help them identify where they currently see themselves and where they would like to be in the future. One example of a vision statement could be asking a parent/carer what they would *like* their children to say about them as parents in 20 years' time – this provides us with the place we want to get to – and comparing this with what they think their children would currently *actually* say about them as parents. Having these two pieces of information can guide you to help the parent/carer identify areas where there are difficulties and what they think might need to change. By undertaking this exercise the parent/carer is given space to think about what *they want* for their children, to identify what is preventing this from being achieved at this time and what changes can be made to move towards this. This is a much more empowering way to approach *difficulties* than a professional *telling* a parent/carer what *they* have identified as difficulties and what *they* think the parent/carer should do about them.

Circular questioning

This aims to get service users to look at things from a different perspective. It can be useful for introducing new ideas and information. Examples of circular questioning might include asking a parent/carer what they think their child would feel about a certain situation, or vice versa. This requires the service user to put themselves in another's shoes and to try to see the situation from a perspective different to their own. This can help to develop an understanding of why different family members react in different ways and can be used to identify possible strategies to diffuse difficult situations. For example, if provided with the response of the person they had been asked about, this can be compared to their own response and the differences, and the reasons for these differences, considered and worked through.

Other examples of circular questioning might include asking a person to describe how another person reacts in a certain situation. For example, mum might say dad 'flies off the handle and shouts and screams over nothing' whereas dad might say he 'had a terrible day, the kids were screaming and shouting and I just wanted some peace and quiet. They made a mess and I yelled at them to get them to tidy it up.' Hearing how others perceive us and our actions can be a transformative experience and can help us to see how what we do and our behaviours appear very differently to others than they do to us, further developing our understanding of our role within the family group and the impact the actions of an individual can have on the group as a whole.

Table 24.1   Benefits and limitations of systemic thinking in social work

Benefits

It locates individuals in their wider context of community and society, moving your thinking from the immediate environment of the family and home.

It encourages you to think sociologically about socio-cultural influences such as values, norms, policy and wider contexts, such as poverty.

It prompts you to consider risks and protective factors in terms of environmental influences.

It directs you away from thinking about people as individual units that are unconnected or unaffected by people or influences around them. Instead, systemic thinking orients you to consider individuals as part of complex systems with complex interrelationships.

(Continued)

Table 24.1   (Continued)

Limitations

Often requires more input with additional family members to address system disturbances, which can be time and resource consuming.

The task of isolating the interconnections of complex family, community, social and cultural systems can be tricky, and thus identifying potential solutions is difficult.

Trevithick (2012) claims that most social workers do not receive training that is adequate in order to apply this approach in ways that influence wider social factors as well as organisational and political systems.

The resources required to work towards a solution are not always available (Jack and Gill, 2003).

CONCLUSION

Child (2000) sums up systemic theory and practice as how the skilled practitioner negotiates the system in terms of how a group or family works positively or negatively with an agency and in terms of how that agency helps or hinders the practitioners who are part of that system. This chapter has set out some of the tools that practitioners can employ to work systemically, along with a summary of the benefits and weaknesses to this social work model.

Having read this chapter, you should be able to:

- Identify different models and frameworks that are underpinned by systems thinking;
- Consider the different systems (micro, meso, macro) that influence an individual's life experiences;
- Consider the barriers and enablers to systemic practice.

RECOMMENDED READING

Goodman, S. and Trowler, I. (eds) (2011) *Social Work Reclaimed: Innovative Frameworks for Child and Family Social Work Practice*. London: Jessica Kingsley.

Jack, G. (2000) Ecological influences on parenting and child development. *British Journal of Social Work*, 30(6): 703–720.

Jack, G. (2012) Ecological perspective. In M. Gray, J. Midegley and S. Webb (eds), *The Sage Handbook of Social Work*. London: Sage.

Michailakis, D. and Schirmer, W. (2014) Social work and social problems: a contribution from systems theory and constructionism. *International Journal of Social Welfare*, 23(4): 431–442.

Narrative Social Work
Jennifer Cooper

Links to the Professional Capabilities Framework

● Professionalism   ● Values and ethics   ● Diversity and equality   ● Knowledge   ● Critical reflection and analysis   ● Skills and interventions

Links to the Knowledge and Skills Statement for Child and Family Practitioners

● Relationships and effective direct work   ● Communication   ● Child development ● Adult mental ill-health, substance misuse, domestic abuse, physical ill-health and disability

Links to the Knowledge and Skills Statement for Social Workers in Adult Services

● Person-centred practice   ● Mental capacity   ● Direct work with individuals and families

Key messages

- A narrative approach to social work draws on a range of theories.
- A practitioner's version of a situation might be very different to a service user's version of the same situation.
- How we perceive a situation or life experience impacts on our understanding and ability to manage it.
- Externalising a problem allows it to be viewed from other perspectives and can help us to address it.
- Strong communication skills such as active listening underpin this approach.

INTRODUCTION

Have you ever been talking with someone about an event that you both experienced, and noticed the differences in your accounts? The different things they remembered, the things that you thought were crucial to the narrative are dealt with as insignificant in their version. Key characters in their account were barely even acknowledged in yours. We all have our own narratives. Your interpretation of experiences and events, and how you perceive them, impacts upon your view of yourself, your life and your story. Importantly, our experiences, self-esteem, confidence and way we view the world – our interpretation of a situation – can impact on mental and psychological health and wellbeing. We might identify patterns that are not objectively there, but because we perceive something in a certain way, this can become a dominant feature in our own narrative.

Using a narrative approach in social work, the aim is to help others to interpret their experience but also to see things that they have experienced from different points of view (see the case study below for an example of two contrasting narratives). Their perception of an event is a crucial part of their story however they may only see in a one-dimensional way, and often only the negatives. Using a **strengths-based approach** (see Chapter 23 'Strengths-Based and Solution-Focused Approaches') you can help service users to reinterpret events in a more positive light, highlighting, for example, their resilience, the positive way they acted in a traumatic situation or the way they have moved on from a situation that they view as the defining moment of their story. This chapter explores this further.

. . . .

Case study: Martha

Practitioner version of a situation

Martha is 23 years old and has two children aged two and three years old. Martha has experienced neglect and abuse growing up and is exposing her children to the same things. Martha has not had good experiences of being parented which makes it hard for her to understand how to parent her children to a good enough standard.

Martha's relationships are characterised by domestic abuse and she uses alcohol as a coping mechanism. This is detrimental to her care of her children and means she is not always physically and emotionally available to them. It also has a negative impact on Martha's financial situation.

Service user version of a situation

I'm only 23 and I've got two little ones. It's really hard at times. My mum and dad fought all the time and I looked after my brother and sister growing up. I tried to be a good parent to them but didn't really know what I was doing but they're both doing alright now.

I've been hit a few times, but that's what love is, isn't it? You argue and fight when things are tough and yeah it might get physical but we make up. My parents have been married for 26 years and they still get into it sometimes but they love each other else they wouldn't still be together. I started drinking when I was about 15, makes me feel better and I don't worry as much. I have a drink sometimes now but never when I've got the girls. My dad used to drink the food money in the pub but I make sure there's food in for my girls and they have nice clothes. They've never been late for nursery and they're happy.

Both of these stories tell you about Martha, her own experiences of growing up and how she looks after her children but reading them, you might be forgiven for thinking they were about different people.

. . . .

WHAT IS A NARRATIVE APPROACH IN SOCIAL WORK?

Taking a narrative approach in social work moves away from the 'traditional' approach of professionals as 'experts', who come in with limited knowledge of the service user, record *their* views and *their* perceptions of the situation and make recommendations based on what *they* perceive to be the issues. This approach does not consider the lived experiences of the service user, their thoughts about why or how a situation has developed or occurred, and their view of their roles in the story of their lives.

White and Epston (1990), drawing on White's interests in family therapy and sociological approaches, are widely acknowledged as pioneering the narrative approach. The family therapy approach 'looks at problems within the systems of relationships in which they occur, and aims to promote change by intervening in the broader system rather than the individual alone' (Burnham, 1984: 2 cited in Walker, 2012). A narrative approach takes a similar stance, attempting to look at problems as entities in themselves; the problem is the problem, rather than a failing in the person themselves.

The family therapy model (which has been adapted for use in social work and is known as the 'Hackney Model' or '**systemic practice**') uses a systemic approach, identifying systems within which a person exists and the influences these systems have on them – either through our interactions with the system, or the influence of the system from the exosystem or macrosystem level (for a discussion of ecological systems theory see Chapter 24 'Systems Theory'). Our individual narratives reflect how we have understood our journey through life, how systems have impacted on us and our interactions with them. However, if someone had been recording our life and this was played back to us on film, it would likely look quite different. How we view ourselves may be quite different to how society views us – and this can be problematic at times. A narrative approach allows for exploration of a story from multiple perspectives, inviting alternative views and a way to view 'the problem as the problem' rather than an integral part of us.

It must be acknowledged that there is some criticism of this approach. For example, Walker (2012) questions if externalising a problem may absolve a person from responsibility for their own actions. Does discussing domestic abuse as the problem rather than the perpetrator's actions assist or support our understanding? Does 'the problem' become the responsibility of others rather than the person taking responsibility for their own behaviour?

USING A NARRATIVE APPROACH IN PRACTICE

Assessments

Almost every service user you work with will require an assessment at some point during your working relationship. It may be this assessment has been undertaken before they were allocated to you or that you may be responsible for undertaking an assessment during your work with them. Most assessments are very structured and formulaic; as a practitioner we go into a meeting or visit with a plan for what information we want to gather as part of the assessment process. In doing so, we may only ever touch on the edges of the service user's story, the specific information we need for our assessment might not reveal the key issues as they see them. If an assessment has already been undertaken, it may be useful to go through this with the service user so you can understand their views on the assessment and identify any areas they feel require further exploration or that they disagree with.

Tools for helping gather information for an assessment which take a narrative approach include the use of **timelines, ecomaps** and **genograms**. These tools are used with service users and allow them to identify key events in their lives, key people and support networks and their family relational history. Be prepared to spend some time with service users when using these tools as they can be quite time consuming. And don't forget to take lots of paper!

Visit the website (https://study.sagepub.com/rogers2e) to access 'How to …' guides for completing timelines, ecomaps and genograms.

Practice example – Assessments: Darren

A single assessment of Darren's parenting of his six-year-old son was undertaken by the referrals and assessment team. They recommended Darren's son was made subject to a child protection plan. There was information from police records included in the report which stated Darren had broken his aunt's arm when his aunt would not give him some money.

Darren repeatedly stated throughout initial visits that he wasn't going to listen or work with services because they lie about everything and make things up and he is never listened to, so what is the point? When this was further unpicked with Darren, it became apparent that Darren had never, in fact, broken his aunt's arm. Both Darren and his aunt reported that the police had attended following an argument between Darren and his aunt and his aunt had told the police Darren grabbed her hand and due to her having osteogenesis imperfecta, this fractured a tiny bone in her hand. There was no further action taken against Darren by the police, nor was the matter followed up – which would seem surprising for such a serious allegation.

This allegation had been included in assessment after assessment despite each time Darren protesting that it did not happen. The view taken by the social worker in the assessment was, of course, reached in good faith on the basis of information shared with them by other professionals, however it provided a very different narrative from that experienced by Darren and his aunt.

Family scripts

Like father, like son, right? Which is great, if your dad is a kind, healthy, hardworking family man. Not so much if he is alcohol dependent who has been in and out of prison for violent crime. Family scripts can be both positive and negative, but it is often the negative ones that receive more prominence and are referred to most often. A family script is a narrative used both within families and outside of them. These can be restrictive and damaging for those trapped within them.

Within a family, a child may be labelled the 'black sheep' of the family if they do not quite fit in or their behaviour is not what parents and families want from them. This exclusion from the family, being marked as 'different', or being labelled in such a way not only influences family members' perceptions of the child, but will influence the way the child sees themselves and if repeated externally – for example with teachers or others working with the family or child – it can influence their understanding and perception of the child and therefore their interactions with and their expectations of the child.

Similarly, as professionals, we can be guilty of reiterating family scripts – every social work office, as well as police station and probation office, has '*that family*', the family that makes the person taking a duty call groan when they hear the name. The family is known throughout the area for a multitude of reoccurring issues and we see them as troublemakers – 'no wonder the children act like that when that's who their parents are'. What chance do these families and future generations have of making changes and breaking free from the problems they have if we, as professionals, perceive them to be inherently entrenched in negative behaviours? And if we as professionals can get stuck in viewing them like that, what chance does a child growing up in that family stand of seeing a different path for themselves? (See Chapter 12 'Interviewing Skills' for an outline of cognitive distortions). The adoption of family scripts may be conscious or unconscious and when working with families, we can work with them to identify these and help unravel where they have come from and support those we work with to break free from the restrictive beliefs that may be holding them back.

Externalising the problem

It is important for our self-esteem and confidence as human beings that we feel heard, understood and valued. When we have difficulties, it is part of our nature to often blame ourselves for these and the problem becomes a part of us, rather than it being a problem in its own right. Indeed, when we internalise a problem, it becomes more difficult to separate it from our 'self' and changing who we are as a person is often viewed as more difficult than changing how we approach the problem.

By externalising the problem, this allows exploration of the problem as something external to the person, thus allowing us to view it from different perspectives and inviting different ways of thinking about it. Then it is no longer something that is intrinsic within the person, but a problem that we can look at and explore from other points of view.

A common way of beginning to explore this approach is asking someone what advice they would give to a friend in a similar situation? It is often easier to give advice to other people than it is to give ourselves advice.

We often ask questions in a way that places the person as the problem, i.e. their behaviour is something intrinsic in them rather than something they can change. By changing the way we ask questions, we can help people see their actions as just that – actions, or reactions, which can then be modified.

Visit the companion website to see 'externalisation' in practice (https://study.sagepub.com/rogers2e).

Reflective activity

Try turning these internalised questions into externalising questions:

- How long have you been depressed?

  Everyone experiences mental health and some people experience difficulties with their mental health at times, such as depression. Can you think of a time when you didn't experience these feelings?

- What makes you drink?

  Are there any patterns that you can think of that lead to you wanting to have a drink? For example, if you have had a bad day at work?

- Why do you shout at the children?

  Are there certain things that the children do that make you get upset or angry? What is going on when you feel yourself getting upset and raising your voice with them?

- The children are always late for nursery and school, why don't you get up earlier?

  What does your morning routine look like? Are there some things we could plan that could be done the night before to make the mornings easier?

LIFE-STORY WORK

Another way that narrative is integrated into social work is through life-story work. Whilst most predominantly associated with children who are permanently removed from their birth families, life-story work can be useful in other areas of social work such as when working with people who have lost family members, or those with memory processing difficulties: for example, with people who have suffered a stroke, traumatic brain injury or older adults living with dementia.

Life-story work with children is mainly associated with adoption, where practitioners will create life-story books, later life letters and parallel stories for children placed for adoption. Adoption legally cuts all ties for children from their birth families and contact is often limited to indirect letterbox contact once a year. This is the process whereby a child or their estranged family member writes a letter and the social worker acts to facilitate the exchange of letters (they are, in effect, the letterbox!). Life-story work prepared by a practitioner (preferably who has worked with the family) provides a narrative account for children of the reasons – from a practitioner's perspective – why the child was removed from their birth family and placed for adoption.

There are several different types of life-story materials practitioners might prepare for a child removed from their parents' care and these might include the following.

Life-story book

A life-story book is a book/story written for a child which provides a child-friendly version of the child's life and social care involvement and the reasons they were removed from their parents' care. Where a child is placed for adoption, a life-story book will often include some information about their adoptive parents, and their life with them as well. Depending on the age of the child placed for adoption, the practitioner might create two books/stories – one for when they are very young which provides a basic story about the child's journey and one for when they are older which provides further detail.

Parallel stories

A parallel story is a story that reflects a child's situation but externalises it and explains their situation in a story format: for example, using an animal family. It might be that a child placed for adoption due to parental illness will have a parallel story about a baby bunny who's mummy rabbit became poorly and was unable to look after them so they went to stay with a friendly foster bunny mummy who looked after them whilst the doctor bunny was trying to make their mummy bunny better and then when mummy bunny wasn't able to get better, they moved to a forever bunny family.

Later life letter

As good as life-story books are at introducing children to their own story, there are often significant adult themes and issues at play that lead to the removal of a child from their birth family which are simply not suitable for children to hear about at a young age. A later life letter is a letter written for the child to open at a future date, usually around their 18th birthday. This letter will provide the young person with a more detailed and adult version of the events that led to their removal, the work social care practitioners undertook with their parents and the steps taken to find them their adoptive family. As noted above, this will be the practitioner's version of events that led to the child's removal and at this time, the young person may be in touch with their birth family. As such it is important to always include a sentence making it clear that this is the practitioner's understanding of the situation and that what they hear from their birth family might be very different.

Life-story work with adults is usually more focused around memory and communicating a person's history to those who are caring for them and working with them. A person with dementia or who has experienced a stroke or traumatic brain injury may not be able to express themselves in the same way they used to and the way they present can be hugely different to the way they were before or how they perceive themselves to be. Life-story work in this situation is about creating a reference point for the person and those working with the person of their life experiences, things they enjoyed doing, important people, places and events that have been a part of their lives. A brief example of this type of work might be a one-page profile which is on a resident's door at a dementia unit; see Figure 25.1 or visit the website to access a 'How to …' guide for undertaking a one-page profile (https://study.sagepub.com/rogers2e). This might include information such as their nickname, what their family members are called, where they used to live, where they worked and what their hobbies were. This allows staff to have a better understanding of the person, things they can talk to them about when undertaking tasks with them and may help them understand why Bob is shouting at the television when Holby City is on - he used to be a doctor and it was not like that at all, but he is no longer able to use his words to explain this to them.

It is not only words or actions that can evoke memories in people, music can trigger memories and emotions that can help soothe people and transport them to a different place. The BBC, in conjunction with the charity Playlist for Life, launched the Music Memories website (https://musicmemories.bbcrewind.co.uk/) in September 2018, which collates thousands of songs and TV theme tunes from the last century which can be used as a resource to create individual memory playlists for people.

Reflective activity

- Think of an assessment you have read either when on placement or when commencing your practice. Do you think the service user it was written about would recognise it as being about their life? If not, why not? If so, how had it been written to ensure that it reflected the service user's experience?
- Put yourself in the shoes of a service user like Martha or Darren (case study and practice example above). How would you feel reading the practitioner's version of your life? How, as a social work practitioner, can you work with service users to ensure their voices are included in your reports?
- There will be times when service users refute everything that is contained in your reports, even when there is factual and objective evidence to support your position. How will you manage this as a practitioner?

My background

- Bob grew up in the East End of London, he uses lots of cockney rhyming slang which he remembers even when he may struggle to retrieve other words.
- Bob worked as a cardiovascular surgeon for over 30 years. He likes watching medical programmes but gets frustrated when he feels they aren't doing things properly.
- Bob spent lots of time in the Lake District and the Peak District on walking holidays, he is an avid bird watcher and loves walking.

My Family

- Bob is the oldest of four siblings, he had two younger brothers called Tim and Reg who have both, sadly died. Bob's younger sister Angela, visits him once a month.
- Bob's wife was called Vera and she has also died but Bob doesn't remember this. He likes to talk about Vera in the present tense.
- Bob has two children, Samantha and George, and four grandchildren, Jemima, Timothy, Laura and Scott. Samantha and George visit on alternate weekends with their children.

Robert 'Bob' Sanderson

What's important to me

- Bob is very methodical and likes to stick to his routine. If Bob is interrupted during his morning routine, he can become frustrated and will start everything all over again. Bob will only have his coffee (milk, one sugar) once he has washed, dressed and made his bed.
- Bob likes watching the gardener, Jim, do the garden and will often offer him advice. Jim likes Bob and is fine with this so there is no need to try and stop Bob talking with Jim – he often follows Bob's advice on planting which brings Bob great joy.
- Bob does not get on with James S, no-one is quite sure why, but the pair do not like each other. If there is nowhere else to sit except next to James in the lounge or at dinner, Bob can become agitated and shout. Betty and Joan are always happy to swap places as they like to feel they are helping out.

Figure 25.1 One-page profile for Bob

CONCLUSION

How we view the world, our own experiences and write our own 'story' impacts on our view of ourselves and the world around us. Using a narrative approach allows us to reframe our experiences from a different perspective, and allows us to take ownership of our story. This empowers us, using a strengths-based model to 'rewrite' our story and allows us to focus on the positives that have come from our experiences.

Using a narrative approach in social work functions to address the imbalance of power and oppression in professional–service user relationships, ensuring the service user's voice is heard and included in the assessment and intervention.

Different tools such as timelines, ecomaps, music and life-story materials are all useful in a narrative approach to social work. They provide us with vehicles for gathering and sharing information in a way that is accessible for service users.

Having read this chapter, you should be able to:

- Consider the impact of the way in which we talk to, and write about, service users;
- Articulate the tools of narrative social work;
- Understand the importance of working with service users to gain their perspective on their lived experiences.

RECOMMENDED READING

Thompson R. (2011) Using life story work to enhance care. *Nursing Older People*, 23(8): 16–21.

Walker, S. (2012) *Effective Social Work with Children, Young People and Families: Putting Systems Theory into Practice*. London: Sage.

Watson, D., Latter, S. and Bellew, R. (2015) Adopters' views on their children's life story books. *Adoption & Fostering*, 39(2): 119–134.

White, M. and Epston, D. (1990) *Narrative Means to Therapeutic Ends*. London: Norton.

Task-Centred Social Work Practice
David Edmondson

Links to the Professional Capabilities Framework

● Values and ethics   ● Knowledge   ● Critical reflection and analysis   ● Skills and interventions

Links to the Knowledge and Skills Statement for Child and Family Practitioners

● Relationships and effective direct work   ● Communication   ● Analysis, decision-making, planning and review

Links to the Knowledge and Skills Statement for Social Workers in Adult Services

● Person-centred practice   ● Safeguarding   ● Effective assessments and outcome-based support planning   ● Direct work with individuals and families

Key messages

- Task-centred social work seeks to help people develop skills and knowledge they can use again and take forward in order to solve future problems on their own, taking more control of their lives.
- It promotes positive change and is premised on the principle of genuine partnership working.
- It is value-led, evidence-based and practical.
- It works with both individuals and groups.

INTRODUCTION

This chapter focuses on using task-centred social work in your practice, providing a practical step-by-step guide to planning and implementing it. For our purposes here, 'task', in relation to task-centred social work practice can be understood as a defined piece of work, sometimes of short or time-limited duration, with activities and actions agreed and assigned between worker and service user. The guide here relates to direct work with individuals, but could be easily adapted to work with families, groups and communities. Done well, it will make your direct work and interventions more effective and help people to make real changes in their lives.

Using a task-centred approach is value-led, evidence-based and practical, promoting positive change, premised on the principle of genuine partnership working. It provides a structured approach for intervention, which social workers can adapt and use across a range of services, settings and roles, flexible enough to be used in work with individuals, groups and communities. It finds its origins in the work of Reid and Shyne (1969), Reid and Epstein (1972), then later through Doel and Marsh (1992) and Marsh and Doel (2005); growing out of the established foundations of social work practice and casework (Payne, 2014), utilising both psychosocial and problem-solving approaches (Hollis, 1972; Perlman, 1957).

> ### Reflective activity
>
> View the following excellent short series of clips authored by Roslyn Edwards and Ruth Forbes, produced and published by Iriss. These take you through the emergence of task-centred work, proposed phases of the model and key skills required to deliver it.
>
> Task centred casework: https://content.iriss.org.uk/taskcentred/

TASKS AND A TASK-CENTRED APPROACH

'T'ain't What You Do (It's the Way That You Do It)' (Song by Melvin 'Sy' Oliver and James 'Trummy' Young, 1939)

For many, contemporary social work practice, notably in England, has become heavily process-led with a focus on formalised assessment and recording in order to complete a set of prescribed agency-led tasks. As we know, social workers will have many legitimate and proper tasks to undertake as part of their roles and responsibilities, influenced by their service and setting. However, this has led to social work becoming narrowly compartmentalised into pockets of assessment, inter-agency meetings, recording, signposting and fundamentally away from direct work with people. Within this restrictive framework, definitions of 'task' frequently feature terms like job, duty, chore and labour; characterised by routine and predictability. Some critics suggest task-centred practice 'is obvious' or the approach is 'just a glorified jobs list'. However, this fundamentally fails to understand its core principles and purpose. It does seek to bring about change but this has to be *alongside* the promotion of learning and skills development which the service user can independently take forward and apply elsewhere to other problems and challenges. To achieve this, the work cannot ever simply be a jobs list allocated out from worker to client, but has to be a shared and transformative relationship, with a desire to share and develop learning and new knowledge through mutual acceptance, trust and support.

Task-centred work is what Doel and Marsh have described as a 'practice method' (2006), with the emphasis on its practical use in direct practice. It is something you will have to learn, practise and develop over time. Reid and Epstein (1972: 95) defined task-centred social work as being essentially concerned with 'efforts to resolve any problem of living'. Thus, task-centred work is seen as being flexible enough to apply across a range of difficulties people may be facing but also with a focus on bringing about positive resolution and change to the lives of the people we work with, through 'problem-solving actions and tasks the client and practitioner undertake' (Reid, 1978: 83). To achieve this, the social worker needs to understand the approach itself but also their professional role and its purpose if it is to achieve all its goals.

PREREQUISITES FOR USING A TASK-CENTRED APPROACH

For task-centred social work to be genuine, social workers have to believe in the ethics and purpose of the profession. Task-centred work is premised on the key values, principles and ambitions of social work: problem-solving and making positive change, empowering people to take control of their own lives, working alongside them and generating working partnerships.

To be most effective, task-centred social work requires understanding and practice of the method; the opportunity and time to work face-to-face with people; and commitment to social work values and principles.

Reflective activity

Read through the BASW Code of Ethics, the PCF and the KSS statements to remind you of the purpose of social work and your own role and work as a professional social worker. Focus on the underlying meaning and requirements you need to be an effective and ethically driven practitioner. Identify which features in the documents you think are most important to helping you be the sort of social worker you intend to be.

As you read through this chapter and begin to plan using a task-centred approach to help people resolve problems in their lives and make real change, keep reminding yourself of the principles you have identified and you seek to live by. They will help you think about *why* and *how* you intend to apply a task-centred approach.

PRINCIPLES OF PRACTICE

As social workers, it is accepted that we have a job to do and tasks to complete that may be heavily directed by our roles, responsibilities and agencies. However, *how* we undertake our work is very much up to us.

Wherever you work, the opportunity to undertake task-centred practice should not be ignored. In essence, task-centred social work practice is as much – if not more – about the way we work with people to resolve problems than what the task or problem is. Thus, task-centred practice is not about taking the problem away from the person you are working with. We want to help people *themselves* to resolve problems and address difficulties in their lives. As far as we can, we want to work *with* people rather than *for* people. The goals in using a task-centred approach in our social work practice reflect core social work values and principles. These include:

- respect for the individuality of the people we work with and assertion that all individuals are capable of change;
- seeking to make positive changes in people's lives by helping them to solve problems, and in learning how to do this, empowering people by helping them learn how to address similar problems for themselves in the future;
- identifying and supporting people's strengths, both actual and potential, and building on rather than discounting or ignoring individual strengths, resources, skills and knowledge;
- helping people towards independence;
- acknowledging and supporting the resilience of others.

In some ways, the opportunity to assess whether or not you are able to use task-centred social work in your practice could be considered a litmus test of the type of social work you are able to practise.

WHAT IS TASK-CENTRED SOCIAL WORK ABOUT?

In essence, task-centred social work *is* about:

- problem identification and solving;
- identifying achievable and realistic outcomes and goals (the changes);
- careful consideration of these problems with the person/s;
- agreeing a step-by-step plan, with a clear set of stages and actions in order to address the problems to be resolved and bring about change.

As importantly, task-centred work practice is *not* about:

- completing agency jobs such as filling in agency forms and records;
- making decisions and taking actions in which service users have had no say;

- doing things on behalf of service users without them having some active involvement;
- ignoring what people see as important to them and discounting their resources and supports;
- assuming our way is *the* right way and the *only* way (the 'we know best' model).

AREAS SUITABLE FOR TASK-CENTRED APPROACHES

Task-centred approaches can be adapted and applied to any aspect of work with adults and children. These may typically include:

- managing scarce resources, e.g. incomes, budgeting, time;
- improving social relations and relationships, e.g. reducing social isolation, improving community engagement, addressing homelessness;
- addressing emotional and psychological distress, e.g. reducing anxiety, stress or unrest; coping with loss, improving and building resilience;
- dealing with behavioural difficulties, e.g. managing anger and aggression, improving parenting skills, helping with sleep problems;
- supporting people through change or transition, e.g. assisting moves towards independent living, moving home or school, starting a new job;
- problems in relation to organisations and services, e.g. improving school attendance, support for care leavers, support to attend regular appointments and commitments;
- medical problems, e.g. improving alcohol and drug management, support with mental health difficulties.

This list is not comprehensive, but gives an indication of the varied challenges and problems where a task-centred approach can be used.

Important note: In selecting to use a task-centred approach it is important to assess its suitability and prospects for success against criteria of timing and setting. Certain things may mitigate against its implementation at a particular moment in time:

- In terms of environment, it requires a certain amount of stability and time to be available to the person you are working with (and to you as well to support delivery of the approach).
- Acute crises, severe disruption or high-risk situations are more suited to some form of crisis intervention than a task-centred approach, particularly for situations where as a worker you may need to take control of a high-risk situation (e.g. acute mental health problems, child protection) or take the major lead in order to address a matter of urgency (e.g. a person is due for eviction).
- Individuals need to be able to engage with the approach in order to get the most out of it, e.g. those with chronic health problems, acute physical or mental distress are less likely to be able to fully participate and engage.
- The circumstances of your first or early meetings with service users will vary from situation to situation, but it is important to consider why you are involved in working

with someone. Some contacts are prompted by legislative duties and responsibilities (e.g. investigating a report of abuse or safeguarding matter; supervising and managing risk), others by self-referral (e.g. perhaps by someone calling in to see a duty worker in your service) or following up a referral request for intervention from other agencies and services (e.g. a referral from a general practitioner, housing department or school). These routes into service impact on what you may have to do, the purpose of your contact and also how you are likely to be perceived and received. This will also inform if and when a task-centred approach may be appropriate to use.

- In addition to the purpose and role of your interventions, your own time and the resources available to you are as important to consider here. Although it can be time-limited as an intervention, it does require you having the time and availability to implement and see it through to a conclusion. Task-centred practice will not fit readily into work that requires only one-off visits and actions. Make sure you look at your diary and can find time for the work and very importantly you will be able to keep appointments and commitments. Changing meetings and cancellations undermine trust and confidence in you and the approach.

GETTING READY TO USE A TASK-CENTRED APPROACH

Task-centred social work is designed to be time-limited, problem-focused and goal-oriented. To achieve change usually takes time, so any plan may require several stages, and several weeks from start to finish. This will obviously vary from situation to situation but it is wise to anticipate a plan which will cover 4–12 weeks. A sample template to plan your task-centred approach has been provided online.

     Visit the website (https://study.sagepub.com/rogers2e) to access an MS Word template you can use and adapt, plus a practical guide and example of a task-centred approach.

STAGES OF TASK-CENTRED SOCIAL WORK PRACTICE

One of the key advantages of using a task-centred social work approach is that it introduces a structure and order to your work and rewards careful planning. It is flexible and adaptable enough to work in a variety of situations and settings and can withstand review and change where unforeseen circumstances arise. It is also an intervention where we have clear goals and actions set out from the start that can be measured and assessed. This helps us assess the work we do and learn from this with regard to identifying how to improve our practice.

Preliminary work and preparation

Regardless of the situation, as in any situation where you are meeting people for the first time, you need to explain who you are, why you are making contact, your duties and responsibilities, the resources and services you may be able to access. A good-quality initial assessment at this early stage should help inform how – from your point of view – to proceed, identifying what needs to be addressed and in what order.

Task-centred work requires a degree of rapport and engagement to have been established. This is important as an early consideration involves discussion with the person you are working with about how they see things, what they see as important, and how you might find ways of working together to address problems an individual cannot resolve on their own. It is important here to note that despite a person presenting with many problems, seemingly persistent and intractable, the people we work with are resourceful and have strengths and assets that can be drawn on, despite their current difficulties.

Identifying and negotiating the problems (the 'tasks') to be addressed

Having made contact, a key activity at this point is to identify the problems to be addressed. This is important and requires sensitivity, given the problems a person may be facing could be causing considerable stress and anxiety and also impacting on other aspects of their life; for example, in working with someone with debt and budgeting problems, or working with a parent to improve managing a child's behaviour. Points of pressure and situations of crisis are quite likely to accompany the problems you are exploring with people and being ready and equipped to address these will fall to you. Thus, being familiar with approaches to crisis intervention and resolution would complement your application of task-centred practice.

This seems an obvious point but is often overlooked. However, it is important not merely so everyone can know what is happening and why but to ensure openness and the opportunity for all to contribute and bring their own knowledge, experience and ways of doing things into play. In the exchange, you may even learn some useful tips yourself such as:

- introducing a task-centred approach to others;
- identifying problems that may be amenable to task-centred practice;
- negotiating roles and activities;
- setting out a potential contract of work.

Such matters require careful consideration of the problems with the person who is actively involved, clarifying the changes wanted from the service user's point of view. Both you and the person you are working with will have to show a willingness to work with each other and cooperate. Good plans include the opportunity to review and revisit how you work together in order to accommodate changes and also manage any possible difficulties, lapses or disagreements. Regularly checking how someone feels things are proceeding, how they are coping and how much help and support is required are worthwhile as they will improve the prospects of a positive outcome.

Agreeing and setting goals and outcomes

A key approach in identifying and agreeing goals is to focus on what is desired and wanted from the intervention for the person you are working with, rather than simply on what is wrong at the moment. Thus, your role here is to help the person you are working with not only identify and define seemingly intractable problems in their lives, but also to re-define these into a set of positive actions and something that – with your support and guidance – can be achieved and changed. Thus, change is presented as a positive set of actions, with the prospect of a positive outcome, rather than merely reacting to what has gone wrong.

Applying task-centred principles to a Signs of Safety model of social work practice

Victoria, a children and families social worker, comments:

> I find that task-centred practice is very much a part of my day-to-day work and when used in the right situations, it can help relationship building with families. I am a Signs of Safety practice leader and since being trained in this process, I have found a task-centred approach has had a positive effect in my work with families.
>
> In the Signs of Safety approach we use the term 'safety goals'. This means identify-ing clear specific goals with the family that are achievable and realistic. A big part of creating these goals is directly involving the family, taking the approach that they know what works best for them.
>
> An agreed safety goal might be, 'Johnny attends school two days a week'. This might not be ideal for education welfare services, but this might be the most realistic and achievable goal for the family. Equally it could be, 'Sonia only drinks alcohol on Friday nights when the children are with grandma and grandad'.
>
> The most valuable information about efficacy of a plan will come from families, and from the children it relates to.
>
> There are many different ways to get feedback from children and their families. One aspect of Signs of Safety is the use of scaling questions, asking children and parents where they would place themselves on a scale of 0–10 in relation to different aspects of their life. For example, if 0 is mum and dad are shouting all the time, I feel very scared and frightened, and 10 is there is no shouting at home, we talk about our problems in a calm way, where would you scale these. The same technique can be used with younger children with a smiley face and a sad face. You can also ask other professionals, who may have a different relationship with a child or young person, to get feedback about how something is working.
>
> Plans that you make in partnership with families will not always work. Sometimes the approach you have taken might not be the right one for the family you are work-ing with. This is not an opportunity to beat yourself up and start to be critical. It is a chance to ask why, to look at what hasn't worked and how it can be changed. Most importantly ask the family, often they will be able to give reasons why part of a plan hasn't worked for them and may even find their own solutions for issues.

SETTING OUT A STRUCTURED PLAN OF ACTION

Having identified the problems and tasks to be addressed and set out some achievable goals and outcomes, the next activity is to negotiate and agree a structured plan of action that links where to start and where to end. A written plan like the one in the sample template, set out in plain terms, is helpful as it means everyone has something to refer to and review. Crucially, this helps each person know what is happening and what they are doing.

It is important to keep to a limited number of stages or steps. This makes the intervention easier to follow, makes it look more achievable and keeps its completion within a reasonable timescale.

MEASURING, EVALUATING AND REVIEWING THE PLAN AND INTERVENTION

Setting out a plan helps participants keep a focus on a target to be reached and the steps to achieving this. Activities linked to end-goals should be capable of being achieved, and in the early stages of using a task-centred approach setting activities that produce quick and easy results is beneficial to confidence building and building momentum.

The plan should be reviewed regularly in order to ensure the plan is being enacted, the person you are working with can review how things are proceeding, identify where things have gone well (and celebrated) and where things may be getting 'stuck' (and need to be revised). Although task-centred work is often time-limited, your availability and speedy intervention could be crucial here and scope for additional time should be built into your own work schedule.

Finally, when the plan has been completed or the time limits for the intervention reached, it is important to review and evaluate how things went. If a problem has been resolved then there is reason to celebrate this success, praise where appropriate and think about how skills and knowledge acquired can be built on and applied to other areas. Even where an intervention has not entirely worked, there are nearly always positives to acknowledge, endorse and build on. Endings here are critical and sufficient time should be incorporated into your work schedule to ensure this is given full attention.

EVIDENCE-BASED PRACTICE

The Families and Schools Together (FAST) programme

The FAST programme uses a task-centred approach to planning and delivering a universal access programme for families with school-aged children, with the aims of: strengthening the bonds within and between families, and between families, the school and the community; enhancing family functioning; preventing school failure; and reducing stress to the family's everyday life.

Visit the website (https://study.sagepub.com/rogers2e) to find out more information on the Families and Schools Together (FAST) programme.

FAST is one of just 23 evidence-based family skills training programmes in the world endorsed and highlighted by the United Nations Office on Drugs and Crime (UNODC).

Visit the website (https://study.sagepub.com/rogers2e) to find out more information on evidence-based models and approaches.

CONCLUSION

Task-centred social work is an approach which is unique and original to social work, rooted in practice-based evidence and a strong tradition of person-led positive and empowering practice. Although not always recognised or fully acknowledged by workers, it is used in day-to-day work by most social workers. Done well, it helps bridge the barrier between worker and client, identifies and clarifies problems and helps in the design and delivery of a credible and effective practical programme for change.

Having read this chapter, you should be able to:

- Better understand the principles, ethics and goals of task-centred social work;
- Identify opportunities where you can use a task-centred approach;
- Design, manage and deliver task-centred social work.

RECOMMENDED READING

Coulshed, V. and Orme, J. (1998) Task-centred practice. *Social Work Practice*. London: Palgrave, pp. 115–132.

Doel, M. (2002) Task-centred work. In R. Adams, L. Dominelli and M. Payne (eds), *Social Work: Themes, Issues and Critical Debates* (2nd edn). Basingstoke: Palgrave Macmillan, pp. 191–199.

Doel, M. and Marsh, P. (2006) Across the divide. Community Care, 8 June. Available at: www.communitycare.co.uk/2006/06/08/across-the-divide/ (accessed 1 September 2015).

Iriss (2019) Task centred casework. Available at: https://content.iriss.org.uk/taskcentred/ (accessed 1 June 2019).

Kanter, J.S. (1983) Reevaluation of task-centered social work practice. *Clinical Social Work Journal*, 11(3): 228–244.

Kelly, M. (2009). Task-centered practice. In T. Mizrahi and L.E. Davis (eds), *Encyclopedia of Social Work* (20th edn). Oxford: Oxford University Press, pp. 197–199.

Person-Centred Social Work

Dawn Whitaker

Links to the Professional Capabilities Framework

• Professionalism • Values and ethics • Diversity and equality • Critical reflection and analysis • Skills and interventions

Links to the Knowledge and Skills Statement for Child and Family Social Workers

• Communication • Relationships and effective direct work • Child development • Adult mental ill-health, substance misuse, domestic violence, physical ill-health and disability • Abuse and neglect of children • Child and family assessment • Analysis, decision-making, planning and review

Links to the Knowledge and Skills Statement for Social Workers in Adult Services

• The role of social workers working with adults • Person-centred practice • Safeguarding • Mental capacity • Effective assessments and outcome-based support planning • Direct work with individuals and families

Key messages

- Person-centred social work is part of the strengths-based approach to practice.
- The relationship is central.
- It requires person-centred communication skills, congruence and empathy, as well as a commitment to enabling growth and change, and the ability to reflect and be reflexive.

INTRODUCTION

As discussed in Chapter 1, person-centred social work originates from the work of Carl Rogers and the development of person-centred counselling. Although not a social work approach as such, its techniques for crafting the conditions required to create a transformative relationship are fundamental to social work intervention. Whilst social workers are not expected to be therapists, this chapter will demonstrate the value of adopting the principles of person-centred counselling in our work.

LEARNING FROM PERSON-CENTRED COUNSELLING

It is difficult to overstate the difference between traditional analytical methods of counselling and the person-centred approach put forward by Rogers. The core difference is that, for Rogers, the 'client knows best' and is therefore the expert in determining how to 'move forward' (Mearns and Thorne, 1999: 1). This is illustrated by Rogers's own description of his change in method:

> I was asking the question: How can I treat, or cure, or change this person? Now I would phrase the question in this way: How can I provide a relationship which this person may use for his own personal growth? (Rogers, 1956: 994)

The crux of Rogers's approach is acknowledging the limitations associated with using professional knowledge to teach others about themselves. Whilst he accepts it is possible to teach a person the characteristics of good parenting, just as a person can be taught budgeting skills and so on, for Rogers such teaching is less effective in helping a person resolve the problems of adjustment and human relationships (Rogers, 1956). In this way of thinking, the client has the answers and it is the therapist's job to help the client find them (Heffner, 2016). Consequently, person-centred counselling shifts emphasis away from professionally driven solutions to the importance of the relationship in enabling people to learn about themselves.

THE IMPORTANCE OF THE RELATIONSHIP

Rogers emphasised the importance of congruence and genuineness. This means faithfully being oneself, rather than presenting an external veneer, whilst hiding an alternative attitude. Basically, it is argued that only by being aware of and providing the genuine reality in ourselves can the other person 'successfully seek the reality' which is in them (Rogers, 1956: 995).

Whilst being genuine is a quality that most people working in the helping professions subscribe to, achieving it in the manner that Rogers intended is not straightforward.

A further condition necessary for the creation of a person centred relationship is acceptance: 'By acceptance I mean a warm regard for him as a person of unconditional self-worth – a person of value no matter what his condition, his behaviour, or his feelings' (Rogers, 1956: 995). This notion of 'acceptance' is often referred to as **unconditional positive regard**. This means relating to the client as a separate person, with his or her own feelings and experiences. Yet Rogers cautions us about the perceived simplicity of achieving unconditional positive regard, namely that acceptance is limited *without* understanding. He argued that it is only when we understand and accept a person's feelings and thoughts as they do that the person can feel 'really free to explore all the hidden nooks and frightening crannies' of their inner experience (Rogers, 1956: 995). One client described this as:

> [The therapist fostered] … my possession of my own experience … that [this] is *my* experience and that I am actually having it: thinking what I think, feeling what I feel, wanting what I want, fearing what I fear: no 'ifs', 'buts' or 'not reallys'. (Rogers, 1957: 98)

Yet for many people, access to positive regard is *conditional* upon them 'living a certain way' (Maclean and Harrison, 2011: 177); for example, '*I should feel* …', or '*I ought to do* …'. However, this can lead to psychological distress as the person's self-experience and self-picture are in conflict (Mearns and Thorne, 1999: 12). Therefore, the ideal person-centred relationship is one in which there is complete transparency and congruence on the part of the worker, and unconditional positive regard towards the other person that enables the worker to empathically understand their private world through their eyes (Rogers, 1956: 995). In doing so, we should acknowledge that we often work with people whose behaviour, lifestyle or attitude differs from our own, and is questionable or even offensive, but ensure that we are congruent and professional in our response (Mathews et al., 2014: 80). We must remember, that according to Rogers (1956), the *purpose* of building a person-centred relationship is to provide the platform for individuals to learn about themselves and achieve constructive personal development and change.

MOTIVATING CHANGE THROUGH PERSON-CENTRED RELATIONSHIPS

Person-centred counselling originates from the theory of humanism, which explains human motivation in terms of an innate desire for personal fulfilment and growth (Lomax and Jones, 2014: 47). On this basis, all individuals have the capacity to achieve '**self-actualisation**' or move forward in their lives, provided they have access to a suitable 'psychological climate' within which it can be released or expressed (Rogers, 1956: 995). For Rogers, this 'suitable climate' can be established through what he refers to as the 'necessary and sufficient conditions of therapeutic personality change', namely:

1   Two persons are in psychological contact.
2   The first, whom we shall term the client, is in a state of incongruence, being distressed or anxious.
3   The second person, whom we shall term the therapist, is congruent, or integrated in the relationship.
4   The therapist experiences unconditional positive regard for the client.
5   The therapist experiences an empathic understanding of the client's internal frame of reference and endeavours to communicate this experience to them.
6   The communication to the client of the therapist's empathic understanding and unconditional positive regard is to a minimal degree achieved.

Whilst the first condition stipulates that minimal psychological contact must exist, the others define the characteristics of the relationship that are necessary in order to achieve change. For Rogers, no other conditions are necessary, and if these six conditions are met, change will follow (1957: 96).

Consequently, a person is able to safely embark on a journey of self-'discovery', in which their 'hates, fears, tensions, feelings of unworthiness' etc., can be felt and explored, including their often-buried positive attitudes and emotions (Rogers, 1956: 996). This must be accompanied by the therapist's empathic understanding of the client's feelings and experience, as if they were their own, although this would be incomplete without the client's awareness of the therapist's acceptance and empathy towards them (Rogers, 1957: 99). This can have powerful effects: 'Empathic understanding restores to the lonely and alienated individual a sense of belonging to the human race' (Mearns and Thorne, 1999: 16). Rogers (1956: 996) provides an illustrative example of how these *necessary and sufficient conditions* can provide a suitable psychological climate for change:

> A father comes to the point where he suddenly realises that love for his children is not an obligatory attitude which he *must* possess, but is a spontaneous, surging, tender feeling in him which he has never dared to recognise because it has seemed unmanly. He sits quietly with tears in his eyes while this feeling flows through him.

According to Rogers, any such realisation is more likely to occur in the context of empathy and unconditional positive regard; that is, 'it permits him to relax the tight defensive structure of his concept of himself, and to admit into awareness and full experience the attitudes which previously he has found too threatening' (Rogers, 1956: 996). The father reorganises his self-picture to include the tenderness and emotionalism which he has previously denied as well as the more masculine feelings which he has experienced (Rogers, 1956: 996). This realisation is bolstered by the person's internalisation of the worker's positive attitude towards them, allowing it to be integrated into their self-picture, thereby enabling them to feel valued and worthy. The new 'self' is discovered in, and defined by, the experience of the relationship. It is argued this means the person is more likely to act in accordance with their new self-picture, even after years of 'futile struggle to change' (Rogers, 1956: 996).

Reflective activity

- Can you identify an intervention either on placement or in practice where you worked in a way that was compatible with Rogers's person-centred approach?
- Reflect on how you were able to achieve this, and the benefits and obstacles in doing so.

WIDER CONSIDERATIONS

Given the *client-as-expert* ethos of person-centred counselling, it is not surprising that Rogers rejected the professional 'pursuit of control or authority over other persons', in favour of a 'commitment to share power and [to] exercise control co-operatively' (Mearns and Thorne, 1999: 19). This 'abdication of power seeking' (Mearns and Thorne, 1999: 19) also included the rejection of 'any type of moral or diagnostic evaluation', which Rogers conceived as threatening to individuals and incompatible with the necessary and sufficient conditions of a person-centred relationship (Rogers, 1956: 995; Rogers, 1957: 101).

Visit the website (https://study.sagepub.com/rogers2e) to find more information on Rogerian person-centred counselling and watch original video footage of Carl Rogers engaged in the therapeutic relationship.

PERSON-CENTRED SOCIAL WORK: A CONTRADICTION IN TERMS?

Rogers asserted that the principles of person-centred counselling are applicable to 'all human relationships', including social work: 'we are seeing the beginnings of a new field of human relationships, in which we may specify that if certain attitudinal conditions exist, then certain definable changes will occur' (Rogers, 1956: 997). However, critics argue that there is 'a mutual incompatibility of the person-centred approach' in the 'context and tasks of modern social work' practice: 'use of the term "person-centred" belies the function of modern social work in which the relationship is for the utilitarian purposes of compliance and externally imposed direction on the service user' (Murphy et al., 2012: 717).

Reflective questions

- Consider to what extent it is possible to achieve Rogers's 'necessary and sufficient conditions' in social work?
- How might this differ in a voluntary or statutory setting?
- Would this be different if your relationship was based on consent or compulsion: for example, an older adult approaching services for assistance to maintain independence vs a court-ordered child protection context?

The debate surrounding the applicability of Rogers's person-centred approach to social work reflects its position as a state-sponsored occupation, and its compatibility or otherwise with genuine **relationship-based approaches**. Whilst social work is often eager to align itself with *skills* that are compatible with person-centred practice, for example empathy, unconditional positive regard and genuineness, critics argue that the *purpose* for which these skills are intended is incompatible with the theoretical foundations of person-centred practice:

> … person-centred practice implies a relationship that is an 'end in itself'. As such, the person-centred practitioner adopts a non-directive attitude in which they have no pre-determined or specific outcomes or intentions for the service user to achieve … [whereas] … social workers who are claiming to be operating in a person-centred way within a relationship-based approach are, in effect, using the relationship instrumentally … to facilitate engagement with the client in order to find out what the client wants, to develop rapport or to gain compliance. (Murphy et al., 2012: 708)

The extent to which the person-centred relationship is intended to be an *end in itself*, or a *means to an end*, reflects what Grant (1990) refers to as the difference between 'principled' and 'instrumental' **non-directiveness**. *Instrumental* non-directiveness refers to the 'therapist's actions to bring about growth or empower clients', whereas in *principled* non-directiveness the therapist does not 'intend to make anything happen', i.e. 'growth', 'insight' or 'self-acceptance' – the aim is to provide the 'therapeutic conditions' under which the client will 'make use of them' (Grant, 1990: 77). On this basis, they are 'done for different reasons, in different spirits' (Grant, 1990: 77).

Utilising Grant's analysis, Murphy et al. (2012: 716–717) argue that it is 'theoretically misleading' to assert that a person-centred approach can be 'fully embraced' in social work, as practitioners are required to act on behalf of the state, meaning that whilst it 'can take an instrumental stance', it 'cannot take a principled stance to nondirectivity in practice'. Whilst we may feel disheartened in response to such criticism, other interpretations of non-directivity are more accessible to social work:

> A client-centered therapist might argue with a client, accompany a client to look for a job, or assist the client to enter a behavior modification program. The issue is not the behavior but whether or not the therapist's actions emerge from the therapist's dedication to the client's frame of reference. (Bozarth and Evans, 2000)

This reflects a broader understanding of non-directiveness, in which the focus is on the client and practitioner's dedication to the client's own frame of reference. This is recognisable in Rogers's response to questioning on this matter:

> … the approach that we developed was a protest against what had been going on and so it was non-directive to separate it from directive, but then it became more and

more focused on the person, then client centered and person-centered became more appropriate terms. I think that those older terms [such as 'non-directive' or 'indirective'] have historical interest but not current value. (Rogers, 1985 in Ellingham, 2005)

In this way of thinking, the issue for social work is *less* about the perils of **directiveness**, and more about ensuring that it reflects a dedication to the client's own frame of reference. Though we should acknowledge Murphy et al.'s representation of statutory social work as a form of utilitarianism, often characterised by protective intervention, risk management and managerialism (2012). This is too broad a generalisation of what is, now more than ever, an increasingly diverse social work landscape, made up of an array of different approaches in statutory and *increasingly* non-statutory practice contexts. Whilst statutory social work does indeed involve elements of **instrumentality**, this does not have to be at the expense of relationship-based practice (Ingram, 2013a). There are opportunities, both within and external to statutory social work, to trust in the self-actualising tendency of people, and recognise their right to self-determination (Lynch, 2014; Milne, 2006). This dilutes Murphy et al.'s blanket assertion that social work is unable to be 'truly person-centred' (2012: 716).

A WAY FORWARD?

Trevithick warns us that the service user–social worker relationship is not an end in itself:

> … some practitioners fell into the deceptive and perilous trap of thinking that forming and maintaining good relationships, sometimes called relationship-building, was an end in itself, rather than a practice approach that provides a foundation on which to build further work. (2003: 166)

Whilst this suggests that the service user–social worker relationship is incompatible with Grant's *principled* non-directiveness, it does not mean that social work is incapable of being person-centred. Indeed, as Bozarth and Evans's (2000) aforementioned broader analysis of non-directiveness asserts, social work *can be* person-centred *provided* the 'work' that stems from the relationship reflects the person's own frame of reference. This echoes research which suggests that although people want social workers to be reliable, warm and approachable, and to listen, understand and be knowledgeable, they *also* want practical help (Holland and Scourfield, 2015: 57). On this basis, we *can* achieve person-centred practice when we are genuinely able to accomplish Rogers's necessary and sufficient conditions, *and* structure our actions around the person's own frame of reference.

Whilst it would be naïve to claim that social work could achieve authentic person-centred practice in *all* situations *all* of the time, we must be careful of eliminating the possibility of doing so, just because it is difficult or not always possible.

> **Reflective activity**
>
> Consider this statement: It is possible to achieve person-centred practice when we are able to accomplish Rogers's necessary and sufficient conditions, and structure our actions around the person's own frame of reference.
>
> - What difficulties might you face in achieving the above in practice?
> - What would you do to overcome these difficulties?

POTENTIAL OBSTACLES AND RESOLUTIONS

- *An inability to accomplish Rogers's necessary and sufficient conditions*: This may be due to relationship difficulties or breakdown; social worker incongruence; or failure to experience and/or communicate unconditional positive regard or empathy. The more we can do to address these issues, and foster Rogers's 'suitable climate', the more we will be able to create the conditions necessary for a genuine person-centred relationship.
- *Conflict between the person's own and our professional frame of reference*: Whilst this is more likely to occur in statutory social work, it is not inevitable. In these circumstances, we should take action to understand and empathise with the person's own frame of reference, and work to close the gap. This might include efforts to negotiate a shared understanding of the 'issue', or action to increase the person's consent by reducing professional power and control.
- *Invisible barriers*: Being congruent means being open and honest, even when addressing difficult subject matter. Explain your role, organisational agenda and associated expectations and limitations. Discuss the nature of your relationship and professional boundaries rather than hide behind an organisational facade. People often know more about the terms of their relationship with an internet provider or utility company than they do about their relationship with their social worker.

It is important to acknowledge the obstacles faced in realising genuine person-centred social work. This means recognising when it *cannot* be achieved, as well as when it can. Otherwise, we risk what Beckett and Horner refer to as a sort of 'pseudo-Rogerian approach', whereby we offer the 'semblance' of acceptance that Rogers describes, without being honest about its limitations or competing agendas (2016: 152).

This suggests that person-centred practice is a work in progress, or as recent research suggests 'an ambition', rather than a 'priority' or reality (National Voices, 2017: 5). However, even where full and genuine person-centred social work is challenging or not possible, the more we adopt the principles of personalised relationship-based practice in our work, the better, as outlined below:

- The person is more likely to share their true self-picture, and we are more likely to accept and understand it.
- We are more likely to understand the person's motivation and recognise them as experts of their own experience.
- We will recognise that everyone has the potential for personal growth.
- The person is more likely to own any identified resolutions.
- Change is likely to be more enduring.
- Practice is likely to be less adversarial, and more successful.

. . . .

Case study

As stated above, 'we can achieve person-centred practice when we are genuinely able to accomplish Rogers's necessary and sufficient conditions, and structure our actions around the person's own frame of reference'.

Preliminary context

It is important to note that most social work intervention is based on assessment, in which the vast bulk of information is social, familial and personal, *as experienced and told by the people themselves*. It is not surprising, therefore, that any relationship that even approaches person-centredness is likely to result in people being more willing and able to communicate with us in a manner that will yield accurate information. In consequence, we are better able to understand and assess the information, because we are tuned into its underpinning frame of reference.

Most social work is involved with changing behaviour in some form. In statutory child care, this generally involves changing adults' behaviour to enable them to be more effective parents and carers. But, as the revolving door of social work engagement shows, the greatest challenge is often maintaining and building on progress.

Case

This case study demonstrates the *beginning* and *end* of a typical person-centred intervention; it is an amalgamation of actual practice situations with identifying features removed or changed. As Ken Kesey said in *One Flew Over the Cuckoo's Nest*, 'it's the truth even if it didn't happen'.
The following case shows how a person-centred relationship with an involuntary service user, *which acknowledged and validated her own lived experience and frame of reference*, allowed her to 'own' not only the issues, but also the solutions.

Emma was in her early thirties, a single parent of two primary-school-age children. The police made a referral to Children's Social Care (CSC) after being called to a 'domestic incident', during which her uncle had tried to force his way into her flat after midnight. According to police the children could be heard crying through the closed door. The uncle had been drunk and abusive, and was arrested 'to prevent a breach of the peace'. However, he was subsequently released without charge when Emma would not make a formal complaint. Police and

(Continued)

housing records showed that he often stayed in her flat, and had been seen to assault her on previous occasions.

The social worker knocked on Emma's door two days later. She initially thought he was a police officer, and was clearly surprised and very frightened when he identified himself as being from social services.

Emma allowed the social worker into her flat and sat on the edge of her seat without speaking. The social worker explained that he was there because the police had informed CSC of the incident two days previously, and raised concerns about her and her children's safety and welfare.

Utilising knowledge of Rogers's core conditions, the social worker used unconditional positive regard and empathy by stating, 'I've spoken to the school and they say only good things about you and the kids.' To which Emma replied: 'You went behind my back?! ... Are you taking them?'

The social worker then demonstrated congruence in his reply: 'No ... I can't and I don't want to ... I want them to stay with you and to be safe, just as much as you do.'

The social worker confirmed that Emma had heard and understood before continuing, 'I think I need to explain what I can and can't do, and what it means when I say I want them to stay with you and be safe. Is that OK?'

The social worker went on to explain both the extent and limits to the local authority's duties and powers under children's legislation and specifically that a social worker could not remove any child without a court order or police intervention. The worker then briefly outlined the research evidence on the impact of domestic abuse on children, and why her uncle's behaviour was considered a threat to their safety and welfare.

The social worker continued using empathy, by stating, 'And I'm wondering if it feels like you've now got another man sitting in your home telling you what to do?', to which Emma nodded and stayed on the edge of her chair.

The social worker responded with congruence, 'That must be hard ... But there's an important difference. The law is clear – the welfare of the child is paramount. That means everything I do must be in the best interest of the children. If you disagree with me, ask me to explain. And if you still disagree, then speak to my manager ... You want the best for your children. Let me prove to you that I want the same thing.'

Commentary

During the intervention, Emma often asked the social worker to explain his decisions, and she spoke to the team manager twice. At the third child protection conference she argued against the assembled professionals, to insist that her children remain on the Child Protection Register, until she was 'back on her feet'. After 10 months of working alongside the social worker and multidisciplinary team, she recognised the value of support that did not stigmatise or blame her. In doing so, she acknowledged that the Child Protection Register was a gateway to services. Six months later she agreed to the children being 'de-registered' and there was no further contact with CSC.

Use of Rogers's necessary and sufficient conditions

1   *Psychological contact between Emma and the worker.* In a social work context, especially in statutory services, the social worker tends to set the initial agenda. Despite this,

something very close to psychological contact can nevertheless be established around a shared commitment to positive change. This was demonstrated when Emma, after a number of months, acknowledged that she and the social worker shared a genuine commitment to her children's welfare.

2 *Client anxious or distressed*: In counselling terms, a client is anxious or distressed when they are in a state of psychological incongruence and recognise that they want or need to make a change. The parallel to this, in social work, is when the service user 'owns the problem' and recognises the need for change. This was achieved after a few weeks when Emma recognised that her uncle's violence, and the risk he presented, had a negative impact on her and her children's lives.

3 *The worker shows congruence*: This was demonstrated by appropriately sharing information that might lessen Emma's anxiety and distress. In particular, explaining that whilst background checks had been undertaken, that only positive information had been disclosed. It was also important that the social worker was clear about his powers and the reason for his involvement.

4 *The worker shows empathy*: This was demonstrated by acknowledging the possible emotional impact of a male worker entering Emma's home to raise concerns about her children, especially when she had recently been disempowered by a man who is part of her family.

5 *The worker shows unconditional positive regard*: This was demonstrated in a number of ways: informing Emma that her children's school was positive about her; explicitly recognising that she wants the best for her children; and encouraging her to challenge the worker's decisions or actions.

6 *The service user experiences the worker's congruence, empathy and positive regard*: It is the worker's responsibility to demonstrate these qualities regardless of the service user's ability or willingness to acknowledge and respond to them. While it is often difficult to demonstrate, Emma's response to the intervention suggests that it had been achieved. This is shown by the extent to which she 'owned' the difficulties and solutions, and continued to engage until she felt able to take full control.

. . . .

CONCLUSION

This chapter introduced the foundations of Rogers's person-centred counselling, before critically exploring its application to social work, and if and how it can be used in practice. It emphasised the importance of the service user–social worker relationship, and the value of adhering to person-centred principles in all we do.

As you will have noted, person-centred social work requires good and effective communication skills, empathy, reflexivity and emotional intelligence. These skills will enable you to better understand the expertise of people who use services and foster resilience in practice – all essential components of strengths-based work. You may wish to revisit each of these subjects in the previous chapters of the book.

Having read this chapter, you should be able to:

- Recognise the importance of relationships in achieving person-centred practice;
- Aim to demonstrate empathy, congruence and unconditional positive regard in your day-to-day work;
- Implement the core features of person-centred social work;
- Overcome the obstacles and resolutions to achieving person-centred social work.

RECOMMENDED READING

Beckett, C. and Horner, N. (2016) *Essential Theory for Social Work Practice* (2nd edn). London: Sage.

Ingram, R. (2013a) Locating emotional intelligence at the heart of social work practice. *British Journal of Social Work*, 43(5): 987–1034.

Mearns, D., Thorne, B. and McLeod, J. (2013) *Person-Centred Counselling in Action* (4th edn). London: Sage.

Murphy, D., Duggan, M. and Joseph. S. (2012) Relationship-based social work and its compatibility with the person-centred approach: principled versus instrumental perspectives. *British Journal of Social Work*, 43(4): 703–719.

Rogers, C. (1957) The necessary and sufficient conditions of therapeutic personality change. *Journal of Consulting Psychology*, 21(2): 95–103.

Group Work
Michaela Rogers

Links to the Professional Capabilities Framework

- Values and ethics   • Diversity and equality   • Knowledge   • Skills and interventions
- Professional leadership

Links to the Knowledge and Skills Statement for Child and Family Practitioners

- Relationships and effective direct work   • Communication   • Analysis, decision-making, planning and review

Links to the Knowledge and Skills Statement for Social Workers in Adult Services

- Person-centred practice   • Effective assessments and outcome-based support planning
- Direct work with individuals and families

Key messages

- Group work can help individuals and groups to meet need and influence change.
- Indeed, participation in groups offers the opportunity for transformation and empowerment.
- Group dynamics are subject to change and can be precarious depending on the different roles that people take.
- Therefore, successful group work relies on good planning and facilitation.

INTRODUCTION

Social work is essentially based on interactions between individuals; this inevitably involves groups (of service users, carers, social workers and other professional groups or any combination of each) both formally and informally. In your work setting, you may be required to work in teams, or become part of a learning set, particularly in your assessed and supported year of employment (ASYE). You may participate in multi-professional group meetings (see Chapter 19 'Inter-Professional Practice and Working Together'). You may coordinate group work (for example, a support group for foster carers) which requires a more formal structure and framework. For the purpose of this chapter, group work is defined as:

> … a method of social work which aims, in an informal way, through purposeful group experiences, to help individuals and groups to meet individual and group need and to influence and change personal, group, organisational and community problems. (Lindsay and Orton, 2011: 7)

It is fair to say that it does not matter which level you are working at (from learner to leadership), or what type of group and setting, as a social worker you should become familiar with and confident in working with groups. Moreover, contrasted with one-to-one work, which can often be focused on what has gone wrong, through group work an individual's strengths and abilities can emerge (see Chapter 23 'Strengths-Based and Solution-Focused Approaches').

GROUP WORK THEORY

Tuckman's (1965) staged model, developed in relation to group formation and dynamics, is well known and oft cited. Tuckman considered that groups should have a purpose, or goal, and he proposed that there are four stages of groups in relation to the achievement of that goal:

Forming: This is the initial stage when people have come together to form a group. The criteria for membership and the aims of the group are known. People start to work together and get to know one another.

Storming: The group then moves into the storming phase, where boundaries may be pushed, goals are questioned or clarified, and there may be conflict between members as different styles of working or personalities emerge. Members may jockey for position as roles are negotiated. Alternatively some members may feel overwhelmed by their role or be disgruntled in terms of the direction the group is taking. Groups can fail at this stage.

Norming: Gradually, the group moves into the norming stage. At this point, people have come to know each other. This helps as differences get resolved, roles are accepted and strengths/weaknesses are acknowledged. Group members develop a strong commitment to the goal of the group as they see progress towards its achievement. There can be an overlap between storming and norming as aspects of the group change (members may join/leave, new tasks may be created).

Performing: The group reaches the performing stage when all the hard work starts to pay off. The structures and processes that have been set up support the achievement of the goal. Disruptions do not have significant impact (such as members leaving) as the group is stable and performing well.

Later, Tuckman added a fifth stage, 'adjourning' (sometimes referred to as 'mourning'), to account for the fact that many groups will be adjourned once the goal is reached. In social work, interventions are usually time-bound and groups are often disbanded once the goal is reached. This is an important aspect in the life of a group and it is essential that the ending is planned for and sufficient time is set aside for the group to mark the ending. It may be prudent to discuss the possibility of the group's end at an earlier stage.

Reflective activity

Think about the groups that you belong to, or have done so in the past, or reflect upon a group that you have facilitated. Can you identify Tuckman's stages in relation to the formation and development of that group?

FUNCTIONS OF GROUP WORK

In social work there are many considerations that need attention when considering group work, such as the purpose, membership and practical arrangements. However, the principal purpose of a group should be to meet the needs of its members. Indeed, there are many positives for individuals including mutual support, increased problem-solving ability, mutual aid, empowerment and positive reinforcement, as well as the belief that individual behaviour can be influenced by group processes.

As groups can have multiple functions, there is also a demand for different types of groups. Some have social benefits as well as being supportive or therapeutic. Formal groups can be established as action groups; for example, a community group that is set up to canvas for a new play area. Thematic groups might be set up in the work environment in order to enable a group of practitioners to look at alternative ways of working with a particular issue, or to implement new policy. Birkenmaier et al. (2014) offer a typology of groups as follows:

- *Support group*: To enable members who share a common experience to provide and gain support (for example, a group for adults who have all experienced childhood abuse).

- *Psychoeducational group*: This focuses on the education of group members regarding a psychological condition (for example, the parents of children with mental health problems).
- *Remedial group*: This type of group focuses on changing behaviour, restoring functioning or promoting coping strategies for the group members (for example, a group for perpetrators of domestic violence and abuse).

- -

Case studies

Consider what might be the type, aims, benefits and limitations of the following groups:

- a young carers social group;
- reminiscence groups for people suffering from dementia;
- bereavement groups for parents who have lost their children;
- a youth group for lesbian, gay, bisexual, trans and queer (LGBTQ) young people;
- an abstinence group for people who misuse alcohol and drugs;
- a community group for people affected by local crime.

- -

Visit the website to explore the benefits of group work (https://study.sagepub.com/rogers2e).

PLANNING GROUPS

The role of a facilitator can be central to the success of a group. As Sharry (2001: 5) notes, 'the aim of the facilitator is to establish the conditions and trust in the group whereby clients can help one another and then to "get out of the way" to allow them to do it'. The facilitator will need to consider various issues, and Moss (2012: 144) defines the key task of the facilitator as simply 'planning': 'Planning is an essential communication skill without which no group work could succeed.' First, it is important to be clear about the identified need or aim of the group. Second, aspects of coordination will take priority and there are many decisions to be made during this stage. These include:

- *Authority and permission*: Does your organisation need to be consulted?
- *Leadership*: Will the facilitator lead the group, or will it be user-led?
- *Membership*: Will group membership be open or closed (the latter means that the membership is fixed throughout the course of the group's life)? Will membership be voluntary or compulsory?
- *Planning and coordination*: Will this be the responsibility of the facilitator or will a planning group, including service users, be established? Who will provide the administration for the group?

- *Group contract*: The expectations need to be clear from the start and may incorporate a group contract. A group contract might include the group's aims, ground rules, confidentiality and expectations of membership (for example, in terms of attendance).
- *Space*: Where is the group going to take place?
- *Days and time*: When is the best time for the group to meet?
- *Length*: How long will group sessions be? Will the group be open-ended or fixed-term?
- *Economy*: How will the group be funded?

In addition, Price and Price (2013) highlight the need for a 'methodology'. The methodology might be agreed in the early stage of the group and might include: discussions; guest speakers; role play; small group tasks; and many other types of activities. Preparing individual sessions, and debriefing after them, is key to successful group management and maintenance, although it is also important to be able to respond to the mood, pace and unexpected occurrences during a group meeting (Doel, 2006).

Best practice case study: Cloverleaf Advocacy Service

Cloverleaf Advocacy Service provides a range of statutory and non-statutory services. Many clients approach the service whilst in crisis, for example, whilst detained under the Mental Health Act 2007 or through the recent statutory obligations of the Care Act 2014. In addition to this, a variety of outreach methods and approaches to engage members of the local community are used, based upon the 'Asset Based Community Development Model' (ABCD).

ABCD is a process of community building that 'starts with the process of locating the assets, skills and capacities of residents, citizens' associations and local institutions' (Kretzman and McKnight 1993 cited in IDeA, 2010: 23).

An example of the ABCD principle is the focus of one particular group, Wednesday's Voice, a weekly session attended by people with learning disabilities and currently facilitated by Cloverleaf. The aims of the sessions are to:

- build confidence and utilise the skills and strengths of people, who have, or are at risk of requiring support services;
- offer mechanisms to ensure the growth of peer-to-peer and self-advocacy skills to enhance resilience both collectively and individually;
- provide greater knowledge and information on which people base their decisions and choices;
- optimise quality of life, independence, choice control, inclusion and safety;
- develop a self-sustaining model of community development;
- ensure the power of decision-making is in the hands of those living within the community.

(Continued)

The group has evolved over the past 18 months and those who attend have chosen the name, while all members were involved in setting the aims and objects as well as agreeing the rules and boundaries, such as treating each other with respect and dignity. Volunteer members complete many of the tasks necessary for each session to maintain itself.

The group recognised the need to pay to attend in order to pay room rental, buy food for 'cook and eat' sessions and provide resources for such things as travel to events they identify as being critical to the group's development. In addition to this they regularly have fund-raising days, sponsored walks, cake and Christmas card sales, all of which are chosen democratically by members.

Members are also involved in consultation events and recently visited a local tourist attraction that is bidding for funds to upgrade its facilities. Members walked around the parkland area and advised the architect which areas could be improved to increase accessibility. The next consultation event will be at the local hospital, where members will visit and evaluate how the hospital environment feels to them with regard to accessibility and sensory experience.

Members have moved on from the group, with one member gaining employment, one feeling confident enough to attend a college course and others gaining confidence to access other community events. In addition to this the 'cook and eat' sessions offer practical skills on how to eat healthily and learning how to cook meals at home.

 Visit the website (https://study.sagepub.com/rogers2e) to read the IDeA paper, 'A glass half full: how an asset approach can improve community health and well-being'.

GROUP DYNAMICS AND PROCESSES

When facilitating groups, a knowledge of group dynamics and process is critical (Price and Price, 2013). A well-planned group that has clear aims and ground rules is a good starting point. This can make members feel confident about the group (which is then reflected in good attendance and contributions) and can enable members to feel supported and welcomed.

Consider your own membership of groups (for example, your student group at university) and think about the formal and informal rules that apply, such as: confidentiality; respect for other people's opinions; challenging a person's behaviour and not the person; anti-oppressive and anti-discriminatory language and behaviour; mobile phone use; turn-taking; punctuality and attendance. Now consider how the group might perform if these rules were not in place. The dynamics of the group would be entirely different and might make participation very difficult if people did not think that the group offered a safe space.

Whilst authors have attempted to analyse group processes and dynamics, according to Lindsay and Orton (2011) Tuckman's linear model of group formation is the best starting point. In using Tuckman's model, however, it is useful to consider the impact of individuals in terms of behaviour and roles.

Reflective activity

Think about your student group at university, or another group to which you belong. Consider the following questions:

1 Are you an active member of the group?
2 Do you take a leadership role?
3 Are you silent or vocally active?
4 Do you feel listened to?
5 Is your point of view heard?
6 Is your point of view congruent with the majority of the group?
7 Are you able to disagree if you want to?
8 Do you feel empowered/disempowered in this group?
9 Do you feel worried if you disagree?
10 Do you 'switch off' and get bored within the group?
11 What do you do if you feel angry/sad/confused?

Being aware of how you function in a group is important as it gives you insight into how others feel about the roles they take within group settings, whilst also being mindful that context is important too. For example, consider a group of women who have all experienced domestic abuse. If one of the group members takes a dominant role, leading conversation and dismissing other people's opinions, imagine how that must feel to the other group members. It may be that the dominant woman is struggling to regain control over her life and this is the only environment where she feels that she can be vocal and take a leading role. In this scenario, it is up to the facilitator to recognise the particular dynamics and encourage different ones to evolve. In fact, the notion of power in relation to its influence on group dynamics is central and for a facilitator to be adept at recognising and managing power, it is essential that they have a good level of self-awareness and sensitivity (Price and Price, 2013). This is to ensure that they remain alert to the power invested in them in their role as well as the power imbalance between them and the group membership. Group diversity in terms of ethnicity, gender, ability and other forms of difference is important too as facilitators should be aware of the barriers and enablers to inclusion and participation.

Reflective activity

For a final time consider your student group at university, or another group to which you belong, and reflect on the roles that people take. Can you identify individuals who adopt the following behaviours and roles:

(Continued)

- the member who monopolises conversations;
- the member who challenges people;
- the one who likes to be different;
- the joker;
- the gatekeeper;
- the member who keeps silent. (Adapted from Doel and Sawdon, 1999)

Table 28.1 Benefits and limitations of group work (adapted from Lindsay, 2013)

Benefits

Groups can provide a source of support as members share life experiences and problems.

As well as experiences, group members can share information about services and relevant issues.

Being part of a group can be empowering as members receive help as well as giving support.

There is an opportunity for transformation as group members can glean insight from others, whilst self-exposure can operate to enable emotional, psychological and cognitive growth.

Group members can learn from one another, but can also invite external people and/or agencies to visit as part of a learning opportunity for the group.

Groups can improve communication between individuals, services and communities.

Groups can offer a safe space for testing new ideas or behaviour.

Limitations

Groups do not always promote community, partnership and/or shared experience; some individuals may dominate, whilst others feel on the margins. In this way, groups can be isolating and disempowering.

Issues of confidentiality and safety can arise.

Groups can be time-consuming and costly.

Groups can even be harmful as vulnerabilities are exposed, and stereotyping or discriminatory behaviour can take place. Are all members equal, or are some marginalised, silenced and excluded?

CONCLUSION

This chapter has explored the processes, dynamics, benefits and limitations of group work. This offers an introduction to some basic techniques and issues that require full consideration when approaching the task of group facilitation. The importance of planning is central to a group's performance, and a structured, well-planned group can help to forge a path through the more challenging stages of Tuckman's (1965) sequential approach to group formation.

Having read this chapter, you should be able to:

- Consider the ways that group work skills benefit social work practice;
- Articulate Tuckman's different stages of group formation;
- Identify the different functions that group work can fill and the range of settings that would be suitable for group work;
- Consider the barriers and enablers to effective group work.

RECOMMENDED READING

Doel, M. and Kelly, T.B. (2014) *The A-Z of Groups and Groupwork*. Basingstoke: Palgrave Macmillan.

Doel, M. and Sawdon, C. (1999) *The Essential Groupworker*. London: Jessica Kingsley.

Lindsay, T. and Orton, S. (2014) *Groupwork Practice in Social Work* (3rd edn). Exeter: Learning Matters.

Attachment Theory: Examining Maternal Sensitivity Scales

Donna Peach

Links to the Professional Capabilities Framework

• Professionalism • Values and ethics • Diversity and equality • Rights, justice and economic wellbeing • Critical reflection and analysis

Links to the Knowledge and Skills Statement for Child and Family Practitioners

• Relationships and effective direct work • Communication • Child development • Child and family assessment

Links to the Knowledge and Skills Statement for Adult Practitioners

• Person-centred practice • Direct work with individuals and families • Supervision, critical reflection and analysis

Key messages

- Attachment theory is a cornerstone of social work practice.
- There are limitations in the application of attachment theory.
- It is embedded in epistemological assumptions about how we relate to others.
- It is vitally important to remain consciously critical when applying attachment theory to the judgements and decisions we make every day in practice.

INTRODUCTION

As social work students, you will have attended lectures and completed reading that informed you of the usefulness of attachment theory. That information will not be repeated in this chapter. Instead you will be encouraged to use and develop your critical evaluative skills to explore a component of attachment theory, the often less-discussed, maternal sensitivity scales developed by Mary Ainsworth. You will have varying degrees of certainty about how attachment theory informs your practice and your confidence in its direct application. After reading this chapter, you will hopefully have a more critical understanding of its theoretical strengths and weaknesses. Although we are limited to a few examples of critique, we proffer a range of lenses with which to examine the construction and application of attachment theory. This critique is not intended to disrupt your practice; quite the contrary, it is hoped that this chapter will increase your confidence to critically analyse theories and their application in practice.

However, this chapter is not a 'how to' guide on observing attachment, because it is difficult to achieve that without unintentionally reaffirming an inherent bias that privileges the perspective of the onlooker. Instead, you will be encouraged to embrace the uncertainty which is integral to social work practice and appreciate that the decisions we make are influenced by our own 'sense-making'. The underpinning social work skill that this chapter focuses on is our ability to begin to recognise the gaps between knowledge and practice and understand how we use our 'self' to fill that space.

Visit the website to listen to Dr Wendy Smith discuss attachment theory (https://study. sagepub.com/rogers2e).

The concepts of epistemology and ontology that are introduced in this chapter are not simple. It could be that you feel overwhelmed by the language and complexity of these theoretical terms. However, these terms are understood by undergraduate psychology students, as they are key to the psychological theories that underpin how we understand children and families. Crucially, social work practice with children is anchored to child development theories, and it is important to encourage you to develop your skill and confidence to engage with these concepts.

Although the content of this chapter interrupts the notion that attachment theory is too established to be unpicked, it does not intend to disrupt your practice. Quite the contrary. It is hoped the increased knowledge will develop your confidence to critically analyse theories and their use. More specifically, understanding the building blocks that founded attachment theory – and an ability to critique these – will assist your ability to form judgements between theoretical constructs and their application to practice.

John Bowlby's (1969/1982) and Mary Ainsworth's (1969) theory of attachment has become a cornerstone of social work practice. However, we need to examine how we transfer knowledge from the original theory, developed almost 50 years ago, to contemporary social work decisions. This chapter interrogates the foundations of mother–child dyadic attachment and considers the implications when social workers are faced with decisions involving the separation of children from members of their birth families. In doing so, it illuminates the need to explore other theoretical concepts, which can assist our determination of a child's individual and relationship needs.

Many students and newly qualified social workers express anxiety about the integration of theory in their written work. Failure to understand theory in a university assignment may affect your grades but doing the same in a written report in practice can have life-changing consequences for the families we work with. This is particularly the case for attachment theory, upon which decisions about interventions into family, or even permanent removal of children from parents and siblings can be based.

To discuss this theory in a critical manner inevitably leads us to question the validity of applying attachment theory in social work practice. This is in itself a challenge as many social workers, psychologists and judges use attachment theory to determine plans for children. However, to not examine this in a critical manner would be a failure of one of the fundamental necessities of social work practice, that of being critically reflexive.

EPISTEMOLOGY

Epistemology is the study of how we know what we know, and is a great starting point for a deconstructive examination of attachment theory. Attachment theory and terms such as 'bonding' are concepts that have been so integrated into our language and understanding of mother–infant relationships that they are often unquestioned. As humans, we love to categorise, to find ways of simplifying knowledge, and attachment theorists have attempted to do this for half a century. Thus, if we want to understand what attachment theory is, we need to consider its origins in the context of their time and place.

Visit the website (https://study.sagepub.com/rogers2e) to find more about epistemology.

Briefly, it is important to recall the socio-political environment that Bowlby and Ainsworth experienced in their lives and the time they developed their theory. This is not to undermine the work they did but to recognise that as researchers our view of the world is situated within the time and place we inhabit. Thus, we cannot divorce attachment theory from the roles that societal cultures construct for women and the influence of white middle-class ideologies of good mothering. To gain further insight into this topic read further about topics such as maternal privation (where a child fails to make an attachment) and maternal deprivation (where an attachment is disrupted or broken).

Visit the website (https://study.sagepub.com/rogers2e) to find out more about maternal privation and maternal deprivation. Watch the video and complete the activity before critically analysing what opinions you have formed.

The concept of maternal relationships and their association to the construction of what we understand to be attachment is particularly important once we begin to consider the assumptions that underpin Ainsworth's maternal sensitivity scale. We will explore these later in this chapter but, for now, it is important to understand the impact that research design has on the knowledge produced. Knowledge derived from research activities is always enabled and constrained by the research methodology. Thus, the research methods used can have a significant impact on our understanding of human behaviour. It is perhaps most easily demonstrated by showing some examples of methods used to understand aspects of child development. Object permanence is a term used to explain how a child knows that an object continues to exist even though they can no longer see it. In Piaget's famous blanket and ball study, he concluded that children were able to form a mental representation of the object at eight months.

Visit the website (https://study.sagepub.com/rogers2e) to watch a video demonstrating Piaget's experiment.

However, the knowledge of when children develop object permanence was limited by the design of the study that required a child to have sufficient physical ability to move and search for the ball. A study by Baillargeon (1986) challenges Piaget's findings by designing an experiment where physical movement of the child was not required. However, in the spirit of continual development of knowledge, Baillargeon's study, which found that children as young as five months demonstrated object permanence, is also contested.

Visit the website (https://study.sagepub.com/rogers2e) to watch a video demonstrating Baillargeon's experiment.

Reflective activity

In light of today's technological advancements, how else do you think we can begin to understand when infants develop awareness of object permanence, and what relationship, if any, does this have on our understanding of the principles of infant attachment to adult caregivers, or more specifically their mothers?

ONTOLOGY

Ontology is a concept that allows us to understand multiple aspects of what it means to be human. Different ontologies that arise from the application of attachment theory include the construction of what it is to be a sensitive or insensitive mother, or a securely or insecurely attached child. In mainstream psychology each of these ontologies are anchored to a view of what it is to be human that is dominated by our cognitive functioning. This focus on the mind and the rational judgements we make leads theories to discover ways that we can interpret what is occurring in the individualistic private world of another (Reuther, 2013). However, there are other ways of contemplating how we can understand one person's experience of their relationship with someone else. This exploration takes us into more philosophical concepts of self and if you are interested you will find Reuther's (2013) paper an excellent discussion on the integration of attachment theory and Heidegger's (1927/1962) phenomenology.

Visit the website (https://study.sagepub.com/rogers2e) to find out more about ontology.

Visit the website (https://study.sagepub.com/rogers2e) to read Reuther's paper 'On our everyday being: Heidegger and attachment theory'.

AINSWORTH'S BALTIMORE STUDY

In many ways, Ainsworth's studies, both in Uganda and later in Baltimore, were innovative and far-reaching. Her contribution to psychology and our understanding of the needs of children is immense. Ainsworth (1970) and Ainsworth et al.'s (1971) seminal 'Strange Situation' observational research, created an environment where a child was left in a room by their mother, both in the presence of a stranger and alone. The child was observed before and during these periods of separation from their mother and upon her return. The following critique is not to question the importance of her overall contribution, but to cast a critical eye over the knowledge produced from her studies to gain a better understanding of the strengths and weaknesses of attachment theory.

One of the innovative methods used by Ainsworth, revealed by Grossmann and Grossmann (1999), was how she undertook observations of mothers and infants up to one year of age in their own homes. The details of whether these infants were the first child born to the mother, issues such as postnatal depression of the mother, or potential needs of the child such as autism are not addressed in available papers (Ainsworth, 1969; Ainsworth et al., 1979). Fundamentally, Ainsworth's work is located in a social cognitive paradigm, which assumes universal truths can be found by coding and quantifying human behaviours. However, this mode of enquiry fails to consider the influence of the researcher(s) and their relationship with the participants, the topic and each other. For example, researchers Frost and Holt (2014) reflected on their 'maternal status' as researchers and the interaction this had within their research.

MATERNAL SENSITIVITY SCALES

Reflective activity

Before reading the next section, visit the website (https://study.sagepub.com/rogers2e) to read Ainsworth's papers from her Baltimore project which define maternal sensitivity scales.

As you read through, make your own notes:

1   Which aspects of the scales do you accept and why?
2   Which would you call into question and why?
3   In your view, do the scales readily transfer to mothers from non-middle-class or ethnic heritage?
4   How might the methods used by Ainsworth influence the knowledge produced?

Then continue reading below.

There is insufficient space here for a detailed critique but let us briefly examine an extract from the paper and consider its implications. Ainsworth's scale of sensitivity versus insensitivity ranges from:

1   Highly insensitive

3   Insensitive

5   Inconsistently sensitive

7   Sensitive

9   Highly sensitive

Inconsistently sensitive

Although this mother can be quite sensitive on occasion, there are some periods in which she is insensitive to B's communications. M's inconsistent sensitivity may occur for any one of several reasons, but the outcome is that she seems to have lacunae in regard to her sensitive dealings with B—being sensitive at some times or in respect to some aspects of his experience, but not in others. Her awareness of B may be intermittent—often fairly keen, but sometimes impervious. Or her perception of B's behavior may be distorted in regard to one or two aspects although it is accurate in other important aspects. She may be prompt and appropriate in response to his communications at times and in most respects, but either inappropriate or slow at other times and in other respects. On the whole, however, she is more frequently sensitive than insensitive. What is striking is that a mother who can be as sensitive as she is on so many occasions can be so insensitive on other occasions. (Ainsworth, 1969: 4)

Apart from the use of language, such as distortion and impervious, the above extract denotes an unspoken assumption and expectation of what constitutes sensitive mothering. There is no critique of what different people may deem to constitute a 'prompt response' and there exists an implied authority that permits the observer to judge whether the mother's behaviour was appropriate or distorted, to the observer's perceptions of the needs of the baby. These issues of power relations are of vital importance not only in the way in which we undertake research, but also as we apply these same judgements in our social work practice.

Visit the website (https://study.sagepub.com/rogers2e) to watch a video of parents interacting with their infant child and use the Ainsworth maternal sensitivity scales to score the participants.

MATERNAL SENSITIVITY AND FOSTER CARE

Ponciano (2010) used home observation of 76 foster children and their foster mothers in Los Angeles. The children were less than four years old and had been in placement for an average of one year. Some of the participating children had already experienced as many as five placements but most (83%) were in their first or second placement. As such, it was recognised that some of the children had previously experienced insecure attachments. In addition to the completion of some questionnaires, the researcher's observations each lasted between three to four hours. The time of these observations is interesting, when we consider the limited observation time that we have in practice with both foster and birth families. The study found evidence of secure attachments in over half of the participating dyads.

One of the measures used by Ponciano, was Waters and Deane's (1985) Attachment Q-Sort. You can read a revised version at http://www.psychology.sunysb.edu/attachment/measures/content/aqs_items.pdf. The AQS items proffer a descriptive 'rationale' that can be used as an educational tool, which you might find useful when interpreting the video data from the 'Strange Situation'.

Usefully the AQS (Waters and Deane, 1985) was subjected to meta-analyses by Ijzendoorn et al. (2004). Their paper describes the construction of the Q-test, a large number of cards, each with the description of 'typical' infant behaviours. The statistical tests they applied found that the observer AQS was a valid measure, but the subjective AQS was not. There is not enough space here to discuss the methodology used in their analysis, but do note that both qualitative and quantitative methods apply a degree of subjective determination. That is not to undermine any contribution but to recognise their limitations. Therefore, it is of interest that the researchers discuss their perplexity that the AQS worked better in Canada and European countries than it did in the US, where it originated. However, you integrate attachment theory and maternal sensitivity scales into your practice, work hard to engage with their complexity. When we are so closely applying what we deem evidence to support the decisions we make about other people's lives, we need to ensure mature critical reflection.

CONTEMPORARY RESEARCH

Still within a social cognitive paradigm, Elizabeth Meins and colleagues explored maternal sensitivity by investigating how mothers respond to their babies (Meins et al., 2001). Their study used Ainsworth's maternal sensitivity scale to assess a mother's interaction with her infant by watching a 20-minute video of the mother–child interaction. Interestingly, although Ainsworth's original paper noted examples of a mother missing the small movement of a baby's mouth, Meins et al.'s (2001) experiment did not include this degree of detail. Instead, one researcher formed an overall view, with a sample of their opinions compared to a second observer. Within this type of experimental model there is a statistical test called the kappa coefficient that can be used to measure the reliability of two different observers. However, the kappa test makes no allowance for the significance of variety of difference between observer views (Viera and Garrett, 2005). Indeed, nor does it provide any analysis of the subjective opinions that each observer may have come to in forming their original decisions.

The videotapes were then coded by two different researchers for maternal mindedness. The dimension for maternal mind-mindedness was developed and five ways of determining whether a mother was treating her infant 'as a mental agent' were defined (Meins et al., 2001: 8):

1   Maternal responsiveness to change in infant's direction of gaze;
2   Maternal responsiveness to infant's object-directed action;
3   Imitation;
4   Encouragement of autonomy;
5   Appropriate mind-related comments.

Maternal responsiveness includes whether the mother was observed looking at the object within her child's gaze or using the object or talking about their child's observation of it. Interestingly, only items labelled 'appropriate mind-related comments' were found to be a predictor of secure attachment. One of the categories for determining the appropriateness of a mother's mind-related comments was that the independent coder agreed with the mother's interpretation of her child's psychological state. This concept of observer bias is interesting and reflective of what happens for social workers observing interactions between parents and their children.

Reflective activity

Using your own observations undertaken in practice or on placement, critically reflect on judgements you have made about the responsiveness of a mother towards her infant. What other factors can you identify which impinge on those decisions?

CONCLUSION

This chapter has provided an introduction into methods we can use to examine underpinning assumptions of attachment theory. It has given some insight into the role of epistemology and ontology in the formation of knowledge which then becomes disseminated and integrated within society. We have highlighted some of the foundational limitations in the construction of maternal sensitivity scales and their methodological use. Attachment theory is deeply embedded in our societal discourses and social work practice. However, we can each work to ensure that we remain critically aware of how we apply this imperfect theory when making decisions that affect the lives of others.

   Visit the website to listen to Dr Wendy Smith discuss implications of attachment theory for the social worker (https://study.sagepub.com/rogers2e).

Having read this chapter, you should be able to:

- Recognise the construct of maternal sensitivity scales;
- Understand the development of research evidence and the need to interrogate the construct of any assessment tool;
- Acknowledge that it is vitally important to remain consciously critical when applying attachment theory to the decisions we make every day in practice.

RECOMMENDED READING

Ainsworth, M., Kiesler, C.A. and Scarr, S. (1979) Infant–mother attachment. *American Psychologist*, 34(10): 932–937.

Brandell, J. and Ringel, S. (2007) Attachment and Dynamic Practice: An Integrative Guide for Social Workers and Other Clinicians. New York: Columbia University Press.

Holmes, P. and Farnfield, S. (2014) *The Routledge Handbook of Attachment Theory*. Abingdon and New York: Routledge.

Ijzendoorn, M.H., Van Vereijken, C.M.J.L., Bakermans-Kranenburg, M.J. and Riksen-Walraven, M.J. (2004) Assessing attachment security with the Attachment Q Sort: meta-analytic evidence for the validity of the observer AQS. *Child Development*, 75(4): 1188–1213.

Grief and Loss
Julie Lawrence

Links to the Professional Capabilities Framework

- Professionalism • Values and ethics • Knowledge • Critical reflection and analysis
- Skills and interventions

Links to the Knowledge and Skills Statement for Child and Family Practitioners

- Relationships and effective direct work • Child development • Abuse and neglect of children • Child and family assessment • Analysis, decision-making, planning and review

Links to the Knowledge and Skills Statement for Social Workers in Adult Services

- Person-centred practice • Effective assessments and outcome-based support planning • Direct work with individuals and families • Supervision, critical reflection and analysis

Key messages

- Grief and loss involve change which often involves struggling with how to make sense of, and live with, grief.
- Grief and loss are important and complex areas of social work practice.
- Traditional theories remain influential, but more contemporary theories encourage us to consider individual and family responses within their social and cultural context.
- Social workers are expected to acknowledge grief and loss in their own lives, in order to relate and support individuals and their unique circumstances.

INTRODUCTION

> Put simply, grief is the price we pay for love, and a natural consequence of forming emotional bonds with people, projects and possessions. All that we value, we will someday lose. (Hall, 2014: 7)

Explanations about grief and loss are usually defined as bereavement, i.e. someone important to the person dying, and that loss brings about a significant and unwanted change. This might include the end of a relationship, losing a job and/or acquiring an illness. Change is, by definition, at the heart of social work and, although viewed in a different sense, it is at the heart of the experience of many service users (Currer, 2007). Grief and loss involves change – some of which is frequently unwanted – and the problems that individuals face often involve struggling with how to make sense of, and live with, grief, underpinned by loss. Whatever our area of practice, social work involves working alongside individuals and families and being involved with them as they engage in solving the problem of how to survive and go forward in the midst of grief and loss (Currer, 2007). They are emotive subjects. Reading reports and considering case examples can trigger emotions and thoughts associated with our own experiences. Therefore, it is advisable to identify a colleague with whom to discuss any reactions and personal issues that have been raised by the material presented in this chapter.

FREUD'S INFLUENCE

Until approximately 20 years ago, theorists of grief and loss were predominantly found to be aligned with the **psychodynamic** tradition (see Freud, 1917/1957). These utilised Freud's work, providing practice models for those professionals (social workers, nurses and psychologists) working with grief and loss (Neimeyer, 2014). Freud's work on loss focused on bereavement and he believed that '*grief work*' involved the painful review and relinquishment of one's 'burden' towards the deceased. Consequently, professionals encouraged individuals to voice their 'troubles' either individually or within a group scenario, whereby 'burdens' could be shared with others, who found themselves in similar situations. The ultimate goal was to encourage people to 'move on' from the deceased and reinvest emotional energy with the living.

DISENFRANCHISED GRIEF

Societies vary in cultural differences and the failure to recognise the loss of a significant attachment can lead to **disenfranchised grief**, a type of grief that the majority of people stigmatise and/or don't feel comfortable talking about (Doka and Martin, 2010). Examples include environments that do not recognise same-sex relationships, suicide, pet loss, a death from an overdose and other losses (such as murder) that are not considered mainstream.

Lloyd (2018) asserts that the failure to recognise the significance of a loss (by family, friends and society) can have devastating effects on the bereaved. In addition to which, she argues:

> Expecting the bereaved to return to 'normal' life very quickly after a death can also lead to disenfranchisement. (Lloyd, 2018: 44)

THE IMPORTANCE OF SOCIAL WORK IN RESPONDING TO GRIEF AND LOSS

We know that service users want social workers who are able to relate to them in a humane way (Romeo, 2017–2018). As such, social workers are expected to be familiar with, and able to acknowledge, grief and loss in their own lives as well as those of service users. In addition to this, social workers often become involved at a time of crisis. Thompson (2012b) argues that a crisis is a time of change and those that involve social work involvement are not usually planned. A crisis can be defined as a turning point in someone's life, a critical moment where the situation will either get better or get worse, but it will not stay the same. A crisis, therefore, can include bereavement and loss situations, all of which will be unique to the people involved and will require a social worker to respond accordingly. This will include giving thoughtful consideration about cultural 'norms' and listening to the needs and wishes of individuals being supported.

Thompson (2012b) sums this up:

> Crisis scenarios have significant echoes of grief situations where, in those circumstances where professional help is needed, the professional helper can again potentially play a key role in helping somebody who is stuck to move forward. (Thompson, 2012b: 41)

In relation to children and young people, for example, changes which can involve grief and loss include family break-up and divorce, death of a close relative (e.g. a grandparent), disability, parental mental health and/or substance misuse, and, not least, the consequences of crime. Current legislation also acknowledges the complex lives that some children and young people lead, in terms of their caring responsibilities for others, which in itself can lead to loss, in terms of childhood and youth. However, section 96 of the Children and Families Act 2014 introduced new rights for young carers (inserted into the Children Act 1989) to improve how young carers and their families are identified and supported. Since April 2015, all young carers are entitled to an assessment of their needs from the local authority. This new provision works alongside measures in the Care Act 2014 for assessing adults to enable a whole family approach (SCIE, 2018). The focus is upon changes, including grief and loss of the 'everyday' faced by some children, young people and adults.

In terms of adults, (in the main) there are also significant developments within **palliative care** and the importance of the role of social work. This is emphasised by the Association of

Palliative Care for Social Workers (2019). Specialist palliative care social workers can offer a wide variety of support to both the person and those who are important to them. This can include sourcing practical help at home, accessing other services, advice around debt or income maintenance, help with housing, advocacy, working with schools or employers, or offering psychosocial support. Palliative care social workers are often skilled in therapeutic work, be it systemic family therapy, counselling or cognitive behaviour therapy. They often work with groups as well as individuals. Additionally, work is undertaken around helping people to prepare for the end of their lives through advanced care planning and psychosocial interventions. The underlining vision of the Association is to uphold core social work values within palliative care and better promote the needs and wishes of people living with palliative illness and those close to them within their organisations, locally and nationally.

 Visit the website to explore the differences between grief for children and adults (https://study.sagepub.com/rogers2e).

TRADITIONAL THEORIES

In many instances the important theory developed by Kübler-Ross (1969, originally) was associated with stages of dying, but is better known as the 'five stages of grief' (Kübler-Ross and Kessler, 2005). Thompson (2012b) argues that this theory has now largely been discredited; however, it continues to be one that is widely used. The basic idea behind the theory is that, when we are grieving, we go through a set of stages and follow a particular pattern. This theory has provided a convenient guide for both professionals and carers alike, due to its accessibility. Kübler-Ross and Kessler (2005) asserted that there were five stages of grief, these being:

1 *Denial*: disbelief about the person's death.
2 *Anger*: the strength of the pain results in anger, including self-anger where the bereaved person blames themselves.
3 *Bargaining*: with a '*god*' to be given another chance, to be able to go back to how things were before.
4 *Depression*: deep sadness about the truth. There can be intense feelings of loneliness and hopelessness.
5 *Acceptance*: the bereaved person needs to recognise the truth of their situation and realise they can carry on, even if they feel the loss of their loved one.

Case study: Samia

Twenty-year-old Samia was a care leaver. She had spent most of her childhood in foster care living with the same family that she was placed with at the age of eight. Samia was now living in supported housing for people with mild to moderate learning disabilities. She shared a house with two other adults. She enjoyed living with them and was studying at college, which she loved. Overall, her childhood had been happy although there was one aspect of family life that caused her continuing upset and anger: she had not seen her brother, Arun, for five years since she was 15 and Arun was 13 years old. This was due to a decision made at the time by Samia and Arun's social workers. However, Samia missed her brother and felt that something was missing from her life as they had been very close in the past (since being taken into care they had always lived with separate foster families, but the relationship with Arun was the only contact that Samia had with someone from her birth family). Samia's social worker, Sally, drew on Kübler-Ross's theory of five stages of grief to make sense of Samia's sense of loss, and Sally concluded that Samia was stuck at the 'anger' stage and would be until there was a change to the situation. Sally contacted Arun's social worker and re-established contact helping the siblings to build their relationship as young adults.

· ·

As mentioned, Thompson (2012b) argues that Kübler-Ross's model has now largely been discredited although it continues to be one that is widely used, as cited in this case study. The counter-argument to this theory is that there was little research evidence to support the idea that people grieve in this linear stage-by-stage way, without reference to how people grieved across time, and what factors impinged upon the recovery process.

   Another model that has 'cast light' on the complexities of grieving is the theory developed by Worden (2010). This theory is linked to developmental psychology in terms of the natural progression of 'life stages'. As humans, we face certain developmental tasks. For example, the transition from being an adolescent to that of an adult is viewed in this sense as a developmental task. This theory has enabled us to better understand what happens when someone is grieving; indeed Worden developed his ideas whilst working alongside adults within mental health settings. Worden's tasks of grieving can be described as follows:

- Accepting the reality of the loss: getting used to the idea that someone is no longer with us in a physical sense.
- Working through the pain of grief: expressing feelings associated with the loss. This is seen as essential.
- Adjusting to a changed environment: implications of the bereavement, which may be practical as well as emotional.
- Emotionally relocating the deceased: moving on with life, whilst continuing to have a meaningful relationship with the deceased in a new context.

It is, however, wise to proceed with caution when faced with these ideas of 'stages' or 'tasks' of grieving. It is simply not enough to explain how individuals grieve in particular social contexts. All societies have expectations of those who grieve, as well as rituals and customs. These can include funerals, placing flowers on the grave on a particular day, scattering ashes, planting trees and keeping memorial albums in order to celebrate a life lived. All or some of these activities may offer comfort in grief and also define socially acceptable behaviours for those who are grieving and other people around them.

Writing from an autobiographical perspective, Dayes (2018) argues:

Our society is hugely influenced by the idea that grief comes at us in stages, each identifiable, each to be worked through, yet this was not what I was observing in my research or practice. The grief I saw in the therapy room did not come in such neat packages. No person's difficulties come into the therapy room as a single entity. They are situated in a web of past and current experiences and difficulties, a strand of which is sometimes overlooked, in grief. (2018: 11)

CONTEMPORARY THEORIES

In the wake of growing scepticism about traditional models of mourning, other new theories have also been proposed. One such theory is the Dual Process Model (DPM) of coping with bereavement formulated by Stroebe and Schut (1999; Stroebe et al., 2017), who argue that grief involves an oscillation between confronting the loss (Loss Orientation) and compartmentalising it, so that the mourner can attend to the life changes necessitated by the death (Restoration Orientation). Neimeyer (2014) argues that this important departure from traditional thinking describes mourning as a cyclical rather than linear and stage-like process. The mourner revisits the loss and its associated emotions, strives to reorganise the relationship to the deceased and to take on new roles imposed by a 'changed world' (Neimeyer, 2014: 126). This theory is helpful in terms of establishing that different people will grieve (and oscillate) at different times. This also affirms the ideas suggested by Dayes (2018) that all individuals bring with them their past and present complexities associated with the deceased person(s) during periods of grief and loss.

Neimeyer (as mentioned above) is a well-known grief expert, who developed the concept of 'meaning making' as an important aspect of grief (Neimeyer and Sands, 2011). He explains that to understand an individual's experience of grief, it is helpful to frame this within the context of the relationship with the person(s) who has died. Meaning making considers how the griever makes sense of their new, different future without that relationship. The aim of those supporting the bereaved is to allow the griever to build new meanings into life after death. This may also include a search for a post-loss identity. Searching for a new identity (e.g. from wife to widow/civil partner to widower) can be multifaceted, which may include addressing questions about the death(s) and challenging faith assumptions.

Attention to the struggle for meaning surrounding bereavement may be crucial in cases of fatal accidents, homicides and suicides where an inability to make sense of the death appears to mediate the impact of violent, as opposed to natural deaths on the adaptation of the survivor(s). Both these contemporary approaches reiterate the importance of 'individual uniqueness' when someone is grieving and therefore disconnect with standardised stages, as previously mentioned.

APPLYING THEORY IN PRACTICE

As a social worker it is important to acknowledge that grief can be a debilitating experience for individuals and their families (as mentioned earlier in this chapter). The application of theory(s) can be complex, due to the broad range of situations which involve grief and loss. Perhaps the best usage of theoretical considerations is to think about a specific aspect of loss as presented in the previous case study and the case study below. Explore the issues raised and, at the same time, give consideration to the positives and limitations attached to each theory presented in this chapter.

. . . .

Case study: Martyn

Martyn had enjoyed a same-sex relationship with Carlos for the past 10 years. They met through mutual friends and found love in later life, Martyn being 40 and Carlos being 52 years old when they met. Martyn described their relationship as being one of close companionship and a comfort to each other in later life. Martyn was an 'out and proud' gay man who shared his lifestyle with his immediate family, including his two sisters, one brother, their families and his mother. Both Martyn and Carlos were invited to family events and Martyn's nephews especially enjoyed their company, due to being football fans.

However, Carlos was a more cautious man, who kept his sexuality and lifestyle separate from his two brothers and their families which included six nephews/nieces. He did not inform his family that he shared an apartment with Martyn and had done so for the past eight years. In turn, his family kept in touch but did not ask too many questions about his lifestyle and/or the people he met. Consequently, he often attended family events alone.

Carlos died suddenly when returning home from work in the city. He was killed instantly in a road accident. Martyn was devastated upon hearing this news, and shared his grief with his immediate family. He wanted to contact Carlos's family to express his condolences. During the initial period of mourning, Carlos's brothers arranged the funeral according to Carlos's wishes. Carlos had stipulated that his family should arrange the funeral. Martyn was unaware of this stipulation in Carlos's will and, as such, his grief was further compounded by his exclusion at Carlos's funeral.

Martyn's sister has approached you as a duty social worker due to concerns about his welfare. Martyn has been absent from work and not contacted his family since Carlos's death some weeks ago. His neighbour saw Martyn standing on the balcony of his apartment a few nights ago and asked him to step down from the balcony for safety reasons.

Reflective questions

- How would you approach Samia and her situation (see earlier case study)?
- How would you approach Martyn and his situation?
- Which grief and loss theory(s) would you refer to in each case, in order to inform your practice?
- What is the legal context in which you would practise in both scenarios?

. . . .

One aspect of social work practice (and interventions) is the necessity to offer grievers 'space and time' to talk about the deceased person(s), which can include the sharing of memories. Thompson (2012b) further argues that we cannot take away the 'pain' of someone who is grieving and that a psychosocial and spiritual understanding of what is required is a positive approach, in order to be *'more helpful in supporting people through grief'* (Thompson, 2012b: 106). Figure 30.1 demonstrates the complex variables which can be involved when someone is grieving. Social workers can offer their professional support at any juncture within a cyclical process of grieving. Emotional and practical support may need to be underpinned by an assessment of risk (to self, to/from others) in some instances. Lloyd (2018) argues that grievers may be uncertain about what they need and may struggle to express themselves, which can make it difficult for social workers to communicate in terms of expectations. One last important point to note is that supporting individuals and families who are grieving can be stressful and upsetting for the social worker involved. It is therefore important that social workers have access and support to effective supervision, which also offers the opportunity to engage with the process of critical reflection, in order to avoid '**compassion fatigue**'.

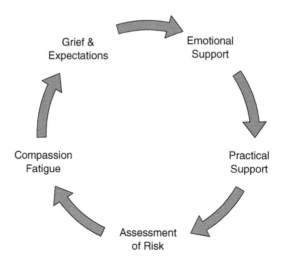

Figure 30.1   Social work interventions during times of grief and loss

CONCLUSION

This chapter has emphasised the important role for social work when involved with individuals and families. The underpinning consideration for social workers involved in supporting people who are experiencing grief and loss is to offer support which is of value to individuals within their specific context(s). Our role should be underpinned by knowledge, skills and values. The various theoretical concepts presented in this chapter may offer some guidance, dependent upon the nature of the loss and how individuals respond over time to their unique circumstances. Critical reflective practice is vital given the nature of the work and must be underpinned by social work (and/or) clinical supervision, to enhance self-care and emotional resilience during periods of involvement.

Having read this chapter, you should be able to:

- Understand that disenfranchised grief and loss is complex and often involves the failure (of others) to recognise the loss of a significant relationship;
- Recognise that there are a number of traditional and contemporary theories associated with grief and loss;
- Understand that both individuals and families are unique in terms of how they deal with grief and loss situations;
- Recognise that social work has an important role in supporting people in times of crisis, associated with grief and loss.

RECOMMENDED READING

Kübler-Ross, E. and Kessler, D. (2005) *On Grief and Grieving: Finding the Meaning of Grief through the Five Stages of Loss*. New York: Scribner.

Lloyd, C. (2018) *Grief Demystified: An Introduction*. London: Jessica Kingsley.

Neimeyer, R. (2014) The changing face of grief: contemporary directions in theory, research and practice. *Progress in Palliative Care*, 22(3): 125–130.

Thompson, N. (2012b) *Grief and its Challenges*. Basingstoke: Palgrave Macmillan.

Crisis Intervention
Donna Peach

Links to the Professional Capabilities Framework

• Professionalism   • Values and ethics   • Critical reflection and analysis   • Skills and interventions

Links to the Knowledge and Skills Statement for Child and Family Practitioners

• Relationships and effective direct work   • Communication   • Adult mental ill-health, substance misuse, domestic abuse, physical ill-health and disability

Links to the Knowledge and Skills Statement for Adult Practitioners

• The role of social workers with adults • Person-centred practice • Safeguarding • Effective assessments and outcome-based support planning • Direct work with individuals and families

Key messages

- Crisis intervention is a concept that has multiple applications in relationship to social work practice.
- A crisis can be created from sources internal or external to individuals and families.
- Trauma-informed approaches support individuals to have effective control over their lives.
- Social work as a profession can itself be subject to crisis.
- Social workers have a role in advocating for social justice for those made vulnerable by our national economic crisis.

INTRODUCTION

There are different ways to situate what is meant by 'crisis intervention' (CI) in social work practice. Although, there is a dearth of contemporary literature on the topic, CI remains an important concept to scaffold interventions created by both internal and external forces (Thompson, 2011). For some, CI includes how social workers respond to the needs of people after a catastrophic event such as a fatal accident or natural disaster (Cacciatore et al., 2011). At other times, CI refers to occasions when we intervene in the lives of individuals who experience deterioration in their mental health (Roberts and Ottens, 2005). Indeed, crisis intervention team (CIT) is the term for a specialist model predominantly used in America and designed to respond to mental health emergencies (Cummins, 2016). It seems fitting that any exploration of CI should also accommodate examination of crises that affect the social work profession, such as political and economic events. Thus, CI will be considered not only in how we assist others, but how we can also support ourselves in times of crisis.

CRISIS: A COMPLEX PHENOMENON

Predominantly, the term crisis intervention is used to describe emergency intervention with a person who has been referred to us for immediate help. How we intervene is of crucial importance to the outcome, so it is vital to understand what we mean when we refer to CI. As in any practice encounter, our use of self and our professional judgement is a contributory factor to the outcome. Therefore, as always, social work students and practitioners need to be ever mindful of the need for critical awareness and reflection. Roberts (2005) provides a useful definition of mental health crisis, which includes the impact it can have upon an individual:

> An acute disruption of psychological homeostasis in which one's usual coping mechanisms fail and there exists evidence of distress and functional impairment. The subjective reaction to a stressful life experience that compromises the individual's stability and ability to cope or function. The main cause of a crisis is an intensely stressful, traumatic, or hazardous event, but two other conditions are also necessary:
>
> 1 the individual's perception of the event as the cause of considerable upset and/or disruption; and
> 2 the individual's inability to resolve the disruption by previously used coping mechanisms.
>
> Crisis also refers to 'an upset in the steady state'. It often has five components: a hazardous or traumatic event, a vulnerable or unbalanced state, a precipitating factor, an active crisis state based on the person's perception, and the resolution of the crisis. (Roberts, 2002: 516)

The above definition assists our understanding of crisis as a complex phenomenon, which includes the event that triggers the crisis, and how individuals experience this. Although our interventions are unlikely to prevent the initial impact of the crisis, we can seek to assist and improve a person's experience of it. A stage model (Figure 31.1) that describes the seven components of intervention necessary to resolve a crisis was proposed by Roberts (1991).

In addition to the seven stages of intervention, the model also implicitly expects the intervening practitioner to not act in a way that creates further anxiety for the individual. Furthermore, it encourages practitioners to support individuals to draw on internal resources to help resolve the effects of the crisis. However, the intervener also has a critical role and, as indicated at stage one of the process, it is to assess whether the individual could be suicidal. Reminding ourselves of that could help to save lives, but Roberts's model suggests it extends even beyond that, creating learning opportunities for all involved in the intervention.

Visit the website to listen to a crisis assessment with a young adult (https://study.sage pub.com/rogers2e).

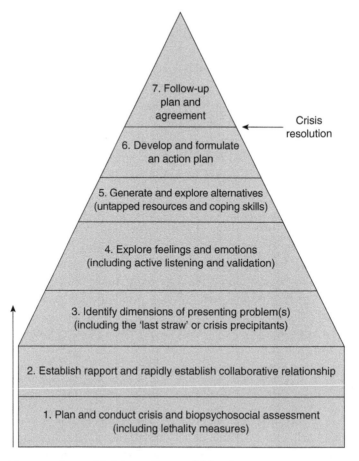

Figure 31.1 Roberts's seven-stage crisis intervention model (1991)

Source: Reprinted with permission of Pearson Education.

Reflective activity

Michael is 19 years old and lives with his parents and two younger siblings. His mother, Joyce, has contacted you to say she is concerned about a marked deterioration in his presentation over the past five weeks. Michael has stopped attending college where he is completing his A levels. She is struggling to get him out of bed in the morning and asking him to wash and dress can lead to bouts of anger. Michael has stopped having contact with his friends from college and refuses to attend his athletics club. He also behaves 'oddly' when his siblings' friends visit and seems to be suspicious of them. Joyce has twice heard Michael talking to himself although he denied this when she questioned him.

Following the seven stages in Roberts's (1991) model, answer the following questions:

1   Who would be involved in planning a biopsychosocial assessment of Michael's needs?
2   What methods would you use to establish a rapport with Michael quickly?
3   What enquiries would you need to make to identify the consequences of the presenting problems?
4   What skills would you draw on to explore Michael's thoughts and feelings?
5   How could you use a strengths-based approach to explore the extent of Michael's internal coping skills?
6   Who would assist you in developing an action plan, what would it include and how might it be implemented?
7   What would be the important components of a follow-up agreement?

More recently, Roberts and Ottens (2005) developed Roberts's earlier model to provide a conceptual framework which enables us to examine in more detail how a worker and an individual in crisis can work together. It is important to recognise the application of his model, not only in our practice with an individual in crisis, but also in how it can be applied to structure teams who are working with people in crisis. Arguably, working in crisis should not be limited to teams of professionals working with individuals or communities in crisis. Indeed, Roberts's model could be used to ensure the needs of practitioners are met at times of meeting acute needs such as in direct response to a crisis. In addition, it could also be adapted to identify chronic needs that arise when practitioners face multiple challenges such as in the current age of austerity that we now experience.

Reflective activity

Consider an occasion during a social work placement when you have engaged with someone who was experiencing a crisis. Then, if you can, identify a time when you or someone personally close to you was experiencing a crisis.

1   Identify the learning that you gained from both practice and personal experiences. Do your experiences reflect the seven stages described by Roberts's model of CI? If not, in

(Continued)

what ways are they different and how do your experiences fit within or go beyond the scope of Roberts's model?
2　How have your student placement and/or personal experiences of crisis influenced your practice?
3　What strategies would you now adopt to identify and intervene with a person who was experiencing a crisis?
4　Identify any gaps in your learning and how you plan to develop your knowledge and skills.

CRISIS IN A COMPLEX LANDSCAPE

In contemporary Britain, the impact of austerity policies is having an increasingly detrimental impact on the most vulnerable in our societies. As a profession, we are also not immune to the impact of austerity, which has dramatically reduced our organisational resources. Thus, in practice, we can experience an absence of available resources to support people in crisis, and this situation can exacerbate the experience of crisis for our service users and ourselves. As a social work student, this scenario may seem overwhelming. It is without a doubt, challenging. However, understanding the complexity of the issues can help to make sense of it and to determine where we must apply our knowledge and skills to do our best at meeting the needs of our service users.

How we challenge and respond to societal crisis is important, and Cooter (2009) suggests a crisis can be viewed as both a disaster and an opportunity. However, it is important to note that it can be difficult to identify opportunities when faced with societal deficits that create social isolation, further marginalise communities and increase deprivation. One key resource we have available is our use of self and the quality of our practice. Strier (2013) proffers a conceptual framework of inclusive social work practice as a means of engaging people in crisis. This moves away from a worker to service user model and suggests a greater democracy of power. The ethos propounded by Strier (2013) is based on fundamental principles of good social work practice. These underpinning values include the encouragement of practical and reflective actions, which can counter feelings of internalised oppression and dependency, due to multiple deprivation. His paper encourages reflection on the current crisis experienced by the social work profession and the complexity of how we support the most vulnerable in society while navigating our own stormy waters.

Reflective activity

Below is an extract from Chris Lee's critical commentary, 'Conservative comforts: some philosophical crumbs for social work', published in the *British Journal of Social Work* in 2014.

Read the extract and reflect on the questions below.

> If there is any resistance to the established order, it is expressed on the front line, in the protection of therapeutic and advocating relationships that practitioners and not just social workers but nurses and occupational therapists and others develop with their mental health service users. That work, that activity which is replete with meaning, acts as a psychological defence against its own devaluation by the reductive dictatorship of the performance agenda. It is not that there has been a complete neo-liberal takeover of social work, because there is contestation both in the academy and in everyday practice. But I believe that it is true to state that, in mental health social work at least, the senior layers of the organisations in which social workers and others are employed have no critical distance from neo-liberal hegemony. All frontline workers can do is conserve. As the time they have to spend with service users is whittled away by the requirements of data collection, they must give up as slowly as they can the very values that led them to the work of caring in the first place. The task is now to retreat at a pace that will outlast the onslaught, to let the defeat be gradual enough to retain hope. (Lee, 2014: 2137)

1   Do you see evidence of 'contestation' or 'conservation' in your social work practice experience? If so, what forms did it take and how effective/ineffective was it?
2   What, if any, aspects of your own practice could be described as 'contestation' or 'conservation'? What aids or inhibits your ability to contest?
3   How have your professional experiences of what Lee terms 'neoliberal hegemony' (the dominance of free-market capitalist ideology) influenced your practice?

A TRAUMA-INFORMED APPROACH

Trauma-informed practice is not new, but the concept is becoming more formalised in both health and social care services. We increasingly recognise that childhood trauma is linked to mental health distress and adult psychosis (Bentall et al., 2014; Varese et al., 2012). Research is beginning to construct evidence of what constitutes a trauma-informed approach (TIA), but achieving that as small changes across large organisations will take about 15 years (Proctor et al., 2009). Using a TIA with a person experiencing crisis can increase the degree of control and influence that the person in crisis feels they have over their lives. That, in turn, reduces the incidence of risk-aversive practices and the imposition of interventions such as Community Treatment Orders (O'Hagan, 2004). Helpfully, Sweeney et al. (2016) produced the key principles of trauma-informed approaches (see Table 31.1).

Indeed, a TIA is embedded in social work values and the core skills that empower others to have effective control of their own lives (Knight, 2015), such as using a strengths-based approach as discussed in Chapter 23. However, it is rare that any individual service will have access to all the resources that an individual who is experiencing trauma might need. These can often include basic safety needs, such as housing. It is notable that Sweeney et al. (2016) have not included, what Maslow considered the most primary of needs, that of having food, warmth and our basic physiological needs met. We should not underestimate the necessity of our basic needs being met before we can engage in effective control of our lives, let alone have the energy required to effectively manage the impact of traumatic events (Laser–Maira et al., 2019).

Table 31.1   Key principles of trauma-informed approaches (Sweeney et al., 2016)

Recognition	Recognise the prevalence, signs and impacts of trauma. This is sometimes referred to as having a trauma lens. This should include routine enquiry about trauma, sensitively asked and appropriately timed. For individual survivors, recognition can create feelings of validation, safety and hope.
Resist retraumatisation	Understand that operational practices, power differentials between staff and survivors, and many other features of psychiatric care can retraumatise survivors (and staff). Take steps to eliminate retraumatisation.
Cultural, historical and gender contexts	Acknowledge community-specific trauma and its impacts. Ensure services are culturally and gender appropriate. Recognise the impact of intersectionalities, and the healing potential of communities and relationships.
Trustworthiness and transparency	Services should ensure decisions taken (organisational and individual) are open and transparent, with the aim of building trust. This is essential to building relationships with trauma survivors who may have experienced secrecy and betrayal.
Collaboration and mutuality	Understand the inherent power imbalance between staff and survivors, and ensure that relationships are based on mutuality, respect, trust, connection and hope. These are critical because abuse of power is typically at the heart of trauma experiences, often leading to feelings of disconnection and hopelessness, and because it is through relationships that healing can occur.
Empowerment, choice and control	Adopt strengths-based approaches, with survivors supported to take control of their lives and develop self-control advocacy. This is vital as trauma experiences are often characterised by a lack of control with long-term feelings of disempowerment.
Safety	Trauma engenders feelings of danger. Give priority to ensuring that everyone within a service feels, and is, emotionally and physically safe. This includes the feelings of safety engendered through choice and control and cultural and gender awareness. Environments must be physically, psychologically, socially, morally and culturally safe.
Survivor partnerships	Understand that peer support and the co-production of services are integral to trauma-informed organisations. This is because the relationships involved in peer support and co-production are based on mutuality and collaboration.
Pathways to trauma-specific care	Survivors should be supported to access appropriate trauma-specific care, where this is desired. Such services should be provided by mental health services and be well resourced.

VICARIOUS TRAUMA – SELF-CARE

In brief, it is vital that we, as a student or practising social worker, take care of ourselves and understand the impact of **vicarious trauma** (VT). In practice, the use of supervision, as discussed in Chapter 20, is an important means of support. Aparicio et al. (2013) examined the psychometric properties of vicarious trauma in social workers, more specifically middle-aged, Caucasian, female social workers. Those who participated showed moderate levels of VT, leading to the recommendation that social workers and their supervisors receive education about the supervisory mitigation of VT. It is important to remember that for practitioners VT can be created from our own personal experiences, societal factors that impede/facilitate our work and the effects of the personal trauma experienced by those we work with.

Reflective activity

Using Sweeney et al.'s (2016) key principles of trauma-informed approaches, in Table 31.1:

- Identify how you can work with your practice supervisor and/or educator to implement these principles to support the supervisory process to address issues relating to vicarious trauma.
- What factors could impact the effects of trauma, e.g. workload, feeling helpless to assist, the distress of other's experiences?

CONCLUSION

This chapter has explored the concept of crisis intervention and its relevance in social work practice. It has encouraged you to extend your contemplation of what constitutes a crisis by examining crises prevalent among individuals that can be caused by both internal and external forces. Central to any intervention with a person in crisis is that it is timely, and that we work to ensure that our action or inaction is designed to provide appropriate levels of empowerment and facilitate recovery. In this chapter you have been encouraged to contemplate the impact of austerity on limiting and creating opportunities for practice in contemporary Britain. The current financial constraints on all our public services are contributing to the loss of public resources at a time when the population's need for support is rising. This dynamic adds a layer of complexity to crisis intervention, when we as social workers may not have the personal and professional resources available to us to support those in crisis. It must also be recognised that a reduction in resources might also mean we work harder to facilitate service users' capacity to meet their own needs. However, practising in such an economically austere climate can equally lead to services imposing higher thresholds designed to reduce access to limited resources. In this scenario, working together, within and across multidisciplinary teams and with service users becomes of increased importance as a means of sharing knowledge and resources.

Having read this chapter, you should be able to:

- Understand the construct of crisis intervention and models of intervention;
- Identify the key principles of trauma-informed approaches;
- Comprehend how a crisis experienced by an individual can be created from both external and internal sources;
- Reflect on your own use of empathy and the impact it can have on the quality of your relationship-based practice.

RECOMMENDED READING

Knight, C. (2015) Trauma-informed social work practice: practice considerations and challenges. *Clinical Social Work Journal*, 43(1): 25–37.

Strier, R. (2013) Responding to the global economic crisis: inclusive social work practice. *Social Work*, 58(4): 344–353.

Sweeney, A., Clement, S., Filson, B. and Kennedy, A. (2016) Trauma-informed mental healthcare in the UK: What is it and how can we further its development? *Mental Health Review Journal*, 21(3): 174–192.

Thompson, N. (2011) *Crisis Intervention* (Theory into Practice series). Lyme Regis: Russell House Publishing.

The Social Models of Disability and Distress

Dawn Whitaker

Links to the Professional Capabilities Framework

• Skills and interventions • Knowledge • Rights, justice and economic wellbeing • Diversity and equality • Values and ethics

Links to the Knowledge and Skills Statement for Child and Family Practitioners

• Communication • Child development • Adult mental ill health, substance use, domestic violence, physical ill health and disability • Abuse and neglect and children • Relationships and effective direct work • Child and family assessment • Analysis, decision making, planning and review • The law and the family and youth justice systems • The role of supervision • Organisational contexts

Links to the Knowledge and Skills Statement for Social Workers in Adult Services

• The role of social workers working with adults • Person-centred practice • Safeguarding • Mental capacity • Effective assessments and outcome-based support planning • Direct work with individuals and families • Supervision, critical reflection and analysis • Professional ethics and leadership

Key messages

• Social work has a lot to learn from disabled people and people who experience distress.
• The social model of disability has had a transformative impact on the lives of many disabled people.
• The social model of disability is a dynamic tool that is continuing to evolve.
• Exciting developments are under way that will move us towards a social model for people who experience distress.

INTRODUCTION

Despite the existence of a relationship between social work and disabled people dating back to the late-nineteenth century, the profession is criticised for being largely uninterested in disability issues (Oliver et al., 2012). Where interest *does* exist, it is often reductionist in nature; dominated by *professionally* driven services aimed at reducing *individual* deficit and need. In contrast, advocates of the social model refute the notion that disability is a *personal* deficit:

> … disability is not an individual problem. Rather, it is a social problem concerned with the effects of hostile physical and social environments upon impaired individuals, or even a societal one concerned with the way the society treats this particular minority group. As such, the base for social work activity with disabled people needs to be broadened, not narrowed. (Oliver et al., 2012: 3)

However, our ability to achieve this 'broadened' activity will be jeopardised, *unless* we challenge the dominant view of disability and distress as an *individual* deficit or tragedy, and refocus practice from *personal* to *social* adjustment. Indeed, Mike Oliver, in his seminal book *Social Work with Disabled People* (originally published in 1983), predicted that social work would 'disappear' unless it was prepared to change. Oliver updated his analysis in 2004, and announced that, regrettably for social work, his prediction had been realised: 'We can probably now announce the death of social work, at least in relation to its involvement in the lives of disabled people' (Oliver, 2004: 10).

This reflects a continued lack of progress by the social work profession to embrace a social approach to disability and distress in practice (Oliver et al., 2012). What is striking, however, is that Oliver used the word 'probably' in his assertion that social work with disabled people was dead, implying that there may be opportunities for change. This is supported by acknowledgement that pockets of good practice exist:

> There have undoubtedly been initiatives by individual social workers or departments which are not based on the individual model and which are indeed perfectly compatible with a **social model of disability**, but social work as a profession has not given systematic attention to developing a theoretical perspective on disability. (Oliver et al., 2012: 20)

We must interpret this both as a final warning *and* an opportunity to build on existing good practice, while at the same time redoubling our efforts to work alongside people in a manner that is meaningful to them.

WHAT IS THE SOCIAL MODEL OF DISABILITY?

During the 1970s and 1980s disabled activists became increasingly vocal in their criticism of the 'individual, medicalized model of disability' (Barnes and Mercer, 2010: 29). This is captured in the 1976 policy statement published by the Union of the Physically Impaired Against Segregation (UPIAS):

> … the traditional way of dealing with disabled people has been for doctors and other professionals to decide what is best for us. … Our Union rejects entirely any idea of medical or other experts having the right to tell us how we should live. … We reject also the whole idea of experts and professionals holding forth on how we should accept our disabilities. … We already know what it feels like to be poor, isolated, segregated, done good to, stared at, and talked down to – far better than any able-bodied expert. We as a Union are not interested in descriptions of how awful it is to be disabled. What we are interested in, are ways of changing our conditions of life, and thus overcoming the disabilities which are imposed on top [of] our impairments by the way this society is organised to exclude us. In our view, it is only the actual impairment which we must accept; the additional and totally unnecessary problems caused by the way we are treated are essentially to be overcome and not accepted. (UPIAS, 1976: 5)

It was Oliver's public expression of this groundbreaking UPIAS statement that formed the basis of what we now understand as the social model of disability (Finkelstein, 2004). This way of thinking turned many disabled people's understanding of disability 'completely on its head', specifically the argument that it is not individual impairments that are 'the main cause' of problems for people, but 'the way society' responds to them (Oliver, 2004: 7).

The central, most radical component of the social model is that it distinguishes between *impairment* and *disability*. Whilst the medical meaning of impairment is 'broadly accepted as an individual attribute', the 'meaning of disability' is 'radically reinterpreted' (Barnes and Mercer, 2010: 30):

> *Impairment* is a characteristic of the mind, body or senses within an individual which is long term and may, or may not, be the result of disease, genetics or injury.

> *Disability* is the disadvantage or restriction of activity caused by the political, economic and cultural norms of a society which takes little or no account of people who have impairments and thus excludes them from mainstream activity [therefore, disability, like racism or sexism, is discrimination and social oppression]. (Oliver et al., 2012: 16)

This way of thinking 'exposes' disability as a form of oppression (Thomas, 2004: 21); that is to say, it is *produced* by social barriers that fail to take disabled people's 'needs into account' (Wallcraft and Hopper, 2015: 85). Unfortunately, examples of these 'disabling social barriers' are all too visible in the everyday lives of people with impairments: for example, 'a wheelchair user or a person with visual impairment [who] cannot access public transport systems, or is not able to obtain a quality education that would enable them to compete for well-paid jobs in the labour market' (Thomas, 2004: 22). However, it is 'not just physical barriers, such as steps or revolving doors' that disable people; 'attitudes towards disabled people (such as pity, charity or fear)' also have significant disabling effects (Rich, 2013).

Reflective activity

Can you identify an example either personally or in practice where a person has been disabled/oppressed, not by their impairment but by *others'/society's* response to it?

CHALLENGES TO THE SOCIAL MODEL

Despite the 'considerable impact' the social model of disability has had on 'public policy, disability politics and disabled people's own understandings of their positions in society', it has also been the subject of 'heated academic and personal debates' (Oliver, 2010: 5).

Critics challenge the model's key 'conceptual distinction' between *impairment* and *disability* (Hughes and Paterson, 1997: 325; Shakespeare and Watson, 2002). Whilst *original* social model advocates consider it risky to focus on the individual experience of impairment, as it could give credibility to the **individual-deficit approach** to disability (Thomas, 2014: 13), others argue this takes insufficient account of the individual experience of living with impairment. For example, Goodley argues that the 'harsh realities of tiredness, the limiting consequences for social interaction, and debilitating experiences associated with some impairments have often become obscured by the structuralist focus of the social model' (2012: 66). This reflects an ongoing debate as to whether people with impairments 'are disabled by society as well as by their bodies', rather than by society alone (Shakespeare, undated: 218). In this context, Thomas developed an extended social-relational model of disability to include both **structural** and **psycho-emotional disablism** (1999). This recognises that oppression operates at both the public *and* personal levels, affecting what people can '*do*' as well as who they can '*be*' (Reeves, 2004: 84):

> Sometimes I don't go into my local town centre because I cannot manage the steps on that day, other times I don't go shopping because I cannot deal with the stares of others. Both of these have the same effect of keeping me out of a public space, both are the result of oppressive social relationships which require changes in the socio-structural and socio-cultural fabric rather than my individual acceptance of disability. (Reeves, 2004: 89)

In consequence, Thomas asserts that the original UPIAS (1976) definition of disability should be amended, to include *any socially produced oppression* that undermines a person with impairment's 'psycho-emotional wellbeing', *as well as* that which stems from **structural disablism** (Thomas, 2004: 25). This reflects what Thomas refers to as '*impairment effects*':

… the direct and unavoidable impacts that 'impairments' (physical, sensory, intellectual, emotional) have on individuals' embodied functioning in the social world. Impairments and impairment effects are always bio-social and culturally constructed in character, and may occur at any stage in the life course. (2014: 14)

This dilutes the presumption that '*all* activity restrictions experienced by individuals with an impairment have a social basis' which can be resolved by social change (Barnes and Mercer, 2010: 35).

In a similar vein to criticism that the social model neglects the personal experience of impairment, it is also faulted for failing to acknowledge identity, namely the diversity of experience *between* disabled people. Critics argue its emphasis on the 'commonalities' of social oppression and need for a collective voice misleadingly portray disability as a homogeneous experience, thereby ignoring the 'differences' that exist between people due to impairment, class, gender, race and ethnicity, sexual orientation and age (Mulvany, 2000: 586). This has led some critics to question whether it is actually possible to 'construct a **grand theory** of disablement that is valid and pertinent for all' (Lang, 2001: 19).

These criticisms are further compounded by mounting objection to the social model's acceptance of the medical nature of *impairment* (Barnes and Mercer, 2010). This is reflected by increasing numbers of theorists calling for a sociological reconceptualisation of it (Lang, 2001: 22):

> … the social model's impairment/disability dualism [split] is problematic because it fails to appreciate that *both* sides of this conceptual dualism are socially constructed and culturally specific. That is, both *impairment* and *disability* are powerful socially generated linguistic categories that divide, govern and control disabled people. (Thomas, 2014: 14)

In this way of thinking 'being or becoming disabled' means being '**socially constructed** and positioned as such' by society (Thomas, 2004: 23). This transforms our understanding of *impairment* from a biological fact to 'a site of social and political debate' (Hughes, 2014: 59). However, as Thomas (2014: 14) states, we must take care not to perform a 'vanishing act' on impairment or, to put it another way, make sure that the body doesn't 'disappear into language and discourse' (Hughes and Paterson, 1997): 'The theoretical elimination of the materiality of the body seems of little value to the disability movement' (Hughes and Paterson, 1997: 334). For Thomas, this means developing a broad theoretical framework that incorporates *both* the '*social dimensions of the biological*', and the '*biological dimensions of the social*' (2014: 14).

Reflective activity

Which version of the social model of disability do you think is most appropriate for social work practice: the original social model; the extended social-relational model; or a *hybrid* of the two?

Reflect on what this might mean for you in practice.

Whilst the challenges and criticisms of the aforementioned *original* social model are insurmountable for some within disability studies, others interpret the dialogue as an essential part of achieving progress. For example, Shakespeare and Watson argue that the *original* model is outdated as 'the world, and social theory, has passed it by' (2002: 29), whereas others have interpreted such 'heightened debate' as 'a sign' of the model's 'political and intellectual' development (Goodley, 2014: 130).

Interestingly, advocates of the *original* model have *readily* acknowledged that it provides 'only a limited and partial explanation for what is happening to disabled people in the modern world' (Oliver, 2013: 1025). For them, its alleged limitations are a 'conceptual misunderstanding' (Oliver, 2004: 8): namely, that the social model was never intended to be 'an all-encompassing framework within which everything that happens to disabled people could be understood or explained' (Oliver, 2013: 1024).

But, what does this mean for social work? In essence, it means working in accordance with the fundamental principle of *all* social approaches; specifically, that we do 'not locate the problem of disability with disabled people because they have "something wrong with them" ... [we must] reject the individual pathology model' (Oliver et al., 2012: 19):

> The social work task is (i) to identify ways in which disability is imposed upon people with impairments with a view to remediation, and (ii) to provide a flexible and accessible service to meet such individual needs as may arise. (Oliver et al., 2012: 49)

MENTAL DISTRESS: SOCIAL MODEL OR SOCIAL APPROACH?

Before proceeding to discuss the application of the social model of disability to mental distress, it is necessary to differentiate between general **social approaches** and the **social model of distress**. General social approaches explore how distress may be understood as 'a response to problematic life experiences', namely:

- *The internalisation or acting out of stressful social experiences* that could not be resolved in other ways ... a person's distress may be seen as an expression (usually indirect) of unresolved issues in relation to what has happened, or is currently happening, to them. Stressful experiences may include loss, discrimination, injustice, abuse or subjection to oppressive expectations made by others.
- *A coping or survival strategy* that a person may be using in order to deal with particular painful or stressful experiences ... distress, such as voice hearing or self harming, may therefore be understood as their best available strategy for coping with life circumstances. ... In this sense, manifestations of mental distress may be seen not as some unfortunate impairment, but as a reflection of people's resourcefulness and ingenuity. (Tew, 2005: 20)

In practice, this means helping people connect their 'inner and outer worlds' to their social experience and circumstance (Tew, 2005: 27). By doing so, social approaches aim to understand the influence of social factors upon the onset, causation and response to distress.

So, while general social approaches are similar to the social model of disability in that they challenge the reductionist nature of the medical, individual-deficit approach to distress, they are '*distinguished*' from the social model due to its emphasis on structural oppression and discrimination, rather than individual causality and experience (Beresford, 2005: 65):

> The social model of disability provides an important framework … by shifting the focus from … individual pathology and deficiency to consideration of oppression and discrimination operating at individual and societal levels. It highlights the barriers thus created and their effects in segregating, excluding, subordinating and marginalising mental health service users. (Beresford, 2005: 66)

Reflective activity

Can you identify an example either personally or in practice where a person has been discriminated against and/or oppressed, not by their mental distress, but by *others'/society's* response to it?

Visit the companion website (https://study.sagepub.com/rogers2e) for videos about general social approaches to mental distress

IS THE SOCIAL MODEL OF DISABILITY APPLICABLE TO MENTAL DISTRESS?

Despite the potential compatibility of the social model of disability to mental distress, mental health service users/survivors have remained on the margins of it (Beresford, 2004: 2). Similarly, whilst there is 'no doubt' that people who experience distress are 'well aware' of the discrimination and oppression they face, this has not sparked an 'equivalent of the social model of disability' to motivate similar 'collective' discussion or action for mental distress (Beresford, 2004: 11). For these reasons, the social model of disability is considered to be valuable to people who experience distress. Indeed, it is argued that it is 'just as useful' to people with 'other impairments' as it has been to disabled people (Oliver et al., 2012: 17).

Yet, notwithstanding an appetite for applying the social model of disability to mental distress, 'we can't just go ahead and "use it" or "apply it" in an easy way' (Spandler, 2012: 14). Although research conducted with people who experience distress identifies parallels with disabled people about the problematic medicalised, individual-deficit approach to practice (Beresford et al., 2010; 2016), a substantial point of contention exists regarding the social model's emphasis on disability and the significance of impairment within it:

… many people were clear that while they could identify in some ways as being disabled, by society or medication, they did not feel they had an impairment. Impairment emerged again as a problematic issue for many mental health service users / survivors. Many do not see their distress as a fixed or permanent state. (Beresford et al., 2016: 33)

Whilst the contested nature of *impairment* in relation to mental distress is similar to that within the social model of disability there is also a fundamental difference. Specifically, that for those 'engaged in the politics of mental health' the *biological* notion of impairment has 'proved particularly problematic':

No matter how far disability scholars may debate impairment in relation to physical disability (… for example, that … impairment is socially constructed), it would be rare for them to dispute the existence of impairment itself. In fact, we could say that the disability movement's demands … *depend on the existence of impairment.* (Sapey et al., 2015: 3)

This way of thinking presents a direct challenge to the application of the social model of disability to mental distress, as 'disablement' in the context of distress isn't necessarily dependent 'upon a pre-existing' physical 'impairment' which is 'oppressed or marginalised by society' (Sapey et al., 2015: 4). This is explained in the example below:

… if we question the very existence of a discrete mental illness such as schizophrenia and frame it instead as, for example, a reaction to trauma, a spiritual crisis or what-ever (as many people are doing), this poses questions for a social model of disability that is based on a priori existence of an impairment. (Spandler, 2012: 15)

This upholds Hughes's earlier assertion regarding the need to reframe *impairment* within the social model of disability; specifically, to 'transform' it from being a biological fact, to a 'site of social and political debate' (2014: 59). In essence, this suggests that in order for the social model of disability to be fully accessible to people who experience distress, impair-ment will need to be reimagined from that of a *biological fact* to a ***psychosocial, socio-political*** entity. Although, given Sapey et al.'s (2015: 3) aforementioned critique that it would be 'rare' for 'disability scholars' to 'dispute' the physical/biological 'existence of impairment', any reconceptualisation of it will have to take place both *within* and *outside* of disability studies.

Yet, in light of our previous discussion, that the *lived experience* of impairment (or distress) may become invisible, if reconceptualised as a socio-political entity, we should remember Thomas's (2014: 14) abovementioned advice and incorporate both the '*social dimensions of the biological*' and the '*biological dimensions of the social*' in practice. This is echoed by research involving mental health service users/survivors, which cautions us against 'drawing over-simplistic distinctions' between the different dimensions of expe-rience, in favour of highlighting their 'interactions' and the 'value of a holistic approach' (Beresford et al., 2016: 59).

Whilst there is no easy answer to these dilemmas, they do illustrate the importance of adopting a person-centred approach to our work. However, in being person-centred, we must remember that the *personal* is *political*.

Reflective activity

Consider to what extent the problematic nature of *impairment* constitutes a barrier to being able to apply the social model of disability to mental distress:

- How might you conceptualise distress as a psychosocial, socio-political experience, rather than a biological fact?

A WAY FORWARD?

It is evident that differences *and* commonalities exist regarding the nature of impairment and disability, both within and between the disabled people's movement and mental health user/survivors. Whilst the notion of impairment, particularly as conceived within the *original* social model, is problematic in both movements (at least for some); there is evidence of an emerging unity between the two. Indeed, current critical debate suggests that both movements share some key concerns: (1) that the *original* social model neglects the individual experience of impairment and distress, and in doing so fails to take account of psycho-emotional disablism; (2) that it misleadingly portrays disability and distress as an homogeneous experience; (3) that it reinforces the medical nature of impairment and distress, to the detriment of broader social dimensions; and (4) that solidarity remains important in taking action against structural disablism. This reflects research conducted with people who experience distress; namely, that like disabled people, they 'are concerned that any understanding of their situation takes full account of the personal issues they face' as well as 'broader social issues and interactions' (Beresford et al., 2010: 30; Beresford et al., 2016).

On this basis, the social model of disability is not fully applicable or accessible to people who experience distress. However, given the commonalities outlined above, there is scope to work with other like-minded groups to discuss and explore shared experiences and build allegiances in this regard. Indeed, Beresford (2015: 245) identifies opportunities that 'may offer a way past the roadblock' in the relationship between disability and distress, namely, building bridges with the **neurodiversity** movement and **mad studies**:

A core principle of neurodiversity is that such conditions are 'real' and neurological in nature; [but] they embody human *diversity* rather than representing pathology or deficiency. Thus, the movement seeks to celebrate neurodiversity and for it to be recognised and valued. It similarly seeks acceptance of identities previously pathologised as mental disorders, as a valid part of human diversity, aiming to 'reclaim' and 'revalue' impairment labels. (Beresford, 2015: 254)

In a similar vein, mad studies provide a collaborative, 'ground-breaking' and inclusive 'body of knowledge' that accords equal value to lived experience, alongside other knowledges from 'outside of the **medical model**' (Beresford, 2015: 258):

> [mad studies is] an umbrella term that is used to embrace the body of knowledge that has emerged from psychiatric survivors, Mad-identified people, anti-psychiatry academics and activists, critical psychiatrists, and radical therapists. This body of knowledge is wide-ranging and includes scholarship that is critical of the mental health system as well as radical and Mad activist scholarship. This field of study is informed by and generated by the perspectives of psychiatric survivors and Mad-identified researchers and academics. (LeFrançois et al., 2013: 337)

We have yet to see how the neurodiversity movement and mad studies will develop, and whether they will form separate disciplines alongside existing disability studies, create a 'broader, more inclusive disability studies', or some other hybrid thereof (Beresford, 2015: 258; McWade et al., 2015: 307). Whichever form this takes, there is no doubt it will share the foundations of both the *original* and *developing* social model of disability, and reject the traditional, individual-deficit discourse of the medical model. Whilst a detailed account of mad studies and the neurodiversity movement is beyond the scope of this chapter, the website contains further information on each of these subjects (https://study.sagepub.com/rogers2e).

In practice, these approaches enable us to step outside of the medical model of disability and distress, by integrating and challenging the 'social and political aspects' of how systems and society disable people and make people 'mad' (Weinstein, 2014: 27). This is reiterated by McDermott's analysis that:

> … making connections with other progressive social and psychological approaches … provide social workers not only with a critical evaluation of mental health, but also with an analysis that can begin to challenge the hegemony of the medical model and its preoccupation with individual deficits, symptomology and pathology. (2014: 63)

For social work, the 'task' should no longer be aimed at supporting people to adjust to 'personal disasters', but rather, working alongside people to 'locate the personal, social, economic and community resources' to enable them to 'live life to the full' (Oliver et al., 2012: 26):

> The rewards for social workers would arise from the enhanced professional and personal satisfaction that stems from both the increased range of tasks in which to exercise professional skills and the greater potential for achieving change. (Oliver et al., 2012: 26)

CONCLUSION

This chapter introduced the social model of disability and reflected on its application to mental distress. It emphasised the importance of problematising the traditional, individual-deficit model, in favour of working according to a more social-relational approach in practice. It concluded by revealing new and exciting opportunities to further develop our approach to social work practice in disability and mental health.

Having read this chapter, you should be able to:

- Understand the problematic consequences of working to a pure medical model alongside people living with disability and/or distress;
- Be familiar with the core features and challenges of the social models of disability and distress;
- Begin to understand the potential allegiances between different disability and mental health activist groups.

RECOMMENDED READING

Beresford, P., Nettle, M. and Perring, R. (2010) *Towards a Social Model of Madness and Distress: Exploring What Service Users Say.* York: Joseph Rowntree Foundation.

Beresford, P., Perring, R., Nettle, M. and Wallcraft, J. (2016) *From Mental Illness to a Social Model of Madness and Distress.* London: Shaping our Lives.

McWade, B., Milton, D. and Beresford, P. (2015) Mad studies and neurodiversity: a dialogue. *Disability and Society*, 30(2): 305–309.

Oliver, M., Sapey, B. and Thomas, P. (2012) *Social Work with Disabled People* (4th edn). Basingstoke: Palgrave Macmillan.

Spandler, H., Anderson, A. and Sapey, B. (eds) (2015) *Madness, Distress and the Politics of Disablement.* Bristol: Policy Press.

Social Work Activism
Donna Peach

Links to the Professional Capabilities Framework

• Professionalism • Values and ethics • Diversity and equality • Rights, justice and economic wellbeing • Contexts and organisations • Professional leadership

Links to the Knowledge and Skills Statement for Child and Family Practitioners

• Communication • Analysis, decision-making, planning and review • Organisational context

Links to the Knowledge and Skills Statement for Adult Practitioners

• Organisational context • Professional ethics and leadership • Effective assessments and outcome-based support planning

Key messages

- Activism is the activity of challenging social injustice, oppression and discrimination.
- Activism is embedded in the professional obligations specified in the British Association of Social Workers' (BASW) Code of Ethics.
- BASW support social work activism and have published a campaign pack to provide guidelines for social workers.
- There are several high-profile campaigns that you can support, and/or learn from, founded by social workers and service users.

INTRODUCTION

As social workers, you are at the forefront of the struggle *to give people some control over their lives, find dignity and self-respect in the most daunting circumstances.* (Ken Loach, Director and Filmmaker, in BASW Campaign Action Pack)

Activism is closely aligned with social justice and therefore entwined with the values and ethics of social work practice. However, it is a term that some feel uncomfortable about and prefer to associate their responsibility as social workers with advocacy. This book addresses advocacy in relation to Group Work (Chapter 28), Conflict Management and Resolution (Chapter 16) and Valuing Difference and Diversity (Chapter 8). As discussed in this book, advocacy is a social work activity that intrinsically must challenge social injustice, oppression and discrimination. When we do that with energy, we call it activism. Activism is work, it is labour; and as Nobel Laureate Jody Williams explains in conversation with Saleh (2012), those who do most of the work grow to be the leaders of those movements.

Visit the website to listen to a discussion on the role of social work advocacy (https://study.sagepub.com/rogers2e).

This chapter presents several examples of social work activism in order to demonstrate the importance of collective action. Indeed, the necessity to fight for social reform and social justice is embedded in the actions of Victorian social reformers such as Octavia Hill (1838–1912), Beatrice Webb (1858–1943) and American counterparts Josephine Shaw Lowel (1843–1905) and social work pioneer Mary Richmond (1861–1928). However, it is an American activist, social worker and author, Jane Addams (1860–1935), who is known as the mother of social work. Notably, the same social challenges that motivated Addams more than a century ago remain prevalent today (Atkinson, 2013). More specifically, today we, like Addams, also face the same loss of professional autonomy and a rise in standardisation that serve to simultaneously impinge and stimulate social work activism. The necessity of our profession's activism is anchored in the continued existence of social oppression and our ethical obligation to combat it.

HISTORICAL, SOCIAL WORK CAMPAIGNING

Social work activism is inherent to our profession's history.

In America during the 1960s and 1970s, Kwame Touré (formerly known as Stokely Carmichael) and political scientist Charles Hamilton constructed a theory of institutional and societal racist oppression of black people. Their articulated views were supported by black social workers who became central to the empowerment of the Black Power movement and the development of American social work profession (Bell, 2015). The Council on Social Work Education (CSWE), which defines social work standards in America, had since 1954 prohibited discriminatory segregation in schools. However, the pressure from black social workers ensured the revision of policy standards devised to define the complete inclusion of black people in education settings (Bell, 2015). Black social workers and members from black schools of social work formed the Black Task Force (BTF), which identified racism as underpinning the lack of attention to black people and their history in the social work curriculum (Bell, 2015). The BTF identified three social work education objectives that they thought were essential to counter inhumane and institutional racism:

1   An understanding of how the economic, social, political and class forces that determine social policies are implicitly influenced by racism;
2   An ability to analyse how social policy is formulated by legislation, by the courts and by government bureaucracies, and how this formulation is influenced by racism;
3   An awareness of the impact of institutional racism on black Americans and other minority ethnic groups, with a particular reference to the distribution of societal resources and the patterns of delivery of educational, health and social services (Bell, 2015: 301).

For social work lecturer Suryia Nayak, collective activism is entwined with theory and their combined strength is inherent within Black feminism. In her paper 'Declaring the activism of black feminist theory', Nayak (2017) demonstrates the multiple forms of Black feminist activism, as a writer, as a co-convenor of events to share grassroots activism and as a co-founder of rape services for Black, Asian and Minoritised Ethnic Women. Nayak weaves reflections of individual determination to make a difference, supported by the rich theoretical foundations offered by black writer and feminist, Audre Lorde. Lorde's poetry is a form of activism, used to articulate experiences of race, gender, class and sexuality – for example, in the poem 'The Politics of Addiction' (1997).

Reflective activity

How far was the content of your social work education programme, your practice placements, or if you're an employed social worker, your place of work, actively aware of institutional racism?

THE BRITISH ASSOCIATION OF SOCIAL WORKERS

The British Association of Social Workers (BASW) is the membership-based, professional organisation for social work in the UK. The association has a Code of Ethics, which specifies the underpinning ethical obligations bestowed on our profession. One of the key principles of the BASW Code of Ethics is to strive for social justice. The box below details the value base that underpins our responsibility to promote social justice in relation not only to those we work with, but to society in general. It identifies five key principles which detail the responsibilities of social workers.

BASW Code of Ethics: Social justice

Value

Social workers have a responsibility to promote social justice, in relation to society generally, and in relation to the people with whom they work.

Principles

1   *Challenging discrimination*: Social workers have a responsibility to challenge discrimination on the basis of characteristics such as ability, age, culture, gender or sex, marital status, socio-economic status, political opinions, skin colour, racial or other physical characteristics, sexual orientation or spiritual beliefs.
2   *Recognising diversity*: Social workers should recognise and respect the diversity of the societies in which they practise, taking into account individual, family, group and community differences.
3   *Distributing resources*: Social workers should ensure that resources at their disposal are distributed fairly, according to need.
4   *Challenging unjust policies and practices*: Social workers have a duty to bring to the attention of their employers, policy makers, politicians and the general public situations where resources are inadequate or where distribution of resources, policies and practice are oppressive, unfair, harmful or illegal.
5   *Working in solidarity*: Social workers, individually, collectively and with others have a duty to challenge social conditions that contribute to social exclusion, stigmatisation or subjugation, and work towards an inclusive society.

In 2015, BASW Vice Chair Fran McDonnell took part in a Task Force as part of the European Anti-Poverty Networks (EAPN) examination of poverty as a violation of human rights. The subsequent handbook can be viewed via this link: www.eapn. eu/wp-content/uploads/2018/07/EAPN-2018-Handbook-on-Poverty-and-Human-Rights-EAPN.pdf. In 2017, led by past BASW UK Chair Guy Shennan and Honorary Officer Jon Dudley, the BASW and the Social Workers Union (SWU) launched the 'Boot Out Austerity Campaign', to highlight the negative impact of austerity on families. The campaign's initial activism comprised of 140 social workers and service users taking part in a 100-mile walk from the BASW UK office in Birmingham to the annual general meeting convened that year in Liverpool (Figure 33.1). BASW has continued to build on this initiative, publishing research about the impact of poverty on children: www.coventry.ac.uk/research/research-directories/current-projects/2014/child-welfare-inequality-uk/cwip-project-outputs/

Furthermore, BASW has convened several workshops around the country to consult on what information should be included in a guide for social workers. In the following activity, you will find the questions that the handbook intends to address.

Figure 33.1   Campaigners walked 100 miles to highlight the negative impact of austerity on families

Source: British Association of Social Workers and Social Workers Union. Reproduced with permission.

Reflective activity

Alone or with a small group of social work students/colleagues address the questions posed by BASW detailed below. When you have listed responses under the three questions, consider which of your proposals are supported by human rights legislation; identify what shortfalls you perceive or have witnessed in practice. Within these gaps identify the organisations who are active in working to fill them, for example, in the absence of food the Trussell Trust run foodbanks (www.trusselltrust.org/), and the end fuel poverty coalition (www.endfuelpoverty.org.uk/).

- What issues should social workers consider in their work with service users who are victims living in poverty?
- In the face of diminishing services arising from austerity, how should social workers involve third sector organisations in statutory work?
- How should social workers address the ethical and human rights issues arising from poverty?

DIGITAL ACTIVISM

As a profession, we have yet to fully examine the ethical challenges of social work activity in digital spaces (Reamer, 2013). Indeed, as a human race we are in the infancy of understanding digital activism. To assist in this endeavour, Neumayer and Svensson (2016) developed a typology of four different types of digital activism. As you will see from Figure 33.2 the four typologies vary according to social and political positioning and the degree to which the activism is law-abiding. Schradie (2018) argues that despite the availability of digital resources there is evidence of digital-activism inequality for people from the working class.

Salon activist

The Salon activist is opposed to accepting the views of the other and believes they should be fought against. They are likely to be political and express verbal hostility, but they are law-abiding, partly through fear of punishment, and therefore unlikely to participate in radical activism.

Contentious activist

The Contentious activist is likely to identify as an activist who is willing to listen to those with views they oppose. They are willing to participate in antisocial behaviour and face prosecution, as a means of achieving change. Their forms of digital activism could include hacking websites and deleting content.

Law-abiding activist

The law-abiding activist holds political opinions and does not accept law-breaking activities. However, they do value and want to listen to views that are opposite to their own. Their online activism takes the form of participating in online debate and social media campaigns.

Gandhian activist

The Gandhian activist is willing to participate in non-violent civil unrest, while simultaneously respecting those with opposite political views. They are positioned by Neumayer and Svensson (2016) as an idealised form of activism from which other forms of participation

Figure 33.2   Typology of activism in the digital age (Neumayer and Svensson, 2016: 140)

should be measured. However, the Gandhian activist is less defined within this model and similarly anticipated to be unnoticed within busy social media debate focused on the damage caused during civil disobedience (Cammaerts, 2013).

Reflective activity

There are multiple types of activists, as a means of some fun exploration, you can use this link to gain some insights into what kind of activist you are: www.quizony.com/what-kind-of-activist-are-you/index.html

---

ARTICLE 39 CAMPAIGN: FIGHTING FOR CHILDREN'S RIGHTS IN INSTITUTIONAL SETTINGS

An example of how a social worker steers collective action to make a difference is the director of the campaign Article 39, Carolyne Willow, who collates data through Freedom of Information requests and uses this research to advocate for improved public policy. The campaign has also found that to effectively protect children's rights it has had to initiate strategic litigation. One issue where they continue to try to effect change relates to the painful restraint of young people living in custodial settings, which came to public attention via the BBC *Panorama* broadcast 'Teenage Prison Abuse Exposed' (https://vimeo.com/199038379).

Article 39 of the UN Convention on the Rights of the Child (UNCRC) declares that the states who are party to the Convention shall 'take all appropriate measures to promote physical and psychological recovery and social reintegration of a child victim of any form of neglect, exploitation, or abuse; torture or any other form of cruel, inhuman or degrading treatment or punishment; or armed conflicts. Such recovery and reintegration shall take place in an environment which fosters the health, self-respect and dignity of the children in environments where their health, self-respect and dignity are nurtured.' The UK signed the Convention on 19 April 1990, in which it makes a commitment that its governments' policy, and practices must comply with the UNCRC. However, the campaign Article 39 (https://article39.org.uk) exists as a means of promoting, monitoring and when necessary taking legal action to safeguard the rights of children who are living in institutional settings when it views the state is failing to do so.

STUDENT SOCIAL WORKERS' VIEWS ON ACTIVISM

Notwithstanding the fundamental need for social work activism, it is not uncommon for social work students and qualified social workers to experience barriers. Gair (2017)

examined student social workers' views in relation to activism, empathy and racism. The participants identified barriers to activism as including perceptions of a lack of time to engage, a lack of subject knowledge and lacking in their self-confidence. However, not all students are inhibited. A content analysis of media coverage of the 2010 UK student protests found they had a willingness to cause damage with the intention of raising awareness of their cause, in order to trigger public debate (Cammaerts, 2013). Their potentially law-breaking activities could be compared to the 'contentious activist' typology, described above in Neumayer and Svensson's (2016) digital activism model.

Despite, the history of social work activism, it is understandable that students and social workers will be wary of acts that break the law. Firstly, there is a requirement for us to undergo a Disclosure and Barring Service (DBS) check, to ensure we are safe to practise. Secondly, we also hold positions where we are required to form views about other people that can affect their lives. Therefore, we need to work to ensure that we live and practise by our professions' values and ethical standards (Pasini, 2015). Jansson and Dodd (2002) explored medical social workers' views of ethical activism, and their findings suggest that social workers are more likely to engage if it will improve the wellbeing of their patients.

CONCLUSION

Activism is woven into the ethical foundations of our social work profession. Our willingness to act collectively in response to social injustice is fundamental to our pursuit of a fair and inclusive society. The historical routes of social work activism have been vital to combating discrimination, and we should feel rightly proud of that history. As in the past, our profession faces multiple and competing demands, which see increased social injustice and a reduction in the resources available to those who need them most. We are faced with unfathomable policies, for example, those which permit state actors to perform painful restraint on children. Most people will be unaware of these hidden truths, and those subject to painful restraint and their families are reliant on campaigners like Carolyne Willow to raise awareness and challenge the policy makers. In turn, campaigns like Article 39 are reliant on those who will add their names to their activities and crowd fundraise to pay for a legal challenge. Social work activism is ethical in its quest for social justice and is always most successful as a collective activity.

Having read this chapter, you should be able to:

- Identify different definitions of activism;
- Understand how activism is an integral and ethically bound aspect of social work;
- Examine the barriers and opportunities for social work activism;
- Reflect on your own use of activism and the role it plays or could play in your social work practice.

RECOMMENDED READING

British Association of Social Workers (2018b) *Leave No Stone Unturned in the Fight Against Austerity.* Campaign action pack. Available at: www.basw.co.uk/system/files/resources/BASW%20 Campaign%20action%20pack.pdf

Pasini, A. (2015) Social workers and moral choices: ethical questions about Giovanna's case. *Ethics and Social Welfare*, 9(4): 403–412.

Saleh, M. (2012) Jody Williams: Nobel Laureate's insights on activism and social work. *Affilia*, 27(1): 51–59.

Conclusion

The original aim of this book was to produce a practical handbook for social work students that gave a brief introduction to the core skills needed for practice. This second edition has the same focus but with an additional acknowledgement that skills and knowledge come hand in hand. We hope that all readers (including students, newly qualified social workers, frontline practitioners, academics and practice educators) will find this book to be helpful and easy to access. We offer practical tips to aid and enhance the development of core skills and knowledge. With the range of chapter topics in mind, we hope that the reader will appreciate the breadth and depth of knowledge and skills involved in social work. The content of the book is not exhaustive in terms of core skills and knowledge, we merely offer what we consider to be the core areas that should be conceived as the foundation for practice.

The website proffers additional material and contains some useful information (for example, the 'How to …' guides and there are two new ones accompanying this second edition). The 'How to …' guides are intended to be used 'on the go' and are, therefore, succinct. The links to Sage journal articles prompts the reader to remember the importance of theory and research-informed knowledge (in addition to Part III of the book, which explores a number of social work theories and methods). However, our motivation to write this book is underpinned, to some degree, by the central theme (skills development). We have retained our adopted theoretical framework of relationship-based practice and person-centred thinking. This, we hope, indicates to the reader the importance of a value-based and human-rights-centred approach to practice.

Michaela Rogers
Dawn Whitaker
David Edmondson
Donna Peach

References

Ahmed, A. (2015) *Retiring to Spain: Women's Narratives of Nostalgia, Belonging and Community*. Bristol: Policy Press.

Ahmed, A. and Rogers, M. (2016) Diversity and exclusion in context. In A. Ahmed and M. Rogers (eds), *Working with Marginalised Groups: From Policy to Practice*. London: Palgrave Macmillan.

Ahmed, A. and Rogers, M. (2017) Interrogating trans and sexual identities through the conceptual lens of translocational positionality. *Sociological Research Online*, 22(1). Available at: www.socresonline.org.uk/22/1/contents.html

Ainsworth, M.D. (1969) *Maternal Sensitivity Scales. The Balti Longitudinal Project*. Johns Hopkins University. Available at: www.psychology.sunysb.edu/attachment/measures/content/maternal%20sensitivity%20scales.pdf

Ainsworth, M.D. and Bell, S.M. (1970) Attachment, exploration, and separation: illustrated by the behavior of one-year-olds in a strange situation. *Child Development*, 41(1): 49–67.

Ainsworth, M.D.S., Bell, S.M. and Stayton, D.J. (1971) Individual differences in Strange Situation behavior of one year olds. In H.R. Schaffer (ed.), *The Origins of Human Social Relations*. New York: Academic Press.

Ainsworth, M., Kiesler, C.A. and Scarr, S. (1979) Infant–mother attachment. *American Psychologist*, 34(10): 932–937.

Anthias, F. (2008) Thinking through the lens of translocational positionality: an intersectionality frame for understanding identity and belonging. *Translocations: Migration and Social Change*, 4(1): 5–20.

Aparicio, E., Michalopoulos, L. and Unick, G. (2013) An examination of the psychometric properties of the vicarious trauma scale in a sample of licensed social workers. *Health & Social Work*, 38(4): 199–206.

Association of Palliative Care for Social Workers (2019) *Social Worker Role*. Available at: https://www.apcsw.org.uk/social-worker-role/ (accessed 13 October 2019).

Atkinson, B. (2013) Was Jane Addams a promiscuous pragmatist? *International Journal of Qualitative Studies in Education*, 26(5): 610–624.

Bailey, D. (2012) *Interdisciplinary Working in Mental Health*. Basingstoke: Palgrave Macmillan.

Baillargeon, R. (1986) Representing the existence and the location of hidden objects: object permanence in 6- to 8-month-old infants. *Cognition*, 23(1): 21–41.

Banks, S. (1995) *Ethics and Values in Social Work*. Basingstoke: Macmillan.

Banks, S. (2012) *Ethics and Values in Social Work* (4th edn). Basingstoke: Palgrave Macmillan.

Banks, S. (2014) *Ethics: Critical and Radical Debates in Social Work*. Bristol: Policy Press.

Barker, R.L. (2003) *The Social Work Dictionary* (5th edn). Washington, DC: The National Association of Social Work Press.

Barnard, A. (2008) Values, ethics and professionalization: a social work history. In A. Barnard, N. Horner and J. Wilde (eds), *The Value Base of Social Work and Social Care: An Active Learning Handbook*. Maidenhead: Open University Press, pp. 5–24.

Barnes, C. and Mercer, G. (2010) *Exploring Disability* (2nd edn). Cambridge: Polity Press.

Bar-On, R. (2006) How important is it to educate people to be emotionally intelligent, can it be done? In R. Bar-On, J.G. Maree and M. Elias (eds), *Educating People to be Emotionally Intelligent*. Johannesburg.

Barrett, G. and Keeping, C. (2005) The processes required for effective interprofessional working. In G. Barrett, D. Sellman and J. Thomas (eds), *Interprofessional Working in Health and Social Care*. Basingstoke: Palgrave Macmillan.

Barrett, G., Sellman, D. and Thomas, J. (2005) *Interprofessional Working and Social Care: Professional Perspectives*. Basingstoke: Palgrave Macmillan.

Barsky, A. (2015) *Conflict Resolution for the Helping Professions* (3rd edn). New York: Oxford University Press.

Bassot, D. (2013) *The Reflective Journal: Capturing your Learning for Person and Professional Development*. Basingstoke: Palgrave Macmillan.

BASW (British Association of Social Workers) (2011) BASW/CoSW England Research on Supervision in Social Work, with Particular Reference to Supervision Practice in Multi Disciplinary Teams: England. Document.BASW/CoSW England Research on Supervision in Social Work, with Particular Reference to Supervision Practice in Multi Disciplinary Teams: England. Birmingham: BASW.

BASW (British Association of Social Workers) (2014) *Code of Ethics for Social Work*. Birmingham: BASW.

BASW (British Association of Social Workers) (2016) Capabilities within the framework. Available at: www.basw.co.uk/pcf/capabilities (accessed 29 February 2016).

BASW (British Association of Social Workers) (2018a) *Professional Capabilities Framework for Social Work in England: The 2018 Refreshed PCF*. Available at: www.basw.co.uk/system/files/resources/Detailed%20level%20descriptors%20for%20all%20domains%20wi%20digital%20aug8.pdf

BASW (British Association of Social Workers) (2018b) *Leave No Stone Unturned in the Fight Against Austerity*. Campaign action pack. Available at: www.basw.co.uk/system/files/resources/BASW%20Campaign%20action%20pack.pdf

Beckett, C. and Horner, N. (2016) *Essential Theory for Social Work Practice* (2nd edn). London: Sage.

Beddoe, L. (2010) Surveillance or reflection: professional supervision in the risk society. *British Journal of Social Work*, 40(4): 1279–1296.

Bell, J. (2018) Values and ethics. In J. Lishman, C. Yuill, G. Brannan and A. Gibson (eds), *Social Work: An Introduction* (2nd edn). London: Sage, pp. 3–18.

Bell, J.M. (2015) The Black Power influence on American schools of social work. *Critical and Radical Social Work*, 3(2): 295–304.

Belli, S. (2010) The construction of an emotion (love) and its relationship with language: a review and discussion of an important area of social sciences. *Razón Y Palabra*, (71).

Bentall, R., de Sousa, P., Varese, F., Wickham, S., Sitko, K., Haarmans, M. and Read, J. (2014) From adversity to psychosis: Pathways and mechanisms from specific adversities to specific symptoms. *Social Psychiatry and Psychiatric Epidemiology*, 49(7): 1011–1022.

Beresford, P. (2002) Thinking about mental health: towards a social model. *Journal of Mental Health*, 11(6): 581–584.

Beresford, P. (2004) Madness, distress, research and a social model. In C. Barnes and G. Mercer (eds), *Implementing the Social Model of Disability: Theory and Research*. Leeds: The Disability Press, pp. 1–21. Available at: http://disability-studies.leeds.ac.uk/files/library/Barnes-implementing-the-social-model-chapter-13.pdf (accessed 21 March 2016).

Beresford, P. (2005) Social work and a social model of madness and distress: developing a viable role for the future. *Social Work and Social Sciences Review*, 12(2): 59–73.

Beresford, P. (2012) Service-user involvement. In M. Gray, J. Midgley and S.A. Webb (eds), *The SAGE Handbook of Social Work*. London: SAGE.

Beresford, P. (2015) Distress and disability: not you, not me, but us? In H. Spandler, A. Anderson and B. Sapey (eds), *Madness, Distress and the Politics of Disablement*. Bristol: Policy Press, pp. 245–259.

Beresford, P., Croft, S. and Adshead, L. (2008) 'We don't see her as a social worker': a service user case study of the importance of the social worker's relationship and humanity. *British Journal of Social Work*, 38(7): 1388–1407.

Beresford, P., Nettle, M. and Perring, R. (2010) *Towards a Social Model of Madness and Distress: Exploring What Service Users Say*. York: Joseph Rowntree Foundation.

Beresford, P., Fleming, J., Glynn, M., Bewley, C., Croft, S., Branfield, F. and Postle, K. (2011) *Supporting People: Towards a Person-Centred Approach*. Bristol: Policy Press.

Beresford, P., Perring, R., Nettle, M. and Wallcraft, J. (2016) *From Mental Illness to a Social Model of Madness and Distress*. London: Shaping our Lives.

Beverley, A. and Worsley, A. (2007) *Learning and Teaching in Social Work Practice*. Basingstoke: Palgrave Macmillan.

Bird, G. and Viding, E. (2014) The self to other model of empathy: providing a new framework for understanding empathy impairments in psychopathy, autism, and alexithymia. *Neuroscience and Biobehavioral Reviews*, 47: 520–532.

Birkenmaier, J., Berg-Weger, M. and Dewees, M.P. (eds) (2014) *The Practice of Generalist Social Work* (3rd edn). New York: Routledge.

Bogg, D. (2012) *Report Writing*. Maidenhead: Open University Press.

Borton, T. (1970) *Reach, Touch and Teach*. London: Hutchinson.

Boud, D., Keogh, R. and Walker, D. (1983) *Reflection: Turning Experience into Learning*. London: Kogan Page.

Bowen, S. (2014) *Act for UK Rights Blog*. Available at: https://actforukrights.wordpress.com/category/european-convention-on-human-rights/ (accessed 31 October 2015).

Bowlby, J. (1969/1982) *Attachment and Loss: Vol. 1. Attachment*. London: Pimlico.

Bozarth, J. and Evans, S. (2000) Non-directiveness in client-centered therapy: A vexed concept. Available at: http://personcentered.com/nondirect.html (accessed 23 October 2019).

Bretherton, I. (1997) Bowlby's legacy to developmental psychology. *Child Psychiatry and Human Development*, 28(1): 33–44.

British Institute of Human Rights (2015) My human rights. Available at: https://www.bihr.org.uk/my-human-rights (accessed 31 October 2015).

Broadhurst, K., Hall, C., Wastell, D., White, S. and Pithouse, A. (2010a) Risk, instrumentalism and the humane project in social work: identifying the informal logics of risk management in children's statutory services. *British Journal of Social Work*, 40(4): 1046–1064.

Broadhurst, K., White, S., Fish, S., Munro, E., Fletcher, K. and Lincoln, H. (2010b) *Ten Pitfalls and how to Avoid Them: What Research Tells Us.* London: NSPCC.

Bronfenbrenner, U. (1979) *The Ecology of Human Development: Experiments by Nature and Design.* Harvard: Harvard University Press.

Brookfield, S. (1987) *Developing Critical Thinkers.* San Francisco, CA: Jossey-Bass.

Bronte-Tinkew, J., Carrano, J., Horowitz, A., and Kinukawa, A. (2008) Involvement Among Resident Fathers and Links to Infant Cognitive Outcomes. *Journal of Family Issues,* 29(9): 1211–1244.

Cacciatore, J., Carlson, B., Michaelis, E., Klimek, B. and Steffan, S. (2011) Crisis intervention by social workers in fire departments: an innovative role for social workers. *Social Work,* 56(1): 81–88.

Calder, M. and Hackett, S. (2013) *Asssessment in Child Care: Using and Developing Frameworks for Practice.* Lyme Regis: Russell House Publishing.

Callaghan, J., Alexander, J., Fellin, L. and Sixsmith, J. (2016) Children's experiences of domestic violence and abuse: siblings' accounts of relational coping. *Clinical Child Psychology and Psychiatry,* 21(4): 649–668.

Cameron, A., Lart, R., Bostock, L. and Coomber, C. (2012) *Research Briefing 41: Factors that Promote and Hinder Joint and Integrated Working between Health and Social Care Services.* London: Social Care Institute for Excellence. Available at: www.scie.org.uk/publications/briefings/files/briefing41.pdf (accessed 13 March 2016).

Cammaerts, B. (2013) The mediation of insurrectionary symbolic damage: the 2010 U.K. student protests. *The International Journal of Press/Politics,* 18(4): 525–548.

Care Act 2014. London: HMSO.

Carers UK (2019) Carers UK: Making life better for carers. Available at: www.carersuk.org/home (accessed 3 June 2019).

Carr, S. (2012) *Personalisation: A Rough Guide.* London: Social Care Institute for Excellence.

Centre for the Advancement of Interprofessional Education (CAIPE) (2007) Available at: www.caipe.org.uk/

Chakrabarti, S. (2012) Human rights or citizen's privileges: the great Bill of Rights swindle. *The Political Quarterly,* 83(3): 454–465.

Chetkow-Yanoov, B.H. (1996) *Social Work Approaches to Conflict Resolution: Making Fighting Obsolete* (Haworth Social Work Practice). Abingdon: Routledge.

Child, N. (2000) *The Potential of Systemic Practice: A Huge Army of Great Workers.* Conference paper, Connections in Practice conference, Stirling, March.

Children Act 1989. London: HMSO.

Children and Families Act 2014. London: HMSO.

Cicchetti, D. (2010) Resilience under conditions of extreme stress: a multilevel perspective. *World Psychiatry,* 9(3): 145–154.

Clark, L.C. (2000) *Social Work Ethics: Politics, Principles and Practices.* London: Macmillan.

Clifford, D. and Burke, B. (2009) *Anti-Oppressive Ethics and Values in Social Work.* Basingstoke: Palgrave Macmillan.

Collins, S. (2009) *Effective Communication: Workbook for Social Care Workers.* London: Jessica Kingsley.

Collins, S. (2015) Alternative psychological approaches for social workers and social work students dealing with stress in the UK: sense of coherence, challenge appraisals, self-efficacy and sense of control. *British Journal of Social Work,* 45(1): 69–85.

Conservative Party (2014) *Protecting Human Rights in the UK: The Conservatives' Proposals for Britain's Human Rights Laws.* Available at: www.conservatives.com/~/media/files/downloadable%20Files/human_rights.pdf (accessed 31 October 2015).

Constable, G. (2013) Written presentation of self. In A. Mantell (ed.), *Skills for Social Work Practice* (2nd edn). Exeter: Learning Matters.

Cooper, P. (2014) *Court and Legal Skills.* Basingstoke: Palgrave Macmillan.

Cooter, R. (2009) Crisis. *The Lancet,* 373(9667): 887.

Cossar, J., Brandon, M. and Jordan, P. (2011) 'Don't make assumptions': Children's and young people's views of the child protection system and messages for change. Office of the Children's Commissioner.

Coulshed, V. and Orme, J. (1998) Task-centred practice. *Social Work Practice.* London: Palgrave, pp. 115–132.

Coulshed, V. and Orme, J. (2012) *Social Work Practice* (5th edn). Basingstoke: Palgrave Macmillan.

Cowden, S. and Singh, G. (2014) A critical analysis of service user struggles. In C. Cocker and T. Hafford-Letchfield (eds), *Rethinking Anti-Discriminatory and Anti-Oppressive Theories for Social Work Practice.* Basingstoke: Palgrave Macmillan, pp. 93–107.

CQC (Care Quality Commission) (2015) *Statement on CQC's Roles and Responsibilities for Safeguarding Children and Adults.* Available at: www.cqc.org.uk/sites/default/files/20150710_CQC_New_Safeguarding_Statement.pdf (accessed 3 March 2019).

Crenshaw, K.W. (1991) Mapping the margins: intersectionality, identity politics, and violence against women of color. *Stanford Law Review,* 32(6): 1241–1299.

Cummins, I. (2016) *Mental Health and the Criminal Justice System: A Social Work Perspective.* Northwich: Critical Publishing.

Currer, C. (2007) *Loss and Social Work.* Exeter: Learning Matters.

Dalrymple, J. and Boylan, J. (2013) *Effective Advocacy in Social Work*. London: Sage.

Dalzell, R. and Chamberlain, C. (2006) *Communicating with Children during Assessment: Training Pack*. London: National Children's Bureau.

Daniel, B. and Wassell, S. (2002a) *The Early Years: Assessing and Promoting Resilience in Vulnerable Children*. London: Jessica Kingsley.

Daniel, B. and Wassell, S. (2002b) *The School Years: Assessing and Promoting Resilience in Vulnerable Children*. London: Jessica Kingsley.

Daniel, B. and Wassell, S. (2002c) *Adolescence: Assessing and Promoting Resilience in Vulnerable Children*. London: Jessica Kingsley.

Daniel, B., Wassell, S. and Gilligan, R. (2010) *Child Development for Child Care and Protection Workers*. London: Jessica Kingsley.

Davies, K. and Jones, R. (eds) (2015) *Skills for Social Work Practice* (4th edn). Basingstoke: Palgrave Macmillan.

Davys, A. and Beddoe, L. (2009) The reflective learning model: supervision of social work students. *Social Work Education: The International Journal*, 28(8): 919–933.

Dayes, J. (2018) *Grief Demystified: An Introduction*. London: Jessica Kingsley.

Derbyshire County Council v. SH [2015] EWFC B102. Available at: www.bailii.org/ew/cases/EWFC/OJ/2015/B102.html (accessed 6 January 2016).

DH (Department of Health) (1988) *Protecting Children: A Guide for Social Workers Undertaking a Comprehensive Assessment*. London: The Stationery Office.

DH (Department of Health) (2000) *Framework for the Assessment of Children in Need and their Families*. London: The Stationery Office.

DH (Department of Health) (2009) Valuing People Now: Summary Report March 2009–September 2010. Including findings from Learning Disability Partnership Board Self Assessments 2009–2010. London: The Stationery Office.

Doel, M. (2002) Task-centred work. In R. Adams, L. Dominelli and M. Payne (eds), *Social Work: Themes, Issues and Critical Debates* (2nd edn). Basingstoke: Palgrave Macmillan, pp. 191–199.

Doel, M. (2006) *Using Groupwork*. London: Routledge/Community Care.

Doel, M. (2010) *Social Work Placements: A Traveller's Guide*. London: Routledge.

Doel, M. and Marsh, P. (1992) *Task-Centred Social Work*. Aldershot: Ashgate.

Doel, M. and Marsh, P. (2006) Across the divide. *Community Care*, 8 June. Available at: www.communitycare.co.uk/2006/06/08/across-the-divide/ (accessed 1 September 2015).

Doel, M. and Sawdon, C. (1999) *The Essential Groupworker*. London: Jessica Kingsley.

Doka, K.J. and Martin, T.L. (2010) *Grieving Beyond Gender: Understanding the Ways Men and Women Mourn*. New York: Brunner-Routledge.

Dominelli, L. (2002) *Anti-oppressive Social Work Theory and Practice*. Basingstoke: Palgrave Macmillan.

Dominelli, L. (2009) Anti-oppressive practice: The challenges of the twenty-first century. In R. Adams, L. Dominelli and M. Payne (eds), *Social Work: Themes, Issues and Debates* (3rd edn). Basingstoke: Palgrave Macmillan, pp. 49–64.

Dowling, S., Manthorpe, J. and Cowley, S. (2006) *Person-Centred Planning in Social Care: A Scoping Review*. York: Joseph Rowntree Foundation.

De Dreu, C. (2007) The virtue and vice of workplace conflict: food for (pessimistic) thought. *Journal of Organizational Behavior*, 29: 5–18.

Duffy, J. and Collins, M. (2010) Macro impacts on case worker decision-making in child welfare: a cross-national comparison. *European Journal of Social Work*, 13(1): 35–54.

Dunhill, A., Elliott, B. and Shaw, A. (2009) *Effective Communication and Engagement with Children and Young People, their Families and Carers*. London: Learning Matters.

Dunstan, R., Lee, A., Matthews, J., Nisbet, G., Pockett, R., Thistlethwaite, J. and White, J. (2009) *Interprofessional Health Education in Australia: The Way Forward*. Sydney: Centre for Research in Learning and Change, University of Technology, Sydney.

Edmondson, D. (2014) *Social Work Practice Learning*. London: Sage.

Edmondson, D. and Rogers, M. (2014) Using supervision, reflective practice and critical thinking. In D. Edmondson, *Social Work Practice Learning: A Student Guide*. London: Sage.

Egan, G. (2007) *The Skilled Helper* (8th edn). Belmont, CA: Thomson.

EHRC (Equality and Human Rights Commissions) (2015) The Public Sector Equality Duty. Available at: www.equalityhumanrights.com/about-us/about-commission/equality-and-diversity/public-sector-equality-duty (accessed 11 February 2016).

Eisenberg, N. and Strayer, J. (1988) *Empathy and its Development*. Cambridge: Cambridge University Press.

Ellingham, I. (2005) Breaking free from 'non-directivity'. *TherapyToday.net*, 16(10). Available at: www.therapytoday.net/article/show/3240/breaking-free-from-non-directivity/

Equal Pay Portal (2018) *Statistics*. Available at: www.equalpayportal.co.uk/statistics/ (accessed 13 October 2019).

Espiner, D. and Hartnett, F. (2011) I felt I was in control of the meeting: facilitating planning with adults within an intellectual disability. *British Journal of Learning Disabilities*, 40(1): 62–70.

Featherstone, B., White, S. and Morris, K. (2014) *Reimagining Child Protection: Towards Humane Social Work with Families*. Bristol: Policy Press.

Ferguson, H. (2005) Working with violence, the emotions and the psycho-social dynamics of child protection: reflections on the Victoria Climbié case. *Social Work Education*, 24(7), 781–795.

Ferguson, H. (2011) *Child Protection Practice*. Basingstoke: Palgrave Macmillan.

Fernald, A., Taeschner, T., Dunn, J., Papousek, M., De Boysson-Bardies, B., and Fukui, I. (1989) A cross-language study of prosodic modifications in mothers' and fathers' speech to preverbal infants *. *Journal of Child Language*, 16(3): 477–501.

Field, P., Jasper, C. and Littler, L. (2014) *Practice Education in Social Work: Achieving Professional Standards*. Northwich: Critical Publishing.

Finkelstein, V. (2004) Representing disability. In J. Swain, S. French, C. Barnes and C. Thomas (eds), *Disabling Barriers – Enabling Environments* (2nd edn). Sage: London, pp. 13–20.

Fink-Samnick, E. (2009) The professional resilience paradigm. *Professional Case Management*, 14(6): 330–332.

Fisher, T. (2005) Fatherhood and the British Fathercraft Movement, 1919–39. *Gender and History*, 17(2): 441–462.

Fishwick, C. (1989) *Court Work* (2nd edn). Birmingham: PEPAR Publications.

Fitzpatrick, G., Reder, P. and Lucey, C. (1995) The child perspective. In P. Reder and C. Lucey (eds), *Assessment of Parenting, Psychiatric and Psychological Contributions*. New York and London: Routledge.

Fook, J. (2002) *Social Work: Critical Theory and Practice*. London: Sage.

Fook, J. and Gardner, F. (2007) *Practising Critical Reflection: A Resource Handbook*. Maidenhead: Open University Press.

Forrester, D., McCambridge, J., Waissbein, C. and Rollnick, S. (2008) How do child and family social workers talk to parents about child welfare concerns? *Child Abuse Review*, 17(1): 23–35.

Fox, J. (2011) *Using Supervision to Promote Excellent Outcomes and Enable Staff Development*. Available at http://docplayer.net/13877400-Effective-supervision.html (accessed 13 October 2019).

Freeth, D., Reeves, S., Koppel, I., Hammick, M. and Barr, H. (2005) *Evaluating Interprofessional Education: A Self-Help Guide*. London: Higher Education Academy Learning and Teaching Support Network for Health Sciences and Practice.

Freud, S. (1917/1957) Mourning and melancholia. In J. Strachey (ed.), *The Complete Psychological Works of Sigmund Freud*. London: Hogarth Press, pp. 152–170.

Frizzo, G., Vivian, B., Piccinini, A. and Lopes, G. (2013) Crying as a form of parent–infant communication in the context of maternal depression. *Journal of Child and Family Studies*, 22(4): 569–581.

Frost, N. and Holt, A. (2014) Mother, researcher, feminist, woman: reflections on 'maternal status' as a researcher identity. *Qualitative Research Journal*, 14(2): 90–102.

Gair, S. (2010) Social work students' thoughts on their (in)ability to empathise with a birth mother's story: pondering the need for a deeper focus on empathy, *Adoption and Fostering*, 34(4): 39–50.

Gair, S. (2017) Pondering the colour of empathy: social work students' reasoning on activism, empathy and racism. *British Journal of Social Work*, 47(1): 162–180.

Gambrill, E. (2006) *Social Work Practice: A Critical Thinker's Guide* (2nd edn). Oxford: Oxford University Press.

Gerdes, K.E. and Segal, E.A. (2009) A social work model of empathy. *Advances in Social Work*, 1(2): 114–127.

Gerdes, K.E., Segal, E.A., Jackson, K.F. and Mullins, J.L. (2011) Teaching empathy: A framework rooted in social cognitive neuroscience and social justice. *Journal of Social Work Education*, 47(1): 109–131.

Gery, I., Miljkovitch, R., Berthoz, S. and Soussignan, R. (2009) Empathy and recognition of facial expressions of emotion in sex offenders, non-sex offenders and normal controls. *Psychiatry Research*, 165(3): 252–262.

Gibbs, G. (1988) Learning by Doing: A Guide to Teaching and Learning Methods. Oxford: Oxford Further Education Unit.

Gillies, V. (2005) Meeting parents' needs? Discourses of 'support' and 'inclusion' in family policy. *Critical Social Policy*, 25(1): 70–90.

Gladstein, G.A. (1984) The historical roots of contemporary empathy research. *Journal of the History of the Behavioral Sciences*, 20(1): 38–59.

Glaister, A. (2008) Introducing critical practice. In S. Fraser and S. Matthews (eds), *The Critical Practitioner in Social Work and Health Care*. London: Sage.

Goleman, D. (1995) *Emotional Intelligence*. London: Basingstoke.

Goodley, D. (2012) Is disability theory ready to engage with the politics of mental health? In J. Anderson, B. Sapey and H. Spandler (eds), *Distress or Disability? Proceedings of a Symposium held at Lancaster University*. Lancaster: Centre for Disability Research, pp. 62–66.

Goodley, D. (2014) Who is disabled? Exploring the scope of the social model of disability. In J. Swain, S. French, C. Barnes and C. Thomas (eds), *Disabling Barriers – Enabling Environments* (3rd edn). London: Sage, pp. 130–137.

Goodman, S. and Trowler, I. (eds) (2011) *Social Work Reclaimed: Innovative Frameworks for Child and Family Social Work Practice*. London: Jessica Kingsley.

Goroff, N.N. (2014) Conflict theories and social work education. *Journal of Sociology & Social Welfare*, 5(4): Article 5.

Grant, B. (1990) Principled and instrumental nondirectiveness in person-centred and client-centred therapy. *Person-Centred Review*, 5(1): 77–88.

Grant, L. and Kinman, G. (2012a) Developing emotional resilience. Practice guidance. Community Care Inform. Available at: www.ccinform.co.uk/practice-guidance/guide-to-developing-social-workers-emotional-resilience/

Grant, L. and Kinman, G. (2012b) Enhancing well-being in social work students: building resilience in the next generation, *Social Work Education*, 31(5): 605–621.

Green, L. (2017) The trouble with touch? New insights and observations on touch for social work and social care. *The British Journal of Social Work*, 47(3): 773–792.

Griffin, H.L. and Vettor, S. (2012) Predicting sexual re-offending in a UK sample of adolescents with intellectual disabilities. *Journal of Sexual Aggression*, 18(1): 64–80.

Grossmann, K.E. and Grossmann, K. (1999) Mary Ainsworth: our guide to attachment research. *Attachment and Human Development*, 1: 224–228.

Grotberg, E.H. (1995) *A Guide to Promoting Resilience in Children: Strengthening the Human Spirit*. The Hague: Bernard van Leer Foundation. Available at: www.bibalex.org/Search4Dev/files/283337/115519.pdf

Gupta, A., Featherstone, B. and White, S. (2016) Reclaiming humanity: from capacities to capabilities in understanding parenting in adversity. *The British Journal of Social Work*, 46(2): 339–354.

Hall, C. (2014) Bereavement theory: recent developments in our understanding of grief and bereavement. *Bereavement Care*, 33(1): 7–12.

Hammick, M., Freeth, D., Copperman, J. and Goodsman, D. (2009) *Being Interprofessional*. Cambridge: Polity Press.

Hatfield, E., Cacioppo, J. and Rapson, R.L. (1994) *Emotional Contagion*. New York: Cambridge University Press.

Health and Care Professions Council (2017) *Standards of Proficiency for Social Workers in England*. London: HCPC.

Health and Care Professions Council (2018) *Standards of Performance, Conduct and Ethics*. London: HCPC.

Healy, M.L. (2008) Exploring the history of social work as a human rights profession. *International Social Work*, 51(6): 735–748.

Healy, K. and Mulholland, J. (2019) *Writing Skills for Social Workers* (3rd edn). London: Sage.

Heffner, C. (2016) Carl Rogers and the client-centered approach. *All Psych*. Available at: http://allpsych.com/personality-synopsis/rogers/

Heidegger, M. (1927/1962) *Being and Time* (J. Macquarrie and E. Robinson, Trans.). New York: Harper

Hester, R. and Taylor, W. (2011) Responding to bereavement, grief and loss: charting the troubled relationship between research and practice in youth offending services. *Mortality*, 16(3): 191–203.

HM Government (2018) *Working Together to Safeguard Children: A Guide to Inter-Agency Working to Safeguard and Promote the Welfare of Children*. Available at: www.gov.uk/government/publications/working-together-to-safeguard-children--2 (accessed 3 March 2019).

Holland, S. and Scourfield, J. (2015) *Social Work: A Very Short Introduction*. Oxford: Oxford University Press.

Hollis, P. (1972) *Casework – A Psychosocial Therapy*. New York: Random House.

Holt, A. (2010) Managing 'spoiled identities': parents' experiences of compulsory parenting support programmes. *Children and Society*, 24(5): 413–423.

Holt, S. (2011) Child care in practice domestic abuse and child contact: positioning children in the decision-making process. *Child Care in Practice*, 17(4): 327–346.

Horne, R.M., Johnson, M.D., Galambos, N.L. and Krahn, H.J. (2017) Time, money, or gender? Predictors of the division of household labour across life stages. *Sex Roles*, 78(11–12): 731–743.

House of Commons Library (2018) *Women in Parliament and Government*. Briefing Paper Number SN01250. London: House of Commons Library.

Howe, D. (2008) *The Emotionally Intelligent Social Worker*. Basingstoke: Palgrave Macmillan.

Howe, D. (2009) *A Brief Introduction to Social Work Theory*. Basingstoke: Macmillan.

Hughes, B. (2014) 'Disability and the body'. In J. Swain, S. French, C. Barnes and C. Thomas (eds), *Disabling Barriers – Enabling Environments* (3rd edn). London: Sage, pp. 55–61.

Hughes, B. and Paterson, K. (1997) The social model of disability and the disappearing body: towards a sociology of impairment. *Disability and Society*, 12(3): 325–340.

Hughes, D.M. (2004) The use of new communications and information technologies for sexual exploitation of women and children. *Net.SeXXX: Reading on Sex, Pornography, and the Internet*, 13(1): 129–148.

Human Rights Act (1998) London: The Stationery Office.

Hutchinson, G.S. and Oltedal, S. (2014) *Five Theories in Social Work*. UiN-rapport.

Iacoboni, M. and Dapretto, M. (2006) The mirror neuron system and the consequences of its dysfunction. *Nature Reviews Neuroscience*, 7(12), 942–951.

IDeA (2010) *A Glass Half Full: How an Asset Approach Can Improve Community Health and Well-being*. London: IDeA.

IFSW (International Federation of Social Workers) (2002) *Social Work and the Rights of the Child: A Professional Training Manual*. Available at: http://cdn.ifsw.org/assets/ifsw_124952-4.pdf (accessed 31 October 2015).

IFSW (International Federation of Social Workers) (2014) Global definition of social work. Available at: http://ifsw.org/policies/definition-of-social-work/ (accessed 13 March 2016).

IFSW (International Federation of Social Workers) (2018) Global Social Work Statement of Ethical Principles. Available at: https://www.ifsw.org/global-social-work-statement-of-ethical-principles/ (accessed 23 October 2019).

Ijzendoorn, M.H., Van Vereijken, C.M.J.L., Bakermans-Kranenburg, M.J. and Riksen-Walraven, M.J. (2004) Assessing attachment security with the Attachment Q Sort: meta-analytic evidence for the validity of the observer AQS. *Child Development*, 75(4): 1188–1213.

Ingram, R. (2013a) Locating emotional intelligence at the heart of social work practice. *British Journal of Social Work*, 43(5): 987–1034.

Ingram, R. (2013b) Emotions, social work practice and supervision: an uneasy alliance? *Journal of Social Work Practice*, 27(1): 5–19.

Iriss (2019) Task centred casework. Available at: https://content.iriss.org.uk/taskcentred/ (accessed 1 June 2019).

Ixer, G. (2003) Developing the relationship between reflective practice and social work values. *Journal of Practice Teaching*, 5(1): 7–22.

Jack, G. (2000) Ecological influences on parenting and child development. *The British Journal of Social Work*, 30(6): 703–720.

Jack, G. and Gill, O (2003) *The Missing Side of the Triangle: Assessing the Importance of Family and Environmental Factors in the Lives of Children*. Ilford: Barnardo's.

Jankowiak-Siuda, K., Rymarczyk, K. and Grabowska, A. (2011) How we empathize with others: a neurobiological perspective. *Medical Science Monitor: International Medical Journal of Experimental and Clinical Research*, 17(1): RA18–24.

Jansson, B. and Dodd, S. (2002) Ethical activism. *Social Work in Health Care*, 36(1): 11–28.

Jay, A. (2014) Independent Inquiry into Child Sexual Exploitation in Rotherham 1997–2013). Available at https://www.rotherham.gov.uk/downloads/file/279/independent-inquiry-into-child-sexual-exploitation-in-rotherham (accessed 18 November 2019).

Jaynes, S. (2014). Using principles of practice-based research to teach evidence-based practice in social work. *Journal of Evidence-Based Social Work*, 11(1–2): 222–235.

Jenkins, R. (2000) Categorization: identity, social process and epistemology. *Current Sociology*, 48(3): 7–25.

Jenkins, R. (2014) *Social Identity* (4th edn). Abingdon: Routledge.

Johns, R. (2017) *Using the Law in Social Work* (7th edn). London: Sage.

Joint Improvement Team Scotland (2009) Health, Social Care and Housing Partnership Working. Chapter 4: Barriers to Partnership Working – Briefing Notes for Practitioners and Managers. Scotland: Scottish Executive Health Department, NHS in Scotland and COSLA.

Jones, R. (2012) Child protection, social work and the media: doing as well as being done to. *Research, Policy and Planning*, 29(2): 83–94.

Jones, R. (2016) Writing skills for social workers. In K. Davies and R. Jones (eds), *Skills for Social Work Practice*. London: Palgrave.

Kanter, J.S. (1983) Reevaluation of task-centered social work practice. *Clinical Social Work Journal*, 11(3): 228–244.

Keefe, T. and Koch, S. (1999) Teaching conflict management in social work. *Journal of Teaching in Social Work*, 18(1/2): 33–52.

Kelly, M. (2009) Task-centered practice. In T. Mizrahi and L.E. Davis (eds), *Encyclopedia of Social Work* (20th edn). Oxford: Oxford University Press, pp. 197–199.

Killgore, W.S., Weber, M.J., Schwab, Z.R., DelDonno, S.L., Kipman, M., Weiner, M. and Rauch, S. (2012) Gray matter correlates of Trait and Ability models of emotional intelligence. *NeuroReport*, 23(9): 551–555.

Kinman, G. and Grant, L. (2011) Exploring stress resilience in trainee social workers: the role of emotional and social competencies. *British Journal of Social Work*, 41(2): 261–275.

Kinsella, P. (2010) Person-centred planning skills. Available at: www.centreforwelfarereform.org/library/by-date/person-centred-planning-tools.html (accessed 10 November 2015).

Knight, C. (2015) Trauma-informed social work practice: practice considerations and challenges. *Clinical Social Work Journal*, 43, 25–37.

Knott, C. and Scragg, T. (2016) *Reflective Practice in Social Work* (4th edn). Exeter: Learning Matters.

Kolb, D.A. (1984) *Experiential Learning: Experience as the Source of Learning and Development*. London: Prentice-Hall.

Koprowska, J. (2008) *Communication and Interpersonal Skills in Social Work* (2nd edn). Exeter: Learning Matters.

Kübler-Ross, E. (1969) *On Death and Dying*. New York: Macmillan.

Kübler-Ross, E. and Kessler, D. (2005) *On Grief and Grieving: Finding the Meaning of Grief through the Five Stages of Loss*. New York and London: Scribner.

Laming, L. (2003) *The Victoria Climbié Inquiry Report*, Cm 5730. London: The Stationery Office.

Lang, R. (2001) The Development and Critique of the Social Model of Disability. Available at: www.ucl.ac.uk/lc-ccr/lccstaff/raymond-lang/developmment_and_critique_of_the_social_model_of_d.pdf (accessed 21 March 2016).

Laser-Maira, J.A., Peach, D.M. and Hounmenou, C.E. (2019) Moving towards self-actualization: a trauma-informed and needs-focused approach to the mental health needs of survivors of commercial child sexual exploitation. *International Journal of Social Work*, 6(2): 27–44.

Leathard, A. (2003) *Interprofessional Collaboration: From Policy to Practice in Health and Social Care*. Hove: Brunner-Routledge.

Lee, C. (2014) Conservative comforts: some philosophical crumbs for social work. *British Journal of Social Work*, 44(8): 2135–2144.

Lefevre, M. (2010) *Communicating with Children and Young People: Making a Difference*. Bristol: Policy Press.

Lefevre, M. (2015) Becoming effective communicators with children: developing practitioner capability through social work education. *British Journal of Social Work*, 45(1): 204–224.

LeFrançois, A.B., Menzies, R. and Reaume, G. (2013) *Mad Matters: A Critical Reader in Canadian Mad Studies*. Toronto: Canadian Scholars' Press.

Leigh, J. (2016) The story of the PPO queen: the development and acceptance of a spoiled identity in child protection social work. *Child and Family Social Work*, 21(4): 412–420.

Leskošek, V. (2011) Historical perspective on the ideologies of motherhood and its impact on social work. *Social Work and Society*, 9(2): 1–10.

Lewis, J. and Erlen, N. (2012) *Resource Pack: Evidence Matters in Family Justice*. Totnes: Research in Practice.

Lexico (2019) *Paralanguage*. Available at: https://www.lexico.com/en/definition/paralanguage

Liebenberg, L., Ungar, M. and LeBlanc, J.C. (2013) The CYRM-12: a brief measure of resilience. *Canadian Journal of Public Health*, 104(2): 131–135.

Lindsay, T. (2013) Groupwork. In T. Lindsay (ed.), *Social Work Intervention* (2nd edn). Exeter: Learning Matters.

Lindsay, T. and Orton, S. (2011) *Groupwork Practice in Social Work* (2nd edn). Exeter: Learning Matters.

Lindsay, T. and Orton, S. (2014) *Groupwork Practice in Social Work* (3rd edn). Exeter: Learning Matters.

Lishman, J. (ed.) (2007) *Handbook for Practice Learning in Social Work and Social Care: Knowledge and Theory*. London: Jessica Kingsley Publishers.

Lishman, J. (2009) *Communication in Social Work* (2nd edn). Basingstoke: Palgrave Macmillan.

Litchfield, M. (1999) Practice wisdom. *Advances in Nursing Studies*, 22(2): 100–110.

Littlechild, B. (2008) Child protection social work: risks of fears and fears of risks – impossible tasks from impossible goals. *Social Policy and Administration*, 42(6): 662–675.

Littlechild, B. and Smith, R. (eds) (2012) *A Handbook for Interprofessional Practice in the Human Services: Learning to Work Together*. Harlow: Pearson.

Lloyd, C. (2018) *Grief Demystified: An Introduction*. London: Jessica Kingsley.

Lomax, R. and Jones, K. (2014) *Surviving your Social Work Placement* (2nd edn). Basingstoke: Palgrave Macmillan.

López-Teijón, M., García-Faura, A. and Prats-Galino, A. (2015) Fetal facial expression in response to intravaginal music emission. *Ultrasound*, 23: 216–223.

Lorde, A. (1997) *The Collected Poems of Audre Lorde*. New York: W.W.Norton & Company. ISBN 0-393-04090-9

Lynch, R. (2014) *Social Work Practice with Older People: A Positive Person Centred Approach*. London: Sage.

Lynch, R. and Garrett, J.P. (2010) 'More than words': touch practices in child and family social work. *Child and Family Social Work*, 15(4): 389–398.

MacDonald, M. and McSherry, D. (2013) Constrained adoptive parenthood and family transition: adopters' experience of unplanned birth family contact in adolescence. *Child and Family Social Work*, 18(1): 87–96.

Maclean, S. and Harrison, R. (2011) *Theory and Practice: A Straightforward Guide for Social Work Students* (2nd edn). Lichfield: Kirwin Maclean Associates.

Mansell, J. and Beadle-Brown, J. (2004) Person-centred planning or person-centred action? Policy and practice in intellectual disability services. *Journal of Applied Research in Intellectual Disabilities*, 17(1): 1–9.

Marsh, P. and Doel, M. (2005) *The Task-Centred Book*. Abingdon: Routledge.

Marshall, W., Hudson, S., Jones, R. and Fernandez, Y. (1995). Empathy in sex offenders. *Clinical Psychology Review*, 15(2): 99–113.

Marshall, L.E. and Marshall, W.L. (2011) Empathy and antisocial behaviour. *The Journal of Forensic Psychiatry & Psychology*, 22(5): 742–759.

Masten, A.S. (2009) Ordinary magic: lessons learned from research on resilience in human development. *Education Canada*, 49(3): 28–32.

Mathews, I., Simpson, D. and Crawford, K. (2014) *Your Social Work Practice Placement: From Start to Finish*. London: Sage.

Mayall, H. and O'Neill, T. (2014) Translating values and ethics into practice. In D. Edmondson, *Social Work Practice Learning – A Student Guide*. London: Sage.

Mayer, J.D., Salovey, P. and Caruso, D.R. (2004) Emotional intelligence: theory, findings, and implications. *Psychological Inquiry*, 15: 197–215.

Mayer, J.D., Panter, A.T. and Caruso, D.R. (2012) Does personal intelligence exist? Evidence from a new ability-based measure. *Journal of Personality Assessment*, 94(2): 124–140.

McDermott, D. (2014) The problem with recovery. In J. Weinstein (ed.), *Mental Health*. Bristol: Policy Press, pp. 63–70.

McDonald, A. (2007) The impact of the UK Human Rights Act 1998 on decision making in adult social care in England and Wales. *Ethics and Social Welfare*, 1(1): 76–94.

McIntosh, B. and Sanderson, H. (2006) Value added. *Community Care*, 20–26 April, pp. 30–31.

McLaughlin, H. (2013) Motherhood, apple pie and interprofessional working. *Social Work Education*, 32(7): 956–963.

McLeod, A. (2010) Thirty years of listening to children? *Adoption and Fostering*, 34(3): 67–73.

McMillen, J.C., Lenze, S.L., Hawley, K.M. and Osborne, V.A. (2009) Revisiting practice-based research networks as a platform for mental health services research. *Administration & Policy in Mental Health & Mental Health Services Research*, 36(5): 308–321. doi:10.1007/s10488-009-0222-2

McWade, B., Milton, D. and Beresford, P. (2015) Mad studies and neurodiversity: a dialogue. *Disability and Society*, 30(2): 305–309.

Meads, G. and Ashcroft, J. (2005) *The Case for Interprofessional Collaboration in Health and Social Care*. Oxford: Blackwell.

Mearns, D. and Thorne, B. (1999) *Person-Centred Counselling in Action* (2nd edn). London: Sage.

Meins, E., Fernyhough, C., Fradley, E. and Tuckey, M. (2001) Rethinking maternal sensitivity: mothers' comments on infants' mental processes predict security of attachment at 12 months. *Journal of Child Psychology and Psychiatry, and Allied Disciplines*, 42(5): 637–648.

Mental Capacity Act (2005) London: HMSO.

Mental Health Act (2007). London: HMSO.

Miller, W.R. and Rollnick, S. (1991) *Motivational Interviewing: Preparing People to Change Addictive Behavior*. New York: Guilford Press.

Miller, W.R. and Rollnick, S. (2002) *Motivational Interviewing: Preparing People to Change Addictive Behaviour* (2nd edn). New York: Guilford Press.

Miller, W.R. and Rollnick, S. (2012) *Motivational Interviewing: Helping People Change* (3rd edn). New York: Guilford Press.

Milne, A. (2006) *The Role of Psychotherapeutic Intervention in the Relationship between Dysfunctional Families and their Social Workers: The Development and Use of an Expanded Rogerian Model of the Person-Centred Approach*. Available at: www.meta-noia.ac.uk/media/1434/ann-milne-abstract.pdf

Milner, J., Myers, J. and O'Byrne, P. (2015) *Assessment in Social Work* (4th edn). London: Macmillan Education.

Mitchell, F. (2011) *Resilience: Concept, Factors and Models for Practice*. Briefing, University of Stirling. Stirling: Scottish Child Care and Protection Network.

Montaño, C. (2012) Social work theory – practice relationship: challenges to overcoming positivist and postmodern fragmentation. *International Social Work*, 55(3): 306–319.

Moon, J. (2004) A Handbook of Reflective and Experiential Learning. London: Routledge Falmer.

Moriarty, J. and Manthorpe, J. (2016) *The Effectiveness of Social Work with Adults: A Systematic Scoping Review*. London: Social Care Workforce Research Unit, King's College London. Available at: www.ripfa.org.uk/latest-news/news-scwru-effectiveness-of-social-work-mar2016/ (accessed 3 March 2019).

Morley, C. (2012) How does critical reflection develop possibilities for emancipatory change? An example from an empirical research project. *British Journal of Social Work*, 42(8): 1513–1532.

Morrison, T. (2007) Emotional intelligence, emotion and social work: context, characteristics, complications and contribution. *British Journal of Social Work*, 37(2): 245–263.

Moss, B. (2012) *Communication Skills in Health and Social Care* (2nd edn). London: Sage.

Mullen, E.J., Bledsoe, S.E. and Bellamy, J.L. (2008) Implementing Evidence-Based Social Work Practice. http://doi.org/10.1177/1049731506297827

Mulvany, J. (2000) Disability, impairment or illness? The relevance of the social model of disability to the study of mental disorder. *Sociology of Health and Illness*, 22(5): 582–601.

Munro, E. (2011) *The Munro Review of Child Protection: Final Report*. London: Department for Education.

Murphy, C. (2019) To what extent are street-level statutory social workers employing their discretion in the post-Munro Review world of child protection? PhD, Manchester Metropolitan University.

Murphy, D., Duggan, M. and Joseph. S. (2012) Relationship-based social work and its compatibility with the person-centred approach: principled versus instrumental perspectives. *British Journal of Social Work*, 43(4): 703–719.

National Voices (2017) *Person-Centred Care in 2017: Evidence from Service Users*. London: National Voices.

Nayak, S. (2017) Declaring the activism of black feminist theory. *Annual Review of Critical Psychology*, 13: 1–12.

Neimeyer, R.A. (2014) The changing face of grief: contemporary directions in theory, research and practice. *Progress in Palliative Care*, 22(3): 125–130.

Neimeyer, R.A. and Sands, D.C. (2011) Meaning reconstruction in bereavement: from principles to practice. In R.A. Neimeyer, D.L. Harris, H.R. Winokuer and G.F. Thornton (eds), *Grief and Bereavement in Contemporary Society: Bridging Research and Practice*. New York: Routledge, pp. 9–22.

Neumayer, C. and Svensson, J. (2016) Activism and radical politics in the digital age: towards a typology. *Convergence. The International Journal of Research into New Media Technologies*, 22(2): 131–146.

Newman, T. (2004) *What Works in Building Resilience*. London: Barnado's.

O'Brien, J. (2004) If person-centred planning did not exist, valuing people would require its intervention. *Journal of Applied Research in Intellectual Disabilities*, 17(1): 11–15.

O'Connell, B. (2001) *Solution Focused Stress Counselling*. London: Sage.

O'Connell, B. and Palmer, S. (eds) (2005) *Handbook of Solution-Focused Therapy*. London: Sage.

O'Connor, L. and Leonard, K. (2014) Decision making in children and families social work: the practitioner's voice. *British Journal of Social Work*, 44(7): 1805–1822.

O'Hagan, M. (2004) Force in mental health services: international user and survivor perspectives (users' views) (cover story). *Mental Health Practice*, 7(5), 12–17.

Oko, J. (2008) *Understanding and Using Theory in Social Work*. Exeter: Learning Matters.

Oliver, C. (2010) *Children's Views and Experiences of their Contact with Social Workers: A Focused Review of the Evidence*. Leeds: CWDC.

Oliver, M. (2004) If I had a hammer: the social model in action. In J. Swain, S. French, C. Barnes and C. Thomas (eds), *Disabling Barriers – Enabling Environments* (2nd edn). Sage: London, pp. 7–12.

Oliver, M. (2010) Foreword. In P. Beresford, M. Nettle and R. Perring (eds), *Towards a Social Model of Madness and Distress: Exploring What Service Users Say*. York: Joseph Rowntree Foundation, p. 5.

Oliver, M. (2013) The social model of disability: thirty years on. *Disability and Society*, 28(7): 1024–1026

Oliver, M., Sapey, B. and Thomas, P. (eds) (2012) *Social Work with Disabled People* (4th edn). Basingstoke: Palgrave Macmillan.

ONS (Office for National Statistics) (2018) Homicide in England and Wales: year ending March 2017. Available at: www.ons.gov.uk/releases/homicideinenglandandwalesyearendingmarch2017

Papoušek, M. (2007) Communication in early infancy: an arena of intersubjective learning. *Infant Behavior & Development*, 30(2): 258–266. doi.org/10.1016/j.infbeh.2007.02.003

Parker, H. (1979) *Social Work and the Courts*. London: Edward Arnold.

Parker, J. (2006) Developing perceptions of competence in practice learning. *British Journal of Social Work*, 36(6): 1017–1036.

Parker, J. (2010) *Effective Practice Learning in Social Work* (2nd edn). Exeter: Learning Matters.

Parley, F. (2001) Person-centred outcomes. *Journal of Learning Disabilities*, 5(4): 299–308.

Parnell, R. and Patsarika, M. (2011) Young people's participation in school design: exploring diversity and power in a UK governmental policy case-study. *Children's Geographies*, 9(3–4): 457–475.

Parton, N. (2011) Child protection and safeguarding in England: changing and competing conceptions of risk and their implications for social work. *British Journal of Social Work*, 41(5): 854–875.

Pasini, A. (2015) Social workers and moral choices: ethical questions about Giovanna's case. *Ethics and Social Welfare*, 9(4): 403–412.

Pattison, S. (1998) Debating point: questioning values. *Health Care Analysis*, 6(1): 352–359.

Pawson, R., Boaz, A., Grayson, L., Lon, A. and Barns, C. (2003) *Knowledge Review 3: Types and Quality of Knowledge in Social Care*. London: Social Care Institute for Excellence.

Payne, M. (2014) *Modern Social Work Theory* (4th edn). Basingstoke: Palgrave Macmillan.

Pemberton, C. (2013) I am now anxious about how the Hackney model is being interpreted and rolled out. *Community Care*, 24 October. Available at: www.communitycare.co.uk/2013/10/24/i-am-now-anxious-about-how-the-hackney-model-is-being-interpreted-and-rolled-out/

Perlman, H.H. (1957) *Social Casework: A Problem Solving Process*. Chicago: University of Chicago Press.

Phelvin, A. (2012) Getting the message: intuition and reflexivity in professional interpretations of non-verbal behaviours in people with profound learning disabilities. *British Journal of Learning Disabilities*, 41(1): 31–37.

Pithers, W.D. (1999). Empathy: definition, enhancement and relevance to the treatment of sexual abusers. *Journal of Interpersonal Violence*, 14: 257–284.

Pollard, J.A., Hawkins, J.D. and Arthur, M.W. (1999) Risk and protection: are both necessary to understand diverse behavioural outcomes in adolescence? *Social Work Research*, 23: 145–158.

Ponciano, L. (2010) Attachment in foster care: the role of maternal sensitivity, adoption, and foster mother experience. *Child and Adolescent Social Work Journal*, 27(2): 97–114.

Preston-Shoot, M. (2014) *Making Good Decisions: Law for Social Work Practice*. Basingstoke: Palgrave Macmillan.

Price, M. and Price, B. (2013) Skills for group work. In A. Mantell (ed.), *Skills for Social Work Practice*. London: Learning Matters.

Prochaska, J. and DiClemente, C. (1983) Stages and processes of self-change of smoking: toward an integrative model of change. *Journal of Consulting and Clinical Psychology*, 51(3): 390–395.

Proctor, E., Landsverk, J., Aarons, G., Chambers, D., Glisson, C. and Mittman, B. (2009) Implementation research in mental health services: an emerging science with conceptual, methodological, and training challenges. *Administration and Policy in Mental Health*, 36(1): 24–34.

Quality Assurance Authority (2016) Subject Benchmark Statement – Social Work. Gloucester: The Quality Assurance Agency for Higher Education.

Quincy, R., Lu, S. and Huang, C-C. (2012) *SWOT Analysis – Raising Capacity of your Organisation in Relation to Social Work.* Beijing: China Philanthropy Research Institute.

Quinney, A. and Hafford-Letchfield, T. (2012) *Interprofessional Social Work: Effective Collaborative Approaches.* London: Learning Matters.

Reamer, F. (2013) Social work in a digital age: ethical and risk management challenges. *Social Work*, 58(2): 163–172.

Reeves, D. (2004) Psycho-emotional dimensions of disability and the social model. In C. Barnes and G. Mercer (eds), *Implementing the Social Model of Disability: Theory and Research.* Leeds: The Disability Press, pp. 83–100.

Reid, W.J. (1978) *The Task-Centered System.* New York: Columbia University Press.

Reid, W.J. and Epstein, L. (1972) *Task-Centred Casework.* New York: Columbia University Press.

Reid, W.J. and Shyne, A.W. (1969) *Brief and Extended Casework.* New York: Columbia University Press.

Reuther, B.T. (2013) On our everyday being: Heidegger and attachment. *Journal of Theoretical and Philosophical Psychology.* Advance online publication. doi:10.1037/a0033040

Riachi, R. (2017) Person-centred communication in dementia care: a qualitative study of the use of the SPECAL® method by care workers in the UK. *Journal of Social Work Practice*, 32(3): 303–321.

Rich, W. (2013) Mental health and the social model (plus a bit of nonsense from the Guardian's sub-editors (updated). Available at: https://arbitraryc.wordpress.com/2013/05/13/mental-health-and-the-social-model/ (accessed 21 March 2016).

RiPfA (Research in Practice for Adults) (2015) Courting evidence: legal literacy in social care. Available at: www.ripfa.org.uk/blog/courting-evidence-legal-literacy-in-social-care/ (accessed 6 January 2016).

Roberts, A.R. (1991) Conceptualizing crisis theory and the crisis intervention model. In A.R. Roberts (ed.), *Contemporary Perspectives on Crisis Intervention and Prevention.* Englewood Cliffs, NJ: Prentice-Hall, pp. 3–17.

Roberts, A.R. (ed.) (2002) *Crisis Intervention Handbook: Assessment, Treatment and Research.* New York: Oxford University Press. pp. 513–529.

Roberts, A.R. (2005) Bridging the past and present to the future of crisis intervention and crisis management. In A.R. Roberts (ed.), *Crisis Intervention Handbook: Assessment, Treatment, and Research* (3rd edn). New York: Oxford University Press, pp. 3–34.

Roberts, A.R. and Ottens, A.J. (2005) The seven-stage crisis intervention model: a road map to goal attainment, problem solving, and crisis resolution. *Brief Treatment and Crisis Intervention*, 5(4): 329–339.

Roberts, A. and Yeager, K. (2006) *Foundations of Evidence-Based Social Work Practice.* Oxford and New York: Oxford University Press.

Roche, W., Teague, P. and Colvin, A. (eds) (2014) *The Oxford Handbook of Conflict Management in Organizations.* New York: Oxford University Press.

Rogers, C. (1956) A counseling approach to human problems. *The American Journal of Nursing*, 56(8): 994–997.

Rogers, C. (1957) The necessary and sufficient conditions of therapeutic personality change. *Journal of Consulting Psychology*, 21(2): 95–103.

Rogers, M. and Allen, D. (2019) *Applying Critical Thinking and Analysis in Social Work.* London: Sage.

Romeo, L. (2017–2018) Chief Social Worker for Adults Annual Report, From Strength to Strength: Strengths-Based Practice and Achieving Better Lives. London: Department of Health and Social Care.

Rosen, A. (2003) Evidence-based social work. *Social Work Research*, 27(4): 197–208.

Ruch, G. (2005) Relationship-based practice and reflective practice: holistic approaches to contemporary child care social work. *Child and Family Social Work*, 10(2): 111–123.

Ruch, G. (2010) *Relationship-based Social Work.* London: Jessica Kingsley.

Ruch, G. (2014) 'Helping children is a human process': researching the challenges social workers face in communicating with children. *British Journal of Social Work*, 44(8): 1–18.

Ruck-Keene, A., Edwards, K., Eldergill, A. and Miles, S. (2014) *Court of Protection Handbook: A User's Guide.* London: Legal Action Group.

Rutter, L. and Brown, K. (2012) *Critical Thinking and Professional Judgement for Social Work* (3rd edn). Exeter: Learning Matters.

Ryde, J. (2009) Being White in the Helping Professions: Developing Effective Intercultural Awareness. London: Jessica Kingsley.

Rymell, S. (2015) Time management: how to feel more in control of your workload. Community Care Inform (Practice Guidance), July. Available at: www.ccinform.co.uk/practice-guidance/guide-to-time-management/

Safe Lives (2014) *SafeLives Dash Risk Checklist.* Available at: www.safelives.org.uk/sites/default/files/resources/Dash%20without%20guidance%20FINAL.pdf

Saleebey, D. (1997) *The Strengths Perspective in Social Work Practice* (2nd edn). Boston: Pearson Education.

Saleebey, D. (2006) *The Strengths Perspective in Social Work Practice* (4th edn). Boston: Pearson Education.

Saleebey, D. (2013) *The Strengths Perspective in Social Work Practice* (6th edn). London: Pearson.

Saleh, M. (2012) Jody Williams: Nobel Laureate's insights on activism and social work. *Affilia*, 27(1): 51–59.

Samson, P.L. (2015) Practice wisdom: the art and science of social work. *Journal of Social Work Practice*, 29(2): 119–131.

Sapey, B., Spandler, H. and Anderson, J. (2015) Introduction. In H. Spandler, A. Anderson and B. Sapey (eds), *Madness, Distress and the Politics of Disablement*. Bristol: Policy Press, pp. 1–9.

Sarkar, S. (2015) Use of technology in human trafficking networks and sexual exploitation: a cross-sectional multi-country study. *Transnational Social Review*, 5(1): 55–68.

Schön, D. (1983) *The Reflective Practitioner*. New York: Basic Books.

Schön, D. (2002) From technical rationality to reflection-in-action. In R. Harrison, F. Reeve, A. Hanson and J. Clarke (eds), *Supporting Lifelong Learning. Volume One. Perspectives on Learning*. Abingdon: Routledge/Open University Press.

Schradie, J. (2018) The digital activism gap: how class and costs shape online collective action. *Social Problems*, 65(1): 51–74.

SCIE (Social Care Institute for Excellence) (2007) *Assessment in Social Work: A Guide for Learning and Teaching*. Available at: www.scie.org.uk/publications/guides/guide18/natureofassessment/reasons.asp

SCIE (Social Care Institute for Excellence) (2012) *At a Glance 9: Think Child, Think Parent, Think Family*. Available at: www.scie.org.uk/publications/ataglance/ataglance09.asp

SCIE (Social Care Institute for Excellence) (2015) *Partnership Working in Child Protection: Cardiff Case Study*. Available at: www.scie.org.uk/socialcaretv/video-player.asp?v=partnership-working-in-child-protection-cardiff

SCIE (Social Care Institute for Excellence) (2018) The Young Carers (Needs Assessment) Regulations 2015. Available at: www.legislation.gov.uk/uksi/2015/527/ (accessed 15 February 2019).

Scragg, T. (2013) Reflective practice. In A. Mantell (ed.), *Skills for Social Work Practice* (2nd edn). Exeter: Learning Matters.

Serano, J. (2007) *Whipping Girl: A Transsexual Woman on Sexism and the Scapegoating of Femininity*. Berkeley, CA: Seal Press.

Series, L., Fennell, P., Clements, L. and Doughty, J. (2015) *Transparency in the Court of Protection*. Technical Report. Cardiff: Cardiff Law School.

Seymour, C. and Seymour, R. (2011) *Courtroom and Report Writing Skills for Social Workers* (2nd edn). Exeter: Learning Matters.

SfC/CWDC (Skills for Care and the Children's Workforce Development Council) (2007) *Providing Effective Supervision: A Workforce Development Tool, including a Unit of Competence and Supporting Guidance*. Available at: http://webarchive.nationalarchives.gov.uk/20130401151715/https://www.education.gov.uk/publications/eOrderingDownload/Providing_Effective_Supervision_unit.pdf

Shakespeare, T. and Watson, N. (2002) The social model of disability: an outdated ideology? Available at: https://www.um.es/discatif/PROYECTO_DISCATIF/Textos_discapacidad/00_Shakespeare2.pdf (accessed 23rd October 2019).

Shakespeare, T. (undated) *The Social Model of Disability*. Available at: www.academia.edu/5144537/The_social_model_of_disability (accessed 20/5/16).

Sharry, J. (2001) *Solution Focused Groupwork*. London: Sage.

Sharland, E., Taylor, I., Jones, L., Orr, D. and Whiting, R. (2007) *Interprofessional Education for Qualifying Social Workers*. London: SCIE.

Shennan, G. (2014) *Solution-Focused Practice*. Basingstoke: Palgrave Macmillan.

Sheppard, M. (2007) Assessment: from reflexivity to process knowledge. In J. Lishman (ed.), *Handbook for Practice Learning in Social Work and Social Care: Knowledge and Theory*. London: Jessica Kingsley.

Simons, H. (2009) *Case Study Research in Practice*. London: Sage.

Slaughter, V., Peterson, C.C. and Carpenter, M. (2009) Maternal mental state talk and infants' early gestural communication. *Journal of Child Language*, 36(5): 1053–1074. doi.org/10.1017/S0305000908009306

Smale, G.G., Tuson, G. and Biehal, T. (1993) *Empowerment, Assessment, Care Management and the Skilled Worker*. London: HMSO.

Smale, G. G., Tuson, G. and Statham, D. (2000) *Social Work and Social Problems: Working toward Social Inclusion and Social Change*. Basingstoke: Palgrave Macmillan.

Spandler, H. (2012) Setting the scene. In J. Anderson, B. Sapey and H. Spandler (eds), *Distress or Disability? Proceedings of a Symposium held at Lancaster University*. Lancaster: Centre for Disability Research, pp. 14–17.

Stake, R.E. (1995) *The Art of Case Study Research*. Thousand Oaks, CA: Sage.

Stark, R. (2008) IFSW Statement on the 60th Anniversary of the Universal Declaration of Human Rights. Available at: http://ifsw.org/news/ifsw-statement-on-the-60th-anniversary-of-the-universal-declaration-of-human-rights-december-10-2008/ (accessed 31 October 2015).

Statista (2018) Distribution of female held CEO positions in FTSE companies in the United Kingdom (UK) as of June 2018. Available at: www.statista.com/statistics/685195/share-of-female-ceo-positions-in-ftse-companies-uk/

Strier, R. (2013) Responding to the global economic crisis: inclusive social work practice. *Social Work*, 58(4): 344–353.

Striker, S. and Kimmel, E. (2004) *The Anti-Colouring Book*. London: Scholastic.

Stroebe, M.S. and Schut, H. (1999) The Dual Process Model of coping with bereavement: rationale and description. *Death Studies*, 23(3): 197–224.

Stroebe, M., Stroebe, W., Schut, H. and Boerner, K. (2017) Grief is not a disease but bereavement merits medical awareness. *The Lancet*, 389(10067): 347–349.

Sutton, C. (1999) *Helping Families with Troubled Children*. Chichester: Wiley and Sons.

Sutton, C. (2006) *Helping Families with Troubled Children: A Preventative Approach* (2nd edn). Chichester: Wiley-Blackwell.

Sweeney, A., Clement, S., Filson, B. and Kennedy, A. (2016) Trauma-informed mental healthcare in the UK: what is it and how can we further its development? *Mental Health Review Journal*, 21(3): 174–192.

SWRB (Social Work Reform Board) (2010) *Building a Safe and Confident Future: One Year On: Overarching Professional Standards for Social Workers in England*. Available at: www.gov.uk/government/uploads/system/uploads/attachment_data/file/180792/DFE-00602-2010-2.pdf (accessed 29 February 2016).

Symonds, J. (2018) Engaging parents with parenting programmes: relationship building in initial conversations. *The British Journal of Social Work*, 48(5): 1296–1314.

Tait, A. (2012) Direct Work with Vulnerable Children: Playful Activities and Strategies for Communication. London: Jessica Kingsley.

Taylor, J. and Taylor, J. (2013) Person-centred planning: evidenced-based practice, challenges, and potential for the 21st century. *Journal of Social Work in Disability and Rehabilitation*, 12(3): 213–235.

Teater, B. (2010) An Introduction to Applying Social Work Theories and Methods. Maidenhead: Open University Press.

Tew, J. (2005) Core themes of social perspectives. In J. Tew (ed.), *Social Perspectives in Mental Health: Developing Social Models to Understand and Work with Mental Distress*. London: Jessica Kingsley, pp. 13–31.

The Children Act 1989. HMSO. London

Thomas, C. (1999) *Female Forms: Experiencing and Understanding Disability*. Buckingham: Open University Press.

Thomas, C. (2004) Disability and impairment. In J. Swain, S. French, C. Barnes and C. Thomas (eds), *Disabling Barriers – Enabling Environments* (2nd edn). Sage: London, pp. 21–27.

Thomas, C. (2014) Disability and impairment. In J. Swain, S. French, C. Barnes and C. Thomas (eds), *Disabling Barriers – Enabling Environments* (3rd edn). Sage: London, pp. 9–16.

Thomas, J. (2004) Using critical incident analysis to promote reflection and holistic assessment. In N. Gould and M. Baldwin (eds), *Social Work, Critical Reflections and the Learning Organisation*. Aldershot: Ashgate.

Thomas, J., Pollard, K. and Sellman, D. (2014) *Interprofessional Working in Health and Social Care* (2nd edn). London: Red Globe Press.

Thompson, N. (2005) *Understanding Social Work: Preparing for Practice*. Basingstoke: Palgrave Macmillan.

Thompson, N. (2006) *Promoting Workbased Learning*. Bristol: Policy Press.

Thompson, N. (2010) *Theorizing Social Work Practice*. Basingstoke: Palgrave Macmillan.

Thompson, N. (2011) *Crisis Intervention: Theory into Practice Series*. Dorset: Russell House Publishing.

Thompson, N. (2012a) *Anti-Discriminatory Practice: Equality, Diversity and Social Justice* (5th edn). Basingstoke: Palgrave Macmillan.

Thompson, N. (2012b) *Grief and its Challenges*. Basingstoke: Palgrave Macmillan

Thompson, N. and Gilbert, P. (2011) *Supervision Skills: A Learning and Development Manual*. Lyme Regis: Russell House Publishing.

Thompson, S. and Thompson, N. (2008) *The Critically Reflective Practitioner*. Basingstoke: Palgrave Macmillan.

Trembath, D., Balandin, S. and Rossi, C. (2005) Cross-cultural practice and autism. *Journal of Intellectual and Developmental Disability*, 30(4): 240–242.

Trevarthen, C. (2005) First things first: infants make good use of the sympathetic rhythm of imitation, without reason or language. *Journal of Child Psychotherapy*, 31(1): 91–113.

Trevarthen, C. and Schore, A.N. (2001) Intrinsic motives for companionship in understanding: their origin, development, and significance for infant mental health. *Infant Mental Health Journal*, 22(1–2): 95–131.

Trevithick, P. (2003) Effective relationship-based practice: a theoretical exploration. *Journal of Social Work Practice*, 17(2): 163–176.

Trevithick, P. (2005) *Social Work Skills*. Milton Keynes: Open University Press.

Trevithick, P. (2012) *Social Work Skills and Knowledge: A Practice Handbook* (2nd edn). Milton Keynes: Open University Press.

Tsang, A.K., Bogo, M. and Lee, L. (2011) Engagement in cross-cultural clinical practice: narrative analysis of first sessions. *Clinical Social Work Journal*, 39(1): 79–90.

Tuckman, B.W. (1965) Developmental sequence in small groups. *Psychological Bulletin*, 63.

Turnell, A. (2012) *The Signs of Safety Comprehensive Briefing Paper*. East Perth: Resolutions Consultancy Pty Ltd. Available at: https://knowledgebank.signsofsafety.net/ArticleDocuments/1435/SofS%20Briefing%20Paper%204th%20ed%20 v1.0.2.pdf.aspx (accessed 18 November 2019).

Turnell, A. and Edwards, S. (1999) Signs of Safety: A Safety and Solution Oriented Approach to Child Protection Casework. New York: W.W. Norton.

Unison and Community Care (2017) *A Day in the Life of Social Work*. London: Unison and Community Care.

UPIAS (1976) *Union of the Physically Impaired Against Segregation: Aims and Policy Statement*. Available at: http://disability-studies.leeds.ac.uk/archiveuk/UPIAS/UPIAS.pdf (accessed 21 March 2016).

Vaiouli, P. and Andreou, G. (2018) Communication and language development of young children with autism: a review of research in music. *Communication Disorders Quarterly*, 39(2): 323–329. https://doi.org/10.1177/1525740117705117

van Nieuwerburgh, C. (2014) *An Introduction to Coaching Skills: A Practical Guide*. London: Sage.

Varese, F., Smeets, F., Drukkers, M., Lieverse, R., Lataster, T., Viechtbauer, W., Read, J., van Os, J. and Bentall, R. (2012) Childhood adversities increase the risk of psychosis: a meta-analysis of patient-control, prospective and cross-sectional cohort studies. *Schizophrenia Bulletin*, 38(4): 661–671.

Viera, A.J. and Garrett, J.M. (2005) Understanding interobserver agreement: the kappa statistic. *Family Medicine*, 37(5): 360–363.

WAFE (2014) *What is Domestic Abuse?* Available at: www.womensaid.org.uk/domestic-violence-articles.asp?section=000100 01002200410001&itemid=1272&itemTitle=What+is+domestic+violence

Waine, B., Tunstill, J., Meadows, P. and Peel, M. (2005) *Developing Social Care: Values and Principles*. London: Social Care Institute for Excellence.

Wallcraft, J. and Hopper, K. (2015) The capabilities approach and the social model of mental health. In H. Spandler, A. Anderson and B. Sapey (eds), *Madness, Distress and the Politics of Disablement*. Bristol: Policy Press, pp. 83–97.

Walker, S. (2012) *Effective Social Work with Children, Young People and Families: Putting Systems Theory into Practice*. London: Sage.

Waltz, T. and Ritchie, H. (2000) Gandhian principles in social work practice: ethics revisited. *Social Work*, 45(3): 213–222.

Warner, J. (2015) *The Emotional Politics of Social Work and Child Protection*. Bristol: Policy Press.

Warner, L., Mariathasan, J., Lawton-Smith, S. and Samele, C. (2006) Choice Literature Review: A Review of the Literature and Consultation on Choice and Decision Making for Users and Carers of Mental Health and Social Care Services. Briefing Paper 31. London: Centre for Mental Health.

Washbrook, E., Waldfogel, J., Bradbury, B., Corak, M. and Ghanghro, A.A. (2012) The development of young children of immigrants in Australia, Canada, the United Kingdom, and the United States. *Child Development*, 83(5): 1591–1607.

Waters, E. and Deane, K.E. (1985) Defining and assessing individual differences in attachment relationships: Q-methodology and the organization of behavior in infancy and early childhood. *Monographs of the Society for Research in Child Development*, 50(1–2, Serial No. 209), 41–65.

Weinstein, J. (2014) *Mental Health*. Bristol: Policy Press.

White, M. and Epston, D. (1990) *Narrative Means to Therapeutic Ends*. London: Norton

Whittington, C. (2007) *Assessment in Social Work: A Guide for Learning and Teaching*. London: Social Care Institute for Excellence.

Whittington, C., Thomas, J. and Quinney, A. (2009) *Interprofessional and Inter-agency Collaboration*. London: Social Care Institute for Excellence. eLearning resource: www.scie.org.uk/publications/elearning/ipiac/index.asp

Wigham, S., Robertson, J., Emerson, E., Hatton, C., Elliot, J., McIntosh, B., Swift, P., Krinjen-Kemp, E., Towers, C., Romeo, R., Knapp, M., Sanderson, H., Routledge, M., Oakes, P. and Joyce, T. (2008) Reported goal setting and benefits of person centred planning for people with intellectual disabilities. *Journal of Intellectual Disabilities*, 12(2): 143–152.

Wöhr, M. and Scattoni, M.L. (2013) Neurobiology of autism. *Behavioural Brain Research*, 251: 1–4.

Woolliams, M., William, K., Butcher, D. and Pye, J. (2011) *Be More Critical: A Practice Guide for Health and Social Care Students*. London: Oxford Brookes University.

Worden, J.W. (2010) *Grief Counselling and Grief Therapy: A Handbook for the Mental Health Practitioner*. London: Routledge.

Yates, T.M. and Masten, A. (2004) Prologue: the promise of resilience research for practice and policy. In T. Newman (ed.) *What Works in Building Resilience*. London: Barnado's.

Yin, R. (1994) *Case Study Research: Design and Methods*. Thousand Oaks, CA: Sage.

Yin, R. (2009) *Case Study Research* (4th edn). Thousand Oaks, CA: Sage.

Index

ABCD model, 295–6
active listening, 14, 22–31, 93–4, 137, 247, 320
  barriers, 29–30
advocacy, 78, 82, 130–1, 295–30, 312, 324, 339
Ainsworth, M., 301–308
alcohol, 128, 129–30, 145, 248, 226, 237, 260–1
analysis, 3, 60, 64–9, 78, 126, 201, 218, 219, 232, 236, 247,
    272, 285, 328, 336
anti-discriminatory/anti-oppressive practice (including
    emancipatory practice), 9, 21, 65–66, 70, 73, 74–75,
    76–78, 82–3, 85, 88, 90, 93–4, 128, 131, 188, 197, 199,
    218, 239, 249, 296
ASPIRE model, 4–6, 119–20, 122, 231
assessment, 5–6, 23, 67, 119–20, 121–31, 134, 138, 173,
    214–5, 231, 233–236, 238, 246, 253–4, 262, 266, 287
attunement, 18, 23, 26–7.

BASW Code of ethics, 2, 76, 90, 154, 156, 271, 340
body language, 13, 15–6, 18, 22, 23, 25, 69, 183, 197
Borton, T., 68
Bowlby, J., 190, 301–302
Bronfenbrenner, U., 170, 253

Care Act 2014, 12, 16, 124, 295, 311
Care Quality Commission, 204
case records, 197, 197–9, 234, 236, 238
  audits, 197
case study approaches, 175–6
child development, 168, 301, 303
Children and Families Act 2014, 311
Children Act 1989, 38, 144, 200, 236, 311
cognitive distortions, 139–40
collaboration 153
communication, 5, 11–21, 22–31, 133, 134–5,
    138–9, 171, 173, 195–7, 202, 218, 236–237,
    259, 279, 282, 294, 298
  barriers, 20–1, 27, 29–31, 33, 138–9
  difficulty, 14, 15–18, 20, 220
  email, 196
  non-verbal, 13–18, 24–5, 27, 29, 160, 183
  paralanguage, 13–6, 25, 197
  paraphrasing, 24, 136–7
  silence, 14, 28

  verbal, 13–18, 22, 23, 29, 135, 236
  written, 13, 149, 194–202, 234–236, 238, 265,
      266, 267, 302
compassion fatigue, 316
conflict, 74, 91, 123, 131
  management and resolution, 175–184
  approaches to conflict management and resolution,
      180–185
  theory, 177
court skills, 6, 230–240
  administration, 234
  giving evidence, 231–234, 237–238
  preparation, 233, 235, 238,
  protocol, 236–237
crisis, 311
crisis intervention, 43, 168, 182, 273, 275, 318–326
critical incident analysis, 68, 69
critical thinking, 21, 63, 97, 195, 201
cross-cultural practice, 89–90
cultural competence, 28–9, 89, 93, 202
cultural humility, 23, 28–30, 31, 89
culture, 29, 34, 36, 40, 61, 71, 78, 89, 90, 129, 215, 58, 66,
    125, 182, 197

decision making, 15–16, 19, 38, 47, 59–61, 74, 76, 84, 87,
    89, 94, 124, 126, 127, 129–31, 138, 143–5, 149, 179,
    195, 197, 199, 201, 230
  group work, 295
definition (IFSW), 75–76, 79, 82, 177
direct work, 5, 33, 39–40, 52, 66–7, 87, 108,
    112, 128, 233
discrimination, 2, 75–80, 87–92, 241, 329, 332–3,
    339, 341, 345
diversity, 2, 69, 75, 78, 83, 84–94, 297, 331, 335–336
domestic violence/domestic abuse, 60, 88, 89, 124, 181,
    189, 191, 231, 260, 288, 294, 297
drugs, 145
duties (legal/statutory), 16, 35, 74, 156, 176, 200,
    210, 274, 288

ecological systems theory, 170, 252–3, 261
ecomap, 139, 199, 255, 262, 268
Egan, G., 23, 26, 29, 135

empathy, 9, 21, 23, 27, 28, 30, 52–62, 69, 76, 90, 129, 131, 137, 171, 279, 282, 286, 288–290
emotional intelligence, 5, 38–41, 42–51, 98, 123–4, 223, 289
emotional literacy 98
empowerment, 79, 87, 88–90, 93, 202, 291, 293
epistemology, 301–302, 307
ethics, 2–3, 73–83, 90, 199, 202
   politicised 76–77, 79, 83
   situated 76–77, 79, 83
equality, 2, 59, 62, 82, 84–94
   Equality Act 2010, 85, 90–94
European Convention on Human Rights (ECHR), 80, 82
Evaluation 220–229
evidence-based approaches, 145, 147, 153, 239
exchange model 159
externalizing, 259, 263–4

family scripts, 263
family therapy, 252, 261, 312
Featherstone, B., 9, 64, 65,149
Freud, S., 34, 310
Ferguson, H., 43–44, 87, 128, 129

genogram, 139, 199, 255, 256, 262
Gibbs, G., 65–67
grief and loss, 309–17
   disenfranchised grief, 310–1
   Dual Process Model, 314
   Worden's life stages model, 313
groupwork, 291–99
   dynamics and processes, 296–8
   function, 293
   planning, 294
   theory, 292–3

Hackney Model, 254, 261
human rights, 2, 73–83, 86–7, 93, 154, 341–2
   Human Rights Act 1998, 79–82
humane social work, 67, 143–151, 158, 165, 180

impairment, 14–16, 18, 248–51, 329–336
interpreters, 139
International Federation of Social Work (IFSW),
   see definition (IFSW)
inter-professional practice, 6, 53, 203–211
   factors impacting on, 206–7
   positive activities to support, 209–11
intersectionality, 85–7, 91
interviewing, 112, 133–42, 173
   barriers, 138–40
   ending, 141

knowledge, 2–4, 23, 64–5, 70–1, 93, 125–7, 195, 213–4, 261, 295
Kolb, D. A., 65, 217
Kübler-Ross, E., 312–3

language, 13–17, 25, 28–30, 77–78, 89, 134, 138, 197, 199, 201, 234–235, 296
life-story work, 264–6
   later life letter, 265
   life-story book, 265
   parallel stories, 265
loss, 309–17 see also grief

mad studies, 335–337
maternal, 35, 189, 191, 300–307,
   mother, 24–25, 60, 86, 136, 147, 169, 189–190, 198, 255
   motherhood, 190,
   mothering, 302, 305
Meins, E., 306
mental capacity, 15, 124, 135, 199
Mental Capacity Act 2005, 15–16, 124, 231
mental health, 49, 81, 87, 136, 139, 199, 231, 311, 313, 333–337
Mental Health Act, 89, 295
Motivational Interviewing, 60, 137–8
Munro, E., 47, 50, 64, 97, 111, 115, 128, 130, 146, 252

narrative social work, 259–68
neurobiology, 56, 58
neurodiversity, 335–337

observation, 36–7, 40, 65, 126, 127–9, 147
one-page profile, 19, 139, 266–7
ontology, 301, 303, 307

palliative care, 311–12
parent/parenting, 24, 66–7, 92, 123–4, 128, 171, 174, 217, 246, 253–4, 256–7, 260, 262, 263, 265
   corporate parent, 200
Parton, N., 147
paternalism, 246
   father, 60, 86, 28, 147–148, 169, 190, 198, 263, 282
   fathercraft, 190
partnership working 134, 152–3, 189, 204–5, 270
person-centred social work 4–6, 8–9, 11–21, 76, 279–290, 335 see also C. Rogers
personalisation, 12, 21
Piaget, J., 34, 191, 303
Positive reframing, 140
power, 2–3, 13, 33, 69, 70, 71, 76–79, 87, 88–9, 195, 218, 239, 245, 268, 283, 286, 288–289, 295, 297
practice wisdom, 65, 70, 125, 126–7, 130
problem solving, 97, 104, 171, 293
professionalism 2, 177, 238–9
professional identity 210,219, 238
protective factors, 167, 169–73, 253, 2567
psychobiology, 34
psychodynamic tradition, 310
psychology, 9, 34, 187, 301, 303–304, 313,

questioning, 77, 124, 134–5, 138, 141–2, 159, 246, 250, 256–7
question, 14, 39, 60
  circular, 257
  closed, 135, 136, 139
  coping, 247
  hypothetical, 136
  indirect, 135, 136
  leading, 238
  miracle, 247
  open, 60, 134, 136
  probing, 135
  reflective, 16
  scaling, 247
  strength-based, 245

reflective practice, 20, 40, 63–72, 21, 222, 241, 317
  barriers, 71–2
  reflection-in-action, 65
  reflection-on-action, 65
  reflection-for-practice, 65
  reflective diary, 72
  reflective thinking 99
reflexivity, 20, 63, 70–72, 91, 95, 188, 223
relationship-based practice, 9, 12, 38, 135, 137, 213, 214, 283–6, 289
report writing 199–202
research, messages from, 114–17, 186–193
resilience, 47, 48, 95–106, 111, 167–174 195, 223, 228, 235, 260, 272, 295, 317
review and evaluation 220–229
risk, 9, 64, 66, 120, 122, 124, 125, 128, 169–70, 172–3, 176, 249, 253, 255–7, 289
Rogers, C., 6, 9, 11–12, 280–290
  person-centred counselling, 12, 280–281, 283, 289, 290
  person-centred social work, 4–5, 21, 242, 279–290
    barriers, 20–21, 286–290
    communication, 11–21
    planning tools, 18–20

safeguarding, 39, 74, 81, 122–124, 143–150, 162, 176, 182, 197, 204, 226, 231
Schön, D., 64–65
Self care 2, 4, 95–106
  promoting, 104–6
self-awareness, 3, 23, 30, 64, 70, 97, 180, 297
service users and carers 6, 65, 150–166
  collaborative working, 153–156, 336
  principles, 156–159

siblings, 174, 198, 302, 313, 321
Signs of Safety, 180, 246
silence, 14, 28
social identity, 86–7, 92–4
social justice, 2, 59, 75–9, 81, 154, 180, 228, 318, 339, 340–1, 345
social model(s) of disability and distress, 7, 327–337
solution-focused approaches, 243–50
statutory social work, 219–20, 285–287
strengths-based approaches, 6, 243–50, 279, 321, 324
supervision, 36, 43, 47, 50, 66–7, 101, 104, 109, 197, 212–20, 254, 255, 316
  barriers, 218–9
  functions, 213–4
  models, 215
systemic practice, 253–4, 256, 258, 261
systems theory, 170, 251–8, 261

task-centred social work 269–278
  areas, 273–4
  prerequisities and principles, 271–2
  stages, 274–277
  review and evaluation, 277
timeline, 125, 262, 268
time management 107–117
touch, 13, 18, 37, 129
Trevarthen, C., 34–35,
Tuckman, B. W., 292–3

unconscious bias, 90, 94
Universal Declaration on Human Rights (UDHR), 79–80, 82,
United Nations Convention on the Rights of Person's with Disabilities (UNCRPD), 16, 79
use of self, 4, 9, 61, 64, 70, 319, 322

values and ethics, 2–3, 5, 29, 69–70, 73–79, 81–83, 90, 93, 97, 113, 130, 171, 253, 256–7
vulnerability, 92, 169–70
Vygotsky, L., 34, 191

working together 203–211
  factors impacting on, 206–7
  positive approaches, 209–11
  problem solving, 276
writing skills, 194–202
  case records, 198–9
  email, 196
  reports, 199–201